VISIONS OF AMERICA

PERSEA ALSO PUBLISHES

Imagining America:
Stories from the Promised Land
Edited by Wesley Brown & Amy Ling

VISIONS OF AMERICA

PERSONAL NARRATIVES
FROM THE PROMISED LAND

Edited by Wesley Brown & Amy Ling

PERSEA BOOKS
NEW YORK

*Since this page cannot legibly accommodate all copyright notices,
pages 366–369 constitute an extension of the copyright page.*

Copyright © 1993 by Wesley Brown and Amy Ling

All rights reserved.

For information, write to the publisher.

*Persea Books, Inc.
60 Madison Avenue
New York, New York 10010*

Library of Congress Cataloging-in-Publication Data

*Visions of America: personal narratives from the promised land/
edited by Wesley Brown & Amy Ling.
p. cm.*
ISBN 0-89255-173-9 : $29.95.—ISBN 0-89255-174-7 (pbk.) : $11.95
*1. Ethnology—United States. 2. United States—Ethnic relations.
3. United States—Emigration and immigration. I. Brown, Wesley,
1945– . II. Ling, Amy.*
E184.A1V67 1992   92-11725
305.8′00973—dc20   CIP

Designed by REM Studio, Inc.

*Set in Century Old Style by ComCom, Allentown, Pennsylvania.
Printed and bound by The Haddon Craftsmen, Scranton, Pennsylvania.
Printed on acid-free, recycled paper.*

First Edition

CONTENTS

CONTENTS

CONTENTS

CONTENTS

INTRODUCTION

JOAN DIDION HAS WRITTEN IN HER REMARKABLY PERCEPTIVE AND singular voice: "We tell ourselves stories in order to live. . . . We interpret what we see, select the most workable of the multiple choices. We live entirely, especially if we are writers, by the imposition of a narrative line upon disparate images." This could be said not only for the invented world of fiction but for the chronicles of our actual experience as well.

We see this anthology of personal narratives and excerpts from memoirs and autobiographies as a companion to our earlier anthology, *Imagining America: Stories from the Promised Land.* While focusing on nonfiction, this book continues the exploration (begun in the previous one) of emigration to and migration within the United States in the twentieth century. However, the scope of this volume has expanded beyond the specific tensions of being an

INTRODUCTION

American with an embattled past and present to include personal essays addressing historical moments that have defined American life during this century. Whatever path these essays follow, they are driven by the attempts of writers to bring coherence to personal and collective experiences that are often contradictory, disorderly, and paradoxical.

We have arranged the essays according to the particular time period that each writer has chosen to recreate; and in many instances they are informed by a perspective many years removed from the time being written about. In the essay "Of the Black Belt," W. E. B. Du Bois recounts his grim train journey through rural Georgia at the turn of the century and finds the remnants of slavery in every effort by blacks to better themselves. Although Sui Sin Far's "Leaves from the Mental Portfolio of an Eurasian" is an often agonizing account of the constant barrage of racial invective she received while growing up in Eastern Canada and then the U.S. during the latter part of the nineteenth century, she remains hopeful.

The resiliency of a Sui Sin Far is indicative of the ways in which many have fortified themselves with some variation of a belief in America as the land of infinite possibility. For Mario Puzo in "Choosing a Dream," the dire circumstances of living in the Hell's Kitchen section of New York during the Depression years of the 1930s were undaunting because of his dream of becoming a writer. Of course, there is no more fitting repository of the American Dream than Hollywood. But in the excerpt from Anzia Yezierska's autobiography, *Red Ribbon on a White Horse,* the sale of the movie rights to her collection of stories to Samuel Goldwyn in 1921 and her subsequent trip to Hollywood makes Yezierska question whether her success is a betrayal of the people on Hester Street whose suffering was the source of her inspiration as a writer. While in Bharati Mukherjee's essay, "Love Me Or Leave Me," the 1950s movie image of Doris Day becomes an example of personal empowerment for her as an oversheltered and overprivileged young girl growing up in Calcutta.

Other essays, including the excerpt from Maxine Hong Kingston's *The Woman Warrior,* Anton Shammas' "Amérka, Amérka," Jessica Hagedorn's "Homesick," Pablo Medina's "Two Cuban Dissidents," and Judith Ortiz Cofer's "Silent Dancing," explore how the "old world" is never left behind but can rear up unexpectedly into the "new" like a living fossil among first and second generation immigrants. For Eva Hoffman (from *Lost in Translation*), the new world is the English language. And her journey to join her Polish sensibility to a new language is enriching as well as exasperating. This notion of language as a homeland is also true for native speakers of English and resonates in Mary Gordon's "I Can't Stand Your Books" and Paule Marshall's "The Making of a Writer: From the Poets in the Kitchen."

Ethnic identity, racial prejudice and their relationship to class, gender, and sexuality are inevitably intertwined in any truthful representation of American society. As the title of her essay "Split at the Root" suggests, Adrienne Rich's journey toward self-discovery was influenced by her ambivalence toward her Jewishness, the racial and class politics of her native Baltimore, her lesbian identity and evolving feminism. The entanglement of class and race continues in Barbara Grizzuti Harrison's "Going Home: Brooklyn Revisited." Harrison's empathy for the people of her Italian, working-class neighborhood of Bensonhurst collides with their virulent racism against black students who attended her former high school during the early 1970s. In "Immigrant Waves," Michael Stephens describes how contracting a fever while teaching for a semester in Hawaii opens him up to the dizzying and hostile racial mix of the islands as well as to the personal demons from his Irish background. And in June Jordan's "Report from the Bahamas" she discovers during her attempts to get help for a black South African woman being abused by her husband that shared experience is a point of genuine connection even among people who share little else.

Twentieth-century America has been shaken to the core by several national tragedies—some of which are addressed by Charles Eastman (a Santee Sioux) in a moving account ("The Ghost Dance War") of his experience as a government doctor called onto the scene after the army massacre of more than two hundred Sioux Indians at Wounded Knee, South Dakota in 1890; Monica Sone's personal account ("Pearl Harbor Echoes in Seattle") of being placed in a Japanese internment camp after the bombing of Pearl Harbor in 1941; James Farmer's powerful on-the-scene report (" 'Tomorrow Is for Our Martyrs' ") on the murder of James Chaney, Andrew Goodman, and Michael Schwerner in Mississippi during the Freedom Summer of 1964; Ron Kovic's harrowing memoir (from *Born on the Fourth of July*), which details his experience as a marine in Vietnam and his return to the United States after suffering wounds that left him paralyzed; and James Baldwin's meditation (from *No Name in the Street*) on the state of the nation and his status as a spokesman for blacks in the aftermath of the assassination of Martin Luther King, Jr.

There are essays here that speak to the emotional breach between generations: in "The Messenger of the Lost Battalion," Gregory Orfalea makes startling discoveries about his deceased father; in "To Begin With," Vivian Gornick takes a wrenching look at her family's allegiance to the utopian vision of the American Communist Party and their crushing disillusionment following the revelations in 1956 about the massive terror in the Soviet Union under Stalin; and in "2G," Sonia Pilcer explores the poignant and ironic experience of being the child of Holocaust survivors.

Specific eras are captured in other pieces. F. Scott Fitzgerald evokes the "age of excess," the 1920s, in "Echoes of the Jazz Age." Geoffrey O'Brien offers a haunting portrait of our national preoccupation with bomb shelters and movies about alien creatures during the A-bomb-threatened years of the 1950s in his essay, "Suburbs." And "The White Album" is Joan Didion's apocalyptic vision of a society skidding dangerously out of control at the end of the 1960s.

Finally, there are essays evoking a vision of America that begins with the land itself. In Gretel Ehrlich's "The Solace of Open Spaces," she tells how living in Wyoming taught her how not to be in an adversarial relationship with nature. This experience of an America that was there before it was obstructed by attempts to bring nature under control is powerfully rendered in an excerpt from N. Scott Momaday's *The Names* in which a schoolhouse in his native Oklahoma is invested with all the properties of the natural world. And in Wendell Berry's "A Native Hill," the loving connection he has to his native Kentucky is informed by "the realization that my people established themselves here by killing or driving out the original possessors, by the awareness that people were once bought and sold here by my people, and by the sense of the violence they have done to their own kind and to each other and to the earth."

The writers in this collection have positioned themselves at or close to the scene of injuries that pulsate throughout this nation. By articulating the ways in which America continues to evolve out of hope as well as hurt, they have made an essential gesture, pointing us in the direction of wisdom and healing.

Many people aided us in the completion of this book. For their encouragement and helpful suggestions we thank Phillip Lopate, Betsy McTiernan, Ken Smith, Rachel Stein, and Naomi Shihab Nye.

WESLEY BROWN
AMY LING

VISIONS OF AMERICA

THE GHOST DANCE WAR

Charles Alexander Eastman

Charles Alexander Eastman (1858–1939), a Santee Sioux, was born in Red
Wood Falls, Minnesota. He graduated from Dartmouth College in 1887 and
earned a medical degree from Boston University in 1890. He wrote nearly one
dozen books on Sioux life and culture. Among them are *Indian Boyhood*
(1902), *The Soul of the Indian: An Interpretation* (1911), and *The Indian
Today* (1915).

"The Ghost Dance War" is chapter seven in his second book of autobiography, *From the Deep Woods to Civilization* (1916), and is a first-hand account
of Eastman's experience as a government doctor called onto the scene after
the battle at Wounded Knee.

A RELIGIOUS CRAZE SUCH AS THAT OF 1890–91 WAS A THING FOREIGN
to the Indian philosophy. I recalled that a hundred years before, on the overthrow
of the Algonquin nations, a somewhat similar faith was evolved by the astute
Delaware prophet, brother to Tecumseh. It meant that the last hope of race
entity had departed, and my people were groping blindly after spiritual relief in
their bewilderment and misery. I believe that the first prophets of the "Red
Christ" were innocent enough and that the people generally were sincere, but
there were doubtless some who went into it for self-advertisement, and who
introduced new and fantastic features to attract the crowd.

The ghost dancers had gradually concentrated on the Medicine Root creek
and the edge of the "Bad Lands," and they were still further isolated by a new
order from the agent, calling in all those who had not adhered to the new religion.

1

Several thousand of these "friendlies" were soon encamped on the White Clay creek, close by the agency. It was near the middle of December, with weather unusually mild for that season. The dancers held that there would be no snow so long as their rites continued.

An Indian called Little had been guilty of some minor offense on the reservation and had hitherto evaded arrest. Suddenly he appeared at the agency on an issue day, for the express purpose, as it seemed, of defying the authorities. The assembly room of the Indian police, used also as a council room, opened out of my dispensary, and on this particular morning a council was in progress. I heard some loud talking, but was too busy to pay particular attention, though my assistant had gone in to listen to the speeches. Suddenly the place was in an uproar, and George burst into the inner office, crying excitedly "Look out for yourself, friend! They are going to fight!"

I went around to see what was going on. A crowd had gathered just outside the council room, and the police were surrounded by wild Indians with guns and drawn knives in their hands. "Hurry up with them!" one shouted, while another held his stone war-club over a policeman's head. The attempt to arrest Little had met with a stubborn resistance.

At this critical moment, a fine-looking Indian in citizen's clothes faced the excited throng, and spoke in a clear, steady, almost sarcastic voice.

"Stop! Think! What are you going to do? Kill these men of our own race? Then what? Kill all these helpless white men, women and children? And what then? What will these brave words, brave deeds lead to in the end? How long can you hold out? Your country is surrounded with a network of railroads; thousands of white soldiers will be here within three days. What ammunition have you? what provisions? What will become of your families? Think, think, my brothers! This is a child's madness."

It was the "friendly" chief, American Horse, and it seems to me as I recall the incident that this man's voice had almost magic power. It is likely that he saved us all from massacre, for the murder of the police, who represented the authority of the Government, would surely have been followed by a general massacre. It is a fact that those Indians who upheld the agent were in quite as much danger from their wilder brethren as were the whites, indeed it was said that the feeling against them was even stronger. Jack Red Cloud, son of the chief, thrust the muzzle of a cocked revolver almost into the face of American Horse. "It is you and your kind," he shouted, "who have brought us to this pass!" That brave man never flinched. Ignoring his rash accuser, he quietly reentered the office; the door closed behind him; the mob dispersed, and for the moment the danger seemed over.

I scarcely knew at the time, but gradually learned afterward, that the Sioux had many grievances and causes for profound discontent, which lay back of and

THE GHOST DANCE WAR

were more or less closely related to the ghost dance craze and the prevailing restlessness and excitement. Rations had been cut from time to time; the people were insufficiently fed, and their protests and appeals were disregarded. Never was more ruthless fraud and graft practiced upon a defenseless people than upon these poor natives by the politicians! Never were there more worthless "scraps of paper" anywhere in the world than many of the Indian treaties and Government documents! Sickness was prevalent and the death rate alarming, especially among the children. Trouble from all these causes had for some time been developing, but might have been checked by humane and conciliatory measures. The "Messiah craze" in itself was scarcely a source of danger, and one might almost as well call upon the army to suppress Billy Sunday and his hysterical followers. Other tribes than the Sioux who adopted the new religion were let alone, and the craze died a natural death in the course of a few months.

Among the leaders of the malcontents at this time were Jack Red Cloud, No Water, He Dog, Four Bears, Yellow Bear, and Kicking Bear. Friendly leaders included American Horse, Young Man Afraid of his Horses, Bad Wound, Three Stars. There was still another set whose attitude was not clearly defined, and among these men was Red Cloud, the greatest of them all. He who had led his people so brilliantly and with such remarkable results, both in battle and diplomacy, was now an old man of over seventy years, living in a frame house which had been built for him within a half mile of the agency. He would come to council, but said little or nothing. No one knew exactly where he stood, but it seemed that he was broken in spirit as in body and convinced of the hopelessness of his people's cause.

It was Red Cloud who asked the historic question, at a great council held in the Black Hills region with a Government commission, and after good Bishop Whipple had finished the invocation, "Which God is our brother praying to now? Is it the same God whom they have twice deceived, when they made treaties with us which they afterward broke?"

Early in the morning after the attempted arrest of Little, George rushed into my quarters and awakened me. "Come quick!" he shouted, "the soldiers are here!" I looked along the White Clay creek toward the little railroad town of Rushville, Nebraska, twenty-five miles away, and just as the sun rose above the knife-edged ridges black with stunted pine, I perceived a moving cloud of dust that marked the trail of the Ninth Cavalry. There was instant commotion among the camps of friendly Indians. Many women and children were coming in to the agency for refuge, evidently fearing that the dreaded soldiers might attack their villages by mistake. Some who had not heard of their impending arrival hurried to the offices to ask what it meant. I assured those who appealed to me that the troops were here only to preserve order, but their suspicions were not easily allayed.

As the cavalry came nearer, we saw that they were colored troopers, wearing buffalo overcoats and muskrat caps; the Indians with their quick wit called them "buffalo soldiers." They halted, and established their temporary camp in the open space before the agency enclosure. The news had already gone out through the length and breadth of the reservation, and the wildest rumors were in circulation. Indian scouts might be seen upon every hill top, closely watching the military encampment.

At this juncture came the startling news from Fort Yates, some two hundred and fifty miles to the north of us, that Sitting Bull had been killed by Indian police while resisting arrest, and a number of his men with him, as well as several of the police. We next heard that the remnant of his band had fled in our direction, and soon afterward, that they had been joined by Big Foot's band from the western part of Cheyenne River agency, which lay directly in their road. United States troops continued to gather at strategic points, and of course the press seized upon the opportunity to enlarge upon the strained situation and predict an "Indian uprising." The reporters were among us, and managed to secure much "news" that no one else ever heard of. Border towns were fortified and cowboys and militia gathered in readiness to protect them against the "red devils." Certain classes of the frontier population industriously fomented the excitement for what there was in it for them, since much money is apt to be spent at such times. As for the poor Indians, they were quite as badly scared as the whites and perhaps with more reason.

General Brooke undertook negotiations with the ghost dancers, and finally induced them to come within reach. They camped on a flat about a mile north of us and in full view, while the more tractable bands were still gathered on the south and west. The large boarding school had locked its doors and succeeded in holding its hundreds of Indian children, partly for their own sakes, and partly as hostages for the good behavior of their fathers. At the agency were now gathered all the government employees and their families, except such as had taken flight, together with traders, missionaries, and ranchmen, army officers, and newspaper men. It was a conglomerate population.

During this time of grave anxiety and nervous tension, the cooler heads among us went about our business, and still refused to believe in the tragic possibility of an Indian war. It may be imagined that I was more than busy, though I had not such long distances to cover, for since many Indians accustomed to comfortable log houses were compelled to pass the winter in tents, there was even more sickness than usual. I had access and welcome to the camps of all the various groups and factions, a privilege shared by my good friend Father Jutz, the Catholic missionary, who was completely trusted by his people.

Three days later, we learned that Big Foot's band of ghost dancers from the Cheyenne river reservation north of us was approaching the agency, and

THE GHOST DANCE WAR

that Major Whiteside was in command of troops with orders to intercept them.

Late that afternoon, the Seventh Cavalry under Colonel Forsythe was called to the saddle and rode off toward Wounded Knee creek, eighteen miles away. Father Craft, a Catholic priest with some Indian blood, who knew Sitting Bull and his people, followed an hour or so later, and I was much inclined to go too, but my fiancée pointed out that my duty lay rather at home with our Indians, and I stayed.

The morning of December 29th was sunny and pleasant. We were all straining our ears toward Wounded Knee, and about the middle of the forenoon we distinctly heard the reports of the Hotchkiss guns. Two hours later, a rider was seen approaching at full speed, and in a few minutes he had dismounted from his exhausted horse and handed his message to General Brooke's orderly. The Indians were watching their own messenger, who ran on foot along the northern ridges and carried the news to the so-called "hostile" camp. It was said that he delivered his message at almost the same time as the mounted officer.

The resulting confusion and excitement was unmistakable. The white teepees disappeared as if by magic and soon the caravans were in motion, going toward the natural fortress of the "Bad Lands." In the "friendly" camp there was almost as much turmoil, and crowds of frightened women and children poured into the agency. Big Foot's band had been wiped out by the troops, and reprisals were naturally looked for. The enclosure was not barricaded in any way and we had but a small detachment of troops for our protection. Sentinels were placed, and machine guns trained on the various approaches.

A few hot-headed young braves fired on the sentinels and wounded two of them. The Indian police began to answer by shooting at several braves who were apparently about to set fire to some of the outlying buildings. Every married employee was seeking a place of safety for his family, the interpreter among them. Just then General Brooke ran out into the open, shouting at the top of his voice to the police: "Stop, stop! Doctor, tell them they must not fire until ordered!" I did so, as the bullets whistled by us, and the General's coolness perhaps saved all our lives, for we were in no position to repel a large attacking force. Since we did not reply, the scattered shots soon ceased, but the situation remained critical for several days and nights.

My office was full of refugees. I called one of my good friends aside and asked him to saddle my two horses and stay by them. "When general fighting begins, take them to Miss Goodale and see her to the railroad if you can," I told him. Then I went over to the rectory. Mrs. Cook refused to go without her husband, and Miss Goodale would not leave while there was a chance of being of service. The house was crowded with terrified people, most of them Christian Indians, whom our friends were doing their best to pacify.

At dusk, the Seventh Cavalry returned with their twenty-five dead and I believe thirty-four wounded, most of them by their own comrades, who had encircled the Indians, while few of the latter had guns. A majority of the thirty or more Indian wounded were women and children, including babies in arms. As there were not tents enough for all, Mr. Cook offered us the mission chapel, in which the Christmas tree still stood, for a temporary hospital. We tore out the pews and covered the floor with hay and quilts. There we laid the poor creatures side by side in rows, and the night was devoted to caring for them as best we could. Many were frightfully torn by pieces of shells, and the suffering was terrible. General Brooke placed me in charge and I had to do nearly all the work, for although the army surgeons were more than ready to help as soon as their own men had been cared for, the tortured Indians would scarcely allow a man in uniform to touch them. Mrs. Cook, Miss Goodale, and several of Mr. Cook's Indian helpers acted as volunteer nurses. In spite of all our efforts, we lost the greater part of them, but a few recovered, including several children who had lost all their relatives and who were adopted into kind Christian families.

On the day following the Wounded Knee massacre there was a blizzard, in the midst of which I was ordered out with several Indian police, to look for a policeman who was reported to have been wounded and left some two miles from the agency. We did not find him. This was the only time during the whole affair that I carried a weapon; a friend lent me a revolver which I put in my overcoat pocket, and it was lost on the ride. On the third day it cleared, and the ground was covered with an inch or two of fresh snow. We had feared that some of the Indian wounded might have been left on the field, and a number of us volunteered to go and see. I was placed in charge of the expedition of about a hundred civilians, ten or fifteen of whom were white men. We were supplied with wagons in which to convey any of whom we might find still alive. Of course a photographer and several reporters were of the party.

Fully three miles from the scene of the massacre we found the body of a woman completely covered with a blanket of snow, and from this point on we found them scattered along as they had been relentlessly hunted down and slaughtered while fleeing for their lives. Some of our people discovered relatives or friends among the dead, and there was much wailing and mourning. When we reached the spot where the Indian camp had stood, among the fragments of burned tents and other belongings we saw the frozen bodies lying close together or piled one upon another. I counted eighty bodies of men who had been in the council and who were almost as helpless as the women and babes when the deadly fire began, for nearly all their guns had been taken from them. A reckless and desperate young Indian fired the first shot when the search for weapons was well under way, and immediately the troops opened fire from all sides, killing not only unarmed men, women, and children, but their own comrades who stood opposite them, for the camp was entirely surrounded.

THE GHOST DANCE WAR

It took all of my nerve to keep my composure in the face of this spectacle, and of the excitement and grief of my Indian companions, nearly every one of whom was crying aloud or singing his death song. The white men became very nervous, but I set them to examining and uncovering every body to see if one were living. Although they had been lying untended in the snow and cold for two days and nights, a number had survived. Among them I found a baby of about a year old warmly wrapped and entirely unhurt. I brought her in, and she was afterward adopted and educated by an army officer. One man who was severely wounded begged me to fill his pipe. When we brought him into the chapel he was welcomed by his wife and daughters with cries of joy, but he died a day or two later.

Under a wagon I discovered an old woman, totally blind and entirely helpless. A few had managed to crawl away to some place of shelter, and we found in a log store near by several who were badly hurt and others who had died after reaching there. After we had dispatched several wagon loads to the agency, we observed groups of warriors watching us from adjacent buttes; probably friends of the victims who had come there for the same purpose as ourselves. A majority of our party, fearing an attack, insisted that some one ride back to the agency for an escort of soldiers, and as mine was the best horse, it fell to me to go. I covered the eighteen miles in quick time and was not interfered with in any way, although if the Indians had meant mischief they could easily have picked me off from any of the ravines and gulches.

All this was a severe ordeal for one who had so lately put all his faith in the Christian love and lofty ideals of the white man. Yet I passed no hasty judgment, and was thankful that I might be of some service and relieve even a small part of the suffering. An appeal published in a Boston paper brought us liberal supplies of much needed clothing, and linen for dressings. We worked on. Bishop Hare of South Dakota visited us, and was overcome by faintness when he entered his mission chapel, thus transformed into a rude hospital.

After some days of extreme tension, and weeks of anxiety, the "hostiles," so called, were at last induced to come in and submit to a general disarmament. Father Jutz, the Catholic missionary, had gone bravely among them and used all his influence toward a peaceful settlement. The troops were all recalled and took part in a grand review before General Miles, no doubt intended to impress the Indians with their superior force.

OF THE BLACK BELT

W. E. B. Du Bois

W. E. B. (William Edward Burghardt) Du Bois (1868–1963) was born in Great Barrington, Massachusetts. An educator, prolific writer, editor, pioneer sociologist, and African American scholar, Du Bois earned a B.A. from Fisk University, another B.A., M.A., and Ph.D. (1896) from Harvard, and pursued further graduate studies at the University of Berlin (1892–94). He wrote and edited some three dozen books, most of which are devoted to the history of people of African descent and the problems of racial prejudice. Du Bois also published six novels, a volume of poems, several plays, and dozens of articles for national periodicals. His best-known work, *The Souls of Black Folk,* from which the following essay is taken, appeared in 1903, but its ideas laid the foundation for the analysis of America's racial dilemma in the twentieth century.

I am black but comely, O ye daughters of Jerusalem,
As the tents of Kedar, as the curtains of Solomon.
Look not upon me, because I am black,
Because the sun hath looked upon me:
My mother's children were angry with me;
They made me the keeper of the vineyards;
But mine own vineyard have I not kept.
—THE SONG OF SOLOMON

OUT OF THE NORTH THE TRAIN THUNDERED, AND WE WOKE TO SEE the crimson soil of Georgia stretching away bare and monotonous right and left. Here and there lay straggling, unlovely villages, and lean men loafed leisurely at the depots; then again came the stretch of pines and clay. Yet we did not nod, nor weary of the scene; for this is historic ground. Right across our track, three hundred and sixty years ago, wandered the cavalcade of Hernando de Soto, looking for gold and the Great Sea; and he and his foot-sore captives disappeared yonder in the grim forests to the west. Here sits Atlanta, the city of a hundred hills, with something Western, something Southern, and something quite its own, in its busy life. And a little past Atlanta, to the southwest, is the land of the Cherokees, and there, not far from where Sam Hose was crucified, you may stand on a spot which is today the center of the Negro problem—the center of those nine million men who are America's dark heritage from slavery and the slave-trade.

Not only is Georgia thus the geographical focus of our Negro population, but in many other respects, both now and yesterday, the Negro problems have seemed to be centered in this State. No other State in the Union can count a million Negroes among its citizens—a population as large as the slave population of the whole Union in 1800; no other State fought so long and strenuously to gather this host of Africans. Oglethorpe thought slavery against law and gospel; but the circumstances which gave Georgia its first inhabitants were not calculated to furnish citizens over-nice in their ideas about rum and slaves. Despite the prohibitions of the trustees, these Georgians, like some of their descendants, proceeded to take the law into their own hands; and so pliant were the judges, and so flagrant the smuggling, and so earnest were the prayers of Whitefield, that by the middle of the eighteenth century all restrictions were swept away, and the slave-trade went merrily on for fifty years and more.

Down in Darien, where the Delegal riots took place some summers ago, there used to come a strong protest against slavery from the Scotch Highlanders; and the Moravians of Ebenezer did not like the system. But not till the Haytian Terror of Toussaint was the trade in men even checked; while the national statute of 1808 did not suffice to stop it. How the Africans poured in!—fifty thousand between 1790 and 1810, and then, from Virginia and from smugglers, two thousand a year for many years more. So the thirty thousand Negroes of Georgia in 1790 were doubled in a decade—were over a hundred thousand in 1810, had reached two hundred thousand in 1820, and half a million at the time of the war. Thus like a snake the black population writhed upward.

But we must hasten on our journey. This that we pass as we leave Atlanta is the ancient land of the Cherokees—that brave Indian nation which strove so long for its fatherland, until Fate and the United States Government drove them beyond the Mississippi. If you wish to ride with me you must come into the "Jim Crow Car." There will be no objection—already four other white men, and a little white girl with her nurse, are in there. Usually the races are mixed in there; but the white coach is all white. Of course this car is not so good as the other, but it is fairly clean and comfortable. The discomfort lies chiefly in the hearts of those four black men yonder—and in mine.

We rumble south in quite a business-like way. The bare red clay and pines of Northern Georgia begin to disappear, and in their place appears a rich rolling land, luxuriant, and here and there well tilled. This is the land of the Creek Indians; and a hard time the Georgians had to seize it. The towns grow more frequent and more interesting, and brand-new cotton mills rise on every side. Below Macon the world grows darker; for now we approach the Black Belt—that strange land of shadows, at which even slaves paled in the past, and whence come now only faint and half-intelligible murmurs to the world beyond. The "Jim Crow Car" grows larger and a shade better; three rough field-hands and two or three white loafers accompany us, and the newsboy still spreads his wares at one end. The sun is setting, but we can see the great cotton country as we enter it—the soil now dark and fertile, now thin and gray, with fruit-trees and dilapidated buildings—all the way to Albany.

At Albany, in the heart of the Black Belt, we stop. Two hundred miles south of Atlanta, two hundred miles west of the Atlantic, and one hundred miles north of the Great Gulf lies Dougherty County, with ten thousand Negroes and two thousand whites. The Flint River winds down from Andersonville, and, turning suddenly at Albany, the county-seat, hurries on to join the Chattahoochee and the sea. Andrew Jackson knew the Flint well, and marched across it once to avenge the Indian Massacre at Fort Mims. That was in 1814, not long before the battle of New Orleans; and by the Creek treaty that followed this campaign, all Dougherty County, and much other rich land, was ceded to Georgia. Still, settlers fought shy of this land, for the Indians were all about, and they were unpleasant neighbors in those days. The panic of 1837, which Jackson bequeathed to Van Buren, turned the planters from the impoverished lands of Virginia, the Carolinas, and east Georgia, toward the West. The Indians were removed to Indian Territory, and settlers poured into these coveted lands to retrieve their broken fortunes. For a radius of a hundred miles about Albany, stretched a great fertile land, luxuriant with forests of pine, oak, ash, hickory, and poplar; hot with the sun and damp with the rich black swamp-land; and here the cornerstone of the Cotton Kingdom was laid.

Albany is today a wide-streeted, placid, Southern town, with a broad sweep of stores and saloons, and flanking rows of homes—whites usually to the north, and blacks to the south. Six days in the week the town looks decidedly too small for itself, and takes frequent and prolonged naps. But on Saturday suddenly the whole county disgorges itself upon the place, and a perfect flood of black peasantry pours through the streets, fills the stores, blocks the sidewalks, chokes the thoroughfares, and takes full possession of the town. They are black, sturdy, uncouth country folk, good-natured and simple, talkative to a degree, and yet far more silent and brooding than the crowds of the Rhine-pfalz, or Naples, or Cracow. They drink considerable quantities of whiskey, but do not get very drunk; they talk and laugh loudly at times, but seldom quarrel or fight. They walk up and down the streets, meet and gossip with friends, stare at the shop windows, buy coffee, cheap candy, and clothes, and at dusk drive home—happy? well no, not exactly happy, but much happier than as though they had not come.

Thus Albany is a real capital—a typical Southern county town, the center of the life of ten thousand souls; their point of contact with the outer world, their center of news and gossip, their market for buying and selling, borrowing and lending, their fountain of justice and law. Once upon a time we knew country life so well and city life so little, that we illustrated city life as that of a closely crowded country district. Now the world has well-nigh forgotten what the country is, and we must imagine a little city of black people scattered far and wide over three hundred lonesome square miles of land, without train or trolley, in the midst of cotton and corn, and wide patches of sand and gloomy soil.

It gets pretty hot in Southern Georgia in July—a sort of dull, determined heat that seems quite independent of the sun; so it took us some days to muster courage enough to leave the porch and venture out on the long country roads, that we might see this unknown world. Finally we started. It was about ten in the morning, bright with a faint breeze, and we jogged leisurely southward in the valley of the Flint. We passed the scattered box-like cabins of the brick-yard hands, and the long tenement-row facetiously called "The Ark," and were soon in the open country, and on the confines of the great plantations of other days. There is the "Joe Fields place"; a rough old fellow was he, and had killed many a "nigger" in his day. Twelve miles his plantation used to run—a regular barony. It is nearly all gone now; only straggling bits belong to the family, and the rest has passed to Jews and Negroes. Even the bits which are left are heavily mortgaged, and, like the rest of the land, tilled by tenants. Here is one of them now—a tall brown man, a hard worker and a hard drinker, illiterate, but versed in farm-lore, as his nodding crops declare. This distressingly new board house is his, and he has just moved out of yonder moss-grown cabin with its one square room.

From the curtains in Benton's house, down the road, a dark comely face is staring at the strangers; for passing carriages are not everyday occurrences here. Benton is an intelligent yellow man with a good-sized family, and manages a plantation blasted by the war and now the broken staff of the widow. He might be well-to-do, they say; but he carouses too much in Albany. And the half-desolate spirit of neglect born of the very soil seems to have settled on these acres. In times past there were cotton-gins and machinery here; but they have rotted away.

The whole land seems forlorn and forsaken. Here are the remnants of the vast plantations of the Sheldons, the Pellots, and the Rensons; but the souls of them are passed. The houses lie in half ruin, or have wholly disappeared; the fences have flown, and the families are wandering in the world. Strange vicissitudes have met these whilom masters. Yonder stretch the wide acres of Bildad Reasor; he died in war-time, but the upstart overseer hastened to wed the widow. Then he went, and his neighbors too, and now only the black tenant remains; but the shadow-hand of the master's grand-nephew or cousin or creditor stretches out of the gray distance to collect the rack-rent remorselessly, and so the land is uncared-for and poor. Only black tenants can stand such a system, and they only because they must. Ten miles we have ridden today and have seen no white face.

A resistless feeling of depression falls slowly upon us, despite the gaudy sunshine and the green cotton-fields. This, then, is the Cotton Kingdom—the shadow of a marvellous dream. And where is the King? Perhaps this is he—the sweating ploughman, tilling his eighty acres with two lean mules, and fighting a hard battle with debt. So we sit musing, until, as we turn a corner on the sandy road, there comes a fairer scene suddenly in view—a neat cottage snugly ensconced by the road, and near it a little store. A tall bronzed man rises from the porch as we hail him, and comes out to our carriage. He is six feet in height, with a sober face that smiles gravely. He walks too straight to be a tenant—yes, he owns two hundred and forty acres. "The land is run down since the boom-days of eighteen hundred and fifty," he explains, and cotton is low. Three black tenants live on his place, and in his little store he keeps a small stock of tobacco, snuff, soap, and soda, for the neighborhood. Here is his gin-house with new machinery just installed. Three hundred bales of cotton went through it last year. Two children he has sent away to school. Yes, he says sadly, he is getting on, but cotton is down to four cents; I know how Debt sits staring at him.

Wherever the King may be, the parks and palaces of the Cotton Kingdom have not wholly disappeared. We plunge even now into great groves of oak and towering pine, with an undergrowth of myrtle and shrubbery. This was the "home-house" of the Thompsons—slave-barons who drove their coach and four in the merry past. All is silence now, and ashes, and tangled weeds. The owner put his whole fortune into the rising cotton industry of the fifties, and with the falling prices of the eighties he packed up and stole away. Yonder is another grove, with unkempt lawn, great magnolias, and grass-grown paths. The Big House stands in half-ruin, its great front door staring blankly at the street, and the back part grotesquely restored for its black tenant. A shabby, well-built Negro he is, unlucky and irresolute. He digs hard to pay rent to the white girl who owns the remnant of the place. She married a policeman, and lives in Savannah.

OF THE BLACK BELT

Now and again we come to churches. Here is one now—Shepherd's, they call it—a great whitewashed barn of a thing, perched on stilts of stone, and looking for all the world as though it were just resting here a moment and might be expected to waddle off down the road at almost any time. And yet it is the center of a hundred cabin homes; and sometimes, of a Sunday, five hundred persons from far and near gather here and talk and eat and sing. There is a school-house near—a very airy, empty shed; but even this is an improvement, for usually the school is held in the church. The churches vary from log-huts to those like Shepherd's, and the schools from nothing to this little house that sits demurely on the county line. It is a tiny plank-house, perhaps ten by twenty, and has within a double row of rough unplaned benches, resting mostly on legs, sometimes on boxes. Opposite the door is a square home-made desk. In one corner are the ruins of a stove, and in the other a dim blackboard. It is the cheerfulest schoolhouse I have seen in Dougherty, save in town. Back of the schoolhouse is a lodge-house two stories high and not quite finished. Societies meet there—societies "to care for the sick and bury the dead"; and these societies grow and flourish.

We had come to the boundaries of Dougherty, and were about to turn west along the county-line, when all these sights were pointed out to us by a kindly old man, black, white-haired, and seventy. Forty-five years he had lived here, and now supports himself and his old wife by the help of the steer tethered yonder and the charity of his black neighbors. He shows us the farm of the Hills just across the county line in Baker—a widow and two strapping sons, who raised ten bales (one need not add "cotton" down here) last year. There are fences and pigs and cows, and the soft-voiced, velvet-skinned young Memnon, who sauntered half-bashfully over to greet the strangers, is proud of his home. We turn now to the west along the county line. Great dismantled trunks of pines tower above the green cotton-fields, cracking their naked gnarled fingers toward the border of living forest beyond. There is little beauty in this region, only a sort of crude abandon that suggests power—a naked grandeur, as it were. The houses are bare and straight; there are no hammocks or easy-chairs, and few flowers. So when, as here at Rawdon's, one sees a vine clinging to a little porch, and home-like windows peeping over the fences, one takes a long breath. I think I never before quite realized the place of the Fence in civilization. This is the Land of the Unfenced, where crouch on either hand scores of ugly one-room cabins, cheerless and dirty. Here lies the Negro problem in its naked dirt and penury. And here are no fences. But now and then the criss-cross rails or straight palings break into view, and then we know a touch of culture is near. Of course Harrison Gohagen—a quiet yellow man, young, smooth-faced, and diligent—of course he is lord of some hundred acres, and we expect to see a vision of well-kept rooms and fat beds and laughing children. For has he not fine fences? And those over yonder, why should they build fences on the rack-rented land? It will only increase their rent.

On we wind, through sand and pines and glimpses of old plantations, till there creeps into sight a cluster of buildings—wood and brick, mills and houses, and scattered cabins. It seemed quite a village. As it came nearer and nearer, however, the aspect changed: the buildings were rotten, the bricks were falling out, the mills were silent, and the store was closed. Only in the cabins appeared now and then a bit of lazy life. I could imagine the place under some weird spell, and was half-minded to search out the princess. An old ragged black man, honest, simple, and improvident, told us the tale. The Wizard of the North—the Capital-ist—had rushed down in the seventies to woo this coy dark soil. He bought a square mile or more, and for a time the field-hands sang, the gins groaned, and the mills buzzed. Then came a change. The agent's son embezzled the funds and ran off with them. Then the agent himself disappeared. Finally the new agent stole even the books, and the company in wrath closed its business and its houses, refused to sell, and let houses and furniture and machinery rust and rot. So the Waters-Loring plantation was stilled by the spell of dishonesty, and stands like some gaunt rebuke to a scarred land.

Somehow that plantation ended our day's journey; for I could not shake off the influence of that silent scene. Back toward town we glided, past the straight and thread-like pines, past a dark tree-dotted pond where the air was heavy with a dead sweet perfume. White slender-legged curlews flitted by us, and the garnet blooms of the cotton looked gay against the green and purple stalks. A peasant girl was hoeing in the field, white-turbaned and black-limbed. All this we saw, but the spell still lay upon us.

How curious a land is this—how full of untold story, of tragedy and laughter, and the rich legacy of human life; shadowed with a tragic past, and big with future promise! This is the Black Belt of Georgia. Dougherty County is the west end of the Black Belt, and men once called it the Egypt of the Confederacy. It is full of historic interest. First there is the Swamp, to the west, where the Chickasa-whatchee flows sullenly southward. The shadow of an old plantation lies at its edge, forlorn and dark. Then comes the pool; pendent gray moss and brackish waters appear, and forests filled with wild-fowl. In one place the wood is on fire, smouldering in dull red anger; but nobody minds. Then the swamp grows beauti-ful; a raised road, built by chained Negro convicts, dips down into it, and forms a way walled and almost covered in living green. Spreading trees spring from a prodigal luxuriance of undergrowth; great dark green shadows fade into the black background, until all is one mass of tangled semi-tropical foliage, marvellous in its weird savage splendor. Once we crossed a black silent stream, where the sad trees and writhing creepers, all glinting fiery yellow and green, seemed like some vast cathedral—some green Milan builded of wildwood. And as I crossed, I seemed to see again that fierce tragedy of seventy years ago. Osceola, the Indian-Negro chieftain, had risen in the swamps of Florida, vowing vengeance. His war-cry reached the red Creeks of Dougherty, and their war-cry rang from the Chattahoochee to the sea. Men and women and children fled and fell before them as they swept into Dougherty. In yonder shadows a dark and hideously painted warrior glided stealthily on—another and another, until three hundred had crept into the treacherous swamp. Then the false slime closing about them called the white men from the east. Waist-deep, they fought beneath the tall trees, until the war-cry was hushed and the Indians glided back into the west. Small wonder the wood is red.

Then came the black slaves. Day after day the clank of chained feet marching from Virginia and Carolina to Georgia was heard in these rich swamp lands. Day after day the songs of the callous, the wail of the motherless, and the muttered curses of the wretched echoed from the Flint to the Chickasawhatchee, until by 1860 there had risen in West Dougherty perhaps the richest slave kingdom the modern world ever knew. A hundred and fifty barons commanded the labor of nearly six thousand Negroes, held sway over farms with ninety thousand acres of tilled land, valued even in times of cheap soil at three millions of dollars. Twenty thousand bales of ginned cotton went yearly to England, New and Old; and men that came there bankrupt made money and grew rich. In a single decade the cotton output increased four-fold and the value of lands was tripled. It was the heyday of the *nouveau riche,* and a life of careless extravagance reigned among the masters. Four and six bob-tailed thoroughbreds rolled their coaches to town; open hospitality and gay entertainment were the rule. Parks and groves were laid out, rich with flower and vine, and in the midst stood the low wide-halled "big house," with its porch and columns and great fire-places.

And yet with all this there was something sordid, something forced—a certain feverish unrest and recklessness; for was not all this show and tinsel built upon a groan? "This land was a little Hell," said a ragged, brown, and grave-faced man to me. We were seated near a roadside blacksmith-shop, and behind was the bare ruin of some master's home. "I've seen niggers drop dead in the furrow, but they were kicked aside, and the plough never stopped. And down in the guard-house, there's where the blood ran."

With such foundations a kingdom must in time sway and fall. The masters moved to Macon and Augusta, and left only the irresponsible overseers on the land. And the result is such ruin as this, the Lloyd "home-place":—great waving oaks, a spread of lawn, myrtles and chestnuts, all ragged and wild; a solitary gate-post standing where once was a castle entrance; an old rusty anvil lying amid rotting bellows and wood in the ruins of a blacksmith shop; a wide rambling old mansion, brown and dingy, filled now with the grandchildren of the slaves who once waited on its tables; while the family of the master has dwindled to two lone women, who live in Macon and feed hungrily off the remnants of an earldom. So we ride on, past phantom gates and falling homes—past the once flourishing farms of the Smiths, the Gandys, and the Lagores—and find all dilapidated and half ruined, even there where a solitary white woman, a relic of other days, sits alone in state among miles of Negroes and rides to town in her ancient coach each day.

This was indeed the Egypt of the Confederacy—the rich granary whence potatoes and corn and cotton poured out to the famished and ragged Confederate troops as they battled for a cause lost long before 1861. Sheltered and secure, it became the place of refuge for families, wealth, and slaves. Yet even then the hard ruthless rape of the land began to tell. The red-clay sub-soil already had begun to peer above the loam. The harder the slaves were driven the more careless and fatal was their farming. Then came the revolution of war and Emancipation, the bewilderment of Reconstruction—and now, what is the Egypt of the Confederacy, and what meaning has it for the nation's weal or woe?

It is a land of rapid contrasts and of curiously mingled hope and pain. Here sits a pretty blue-eyed quadroon hiding her bare feet; she was married only last week, and yonder in the field is her dark young husband, hoeing to support her, at thirty cents a day without board. Across the way is Gatesby, brown and tall, lord of two thousand acres shrewdly won and held. There is a store conducted by his black son, a blacksmith shop, and a ginnery. Five miles below here is a town owned and controlled by one white New Englander. He owns almost a Rhode Island county, with thousands of acres and hundreds of black laborers. Their cabins look better than most, and the farm, with machinery and fertilizers, is much more business-like than any in the county, although the manager drives hard bargains in wages. When now we turn and look five miles above, there on the edge of town are five houses of prostitutes—two of blacks and three of whites; and in one of the houses of the whites a worthless black boy was harbored too openly two years ago; so he was hanged for rape. And here, too, is the high whitewashed fence of the "stockade," as the county prison is called; the white folks say it is ever full of black criminals—the black folks say that only colored boys are sent to jail, and they not because they are guilty, but because the State needs criminals to eke out its income by their forced labor.

The Jew is the heir of the slave-baron in Dougherty; and as we ride westward, by wide stretching cornfields and stubby orchards of peach and pear, we see on all sides within the circle of dark forest a Land of Canaan. Here and there are tales of projects for money-getting, born in the swift days of Reconstruction—"improvement" companies, wine companies, mills and factories; nearly all failed, and the Jew fell heir. It is a beautiful land, this Dougherty, west of the Flint. The forests are wonderful, the solemn pines have disappeared, and this is the

"Oakey Woods," with its wealth of hickories, beeches, oaks, and palmettos. But a pall of debt hangs over the beautiful land; the merchants are in debt to the wholesalers, the planters are in debt to the merchants, the tenants owe the planters, and laborers bow and bend beneath the burden of it all. Here and there a man has raised his head above these murky waters. We passed one fenced stock-farm, with grass and grazing cattle, that looked very homelike after endless corn and cotton. Here and there are black freeholders: there is the gaunt dull-black Jackson, with his hundred acres. "I says, 'Look up! If you don't look up you can't get up.' " remarks Jackson, philosophically. And he's gotten up. Dark Carter's neat barns would do credit to New England. His master helped him to get a start, but when the black man died last fall the master's sons immediately laid claim to the estate. "And them white folks will get it, too," said my yellow gossip.

I turn from these well-tended acres with a comfortable feeling that the Negro is rising. Even then, however, the fields, as we proceed, begin to redden and the trees disappear. Rows of old cabins appear filled with renters and laborers—cheerless, bare, and dirty, for the most part, although here and there the very age and decay makes the scene picturesque. A young black fellow greets us. He is twenty-two, and just married. Until last year he had good luck renting; then cotton fell, and the sheriff seized and sold all he had. So he moved here, where the rent is higher, the land poorer, and the owner inflexible; he rents a forty-dollar mule for twenty dollars a year. Poor lad!—a slave at twenty-two. This plantation, owned now by a Russian Jew, was a part of the famous Bolton estate. After the war it was for many years worked by gangs of Negro convicts—and black convicts then were even more plentiful than now; it was a way of making Negroes work, and the question of guilt was a minor one. Hard tales of cruelty and mistreatment of the chained free men are told but the county authorities were deaf until the free-labor market was nearly ruined by wholesale migration. Then they took the convicts from the plantations, but not until one of the fairest regions of the "Oakey Woods" had been ruined and ravished into a red waste, out of which only a Yankee or a Jew could squeeze more blood from debt-cursed tenants.

No wonder that Luke Black, slow, dull, and discouraged, shuffles to our carriage and talks hopelessly. Why should he strive? Every year finds him deeper in debt. How strange that Georgia, the world-heralded refuge of poor debtors, should bind her own to sloth and misfortune as ruthlessly as ever England did! The poor land groans with its birth-pains, and brings forth scarcely a hundred pounds of cotton to the acre, where fifty years ago it yielded eight times as much. Of this meager yield the tenant pays from a quarter to a third in rent, and most of the rest in interest on food and supplies bought on credit. Twenty years yonder sunken-cheeked, old black man has labored under that system, and now, turned day-laborer, is supporting his wife and boarding himself on his wages of a dollar and a half a week, received only part of the year.

The Bolton convict farm formerly included the neighboring plantation. Here it was that the convicts were lodged in the great log prison still standing. A dismal place it still remains, with rows of ugly huts filled with surly ignorant tenants. "What rent do you pay here?" I inquired. "I don't know—what is it, Sam?" "All we make," answered Sam. It is a depressing place—bare, unshaded, with no charm of past association, only a memory of forced human toil—now, then, and before the war. They are not happy, these black men whom we meet throughout this region. There is little of the joyous abandon and playfulness which we are wont to associate with the plantation Negro. At best, the natural good-nature is edged with complaint or has changed into sullenness and gloom. And now and then it blazes forth in veiled but hot anger. I remember one big red-eyed black whom we met by the roadside. Forty-five years he had labored on this farm, beginning with nothing, and still having nothing. To be sure, he had given four children a common-school training, and perhaps if the new fence-law had not allowed unfenced crops in West Dougherty he might have raised a little stock and kept ahead. As it is, he is hopelessly in debt, disappointed, and embittered. He stopped us to inquire after the black boy in Albany, whom it was said a policeman had shot and killed for loud talking on the sidewalk. And then he said slowly: "Let a white man touch me, and he dies; I don't boast this—I don't say it around loud, or before the children—but I mean it. I've seen them whip my father and my old mother in them cotton-rows till the blood ran; by—" and we passed on.

Now Scars, whom we met next lolling under the chubby oak-trees, was of quite different fiber. Happy?—Well, yes; he laughed and flipped pebbles, and thought the world was as it was. He had worked here twelve years and has nothing but a mortgaged mule. Children? Yes, seven; but they hadn't been to school this year—couldn't afford books and clothes, and couldn't spare their work. There go part of them to the fields now—three big boys astride mules, and a strapping girl with bare brown legs. Careless ignorance and laziness here, fierce hate and vindictiveness there—these are the extremes of the Negro problem which we met that day, and we scarce knew which we preferred.

Here and there we meet distinct characters quite out of the ordinary. One came out of a piece of newly cleared ground, making a wide detour to avoid the snakes. He was an old, hollow-cheeked man, with a drawn and characterful brown face. He had a sort of self-contained quaintness and rough humor impossible to describe; a certain cynical earnestness that puzzled one. "The niggers were jealous of me over on the other place," he said, "and so me and the old woman begged this piece of woods, and I cleared it up myself. Made nothing for two years, but I reckon I've got a crop now." The cotton looked tall and rich, and we praised it. He curtsied low, and then bowed almost to the ground, with an imperturbable gravity that seemed almost suspicious. Then he continued, "My mule died last week"—a calamity in this land equal to a devastating fire in town—"but a white man loaned me another." Then he added, eyeing us, "Oh, I gets along with white folks." We turned the conversation. "Bears? deer?" he answered, "well, I should say there were," and he let fly a string of brave oaths, as he told hunting-tales of the swamp. We left him standing still in the middle of the road looking after us, and yet apparently not noticing us.

The Whistle place, which includes his bit of land, was bought soon after the war by an English syndicate, the "Dixie Cotton and Corn Company." A marvellous deal of style their factor put on, with his servants and coach-and-six; so much so that the concern soon landed in inextricable bankruptcy. Nobody lives in the old house now, but a man comes each winter out of the North and collects his high rents. I know not which are the more touching—such old empty houses, or the homes of the masters' sons. Sad and bitter tales lie hidden back of those white doors—tales of poverty, of struggle, of disappointment. A revolution such as that of '63 is a terrible thing; they that rose rich in the morning often slept in paupers' beds. Beggars and vulgar speculators rose to rule over them, and their children went astray. See yonder sad-colored house, with its cabins and fences and glad crops? It is not glad within; last month the prodigal son of the struggling father wrote home from the city for money. Money! Where was it to come from? And so the son rose in the night and killed his baby, and killed his wife, and shot himself dead. And the world passed on.

I remember wheeling around a bend in the road beside a graceful bit of forest and a singing brook. A long low house faced us, with porch and flying pillars, great oaken door, and a broad lawn shining in the evening sun. But the window-panes were gone, the pillars were worm-eaten, and the moss-grown roof was falling in. Half curiously I peered through the unhinged door, and saw where, on the wall across the hall, was written in once gay letters a faded "Welcome."

Quite a contrast to the southwestern part of Dougherty County is the northwest. Soberly timbered in oak and pine, it has none of that half-tropical luxuriance of the southwest. Then, too, there are fewer signs of a romantic past, and more of systematic modern land-grabbing and money-getting. White people are more in evidence here, and farmer and hired labor replace to some extent the absentee landlord and rack-rented tenant. The crops have neither the luxuriance of the richer land nor the signs of neglect so often seen, and there were fences and meadows here and there. More of this land was poor, and beneath the notice of the slave-baron, before the war. Since then his nephews and the poor whites and the Jews have seized it. The returns of the farmer are too small to allow much for wages, and yet he will not sell off small farms. There is the

Negro Sanford; he has worked fourteen years as overseer on the Ladson place, and "paid out enough for fertilizers to have bought a farm," but the owner will not sell off a few acres.

Two children—a boy and a girl—are hoeing sturdily in the fields on the farm where Corliss works. He is smooth-faced and brown, and is fencing up his pigs. He used to run a successful cotton-gin, but the Cotton Seed Oil Trust has forced the price of ginning so low that he says it hardly pays him. He points out a stately old house over the way as the home of "Pa Willis." We eagerly ride over, for "Pa Willis" was the tall and powerful black Moses who led the Negroes for a generation, and led them well. He was a Baptist preacher, and when he died two thousand black people followed him to the grave; and now they preach his funeral sermon each year. His widow lives here—a weazened, sharp-featured little woman, who curtsied quaintly as we greeted her. Further on lives Jack Delson, the most prosperous Negro farmer in the county. It is a joy to meet him—a great broad-shouldered, handsome black man, intelligent and jovial. Six hundred and fifty acres he owns, and has eleven black tenants. A neat and tidy home nestled in a flower-garden, and a little store stands beside it.

We pass the Munson place, where a plucky white widow is renting and struggling; and the eleven hundred acres of the Sennet plantation, with its Negro overseer. Then the character of the farms begins to change. Nearly all the lands belong to Russian Jews; the overseers are white, and the cabins are bare board-houses scattered here and there. The rents are high, and day-laborers and "contract" hands abound. It is a keen, hard struggle for living here, and few have time to talk. Tired with the long ride, we gladly drive into Gillonsville. It is a silent cluster of farm-houses standing on the cross-roads, with one of its stores closed and the other kept by a Negro preacher. They tell great tales of busy times at Gillonsville before all the railroads came to Albany; now it is chiefly a memory. Riding down the street, we stop at the preacher's and seat ourselves before the door. It was one of those scenes one cannot soon forget—a wide, low, little house, whose motherly roof reached over and sheltered a snug little porch. There we sat, after the long hot drive, drinking cool water—the talkative little store-keeper who is my daily companion; the silent old black woman patching pantaloons and saying never a word; the ragged picture of helpless misfortune who called in just to see the preacher; and finally the neat matronly preacher's wife, plump, yellow, and intelligent. "Own land?" said the wife; "well, only this house." Then she added quietly, "We did buy seven hundred acres up yonder, and paid for it; but they cheated us out of it. Sells was the owner." "Sells!" echoed the ragged misfortune, who was leaning against the balustrade and listening, "he's a regular cheat. I worked for him thirty-seven days this spring, and he paid me in cardboard checks which were to be cashed at the end of the month. But he never cashed them—kept putting me off. Then the sheriff came and took my mule and corn and furniture—" "Furniture?" I asked; "but furniture is exempt from seizure by law." "Well, he took it just the same," said the hard-faced man.

LEAVES FROM THE MENTAL PORTFOLIO
OF AN EURASIAN

Sui Sin Far

Sui Sin Far (1865–1914) was born Edith Maud Eaton in Macclesfield, England, to a Chinese mother and an English father. She grew up in Montreal, worked as a journalist and writer of short fiction on the island of Jamaica and in San Francisco, Seattle, and Boston. Her collected stories, *Mrs. Spring Fragrance* (1912), was the first fiction published by an Asian American in the United States, and she was the first to write of Eurasian themes.

The following essay appeared in the progressive journal *The Independent* on January 21, 1909.

WHEN I LOOK BACK OVER THE YEARS I SEE MYSELF, A LITTLE CHILD of scarcely four years of age, walking in front of my nurse, in a green English lane, and listening to her tell another of her kind that my mother is Chinese. "Oh, Lord!" exclaims the informed. She turns me around and scans me curiously from head to foot. Then the two women whisper together. Though the word "Chinese" conveys very little meaning to my mind, I feel that they are talking about my father and mother and my heart swells with indignation. When we reach home I rush to my mother and try to tell her what I have heard. I am a young child. I fail to make myself intelligible. My mother does not understand, and when the nurse declares to her, "Little Miss Sui is a story-teller," my mother slaps me.

Many a long year has past over my head since that day—the day on which

22

LEAVES FROM THE MENTAL PORTFOLIO

I first learned that I was something different and apart from other children, but though my mother has forgotten it, I have not.

I see myself again, a few years older. I am playing with another child in a garden. A girl passes by outside the gate. "Mamie," she cries to my companion. "I wouldn't speak to Sui if I were you. Her mamma is Chinese."

"I don't care," answers the little one beside me. And then to me, "Even if your mamma is Chinese, I like you better than I like Annie."

"But I don't like you," I answer, turning my back on her. It is my first conscious lie.

I am at a children's party, given by the wife of an Indian officer whose children were school fellows of mine. I am only six years of age, but have attended a private school for over a year, and have already learned that China is a heathen country, being civilized by England. However, for the time being, I am a merry romping child. There are quite a number of grown people present. One, a white haired old man, has his attention called to me by the hostess. He adjusts his eyeglasses and surveys me critically. "Ah, indeed!" he exclaims, "Who would have thought it at first glance. Yet now I see the difference between her and other children. What a peculiar coloring! Her mother's eyes and hair and her father's features, I presume. Very interesting little creature!"

I had been called from my play for the purpose of inspection. I do not return to it. For the rest of the evening I hide myself behind a hall door and refuse to show myself until it is time to go home.

My parents have come to America. We are in Hudson City, New York, and we are very poor. I am out with my brother, who is ten months older than myself. We pass a Chinese store, the door of which is open. "Look!" says Charlie, "Those men in there are Chinese!" Eagerly I gaze into the long low room. With the exception of my mother, who is English bred with English ways and manner of dress, I have never seen a Chinese person. The two men within the store are uncouth specimens of their race, dressed in working blouses and pantaloons with queues hanging down their backs. I recoil with a sense of shock.

"Oh, Charlie," I cry, "Are we like that?"

"Well, we're Chinese, and they're Chinese, too, so we must be!" returns my seven-year-old brother.

"Of course you are," puts in a boy who has followed us down the street, and who lives near us and has seen my mother: "Chinky, Chinky, Chinaman, yellow-face, pig-tail, rat-eater." A number of other boys and several little girls join in with him.

"Better than you," shouts my brother, facing the crowd. He is younger and smaller than any there, and I am even more insignificant than he; but my spirit revives.

"I'd rather be Chinese than anything else in the world," I scream.

They pull my hair, they tear my clothes, they scratch my face, and all but lame my brother; but the white blood in our veins fights valiantly for the Chinese half of us. When it is all over, exhausted and bedraggled, we crawl home, and report to our mother that we have "won the battle."

"Are you sure?" asks my mother doubtfully.

"Of course. They ran from us. They were frightened," returns my brother.

My mother smiles with satisfaction.

"Do you hear?" she asks my father.

"Umm," he observes, raising his eyes from his paper for an instant. My childish instinct, however, tells me that he is more interested than he appears to be.

It is tea time, but I cannot eat. Unobserved I crawl away. I do not sleep that night. I am too excited and I ache all over. Our opponents had been so very much stronger and bigger than we. Toward morning, however, I fall into a doze from which I awake myself, shouting:

"Sound the battle cry;
See the foe is nigh."

My mother believes in sending us to Sunday school. She has been brought up in a Presbyterian college.

The scene of my life shifts to Eastern Canada. The sleigh which has carried us from the station stops in front of a little French Canadian hotel. Immediately we are surrounded by a number of villagers, who stare curiously at my mother as my father assists her to alight from the sleigh. Their curiosity, however, is tempered with kindness, as they watch, one after another, the little black heads of my brothers and sisters and myself emerge out of the buffalo robe, which is part of the sleigh's outfit. There are six of us, four girls and two boys; the eldest, my brother, being only seven years of age. My father and mother are still in their twenties. "Les pauvres enfants," the inhabitants murmur, as they help to carry us into the hotel. Then in lower tones: "Chinoise, Chinoise."

For some time after our arrival, whenever we children are sent for a walk, our footsteps are dogged by a number of young French and English Canadians, who amuse themselves with speculations as to whether, we being Chinese, are susceptible to pinches and hair pulling, while older persons pause and gaze upon us, very much in the same way that I have seen people gaze upon strange animals in a menagerie. Now and then we are stopped and plied with questions as to what we eat and drink, how we go to sleep, if my mother understands what my father says to her, if we sit on chairs or squat on floors, etc., etc., etc.

There are many pitched battles, of course, and we seldom leave the house

LEAVES FROM THE MENTAL PORTFOLIO

without being armed for conflict. My mother takes a great interest in our battles, and usually cheers us on, though I doubt whether she understands the depth of the troubled waters through which her little children wade. As to my father, peace is his motto, and he deems it wisest to be blind and deaf to many things.

School days are short, but memorable. I am in the same class with my brother, my sister next to me in the class below. The little girl whose desk my sister shares shrinks close against the wall as my sister takes her place. In a little while she raises her hand.

"Please, teacher!"

"Yes, Annie."

"May I change my seat?"

"No, you may not!"

The little girl sobs. "Why should she have to sit beside a——"

Happily my sister does not seem to hear, and before long the two little girls become great friends. I have many such experiences.

My brother is remarkably bright; my sister next to me has a wonderful head for figures, and when only eight years of age helps my father with his night work accounts. My parents compare her with me. She is of sturdier build than I, and, as my father says, "Always has her wits about her." He thinks her more like my mother, who is very bright and interested in every little detail of practical life. My father tells me that I will never make half the woman that my mother is or that my sister will be. I am not as strong as my sisters, which makes me feel somewhat ashamed, for I am the eldest little girl, and more is expected of me. I have no organic disease, but the strength of my feelings seems to take from me the strength of my body. I am prostrated at times with attacks of nervous sickness. The doctor says that my heart is unusually large; but in the light of the present I know that the cross of the Eurasian bore too heavily upon my childish shoulders. I usually hide my weakness from the family until I cannot stand. I do not understand myself, and I have an idea that the others will despise me for not being as strong as they. Therefore, I like to wander away alone, either by the river or in the bush. The green fields and flowing water have a charm for me. At the age of seven, as it is today, a bird on the wing is my emblem of happiness.

I have come from a race on my mother's side which is said to be the most stolid and insensible to feeling of all races, yet I look back over the years and see myself so keenly alive to every shade of sorrow and suffering that it is almost a pain to live.

If there is any trouble in the house in the way of a difference between my father and mother, or if any child is punished, how I suffer! And when harmony is restored, heaven seems to be around me. I can be sad, but I can also be glad. My mother's screams of agony when a baby is born almost drive me wild, and long after her pangs have subsided I feel them in my own body. Sometimes it is a week before I can get to sleep after such an experience.

A debt owing by my father fills me with shame. I feel like a criminal when I pass the creditor's door. I am only ten years old. And all the while the question of nationality perplexes my little brain. Why are we what we are? I and my brothers and sisters. Why did God make us to be hooted and stared at? Papa is English, mamma is Chinese. Why couldn't we have been either one thing or the other? Why is my mother's race despised? I look into the faces of my father and mother. Is she not every bit as dear and good as he? Why? Why? She sings us the songs she learned at her English school. She tells us tales of China. Though a child when she left her native land she remembers it well, and I am never tired of listening to the story of how she was stolen from her home. She tells us over and over again of her meeting with my father in Shanghai and the romance of their marriage. Why? Why?

I do not confide in my father and mother. They would not understand. How could they? He is English, she is Chinese. I am different to both of them—a stranger, though their own child. "What are we?" I ask my brother. "It doesn't matter, sissy," he responds. But it does. I love poetry, particularly heroic pieces. I also love fairy tales. Stories of everyday life do not appeal to me. I dream dreams of being great and noble; my sisters and brothers also. I glory in the idea of dying at the stake and a great genie arising from the flames and declaring to those who have scorned us: "Behold, how great and glorious and noble are the Chinese people!"

My sisters are apprenticed to a dressmaker; my brother is entered in an office. I tramp around and sell my father's pictures, also some lace which I make myself. My nationality, if I had only known it at that time, helps to make sales. The ladies who are my customers call me "The Little Chinese Lace Girl." But it is a dangerous life for a very young girl. I come near to "mysteriously disappearing" many a time. The greatest temptation was in the thought of getting far away from where I was known, to where no mocking cries of "Chinese! Chinese!" could reach.

Whenever I have the opportunity I steal away to the library and read every book I can find on China and the Chinese. I learn that China is the oldest civilized nation on the face of the earth and a few other things. At eighteen years of age what troubles me is not that I am what I am, but that others are ignorant of my superiority. I am small, but my feelings are big—and great is my vanity.

My sisters attend dancing classes, for which they pay their own fees. In spite of covert smiles and sneers, they are glad to meet and mingle with other young folk. They are not sensitive in the sense that I am. And yet they understand. One of them tells me that she overheard a young man say to another that he would rather marry a pig than a girl with Chinese blood in her veins.

LEAVES FROM THE MENTAL PORTFOLIO

In course of time I too learn shorthand and take a position in an office. Like my sister, I teach myself, but, unlike my sister, I have neither the perseverance nor the ability to perfect myself. Besides, to a temperament like mine, it is torture to spend the hours in transcribing other people's thoughts. Therefore, although I can always earn a moderately good salary, I do not distinguish myself in the business world as does she.

When I have been working for some years I open an office of my own. The local papers patronize me and give me a number of assignments, including most of the local Chinese reporting. I meet many Chinese persons, and when they get into trouble am often called upon to fight their battles in the papers. This I enjoy. My heart leaps for joy when I read one day an article signed by a New York Chinese in which he declares "The Chinese in America owe an everlasting debt of gratitude to Sui Sin Far for the bold stand she has taken in their defense."

The Chinaman who wrote the article seeks me out and calls upon me. He is a clever and witty man, a graduate of one of the American colleges and as well a Chinese scholar. I learn that he has an American wife and several children. I am very much interested in these children, and when I meet them my heart throbs in sympathetic tune with the tales they relate of their experience as Eurasians. "Why did papa and mamma born us?" asks one. Why?

I also meet other Chinese men who compare favorably with the white men of my acquaintance in mind and heart qualities. Some of them are quite handsome. They have not as finely cut noses and as well developed chins as the white men, but they have smoother skins and their expression is more serene; their hands are better shaped and their voices softer.

Some little Chinese women whom I interview are very anxious to know whether I would marry a Chinaman. I do not answer No. They clap their hands delightedly, and assure me that the Chinese are much the finest and best of all men. They are, however, a little doubtful as to whether one could be persuaded to care for me, full-blooded Chinese people having a prejudice against the half white.

Fundamentally, I muse, all people are the same. My mother's race is as prejudiced as my father's. Only when the whole world becomes as one family will human beings be able to see clearly and hear distinctly. I believe that some day a great part of the world will be Eurasian. I cheer myself with the thought that I am but a pioneer. A pioneer should glory in suffering.

"You were walking with a Chinaman yesterday," accuses an acquaintance.

"Yes, what of it?"

"You ought not to. It isn't right."

"Not right to walk with one of my mother's people? Oh, indeed!"

I cannot reconcile his notion of righteousness with my own.

.   .   .

I am living in a little town away off on the north shore of a big lake. Next to me at the dinner table is the man for whom I work as a stenographer. There are also a couple of business men, a young girl and her mother.

Some one makes a remark about the cars full of Chinamen that passed that morning. A transcontinental railway runs through the town.

My employer shakes his rugged head. "Somehow or other," says he, "I cannot reconcile myself to the thought that the Chinese are humans like ourselves. They may have immortal souls, but their faces seem to be so utterly devoid of expression that I cannot help but doubt."

"Souls," echoes the town clerk. "Their bodies are enough for me. A chinaman is, in my eyes, more repulsive than a nigger."

"They always give me such a creepy feeling," puts in the young girl with a laugh.

"I wouldn't have one in my house," declares my landlady.

"Now, the Japanese are different altogether. There is something bright and likeable about those men," continues Mr. K.

A miserable, cowardly feeling keeps me silent. I am in a Middle West town. If I declare what I am, every person in the place will hear about it the next day. The population is in the main made up of working folks with strong prejudices against my mother's countrymen. The prospect before me is not an enviable one—if I speak. I have no longer an ambition to die at the stake for the sake of demonstrating the greatness and nobleness of the Chinese people.

Mr. K. turns to me with a kindly smile.

"What makes Miss Far so quiet?" he asks.

"I don't suppose she finds the 'washee washee men' particularly interesting subjects of conversation," volunteers the young manager of the local bank.

With a great effort I raise my eyes from my plate. "Mr. K.," I say, addressing my employer, "the Chinese people may have no souls, no expression on their faces, be altogether beyond the pale of civilization, but whatever they are, I want you to understand that I am—I am a Chinese."

There is silence in the room for a few minutes. Then Mr. K. pushes back his plate and, standing up beside me, says:

"I should not have spoken as I did. I know nothing whatever about the Chinese. It was pure prejudice. Forgive me!"

I admire Mr. K.'s moral courage in apologizing to me; he is a conscientious Christian man, but I do not remain much longer in the little town.

I am under a tropic sky, meeting frequently and conversing with persons who are almost as high up in the world as birth, education and money can set them. The environment is peculiar, for I am also surrounded by a race of people, the reputed descendants of Ham, the son of Noah, whose offspring, it was prophesied, should be the servants of the sons of Shem and Japheth. As I am a descendant, according to the Bible, of both Shem and Japheth, I have a perfect right to set my heel upon the Ham people; but though I see others around me following out the Bible suggestion, it is not in my nature to be arrogant to any but those who seek to impress me with their superiority, which the poor black maid who has been assigned to me by the hotel certainly does not. My employer's wife takes me to task for this. "It is unnecessary," she says, "to thank a black person for a service."

The novelty of life in the West Indian island is not without its charm. The surroundings, people, manner of living, are so entirely different from what I have been accustomed to up North that I feel as if I were "born again." Mixing with people of fashion, and yet not of them, I am not of sufficient importance to create comment or curiosity. I am busy nearly all day and often well into the night. It is not monotonous work, but it is certainly strenuous. The planters and business men of the island take me as a matter of course and treat me with kindly courtesy. Occasionally an Englishman will warn me against the "brown boys" of the island, little dreaming that I too am of the "brown people" of the earth.

When it begins to be whispered about the place that I am not all white, some of the "sporty" people seek my acquaintance. I am small and look much younger than my years. When, however, they discover that I am a very serious and sober-minded spinster indeed, they retire quite gracefully, leaving me a few amusing reflections.

One evening a card is brought to my room. It bears the name of some naval officer. I go down to my visitor, thinking he is probably some one who, having been told that I am a reporter for the local paper, has brought me an item of news. I find him lounging in an easy chair on the veranda of the hotel—a big, blond, handsome fellow, several years younger than I.

"You are Lieutenant——?" I inquire.

He bows and laughs a little. The laugh doesn't suit him somehow—and it doesn't suit me, either.

"If you have anything to tell me, please tell it quickly, because I'm very busy."

"Oh, you don't really mean that," he answers, with another silly and offensive laugh. "There's always plenty of time for good times. That's what I am here for. I saw you at the races the other day and twice at King's House. My ship will be here for——weeks."

"Do you wish that noted?" I ask.

"Oh, no! Why—I came just because I had an idea that you might like to know me. I would like to know you. You look such a nice little body. Say, wouldn't you like to go out for a sail this lovely night? I will tell you all about the sweet little Chinese girls I met when we were at Hong Kong. They're not so shy!"

VISIONS OF AMERICA

. . .

I leave Eastern Canada for the Far West, so reduced by another attack of rheumatic fever that I only weigh eighty-four pounds. I travel on an advertising contract. It is presumed by the railway company that in some way or other I will give them full value for their transportation across the continent. I have been ordered beyond the Rockies by the doctor, who declares that I will never regain my strength in the East. Nevertheless, I am but two days in San Francisco when I start out in search of work. It is the first time that I have sought work as a stranger in a strange town. Both of the other positions away from home were secured for me by home influence. I am quite surprised to find that there is no demand for my services in San Francisco and that no one is particularly interested in me. The best I can do is to accept an offer from a railway agency to typewrite their correspondence for $5 a month. I stipulate, however, that I shall have the privilege of taking in outside work and that my hours shall be light. I am hopeful that the sale of a story or newspaper article may add to my income, and I console myself with the reflection that, considering that I still limp and bear traces of sickness, I am fortunate to secure any work at all.

The proprietor of one of the San Francisco papers, to whom I have a letter of introduction, suggests that I obtain some subscriptions from the people of Chinatown, that district of the city having never been canvassed. This suggestion I carry out with enthusiasm, though I find that the Chinese merchants and people generally are inclined to regard me with suspicion. They have been imposed upon so many times by unscrupulous white people. Another drawback—save for a few phrases, I am unacquainted with my mother tongue. How, then, can I expect these people to accept me as their own countrywoman? The Americanized Chinamen actually laugh in my face when I tell them that I am of their race. However, they are not all "doubting Thomases." Some little women discover that I have Chinese hair, color of eyes and complexion, also that I love rice and tea. This settles the matter for them—and for their husbands.

My Chinese instincts develop. I am no longer the little girl who shrank against my brother at the first sight of a Chinaman. Many and many a time, when alone in a strange place, has the appearance of even an humble laundryman given me a sense of protection and made me feel quite at home. This fact of itself proves to me that prejudice can be eradicated by association.

I meet a half Chinese, half white girl. Her face is plastered with a thick white coat of paint and her eyelids and eyebrows are blackened so that the shape of her eyes and the whole expression of her face is changed. She was born in the East, and at the age of eighteen came West in answer to an advertisement. Living for many years among the working class, she had heard little but abuse of the Chinese. It is not difficult, in a land like California, for a half Chinese, half white girl to pass as one of Spanish or Mexican origin. This the poor child does, though

LEAVES FROM THE MENTAL PORTFOLIO

she lives in nervous dread of being "discovered." She becomes engaged to a young man, but fears to tell him what she is, and only does so when compelled by a fearless American girl friend. This girl, who knows her origin, realizing that the truth sooner or later must be told, and better soon than late, advises the Eurasian to confide in the young man, assuring her that he loves her well enough not to allow her nationality to stand, a bar sinister, between them. But the Eurasian prefers to keep her secret, and only reveals it to the man who is to be her husband when driven to bay by the American girl, who declares that if the halfbreed will not tell the truth she will. When the young man hears that the girl he is engaged to has Chinese blood in her veins, he exclaims: "Oh, what will my folks say?" But that is all. Love is stronger than prejudice with him, and neither he nor she deems it necessary to inform his "folks."

The Americans having for many years manifested a much higher regard for the Japanese than for the Chinese, several half Chinese young men and women, thinking to advance themselves, both in a social and business sense, pass as Japanese. They continue to be known as Eurasians; but a Japanese Eurasian does not appear in the same light as a Chinese Eurasian. The unfortunate Chinese Eurasians! Are not those who compel them to thus cringe more to be blamed than they?

People, however, are not all alike. I meet white men, and women, too, who are proud to mate with those who have Chinese blood in their veins, and think it a great honor to be distinguished by the friendship of such. There are also Eurasians and Eurasians. I know of one who allowed herself to become engaged to a white man after refusing him nine times. She had discouraged him in every way possible, had warned him that she was half Chinese; that her people were poor, that every week or month she sent home a certain amount of her earnings, and that the man she married would have to do as much, if not more; also, most uncompromising truth of all, that she did not love him and never would. But the resolute and undaunted lover swore that it was a matter of indifference to him whether she was a Chinese or a Hottentot, that it would be his pleasure and privilege to allow her relations double what it was in her power to bestow, and as to not loving him—that did not matter at all. He loved her. So, because the young woman had a married mother and married sisters, who were always picking at her and gossiping over her independent manner of living, she finally consented to marry him, recording the agreement in her diary thus:

"I have promised to become the wife of —— —— on —— ——, 189–, because the world is so cruel and sneering to a single woman—and for no other reason."

Everything went smoothly until one day. The young man was driving a pair of beautiful horses and she was seated by his side, trying very hard to imagine herself in love with him, when a Chinese vegetable gardener's cart came rumbling along. The Chinaman was a jolly-looking individual in blue cotton blouse and pantaloons, his rakish looking hat being kept in place by a long queue which was pulled upward from his neck and wound around it. The young woman was suddenly possessed with the spirit of mischief. "Look!" she cried, indicating the Chinaman, "there's my brother. Why don't you salute him?"

The man's face fell a little. He sank into a pensive mood. The wicked one by his side read him like an open book.

"When we are married," said she. "I intend to give a Chinese party every month."

No answer.

"As there are very few aristocratic Chinese in this city, I shall fill up with the laundrymen and vegetable farmers. I don't believe in being exclusive in democratic America, do you?"

He hadn't a grain of humor in his composition, but a sickly smile contorted his features as he replied:

"You shall do just as you please, my darling. But—but—consider a moment. Wouldn't it be just a little pleasanter for us if, after we are married, we allowed it to be presumed that you were—er—Japanese? So many of my friends have inquired of me if that is not your nationality. They would be so charmed to meet a little Japanese lady."

"Hadn't you better oblige them by finding one?"

"Why—er—what do you mean?"

"Nothing much in particular. Only—I am getting a little tired of this," taking off his ring.

"You don't mean what you say! Oh, put it back, dearest! You know I would not hurt your feelings for the world!"

"You haven't. I'm more than pleased. But I do mean what I say."

That evening the "ungrateful" Chinese Eurasian diaried, among other things, the following:

"Joy, oh, joy! I'm free once more. Never again shall I be untrue to my own heart. Never again will I allow any one to 'hound' or 'sneer' me into matrimony."

I secure transportation to many California points. I meet some literary people, chief among whom is the editor of the magazine who took my first Chinese stories. He and his wife give me a warm welcome to their ranch. They are broadminded people, whose interest in me is sincere and intelligent, not affected and vulgar. I also meet some funny people who advise me to "trade" upon my nationality. They tell me that if I wish to succeed in literature in America I should dress in Chinese costume, carry a fan in my hand, wear a pair of scarlet beaded slippers, live in New York, and come of high birth. Instead of making myself familiar with the Chinese-Americans around me, I should discourse on my spirit acquaintance with Chinese ancestors and quote in between the "Good mornings" and "How d'ye dos" of editors.

> "Confucius, Confucius, how great is Confucius, Before Confucius, there never was Confucius. After Confucius, there never came Confucius," etc., etc., etc.,

or something like that, both illuminating and obscuring, don't you know. They forget, or perhaps they are not aware that the old Chinese sage taught "The way of sincerity is the way of heaven."

My experiences as an Eurasian never cease; but people are not now as prejudiced as they have been. In the West, too, my friends are more advanced in all lines of thought than those whom I know in Eastern Canada—more genuine, more sincere, with less of the form of religion, but more of its spirit.

So I roam backward and forward across the continent. When I am East, my heart is West. When I am West, my heart is East. Before long I hope to be in China. As my life began in my father's country it may end in my mother's.

After all I have no nationality and am not anxious to claim any. Individuality is more than nationality. "You are you and I am I," says Confucius. I give my right hand to the Occidentals and my left to the Orientals, hoping that between them they will not utterly destroy the insignificant "connecting link." And that's all.

THE MYTH THAT MADE HOLLYWOOD

Anzia Yezierska

Anzia Yezierska (1881?–1970) was born in the Russian-Polish ghetto of
Plotsk, and emigrated to New York City with her family in 1890. She worked
as a servant, a laundress, and as a button sewer in sweatshops on the Lower
East Side. She also attended night school and in 1904 graduated from Columbia Teachers College. By writing about the lives of immigrant Jews like
herself, she earned a reputation and, for a time, considerable financial success
as a writer. She is the author of two volumes of short stories, *Hungry Hearts*
(1920), which was sold to Hollywood, and *Children of Loneliness* (1923)—
now published together in *How I Found America: Collected Stories of Anzia
Yezierska*. She also wrote five novels, including the classic *Bread Givers*
(1925). The following selection is chapter five of her last book, *Red Ribbon
on a White Horse* (1950), a memoir.

AFTER MY DÉBUT INTO HOLLYWOOD SOCIETY WILL ROGERS IN-
vited me to visit his family at his Santa Monica ranch. Like millions of people
throughout the country, I used to read Rogers' column in *The New York Times*
and his adventures as "The Self-Appointed Ambassador of Good-Will" in *The
Saturday Evening Post.* But I did not know his power until I had heard him speak
to the Jewish Actors' Guild on behalf of Eddie Cantor's camp for poor boys' free
vacations. He said that there were certain things that no money could buy, that
only the privileged poor could enjoy. When he had visited Eddie's camp he had
been so impressed he wanted his own boy to spend a summer there. But no
money could buy admission to Eddie's happy hunting grounds for kids. Talk
about the privileges of poverty! Any poor kid had a chance to enjoy the luxuries
denied to the rich!

THE MYTH THAT MADE HOLLYWOOD

An Oklahoma cowboy, with his simple gift of fellowship, he had that hallful of people in the palm of his hand. With his power to impart his ease, his joy in life, he made a crowd of Jews laugh away their heritage of sorrow.

The same spirit that had impelled Rogers to speak in behalf of the poor boys' camp made him go out of his way to befriend me. He saw how lost I was in Hollywood and had invited me to spend a week end with his wife and children. I felt I must celebrate the occasion in some special way. All at once my old clothes could no longer contain me. I was letting myself go into a new world. New clothes were part of this new world! I was going to enjoy all the things I had done without, but enjoy people most of all. I decided to go shopping with my secretary. She would know her way about when it came to clothes.

She was waiting for me as usual in the inner room of my office. I was in such a magnanimous mood I could not only forgive Miss Young her youth, her beauty, but even find pleasure in her company. I was getting used to my secretary as I was getting used to my private car and chauffeur.

"It's a grand day," I said.

Her head was bent over her typewriter. She seemed not to see or hear me.

"What perfect weather!" I took off my gloves. "Doesn't it ever rain here?"

She gave me a quick glance and began dusting the typewriter. I looked at her slim young legs in sheer silk stockings and patent-leather pumps. She wore a blouse and skirt with the grace and style of a French model.

"I'm going shopping today," I said. "Come along. Show me where you buy your clothes. You have such good taste."

"A lot of good it does me."

"What's the matter?" I asked.

For the first time she looked at me.

"Try getting a five-dollar raise and being told a hundred girls are waiting to step into your shoes," she said. "All I get is twenty-five dollars a week—and on that I have to look like a fashion plate!"

"You mean to say you're making only twenty-five a week? How can you dress the way you do?"

"I'm part of the stage-set," she said bitterly. "If I didn't dress the part, I'd lose my job—"

The bones in her face stood out sharply under her make-up. Perhaps she had not had enough to eat that morning, but she had covered hunger with the paint of a beauty parlor. When I had been poor I had walked about in rags. But this girl had to wear silk stockings, have her hair waved, nails manicured—on twenty-five dollars a week. This dressed-up poverty was as different from the poverty I had known as Hollywood was different from the ghetto.

"You need more than a diploma from a business college to hold down this job—"

"I'll speak to the personnel manager about you at once," I told her and phoned for an appointment.

Without stopping to think what I would say, I went to his office. He rose from his huge desk, turned on his executive smile.

"What can I do for you?" He drew up a chair for me.

"My secretary . . ." I began, wilted by the slick business face.

"Isn't she okay?"

"More than okay. Why don't you give her a raise?"

He relit his cigar, took a few puffs, his eyes following the smoke to the ceiling. "My job is to run the office force with economy and efficiency. Wages are a matter of supply and demand. So many girls flock to Hollywood, they're begging to work for less than twenty a week. . . ."

"But how can they exist on those wages? Their clothes cost so much."

"Don't let it get you." He smiled. "She's only a stenographer. There are millions of them. If they want to dress like the stars, it's their hard luck."

The smile on his self-satisfied face sickened me. He ate up the air, ate the words out of my mouth.

"The picture business is a game," he said importantly. "The toughest game in the world. Those who can't take it had better get out."

Smoking his cigar, he reminded me of my first boss in the shirt factory. I had protested against overtime work without pay. "Nightwork for nothing is too much."

I was immediately fired for my moment's rebellion.

And now in Hollywood it seemed I had merely reversed my position, joined hands with those who grew rich at the expense of the poor.

I walked out, feeling like a dumb, bewildered immigrant again. And then I remembered the friendly talk I had had with Will Rogers the night before. He would know how to help my secretary get her raise.

I had an appointment with Elinor Glyn for lunch that day in the studio dining room where Rogers often ate. Hurrying to meet her, I passed the "Bear Pit," the cafeteria where the anonymous small fry struggled with their trays at the steam tables. Beyond this noisy crowd was the dining room where the box-office names, the stars, directors, authors, were served by obsequious waiters who catered to their individual diets.

Miss Glyn was waiting for me at her table.

"It's nice to see you again," she said, holding out her hand.

Will Rogers sauntered over. His presence seemed to fling open all the windows of the room.

"We got the barn ready for your visit next Friday," he said.

"Only the barn? I thought, since you're the mayor of Santa Monica, I'd stay in City Hall. I was going to get a new outfit for the occasion. But if I'm to stay at the barn, my old clothes are good enough."

"Well, if you're coming in your glad rags we'll have to put you in the parlor." He threw a piece of chewing gum in his mouth. "Mind if I eat with you?" he asked.

"Come, sit down," I said. "I'm in great need of your advice."

"Where's the fire now, gal?"

I told him of the time I had wasted trying to persuade the personnel manager to raise Miss Young's salary.

"Relax," said Will Rogers. "How about some chow?"

"I'd rather talk than eat—"

"Go ahead and talk, but me—I'm eating." Rogers laughed, reaching for a roll.

Still smarting from my encounter with the personnel manager, I went on: "Did you ever meet a man you hated at sight?"

"I never met a man I didn't like," he said.

"You never met a man you didn't like?" I looked at him. He was so pleasing to people because he found them so pleasant. His sunburned face had the vitality of a man unacquainted with grief, unaware of defeat. He had been unanimously elected mayor of his town. He loved his wife. He worshiped his children. He was such a perfect salesman of himself he could have become a self-satisfied citizen, but he had never stopped being himself—a warm human being.

"When I was a kid on the farm the cow hands usta talk about mean horses or stubborn yearlings. But I never met a calf or any other critter I didn't understand and that didn't understand me. I saw mighty little difference between 'em. Some was more ornery, and some less, but I got along with 'em all."

"Could you get along with them all in a crowded tenement in Hester Street?"

"We-l-l-l," he spun out slowly, "I never lived in Hester Street, but folks are pretty much the same in Hester Street or Kalamazoo. . . ."

Elinor Glyn turned to me, laughing. "He loves everybody, the way the clown loves his audience, the human material for his wisecracks."

"All of us here are clowning for pay, except people like my secretary," I said.

"And what are you clowning for?" the gum-chewing philosopher demanded. "For the glory of the woiking goil?"

Miss Glyn straightened the silver at her plate with carefully manicured fingers. The royal lift of her head declared she lived in an orderly world where values were fixed.

"Something is wrong when my secretary, with her youth and intelligence, has it so hard—" I went on.

VISIONS OF AMERICA

"After all, you got here," said Elinor Glyn.

"I got here by an odd streak of luck," I said.

"Don't be a sourpuss," Rogers admonished. "Don't mock our faith in good luck, or you'll destroy the myth that made Hollywood."

"You could give your secretary a raise out of your own pocket, if it would make you feel better," Elinor Glyn said. "But would that solve the problem of the others?"

Rogers shook his finger and winked at me. "You ought to know that poverty develops character. Don't weaken the girl's fiber with charity. Blessed are the poor. For them is the kingdom."

Everything he said weakened the kinship that the wine and the cocktails had made me feel the night before.

I looked at Elinor Glyn's queenlike neck and shoulders. Here was a woman against whom fate had no weapons. As for Rogers, he laughed so easily. But why shouldn't he laugh? He had no need to change himself, no urge to change the world.

I watched the relish with which he swallowed his last morsel of deep-dish apple pie. Elinor Glyn daintily spooned whipped cream and cherry from her parfait glass. They ate with pleasure. They lived with pleasure.

For a moment I felt I was watching a scene from my past when I had stood outside Childs Restaurant window, seeing the flapjacks turn golden-brown on the griddle—for others to eat.

"Sad, sad, sad little sister." Rogers patted my cheek. "You got success on a tear-jerker the hard way. Must you fiddle the same tune forever? Suppose you give us another number?"

"Have you ever wanted what you couldn't be, or what you couldn't do?"

Rogers took a gulp of water and flung his napkin on the table.

"Gal! You're like a punch-drunk prize fighter, striking an opponent no longer there. You've won your fight and you don't know it. . . ."

"How long has it been since you were poor?" I asked.

"Not so long ago," Rogers retorted. "But I gave them what they wanted. You did too. Lap up the cream while the going's good."

That afternoon when I walked out on the lot, the chauffeur was waiting for me as usual. He opened the door of the car. I was about to step in, but the fine upholstery, the neatly folded rug, and the chauffeur in his smooth-fitting uniform made me feel as if I were part of a stage-set.

"How can I get back to my hotel by trolley?" I asked.

"The trolley is a long roundabout way," he said. "I can get you back in forty minutes—"

"I don't want the car. Give me directions for the trolley."

Outside the gates of the studio. I joined the crowd waiting for the trolley:

stagehands, stenographers, nameless office workers who punched the clock morning and night. It was like the warmth of an open log fire after the artificial fireplace in my office. Here's where I belong, I thought. I felt myself relax, for the first time at ease in Hollywood. When the trolley finally arrived, every seat was jammed. I squeezed in among the straphangers, stimulated by the crowdedness, the physical discomfort. On one side of me, a big-boned Negro washwoman; on the other, a grimy mechanic, a lifetime's hard labor in the lines of his face.

Before the trip was half over, I was exhausted. If I could only slump into a seat. And then a man in front of me got up. Before I had a chance to sit down, a Mexican day laborer pushed past me into the seat. A smell of garlic and the sickening odor of sweat turned my stomach. Too weary to hold onto the strap any longer, I surrendered to the pitching and tossing of the crowd at every turn of the trolley. At last, after many stops, we got to West Los Angeles station, just as the bus to Santa Monica began to pull out. I had missed my connection by less than a minute. The next bus would not be due for half an hour. Another half-hour of waiting in this noisy, pushing mob was too much. Confused, unnerved by the roaring traffic, I hailed a taxi.

As I watched the meter tick off the dimes and dollars, I began to laugh at my silly, stupid contradictions. What a fool and a faker I was to think that giving up the car and riding in the trolley would still my guilty conscience!

ECHOES OF THE JAZZ AGE

F. Scott Fitzgerald

F. Scott Fitzgerald (1896–1940) was born and reared in St. Paul, Minnesota.
In 1917 he left Princeton during his senior year to join the army. Two years
later, he published his first novel, *This Side of Paradise*. Fitzgerald's most
productive period was the decade of the twenties, which saw the publication
of seven books, including his best-known novel, *The Great Gatsby* (1925).
The following essay has been collected in *The Crack-Up* (1945).

November, 1931

It is too soon to write about the jazz age with perspective, and without being
suspected of premature arteriosclerosis. Many people still succumb to violent
retching when they happen upon any of its characteristic words—words which
have since yielded in vividness to the coinages of the underworld. It is as dead
as were the Yellow Nineties in 1902. Yet the present writer already looks back
to it with nostalgia. It bore him up, flattered him and gave him more money than
he had dreamed of, simply for telling people that he felt as they did, that
something had to be done with all the nervous energy stored up and unexpended
in the War.

The ten-year period that, as if reluctant to die outmoded in its bed, leaped

E C H O E S   O F   T H E   J A Z Z   A G E

to a spectacular death in October, 1929, began about the time of the May Day riots in 1919. When the police rode down the demobilized country boys gaping at the orators in Madison Square, it was the sort of measure bound to alienate the more intelligent young men from the prevailing order. We didn't remember anything about the Bill of Rights until Mencken began plugging it, but we did know that such tyranny belonged in the jittery little countries of South Europe. If goose-livered business men had this effect on the government, then maybe we had gone to war for J. P. Morgan's loans after all. But, because we were tired of Great Causes, there was no more than a short outbreak of moral indignation, typified by Dos Passos' *Three Soldiers.* Presently we began to have slices of the national cake and our idealism only flared up when the newspapers made melo-drama out of such stories as Harding and the Ohio Gang or Sacco and Vanzetti. The events of 1919 left us cynical rather than revolutionary, in spite of the fact that now we are all rummaging around in our trunks wondering where in hell we left the liberty cap—"I know I *had* it"—and the moujik blouse. It was character-istic of the Jazz Age that it had no interest in politics at all.

It was an age of miracles, it was an age of art, it was an age of excess, and it was an age of satire. A Stuffed Shirt, squirming to blackmail in a lifelike way, sat upon the throne of the United States; a stylish young man hurried over to represent to us the throne of England. A world of girls yearned for the young Englishman; the old American groaned in his sleep as he waited to be poisoned by his wife, upon the advice of the female Rasputin who then made the ultimate decision in our national affairs. But such matters apart, we had things our way at last. With Americans ordering suits by the gross in London, the Bond Street tailors perforce agreed to moderate their cut to the American long-waisted figure and loose-fitting taste, something subtle passed to America, the style of man. During the Renaissance, Francis the First looked to Florence to trim his leg. Seventeenth-century England aped the court of France, and fifty years ago the German Guards officer bought his civilian clothes in London. Gentlemen's clothes—symbol of "the power that man must hold and that passes from race to race."

We were the most powerful nation. Who could tell us any longer what was fashionable and what was fun? Isolated during the European War, we had begun combing the unknown South and West for folkways and pastimes, and there were more ready to hand.

The first social revelation created a sensation out of all proportion to its novelty. As far back as 1915 the unchaperoned young people of the smaller cities had discovered the mobile privacy of that automobile given to young Bill at sixteen to make him "self-reliant." At first petting was a desperate adventure even under such favorable conditions, but presently confidences were exchanged

VISIONS OF AMERICA

and the old commandment broke down. As early as 1917 there were references to such sweet and casual dalliance in any number of the *Yale Record* or the *Princeton Tiger.*

But petting in its more audacious manifestations was confined to the wealthier classes—among other young people the old standard prevailed until after the War, and a kiss meant that a proposal was expected, as young officers in strange cities sometimes discovered to their dismay. Only in 1920 did the veil finally fall—the Jazz Age was in flower.

Scarcely had the staider citizens of the republic caught their breaths when the wildest of all generations, the generation which had been adolescent during the confusion of the War, brusquely shouldered my contemporaries out of the way and danced into the limelight. This was the generation whose girls dramatized themselves as flappers, the generation that corrupted its elders and eventually overreached itself less through lack of morals than through lack of taste. May one offer in exhibit the year 1922! That was the peak of the younger generation, for though the Jazz Age continued, it became less and less an affair of youth.

The sequel was like a children's party taken over by the elders, leaving the children puzzled and rather neglected and rather taken aback. By 1923 their elders, tired of watching the carnival with ill-concealed envy, had discovered that young liquor will take the place of young blood, and with a whoop the orgy began. The younger generation was starred no longer.

A whole race going hedonistic, deciding on pleasure. The precocious intimacies of the younger generation would have come about with or without prohibition—they were implicit in the attempt to adapt English customs to American conditions. (Our South, for example, is tropical and early maturing—it has never been part of the wisdom of France and Spain to let young girls go unchaperoned at sixteen and seventeen.) But the general decision to be amused that began with the cocktail parties of 1921 had more complicated origins.

The word jazz in its progress toward respectability has meant first sex, then dancing, then music. It is associated with a state of nervous stimulation, not unlike that of big cities behind the lines of a war. To many English the War still goes on because all the forces that menace them are still active—Wherefore eat, drink and be merry, for tomorrow we die. But different causes had now brought about a corresponding state in America—though there were entire classes (people over fifty, for example) who spent a whole decade denying its existence even when its puckish face peered into the family circle. Never did they dream that they had contributed to it. The honest citizens of every class, who believed in a strict public morality and were powerful enough to enforce the necessary legislation, did not know that they would necessarily be served by criminals and quacks, and do not really believe it today. Rich righteousness had always been able to buy honest and intelligent servants to free the slaves or the Cubans, so when this attempt collapsed our elders stood firm with all the stubbornness of people involved in a weak case, preserving their righteousness and losing their children. Silver-haired women and men with fine old faces, people who never did a consciously dishonest thing in their lives, still assure each other in the apartment hotels of New York and Boston and Washington that "there's a whole generation growing up that will never know the taste of liquor." Meanwhile their granddaughters pass the well-thumbed copy of *Lady Chatterley's Lover* around the boarding-school and, if they get about at all, know the taste of gin or corn at sixteen. But the generation who reached maturity between 1875 and 1895 continue to believe what they want to believe.

Even the intervening generations were incredulous. In 1920 Heywood Broun announced that all this hubbub was nonsense, that young men didn't kiss but told anyhow. But very shortly people over twenty-five came in for an intensive education. Let me trace some of the revelations vouchsafed them by reference to a dozen works written for various types of mentality during the decade. We begin with the suggestion that Don Juan leads an interesting life (*Jurgen*, 1919); then we learn that there's a lot of sex around if we only knew it (*Winesburg, Ohio,* 1920), that adolescents lead very amorous lives (*This Side of Paradise,* 1920), that there are a lot of neglected Anglo-Saxon words (*Ulysses,* 1921), that older people don't always resist sudden temptations (*Cytherea,* 1922), that girls are sometimes seduced without being ruined (*Flaming Youth,* 1922), that even rape often turns out well (*The Sheik,* 1922), that glamorous English ladies are often promiscuous (*The Green Hat,* 1924), that in fact they devote most of their time to it (*The Vortex,* 1926), that it's a damn good thing too (*Lady Chatterley's Lover,* 1928), and finally that there are abnormal variations (*The Well of Loneliness,* 1928, and *Sodom and Gomorrah,* 1929).

In my opinion the erotic element in these works, even *The Sheik* written for children in the key of *Peter Rabbit,* did not one particle of harm. Everything they described, and much more, was familiar in our contemporary life. The majority of the theses were honest and elucidating—their effect was to restore some dignity to the male as opposed to the he-man in American life. ("And what is a 'He-man'?" demanded Gertrude Stein one day. "Isn't it a large enough order to fill out to the dimensions of all that 'a man' has meant in the past? A 'He-man'!") The married woman can now discover whether she is being cheated, or whether sex is just something to be endured, and her compensation should be to establish a tyranny of the spirit, as her mother may have hinted. Perhaps many women found that love was meant to be fun. Anyhow the objectors lost their tawdry little case, which is one reason why our literature is now the most living in the world.

Contrary to popular opinion, the movies of the Jazz Age had no effect upon its morals. The social attitude of the producers was timid, behind the times and banal—for example, no picture mirrored even faintly the younger generation until 1923, when magazines had already been started to celebrate it and it had long ceased to be news. There were a few feeble splutters and then Clara Bow in *Flaming Youth;* promptly the Hollywood hacks ran the theme into its cinematographic grave. Throughout the Jazz Age the movies got no farther than Mrs. Jiggs, keeping up with its most blatant superficialities. This was no doubt due to the censorship as well as to innate conditions in the industry. In any case, the Jazz Age now raced along under its own power, served by great filling stations full of money.

The people over thirty, the people all the way up to fifty, had joined the dance. We graybeards (to tread down F. P. A.) remember the uproar when in 1912 grandmothers of forty tossed away their crutches and took lessons in the Tango and the Castle-Walk. A dozen years later a woman might pack the Green Hat with her other affairs as she set off for Europe or New York, but Savonarola was too busy flogging dead horses in Augean stables of his own creation to notice. Society, even in small cities, now dined in separate chambers, and the sober table learned about the gay table only from hearsay. There were very few people left at the sober table. One of its former glories, the less sought-after girls who had become resigned to sublimating a probable celibacy, came across Freud and Jung in seeking their intellectual recompense and came tearing back into the fray.

By 1926 the universal preoccupation with sex had become a nuisance. (I remember a perfectly mated, contented young mother asking my wife's advice about "having an affair right away," though she had no one especially in mind, "because don't you think it's sort of undignified when you get much over thirty?") For a while bootleg Negro records with their phallic euphemisms made everything suggestive, and simultaneously came a wave of erotic plays—young girls from finishing-schools packed the galleries to hear about the romance of being a Lesbian and George Jean Nathan protested. Then one young producer lost his head entirely, drank a beauty's alcoholic bath-water and went to the penitentiary. Somehow his pathetic attempt at romance belongs to the Jazz Age, while his contemporary in prison, Ruth Snyder, had to be hoisted into it by the tabloids—she was, as *The Daily News* hinted deliciously to gourmets, about "to cook, *and sizzle, AND FRY!*" in the electric chair.

The gay elements of society had divided into two main streams, one flowing toward Palm Beach and Deauville, and the other, much smaller, toward the summer Riviera. One could get away with more on the summer Riviera, and whatever happened seemed to have something to do with art. From 1926 to 1929, the great years of the Cap d'Antibes, this corner of France was dominated by a group quite distinct from that American society which is dominated by Europeans. Pretty much of anything went at Antibes—by 1929, at the most

ECHOES OF THE JAZZ AGE

gorgeous paradise for swimmers on the Mediterranean no one swam any more, save for a short hang-over dip at noon. There was a picturesque graduation of steep rocks over the sea and somebody's valet and an occasional English girl used to dive from them, but the Americans were content to discuss each other in the bar. This was indicative of something that was taking place in the home-land—Americans were getting soft. There were signs everywhere: we still won the Olympic games but with champions whose names had few vowels in them—teams composed, like the fighting Irish combination of Notre Dame, of fresh overseas blood. Once the French became really interested, the Davis Cup gravi-tated automatically to their intensity in competition. The vacant lots of the Middle-Western cities were built up now—except for a short period in school, we were not turning out to be an athletic people like the British, after all. The hare and the tortoise. Of course if we wanted to we could be in a minute; we still had all those reserves of ancestral vitality, but one day in 1926 we looked down and found we had flabby arms and a fat pot and couldn't say boop-boop-a-doop to a Sicilian. Shades of Van Bibber!—no utopian ideal, God knows. Even golf, once considered an effeminate game, had seemed very strenuous of late—an emasculated form appeared and proved just right.

By 1927 a wide-spread neurosis began to be evident, faintly signalled, like a nervous beating of the feet, by the popularity of cross-word puzzles. I remem-ber a fellow expatriate opening a letter from a mutual friend of ours, urging him to come home and be revitalized by the hardy, bracing qualities of the native soil. It was a strong letter and it affected us both deeply, until we noticed that it was headed from a nerve sanitarium in Pennsylvania.

By this time contemporaries of mine had begun to disappear into the dark maw of violence. A classmate killed his wife and himself on Long Island, another tumbled "accidently" from a skyscraper in Philadelphia, another purposely from a skyscraper in New York. One was killed in a speak-easy in Chicago; another was beaten to death in a speak-easy in New York and crawled home to the Princeton Club to die; still another had his skull crushed by a maniac's axe in an insane asylum where he was confined. These are not catastrophes that I went out of my way to look for—these were my friends; moreover, these things happened not during the depression but during the boom.

In the spring of '27, something bright and alien flashed across the sky. A young Minnesotan who seemed to have had nothing to do with his generation did a heroic thing, and for a moment people set down their glasses in country clubs and speakeasies and thought of their old best dreams. Maybe there was a way out by flying, maybe our restless blood could find frontiers in the illimitable air. But by that time we were all pretty well committed; and the Jazz Age continued; we would all have one more.

Nevertheless, Americans were wandering ever more widely—friends seemed eternally bound for Russia, Persia, Abyssinia and Central Africa. And by 1928 Paris had grown suffocating. With each new shipment of Americans spewed up by the boom the quality fell off, until toward the end there was something sinister about the crazy boatloads. They were no longer the simple pa and ma and son and daughter, infinitely superior in their qualities of kindness and curiosity to the corresponding class in Europe, but fantastic neanderthals who believed something, something vague, that you remembered from a very cheap novel. I remember an Italian on a steamer who promenaded the deck in an American Reserve Officer's uniform picking quarrels in broken English with Americans who criticized their own institutions in the bar. I remember a fat Jewess, inlaid with diamonds, who sat behind us at the Russian ballet and said as the curtain rose, "Thad's luffly, dey ought to baint a bicture of it." This was low comedy, but it was evident that money and power were falling into the hands of people in comparison with whom the leader of a village Soviet would be a gold-mine of judgment and culture. There were citizens travelling in luxury in 1928 and 1929 who, in the distortion of their new condition, had the human value of Pekinese, bivalves, cretins, goats. I remember the Judge from some New York district who had taken his daughter to see the Bayeux Tapestries and made a scene in the papers advocating their segregation because one scene was immoral. But in those days life was like the race in *Alice in Wonderland,* there was a prize for every one.

The Jazz Age had had a wild youth and a heady middle age. There was the phase of the necking parties, the Leopold-Loeb murder (I remember the time my wife was arrested on Queensborough Bridge on the suspicion of being the "Bob-haired Bandit") and the John Held Clothes. In the second phase such phenomena as sex and murder became more mature, if much more conventional. Middle age must be served and pajamas came to the beach to save fat thighs and flabby calves from competition with the one-piece bathing-suit. Finally skirts came down and everything was concealed. Everybody was at scratch now. Let's go—

But it was not to be. Somebody had blundered and the most expensive orgy in history was over.

It ended two years ago,* because the utter confidence which was its essential prop received an enormous jolt, and it didn't take long for the flimsy structure to settle earthward. And after two years the Jazz Age seems as far away as the days before the War. It was borrowed time anyhow—the whole upper tenth of a nation living with the insouciance of grand ducs and the casualness of chorus girls. But moralizing is easy now and it was pleasant to be in one's twenties in such a certain and unworried time. Even when you were broke you didn't worry

*1929

ECHOES OF THE JAZZ AGE

about money, because it was in such profusion around you. Toward the end one had a struggle to pay one's share; it was almost a favor to accept hospitality that required any travelling. Charm, notoriety, mere good manners weighed more than money as a social asset. This was rather splendid, but things were getting thinner and thinner as the eternal necessary human values tried to spread over all that expansion. Writers were geniuses on the strength of one respectable book or play; just as during the War officers of four months' experience commanded hundreds of men, so there were now many little fish lording it over great big bowls. In the theatrical world extravagant productions were carried by a few second-rate stars, and so on up the scale into politics, where it was difficult to interest good men in positions of the highest importance and responsibility, importance and responsibility far exceeding that of business executives but which paid only five or six thousand a year.

Now once more the belt is tight and we summon the proper expression of horror as we look back at our wasted youth. Sometimes, though, there is a ghostly rumble among the drums, an asthmatic whisper in the trombones that swings me back into the early twenties when we drank wood alcohol and every day in every way grew better and better, and there was a first abortive shortening of the skirts, and girls all looked alike in sweater dresses, and people you didn't want to know said "Yes, we have no bananas," and it seemed only a question of a few years before the older people would step aside and let the world be run by those who saw things as they were—and it all seems rosy and romantic to us who were young then, because we will never feel quite so intensely about our surroundings any more.

CHOOSING A DREAM:
ITALIANS IN HELL'S KITCHEN

Mario Puzo

Mario Puzo was born in New York City and attended the New School for
Social Research and Columbia University. His novels include *The Dark Arena*
(1955), *The Fortunate Pilgrim* (1964), *The Godfather* (1969), and *The Fourth
K* (1991). Puzo is also the author of a collection of essays, *The Godfather
Papers and Other Confessions* (1972).

AS A CHILD AND IN MY ADOLESCENCE, LIVING IN THE HEART OF NEW
York's Neapolitan ghetto, I never heard an Italian singing. None of the grown-ups
I knew were charming or loving or understanding. Rather they seemed coarse,
vulgar, and insulting. And so later in my life when I was exposed to all the clichés
of lovable Italians, singing Italians, happy-go-lucky Italians, I wondered where
the hell the moviemakers and storywriters got all their ideas from.

At a very early age I decided to escape these uncongenial folk by becoming
an artist, a writer. It seemed then an impossible dream. My father and mother
were illiterate, as were their parents before them. But, practicing my art, I tried
to view the adults with a more charitable eye and so came to the conclusion that
their only fault lay in their being foreigners: I was an American. This didn't really

CHOOSING A DREAM

help because I was only half right. I was the foreigner. They were already more "American" than I could ever become.

But it did seem then that the Italian immigrants, all the fathers and mothers that I knew, were a grim lot; always shouting, always angry, quicker to quarrel than embrace. I did not understand that their lives were a long labor to earn their daily bread and that physical fatigue does not sweeten human natures.

And so even as a very small child I dreaded growing up to be like the adults around me. I heard them saying too many cruel things about their dearest friends, saw too many of their false embraces with those they had just maligned, observed with horror their paranoiac anger at some small slight or a fancied injury to their pride. They were, always, too unforgiving. In short, they did not have the careless magnanimity of children.

In my youth I was contemptuous of my elders, including a few under thirty. I thought my contempt special to their circumstances. Later when I wrote about these illiterate men and women, when I thought I understood them, I felt a condescending pity. After all, they had suffered, they had labored all the days of their lives. They had never tasted luxury, knew little more economic security than those ancient Roman slaves who might have been their ancestors. And alas, I thought, with newfound artistic insight, they were cut off from their children because of the strange American tongue, alien to them, native to their sons and daughters.

Already an artist but not yet a husband or father, I pondered omnisciently on their tragedy, again thinking it special circumstance rather than a constant in the human condition. I did not yet understand why these men and women were willing to settle for less than they deserved in life and think that "less" quite a bargain. I did not understand that they simply could not afford to dream; I myself had a hundred dreams from which to choose. For I was already sure that I would make my escape, that I was one of the chosen. I would be rich, famous, happy. I would master my destiny.

And so it was perhaps natural that as a child, with my father gone, my mother the family chief, I, like all the children in all the ghettos of America, became locked in a bitter struggle with the adults responsible for me. It was inevitable that my mother and I became enemies.

As a child I had the usual dreams. I wanted to be handsome, specifically as cowboy stars in movies were handsome. I wanted to be a killer hero in a worldwide war. Or if no wars came along (our teachers told us another was impossible), I wanted at the very least to be a footloose adventurer. Then I branched out and thought of being a great artist, and then, getting ever more sophisticated, a great criminal.

My mother, however, wanted me to be a railroad clerk. And that was her *highest* ambition; she would have settled for less. At the age of sixteen, when I let everybody know that I was going to be a great writer, my friends and family took the news quite calmly, my mother included. She did not become angry. She quite simply assumed that I had gone off my nut. She was illiterate, and her peasant life in Italy made her believe that only a son of the nobility could possibly be a writer. Artistic beauty after all could spring only from the seedbed of fine clothes, fine food, luxurious living. So then how was it possible for a son of hers to be an artist? She was not too convinced she was wrong even after my first two books were published many years later. It was only after the commercial success of my third novel that she gave me the title of poet.

My family and I grew up together on Tenth Avenue, between Thirtieth and Thirty-first streets, part of the area called Hell's Kitchen. This particular neighborhood could have been a movie set for one of the Dead End Kid flicks or for the social drama of the East Side in which John Garfield played the hero. Our tenements were the western wall of the city. Beneath our windows were the vast black iron gardens of the New York Central Railroad, absolutely blooming with stinking boxcars freshly unloaded of cattle and pigs for the city slaughterhouse. Steers sometimes escaped and loped through the heart of the neighborhood followed by astonished young boys who had never seen a live cow.

The railroad yards stretched down to the Hudson River, beyond whose garbagey waters rose the rocky Palisades of New Jersey. There were railroad tracks running downtown on Tenth Avenue itself to another freight station called St. Johns Park. Because of this, because these trains cut off one side of the street from the other, there was a wooden bridge over Tenth Avenue, a romantic-looking bridge despite the fact that no sparkling water, no silver flying fish darted beneath it; only heavy dray carts drawn by tired horses, some flat-boarded trucks, tin lizzie automobiles and, of course, long strings of freight cars drawn by black, ugly engines.

What was really great, truly magical, was sitting on the bridge, feet dangling down, and letting the engine under you blow up clouds of steam that made you disappear, then reappear all damp and smelling of fresh ironing. When I was seven years old, I fell in love for the first time with the tough little girl who held my hand and disappeared with me in that magical cloud of steam. This experience was probably more traumatic and damaging to my later relationships with women than one of those ugly childhood adventures Freudian novelists use to explain why their hero has gone bad.

My father supported his wife and seven children by working as a trackman laborer for the New York Central Railroad. My oldest brother worked for the railroad as a brakeman; another brother was a railroad shipping clerk in the freight office. Eventually I spent some of the worst months of my life as the railroad's worst messenger boy.

CHOOSING A DREAM

My oldest sister was just as unhappy as a dressmaker in the garment industry. She wanted to be a schoolteacher. At one time or another my other two brothers also worked for the railroad—it got all six males in the family. The two girls and my mother escaped, though my mother felt it her duty to send all our bosses a gallon of homemade wine on Christmas. But everybody hated their jobs except my oldest brother, who had a night shift and spent most of his working hours sleeping in freight cars. My father finally got fired because the foreman told him to get a bucket of water for the crew and not to take all day. My father took the bucket and disappeared forever.

Nearly all the Italian men living on Tenth Avenue supported their large families by working on the railroad. Their children also earned pocket money by stealing ice from the refrigerator cars in summer and coal from the open stoking cars in the winter. Sometimes an older lad would break the seal of a freight car and take a look inside. But this usually brought down the "Bulls," the special railroad police. And usually the freight was "heavy" stuff, too much work to cart away and sell, something like fresh produce or boxes of cheap candy that nobody would buy.

The older boys, the ones just approaching voting age, made their easy money by hijacking silk trucks that loaded up at the garment factory on Thirty-first Street. They would then sell the expensive dresses door to door, at bargain prices no discount house could match. From this some graduated into organized crime, whose talent scouts alertly tapped young boys versed in strong arm. Yet despite all this, most of the kids grew up honest, content with fifty bucks a week as truck drivers, deliverymen, and white-collar clerks in the Civil Service.

I had every desire to go wrong but I never had a chance. The Italian family structure was too formidable.

I never came home to an empty house; there was always the smell of supper cooking. My mother was always there to greet me, sometimes with a policeman's club in her hand (nobody ever knew how she acquired it). But she was always there, or her authorized deputy, my older sister, who preferred throwing empty milk bottles at the heads of her little brothers when they got bad marks on their report cards. During the great Depression of the 1930s, though we were the poorest of the poor, I never remember not dining well. Many years later as a guest of a millionaire's club, I realized that our poor family on home relief ate better than some of the richest people in America.

My mother would never dream of using anything but the finest imported olive oil, the best Italian cheeses. My father had access to the fruits coming off ships, the produce from railroad cars, all before it went through the stale process of middlemen; and my mother, like most Italian women, was a fine cook in the peasant style.

My mother was as formidable a personage as she was a cook. She was not to be treated cavalierly. My oldest brother at age sixteen had his own tin lizzie Ford and used it to further his career as the Don Juan of Tenth Avenue. One day my mother asked him to drive her to the market on Ninth Avenue and Fortieth Street, no more than a five-minute trip. My brother had other plans and claimed he was going to work on a new shift on the railroad. Work was an acceptable excuse even for funerals. But an hour later when my mother came out of the door of the tenement, she saw the tin lizzie loaded with three pretty neighborhood girls, my Don Juan brother about to drive them off. Unfortunately there was a cobblestone lying loose in the gutter. My mother dropped her black leather shopping bag and picked up the stone with both hands. As we all watched in horror, she brought the boulder down on the nearest fender of the tin lizzie, demolishing it. Then she picked up her bag and marched off to Ninth Avenue to do her shopping. To this day, forty years later, my brother's voice still has a surprised horror and shock when he tells the story. He still doesn't understand how she could have done it.

My mother had her own legends and myths on how to amass a fortune. There was one of our uncles who worked as an assistant chef in a famous Italian-style restaurant. Every day, six days a week, this uncle brought home, under his shirt, six eggs, a stick of butter, and a small bag of flour. By doing this for thirty years he was able to save enough money to buy a fifteen-thousand-dollar house on Long Island and two smaller houses for his son and daughter. Another cousin, blessed with a college degree, worked as a chemist in a large manufacturing firm. By using the firm's raw materials and equipment he con-cocted a superior floor wax which he sold door to door in his spare time. It was a great floor wax, and with his low overhead, the price was right. My mother and her friends did not think this stealing. They thought of it as being thrifty.

The wax-selling cousin eventually destroyed his reputation for thrift by buying a sailboat; this was roughly equivalent to the son of a Boston Brahmin spending a hundred grand in a whorehouse.

As rich men escape their wives by going to their club, I finally escaped my mother by going to the Hudson Guild Settlement House. Most people do not know that a setlement house is really a club combined with social services. The Hudson Guild, a five-story field of joy for slum kids, had ping-pong rooms and billiard rooms, a shop in which to make lamps, a theater for putting on amateur plays, a gym to box and play basketball in. And then there were individual rooms, where your particular club could meet in privacy. The Hudson Guild even sus-pended your membership for improper behavior or failure to pay the tiny dues. It was a heady experience for a slum kid to see his name posted on the billboard to the effect that he was suspended by the Board of Governors.

There were young men who guided us as counselors whom I remember with fondness to this day. They were more like friends than adults assigned to watch over us. I still remember one helping us eat a box of stolen chocolates rather than reproaching us. Which was exactly the right thing for him to do; we trusted him after that. The Hudson Guild kept more kids out of jail than a thousand policemen. It still exists today, functioning for the new immigrants, the blacks, and the Puerto Ricans.

There was a night when the rich people of New York, including the Ethical Culture Society, attended a social function at the Hudson Guild in order to be conned into contributing huge sums of money for the settlement house program. I think it was a dinner and amateur theater presentation that was costing them a hundred bucks a head. Their chauffeurs parked the limousines all along the curbs of Twenty-seventh Street and Tenth Avenue. Us deprived kids, myself the leader, spent the night letting the air out of our benefactors' tires. *Noblesse oblige.*

But we weren't all bad. In our public schools one year an appeal was made to every child to try to bring a can of food to fill Thanksgiving baskets for the poor. The teachers didn't seem to realize *we* were the poor. We didn't either. Every kid in that public school, out of the goodness of his heart, went out and stole a can of food from a local grocery store. Our school had the best contributor record of any school in the city.

Some of the most exciting days in my life were spent at the Hudson Guild. At the age of eleven I became captain of my club football team for seven years and president of the Star Club, an office I held for five. I enjoyed that success more than any other in my life. And learned a great deal from it. At the age of fifteen I was as thoroughly corrupted by power as any dictator until I was overthrown by a coalition of votes; my best friends joining my enemies to depose me. It was a rare lesson to learn at fifteen.

The Star Club was made up of boys my own age, a gang, really, which had been pacified by the Hudson Guild Settlement House. We had a football team, a baseball team, a basketball team. We had a yearbook. We had our own room, where we could meet, and a guidance counselor, usually a college boy. We had one named Ray Dooley whom I remember with affection to this day. He took us for outings in the country, to the Hudson Guild Farm in New Jersey for winter weekends, where we hitched our sleds to his car, towed at thirty miles an hour. We repaid him by throwing lye into his face and almost blinding him. We thought it was flour. He never reproached us and it wound up okay. We idolized him after that. I liked him because he never tried to usurp my power, not so that I could notice.

The Hudson Guild was also responsible for absolutely the happiest times of my childhood. When I was about nine or ten they sent me away as a Fresh Air Fund kid. This was a program where slum children were boarded on private families in places like New Hampshire for two weeks.

As a child I knew only the stone city. I had no conception of what the countryside could be. When I got to New Hampshire, when I smelled grass and flowers and trees, when I ran barefoot along the dirt country roads, when I drove the cows home from pasture, when I darted through fields of corn and waded through clear brooks, when I gathered warm brown-speckled eggs in the hen-house, when I drove a hay wagon drawn by two great horses—when I did all these things—I nearly went crazy with the joy of it. It was quite simply a fairy tale come true.

The family that took me in, a middle-aged man and woman, childless, were Baptists and observed Sunday so religiously that even checker playing was not allowed on the Lord's day of rest. We went to church on Sunday for a good three hours, counting Bible class, then again at night. On Thursday evenings we went to prayer meetings. My guardians, out of religious scruple, had never seen a movie. They disapproved of dancing, they were no doubt political reactionaries; they were everything that I came later to fight against.

And yet they gave me those magical times children never forget. For two weeks every summer from the time I was nine to fifteen I was happier than I have ever been before or since. The man was good with tools and built me a little playground with swings, sliding ponds, seesaws. The woman had a beautiful flower and vegetable garden and let me pick from it. A cucumber or strawberry in the earth was a miracle. And then when they saw how much I loved picnics, the sizzling frankfurters on a stick over the wood fire, the yellow roasted corn, they drove me out on Sunday afternoons to a lovely green grass mountainside. Only on Sundays it was never called a picnic; it was called "taking our lunch outside." I found it then—and now—a sweet hypocrisy.

The Baptist preacher lived in the house a hundred yards away, and some-times he, too, took his lunch "out" with us on a Sunday afternoon, he and his wife and children. Outside of his church he was a jolly fat man, a repressed comedian. Also a fond father, he bought his children a great many toys. I borrowed those toys and on one late August day I sailed his son's huge motor launch down a quiet, winding brook, and when it nosed into a wet mossy bank. I buried the toy there to have the following year when I came back. But I never found it.

There came a time, I was fifteen, when I was told I was too old to be sent away to the country as a Fresh Air Fund kid. It was the first real warning that I must enter the adult world, ready or not. But I always remembered that man and woman with affection, perhaps more. They always bought me clothing during my visits, my very first pajamas. They sent me presents at Christmastime, and when I was about to go into the Army, I visited them as a young man of twenty-one. The young were excessively grateful then, so I did not smoke in their house nor did I follow up on a local maid who seemed promising.

I believed then, as a child, that the state of New Hampshire had some sort

CHOOSING A DREAM

of gates at which all thieves and bad guys were screened out. I believed this, I think, because the house was left unlocked when we went to church on Sundays and Thursday nights. I believed it because I never heard anyone curse or quarrel with raised voices. I believed it because it was beautiful to believe.

When I returned home from these summer vacations I had a new trick. I said grace with bowed head before eating the familiar spaghetti and meat balls. My mother always tolerated this for the few days it lasted. After all, the two weeks' vacation from her most troublesome child was well worth a Baptist prayer.

From this Paradise I was flung into Hell. That is, I had to help support my family by working on the railroad. After school hours, of course. This was the same railroad that had supplied free coal and free ice to the whole Tenth Avenue when I was young enough to steal with impunity. After school finished at 3 P.M. I went to work in the freight office as a messenger. I also worked Saturdays and Sundays when there was work available.

I hated it. One of my first short stories was about how I hated that job. But of course what I really hated was entering the adult world. To me the adult world was a dark enchantment, unnatural. As unnatural to the human dream as death. And as inevitable.

The young are impatient about change because they cannot grasp the power of time itself; not only as the enemy of flesh, the very germ of death, but as a benign cancer. As the young cannot grasp really that love must be a victim of time, so too they cannot grasp that injustices, the economic and family traps of living, can also fall victim to time.

And so I really thought that I would spend the rest of my life as a railroad clerk. That I would never be a writer. That I would be married and have children and go to christenings and funerals and visit my mother on a Sunday afternoon. That I would never own an automobile or a house. That I would never see Europe, the Paris and Rome and Greece I was reading about in books from the public library. That I was hopelessly trapped by my family, by society, by my lack of skills and education.

But I escaped again. At the age of eighteen I started dreaming about the happiness of my childhood. As later at the age of thirty I would dream about the joys of my lost adolescence, as at the age of thirty-five I was to dream about the wonderful time I had in the Army which I had hated being in. As at the age of forty-five I dreamed about the happy, struggling years of being a devoted husband and loving father. I had the most valuable of human gifts, that of retrospective falsification: remembering the good and not the bad.

I still dreamed of future glory. I still wrote short stories, one or two a year. I still *knew* I would be a great writer, but I was beginning to realize that accidents

VISIONS OF AMERICA

could happen and my second choice, that of being a great criminal, was coming up fast. But for the young everything goes so slowly, I could wait it out. The world would wait for me. I could still spin out my life with dreams.

In the summertime I was one of the great Tenth Avenue athletes, but in the wintertime I became a sissy. I read books. At a very early age I discovered libraries, the one in the Hudson Guild and the public ones. I loved reading in the Hudson Guild where the librarian became a friend. I loved Joseph Altsheler's (I don't even have to look up his name) tales about the wars of the New York State Indian tribes, the Senecas and the Iroquois. I discovered Doc Savage and the Shadow and then the great story-teller Sabatini. Part of my character to this day is Scaramouche, I like to think. And then maybe at the age of fourteen or fifteen or sixteen I discovered Dostoevski. I read books, all of them I could get. I wept for Prince Myshkin in *The Idiot,* I was as guilty as Raskolnikov. And when I finished *The Brothers Karamazov* I understood for the first time what was really happening to me and the people around me. I had always hated religion even as a child, but now I became a true believer. I believed in art. A belief that has helped me as well as any other.

My mother looked on all this reading with a fishy Latin eye. She saw no profit in it, but since all her children were great readers, she was a good enough general to know she could not fight so pervasive an insubordination. And there may have been some envy. If she had been able to, she would have been the greatest reader of us all.

My direct ancestors for a thousand years have most probably been illiterate. Italy, the golden land, so loving to vacationing Englishmen, so majestic in its language and cultural treasures (they call it, I think, the cradle of civilization), has never cared for its poor people. My father and mother were both illiterates. Both grew up on rocky, hilly farms in the countryside adjoining Naples. My mother remembers never being able to taste the ham from the pig they slaughtered every year. It brought too high a price in the marketplace and cash was needed. My mother was also told the family could not afford the traditional family gift of linens when she married, and it was this that decided her to emigrate to America to marry her first husband, a man she barely knew. When he died, in a tragic work accident on the docks, she married my father, who assumed responsibility for a widow and her four children perhaps out of ignorance, perhaps out of compassion, perhaps out of love. Nobody ever knew. He was a mystery, a Southern Italian with blue eyes, who departed from the family scene three children later when I was twelve. But he cursed Italy even more than my mother did. Then again, he wasn't too pleased with America either. My mother never heard of Michelangelo; the great deeds of the Caesars had not yet reached her ears. She never heard the great music of her native land. She could not sign her name.

CHOOSING A DREAM

And so it was hard for my mother to believe that her son could become an artist. After all, her one dream in coming to America had been to earn her daily bread, a wild dream in itself. And looking back she was dead right. Her son an artist? To this day she shakes her head. I shake mine with her.

America may be a Fascistic, warmongering, racially prejudiced country today. It may deserve the hatred of its revolutionary young. But what a miracle it once was! What has happened here has never happened in any other country in any other time. The poor, who had been poor for centuries—hell, since the beginning of Christ—whose children had inherited their poverty, their illiteracy, their hopelessness, achieved some economic dignity and freedom. You didn't get it for nothing, you had to pay a price in tears, in suffering, but why not? And some even became artists.

Not even my gift for retrospective falsification can make my eighteenth to twenty-first years seem like a happy time. I hated my life. I was being dragged into the trap I feared and had foreseen even as a child. It was all there, the steady job, the nice girl who would eventually get knocked up, and then the marriage and fighting over counting pennies to make ends meet. I noticed myself acting more unheroic all the time. I had to tell lies in pure self-defense, I did not forgive so easily.

But I was delivered. When World War II broke out, I was delighted. There is no other word, terrible as it may sound. My country called. I was delivered from my mother, my family, the girl I was loving passionately but did not love. And delivered *without guilt.* Heroically. My country called, ordered me to defend it. I must have been one of millions—sons, husbands, fathers, lovers—making their innocent getaway from baffled loved ones. And what an escape it was. The war made all my dreams come true. I drove a jeep, toured Europe, had love affairs, found a wife, and lived the material for my first novel. But of course it is perhaps for the best that the revolutionary young make their escape by attacking their own rulers.

Then why five years later did I walk back into the trap with a wife and child and a Civil Service job I was glad to get? After five years of the life I had dreamed about, plenty of women, plenty of booze, plenty of money, hardly any work, interesting companions, travel, etc., why did I walk back into that cage of family and duty and a steady job?

For the simple reason, of course, that I had never really escaped, not my mother, not my family, not the moral pressures of our society. Time again had done its work. I was back in my cage and I was, I think, happy. In the next twenty years I wrote three novels. Two of them were critical successes but I didn't make much money. The third novel, not as good as the others, made me rich. And free at last. Or so I thought.

Then why do I dream of those immigrant Italian peasants as having been happy? I remember how they spoke of their forebears, who spent all their lives farming the arid mountain slopes of Southern Italy. "He died in that house in which he was born," they say enviously. "He was never more than an hour from his village, not in all his life." They sigh. And what would they make of a phrase like "retrospective falsification"?

No, really, we are all happier now. It is a better life. And after all, as my mother always said, "Never mind about being happy. Be glad you're alive."

When I came to my "autobiographical novel," the one every writer does about himself, I planned to make myself the sensitive, misunderstood hero, much put upon by his mother and family. To my astonishment my mother took over the book and instead of my revenge I got another comeuppance. But it is, I think, my best book. And all those old-style grim conservative Italians whom I hated, then pitied so patronizingly, they also turned out to be heroes. Through no desire of mine, I was surprised. The thing that amazed me most was their courage. Where were their Congressional Medals of Honor? Their Distinguished Service Crosses? How did they ever have the balls to get married, have kids, go out to earn a living in a strange land, with no skills, not even knowing the language? They made it without tranquilizers, without sleeping pills, without psychiatrists, without even a dream. Heroes. Heroes all around me. I never saw them.

But how could I? They wore lumpy work clothes and handlebar mustaches, they blew their noses on their fingers, and they were so short that their high school children towered over them. They spoke a laughable broken English and the furthest limit of their horizon was their daily bread. Brave men, brave women, they fought to live their lives without dreams. Bent on survival, they narrowed their minds to the thinnest line of existence.

It is no wonder that in my youth I found them contemptible. And yet they had left Italy and sailed the ocean to come to a new land and leave their sweated bones in America. Illiterate Colombos, they dared to seek the promised land. And so they, too, dreamed a dream.

Forty years ago, in 1930, when I was ten, I remember gas light, spooky, making the tenement halls and rooms alive with ghosts.

We had the best apartment on Tenth Avenue, a whole top floor of six rooms, with the hall as our storage cellar and the roof as our patio. Two views, one of the railroad yards backed by the Jersey shore, the other of a backyard teeming with tomcats everybody shot at with BB guns. In between these two rooms with a view were three bedrooms without windows—the classic railroad flat pattern. The kitchen had a fire escape that I used to sneak out at night. I liked that apartment, though it had no central heating, only a coal stove at one end and an oil stove at the other. I remember it as comfortable, slum or not.

My older brothers listened to a crystal radio on homemade headsets. I

CHOOSING A DREAM

hitched a ride on the backs of horses and wagons; my elders daringly rode the trolley cars. Only forty years ago in calendar time, it is really a thousand years in terms of change in our physical world. There are the jets, TV, penicillin for syphilis, cobalt for cancer, equal sex for single girls; yet still always the contempt of the young for their elders.

But maybe the young are on the right track this time. Maybe they know that the dreams of our fathers were malignant. Perhaps it is true that the only real escape is in the blood magic of drugs. All the Italians I knew and grew up with have escaped, have made their success. We all are Americans now, we all are successes now. And yet the most successful Italian man I know admits that, though the one human act he never could understand was suicide, he understood it when he became a success. Not that he ever would do such a thing; no man with Italian blood ever commits suicide or becomes a homosexual in his belief. But suicide has crossed his mind. And so to what avail the finding of the dream? He went back to Italy and tried to live like a peasant again. But he can never again be unaware of more subtle traps than poverty and hunger.

There is a difference between having a good time in life and being happy. My mother's life was a terrible struggle and yet I think it was a happy life. One tentative proof is that at the age of eighty-two she is positively indignant at the thought that death dares approach her. But it's not for everybody, that kind of life.

Thinking back, I wonder why I became a writer. Was it the poverty or the books I read? Who traumatized me, my mother or the Brothers Karamazov? Being Italian? Or the girl sitting with me on the bridge as the engine steam deliciously made us vanish? Did it make any difference that I grew up Italian rather than Irish or black?

No matter. The good times are beginning, I am another Italian success story. Not as great as DiMaggio or Sinatra, but quite enough. It will serve. Yet I can escape again. I have my retrospective falsification (how I love that phrase). I can dream now about how happy I was in my childhood, in my tenement, playing in those dirty but magical streets—living in the poverty that made my mother weep. True, I was a deposed dictator at fifteen, but they never hanged me. And now I remember all those impossible dreams strung out before me, waiting for me to choose, not knowing that the life I was living then, as a child, would become my final dream.

from AMERICA IS IN THE HEART

Carlos Bulosan

Carlos Bulosan (1913–1956) was born in Binalonan in the Philippines. He landed in Seattle at the age of sixteen, having traveled steerage class. Working many years as a migrant farm laborer and dishwasher, Bulosan became involved in labor organizing and wrote for the union newspaper. Throughout the Second World War, his stories, essays, and books had high national visibility, but he died in poverty and obscurity. His books include *The Voice of Bataan* (1943), *The Dark People* (1944), *Laughter of My Father* (1944), *America Is in the Heart: A Personal History* (1946), and *The Power of the People,* published posthumously in 1977.

WE ARRIVED IN SEATTLE ON A JUNE DAY. MY FIRST SIGHT OF THE approaching land was an exhilarating experience. Everything seemed native and promising to me. It was like coming home after a long voyage, although as yet I had no home in this city. Everything seemed familiar and kind—the white faces of the buildings melting in the soft afternoon sun, the gray contours of the surrounding valleys that seemed to vanish in the last periphery of light. With a sudden surge of joy, I knew that I must find a home in this new land.

I had only twenty cents left, not even enough to take me to Chinatown where, I had been informed, a Filipino hotel and two restaurants were located. Fortunately two oldtimers put me in a car with four others, and took us to a hotel on King Street, the heart of Filipino life in Seattle. Marcelo, who was also in the car, had a cousin named Elias who came to our room with another oldtimer. Elias and his unknown friend persuaded my companions to play a strange kind of card game. In a little while Elias got up and touched his friend suggestively; then they disappeared and we never saw them again.

It was only when our two countrymen had left that my companions realized what happened. They had taken all their money. Marcelo asked me if I had any money. I gave him my twenty cents. After collecting a few more cents from the others, he went downstairs and when he came back he told us that he had telegraphed for money to his brother in California.

All night we waited for the money to come, hungry and afraid to go out in the street. Outside we could hear shouting and singing; then a woman screamed lustily in one of the rooms down the hall. Across from our hotel a jazz band was playing noisily; it went on until dawn. But in the morning a telegram came to Marcelo which said:

YOUR BROTHER DIED AUTOMOBILE ACCIDENT LAST WEEK

Marcelo looked at us and began to cry. His anguish stirred an aching fear in me. I knelt on the floor looking for my suitcase under the bed. I knew that I had to go out now—alone. I put the suitcase on my shoulder and walked toward the door, stopping for a moment to look back at my friends who were still standing silently around Marcelo. Suddenly a man came into the room and announced that he was the proprietor.

"Well, boys," he said, looking at our suitcases, "where is the rent?"

"We have no money, sir," I said, trying to impress him with my politeness.

"That is too bad," he said quickly, glancing furtively at our suitcases again. "That is just too bad." He walked outside and went down the hall. He came back with a short, fat Filipino, who looked at us stupidly with his dull, small eyes, and spat his cigar out of the window.

"There they are, Jake," said the proprietor.

Jake looked disappointed. "They are too young," he said.

"You can break them in, Jake," said the proprietor.

"They will be sending babies next," Jake said.

"You can break them in, can't you, Jake?" the proprietor pleaded. "This is not the first time you have broken babies in. You have done it in the sugar plantations in Hawaii, Jake!"

"Hell!" Jake said, striding across the room to the proprietor. He pulled a fat roll of bills from his pocket and gave twenty-five dollars to the proprietor. Then he turned to us and said, "All right, Pinoys, you are working for me now. Get your hats and follow me."

We were too frightened to hesitate. When we lifted our suitcases the proprietor ordered us not to touch them.

"I'll take care of them until you come back from Alaska," he said. "Good fishing, boys!"

In this way we were sold for five dollars each to work in the fish canneries in Alaska, by a Visayan from the island of Leyte to an Ilocano from the province of La Union. Both were oldtimers; both were tough. They exploited young immigrants until one of them, the hotel proprietor, was shot dead by an unknown assailant. We were forced to sign a paper which stated that each of us owed the contractor twenty dollars for bedding and another twenty for luxuries. What the luxuries were, I have never found out. The contractor turned out to be a tall, heavy-set, dark Filipino, who came to the small hold of the boat barking at us like a dog. He was drunk and saliva was running down his shirt.

"And get this, you devils!" he shouted at us. "You will never come back alive if you don't do what I say!"

It was the beginning of my life in America, the beginning of a long flight that carried me down the years, fighting desperately to find peace in some corner of life.

I had struck up a friendship with two oldtimers who were not much older than I. One was Conrado Torres, a journalism student at a university in Oregon, who was fired with a dream to unionize the cannery workers. I discovered that he had come from Binalonan, but could hardly remember the names of people there because he had been very young when he had come to America. Conrado was small and dark, with slant eyes and thick eyebrows; but his nose was thin above a wise, sensuous mouth. He introduced me to Paulo Lorca, a gay fellow, who had graduated from law school in Los Angeles. This surreptitious meeting at a cannery in Rose Inlet was the beginning of a friendship that grew simultaneously with the growth of the trade union movement and progressive ideas among the Filipinos in the United States.

In those days labor unions were still unheard of in the canneries, so the contractors rapaciously exploited their workers. They had henchmen in every cannery who saw to it that every attempt at unionization was frustrated and the instigators of the idea punished. The companies also had their share in the exploitation; our bunkhouses were unfit for human habitation. The lighting system was bad and dangerous to our eyes, and those of us who were working in the semi-darkness were severely affected by the strong ammonia from the machinery.

I was working in a section called "wash lye." Actually a certain amount of lye was diluted in the water where I washed the beheaded fish that came down on a small escalator. One afternoon a cutter above me, working in the poor light, slashed off his right arm with the cutting machine. It happened so swiftly he did not cry out. I saw his arm floating down the water among the fish heads.

AMERICA IS IN THE HEART

It was only at night that we felt free, although the sun seemed never to disappear from the sky. It stayed on in the western horizon and its magnificence inflamed the snows on the island, giving us a world of soft, continuous light, until the moon rose at about ten o'clock to take its place. Then trembling shadows began to form on the rise of the brilliant snow in our yard, and we would come out with baseball bats, gloves and balls, and the Indian girls who worked in the cannery would join us, shouting huskily like men.

We played far into the night. Sometimes a Filipino and an Indian girl would run off into the moonlight; we could hear them chasing each other in the snow. Then we would hear the girl giggling and laughing deliciously in the shadows. Paulo was always running off with a girl named La Belle. How she acquired that name in Alaska, I never found out. But hardly had we started our game when off they ran, chasing each other madly and suddenly disappearing out of sight.

Toward the end of the season La Belle gave birth to a baby. We were sure, however, that the father was not in our group. We were sure that she had got it from one of the Italian fishermen on the island. La Belle did not come to work for two days, but when she appeared on the third day with the baby slung on her back, she threw water into Conrado's face.

"Are you going to marry me or not?" she asked him.

Conrado was frightened. He was familiar with the ways of Indians, so he said: "Why should I marry you?"

"We'll see about that!" La Belle shouted, running to the door. She came back with an official of the company. "That's the one!" she said, pointing to Conrado.

"You'd better come to the office with us," said the official.

Conrado did not know what to do. He looked at me for help. Paulo left his washing machine and nodded to me to follow him. We went with them into the building which was the town hall.

"You are going to marry this Indian girl and stay on the island for seven years as prescribed by law," said the official to Conrado. "And as the father of the baby, you must support both mother and child, and, if you have four more children by the time your turn is up, you will be sent back to the mainland with a bonus."

"But, sir, the baby is not mine," said Conrado weakly.

Paulo stepped up quickly beside him and said: "The baby is mine, sir. I guess I'll have to stay."

La Belle looked at Paulo with surprise. After a moment, however, she began to smile with satisfaction. Paulo was well-educated and spoke good English. But I think what finally drove Conrado from La Belle's primitive mind were Paulo's curly hair, his even, white teeth. Meekly she signed the paper after Paulo.

"I'll stay here for seven years, all right," Paulo said to me. "I'm in a mess in Los Angeles anyway—so I'll stay with this dirty Indian girl."

"Stop talking like that if you know what is good for you," La Belle said, giving him the baby.

"I guess you are right," Paulo said.

"You shouldn't have done it for me," Conrado said.

"It's all right," Paulo laughed. "I'll be in the United States before you know it."

I still do not understand why Paulo interceded for Conrado. When the season was over Paulo came to our bunks in the boat and asked Conrado to send him something to drink. I did not see him again.

———

When I landed in Seattle for the second time, I expected a fair amount of money from the company. But the contractor, Max Feuga, came into the play room and handed us slips of paper. I looked at mine and was amazed at the neatly itemized expenditures that I was supposed to have incurred during the season. Twenty-five dollars for withdrawals, one hundred for board and room, twenty for bedding, and another twenty for something I do not now remember. At the bottom was the actual amount I was to receive after all the deductions: *thirteen dollars!*

I could do nothing. I did not even go to the hotel where I had left my suitcase. I went to a Japanese dry goods store on Jackson Street and bought a pair of corduroy pants and a blue shirt. It was already twilight and the cannery workers were in the crowded Chinese gambling houses, losing their season's earnings and drinking bootleg whisky. They became quarrelsome and abusive to their own people when they lost, and subservient to the Chinese gambling lords and marijuana peddlers. They pawed at the semi-nude whores with their dirty hands and made suggestive gestures, running out into the night when they were rebuffed for lack of money.

I was already in America, and I felt good and safe. I did not understand why. The gamblers, prostitutes and Chinese opium smokers did not excite me, but they aroused in me a feeling of flight. I knew that I must run away from them, but it was not that I was afraid of contamination. I wanted to see other aspects of American life, for surely these destitute and vicious people were merely a small part of it. Where would I begin this pilgrimage, this search for a door into America?

I went outside and walked around looking into the faces of my countrymen, wondering if I would see someone I had known in the Philippines. I came to a building which brightly dressed white women were entering, lifting their diaphanous gowns as they climbed the stairs. I looked up and saw the huge sign:

MANILA DANCE HALL

The orchestra upstairs was playing; Filipinos were entering. I put my hands in my pockets and followed them, beginning to feel lonely for the sound of home.

The dance hall was crowded with Filipino cannery workers and domestic servants. But the girls were very few, and the Filipinos fought over them. When a boy liked a girl he bought a roll of tickets from the hawker on the floor and kept dancing with her. But the other boys who also liked the same girl shouted at him to stop, cursing him in the dialects and sometimes throwing rolled wet papers at him. At the bar the glasses were tinkling, the bottles popping loudly, and the girls in the back room were smoking marijuana. It was almost impossible to breathe.

Then I saw Marcelo's familiar back. He was dancing with a tall blonde in a green dress, a girl so tall that Marcelo looked like a dwarf climbing a tree. But the girl was pretty and her body was nicely curved and graceful, and she had a way of swaying that aroused confused sensations in me. It was evident that many of the boys wanted to dance with her; they were shouting maliciously at Marcelo. The way the blonde waved to them made me think that she knew most of them. They were nearly all oldtimers and strangers to Marcelo. They were probably gamblers and pimps, because they had fat rolls of money and expensive clothing.

But Marcelo was learning very fast. He requested one of his friends to buy another roll of tickets for him. The girl was supposed to tear off one ticket every three minutes, but I noticed that she tore off a ticket for every minute. That was ten cents a minute. Marcelo was unaware of what she was doing; he was spending his whole season's earnings on his first day in America. It was only when one of his friends shouted to him in the dialect that he became angry at the girl. Marcelo was not tough, but his friend was an oldtimer. Marcelo pushed the girl toward the gaping bystanders. His friend opened a knife and gave it to him.

Then something happened that made my heart leap. One of the blonde girl's admirers came from behind and struck Marcelo with a piece of lead pipe. Marcelo's friend whipped out a pistol and fired. Marcelo and the boy with the lead pipe fell on the floor simultaneously, one on top of the other, but the blonde girl ran into the crowd screaming frantically. Several guns banged at once, and the lights went out. I saw Marcelo's friend crumple in the fading light.

At once the crowd seemed to flow out of the windows. I went to a side window and saw three heavy electric wires strung from the top of the building to the ground. I reached for them and slid to the ground. My palms were burning when I came out of the alley. Then I heard the sirens of police cars screaming infernally toward the place. I put my cap in my pocket and ran as fast as I could in the direction of a neon sign two blocks down the street.

It was a small church where Filipino farm workers were packing their suitcases and bundles. I found out later that Filipino immigrants used their churches as rest houses while they were waiting for work. There were two large trucks outside. I went to one of them and sat on the running board, holding my hands over my heart for fear it would beat too fast. The lights in the church went out and the workers came into the street. The driver of the truck in which I was sitting pointed a strong flashlight at me.

"Hey, you, are you looking for a job?" he asked.

"Yes, sir," I said.

"Get in the truck," he said, jumping into the cab. "Let's go, Flo!" he shouted to the other driver.

I was still trembling with excitement. But I was glad to get out of Seattle—to anywhere else in America. I did not care where so long as it was in America. I found a corner and sat down heavily. The drivers shouted to each other. Then we were off to work.

It was already midnight and the lights in the city of Seattle were beginning to fade. I could see the reflections on the bright lake in Bremerton. I was reminded of Baguio. Then some of the men began singing. The driver and two men were arguing over money. A boy in the other truck was playing a violin. We were on the highway to Yakima Valley.

After a day and a night of driving we arrived in a little town called Moxee City. The apple trees were heavy with fruit and the branches drooped to the ground. It was late afternoon when we passed through the town; the hard light of the sun punctuated the ugliness of the buildings. I was struck dumb by its isolation and the dry air that hung oppressively over the place. The heart-shaped valley was walled by high treeless mountains, and the hot breeze that blew in from a distant sea was injurious to the apple trees.

The leader of our crew was called Cornelio Paez; but most of the oldtimers suspected that it was not his real name. There was something shifty about him, and his so-called bookkeeper, a pockmarked man we simply called Pinoy (which is a term generally applied to all Filipino immigrant workers), had a strange trick of squinting sideways when he looked at you. There seemed to be an old animosity between Paez and his bookkeeper.

But we were drawn together because the white people of Yakima Valley were suspicious of us. Years before, in the town of Toppenish, two Filipino apple pickers had been found murdered on the road to Sunnyside. At that time, there

AMERICA IS IN THE HEART

was ruthless persecution of the Filipinos throughout the Pacific Coast, instigated by orchardists who feared the unity of white and Filipino workers. A small farmer in Wapato who had tried to protect his Filipino workers had had his house burned. So however much we distrusted each other under Paez, we knew that beyond the walls of our bunkhouses were our real enemies, waiting to drive us out of Yakima Valley.

I had become acquainted with an oldtimer who had had considerable experience in the United States. His name was Julio, and it seemed that he was hiding from some trouble in Chicago. At night, when the men gambled in the kitchen, I would stand silently behind him and watch him cheat the other players. He was very deft, and his eyes were sharp and trained. Sometimes when there was no game, Julio would teach me tricks.

Mr. Malraux, our employer, had three daughters who used to work with us after school hours. He was a Frenchman who had gone to Moxee City when it consisted of only a few houses. At that time the valley was still a haven for Indians, but they had been gradually driven out when farming had been started on a large scale. Malraux had married an American woman in Spokane and begun farming; the girls came one by one, helping him on the farm as they grew. When I arrived in Moxee City they were already in their teens.

The oldest girl was called Estelle; she had just finished high school. She had a delightful disposition and her industry was something that men talked about with approval. The other girls, Maria and Diane, were still too young to be going about so freely; but whenever Estelle came to our bunkhouse they were always with her.

It was now the end of summer and there was a bright moon in the sky. Not far from Moxee City was a wide grassland where cottontails and jack rabbits roamed at night. Estelle used to drive her father's old car and would pick up some of us at the bunkhouse; then we would go hunting with their dogs and a few antiquated shotguns.

When we came back from hunting we would go to the Malraux house with some of the men who had musical instruments. We would sit on the lawn for hours singing American songs. But when they started singing Philippine songs their voices were so sad, so full of yesterday and the haunting presence of familiar seas, as if they had reached the end of creation, that life seemed ended and no bright spark was left in the world.

But one afternoon toward the end of the season, Paez went to the bank to get our paychecks and did not come back. The pockmarked bookkeeper was furious.

"I'll get him this time!" he said, running up and down the house. "He did that last year in California and I didn't get a cent. I know where to find the bastard!"

Julio grabbed him by the neck. "You'd better tell me where to find him if you know what is good for you," he said angrily, pushing the frightened bookkeeper toward the stove.

"Let me alone!" he shouted.

Julio hit him between the eyes, and the bookkeeper struggled violently. Julio hit him again. The bookkeeper rolled on the floor like a baby. Julio picked him up and threw him outside the house. I thought he was dead, but his legs began to move. Then he opened his eyes and got up quickly, staggering like a drunken stevedore toward the highway. Julio came out of the house with brass knuckles, but the bookkeeper was already disappearing behind the apple orchard. Julio came back and began hitting the door of the kitchen with all his force, in futile anger.

I had not seen this sort of brutality in the Philippines, but my first contact with it in America made me brave. My bravery was still nameless, and waiting to express itself. I was not shocked when I saw that my countrymen had become ruthless toward one another, and this sudden impact of cruelty made me insensate to pain and kindness, so that it took me a long time to wholly trust other men. As time went by I became as ruthless as the worst of them, and I became afraid that I would never feel like a human being again. Yet no matter what bestiality encompassed my life, I felt sure that somewhere, sometime, I would break free. This faith kept me from completely succumbing to the degradation into which many of my countrymen had fallen. It finally paved my way out of our small, harsh life, painfully but cleanly, into a world of strange intellectual adventures and self-fulfillment.

———

I began to be afraid, riding alone in the freight train. I wanted suddenly to go back to Stockton and look for a job in the tomato fields, but the train was already traveling fast. I was in flight again, away from an unknown terror that seemed to follow me everywhere. Dark flight into another place, toward other enemies. But there was a clear sky and the night was ablaze with stars. I could still see the faint haze of Stockton's lights in the distance, a halo arching above it and fading into a backdrop of darkness.

In the early morning the train stopped a few miles from Niles, in the midst of a wide grape field. The grapes had been harvested and the bare vines were falling to the ground. The apricot trees were leafless. Three railroad detectives jumped out of a car and ran toward the boxcars. I ran to the vineyard and hid behind a smudge pot, waiting for the next train from Stockton. A few bunches of grapes still hung on the vines, so I filled my pockets and ran for the tracks when the train came. It was a freight and it stopped to pick up carloads of grapes; when it started moving again the empties were full of men.

I crawled to a corner of a car and fell asleep. When I awakened the train was already in San Jose. I jumped outside and found another freight going south. I swung aboard and found several hoboes drinking cans of beer. I sat and watched them sitting solemnly, as though there were no more life left in the world. They talked as though there were no more happiness left, as though life had died and would not live again. I could not converse with them, and this barrier made me a stranger. I wanted to know them and to be a part of their life. I wondered what I had in common with them beside the fact that we were all on the road rolling to unknown destinations.

When I reached Salinas, I walked to town and went to a Mexican restaurant on Soledad Street. I was drinking coffee when I saw the same young girl who had disappeared in the night. She was passing by with an old man. I ran to the door and called to her, but she did not hear me. I went back to my coffee wondering what would become of her.

I avoided the Chinese gambling houses, remembering the tragedy in Stockton. Walking on the dark side of the street as though I were hunted, I returned eagerly to the freight yards. I found the hoboes sitting gloomily in the dark. I tried a few times to jump into the boxcars, but the detectives chased me away. When the freights had gone the detectives left.

Then an express from San Francisco came and stopped to pick up a few passengers. The hoboes darted out from the dark and ran to the rods. When I realized that I was the only one left, I grabbed the rod between the coal car and the car behind it. Then the express started, gathering speed as it nosed its way through the night.

I almost fell several times. The strong, cold wind lashed sharply at my face. I put the crook of my arm securely about the rod, pinching myself when I feared that I was going to sleep. It was not yet autumn and the sky was clear, but the wind was bitter and sharp and cut across my face like a knife. When my arm went to sleep, I beat it to life with my fist. It was the only way I could save myself from falling to my death.

I was so exhausted and stiff with the cold when I reached San Luis Obispo that I could scarcely climb down. I stumbled when I reached the ground, rolling over on my stomach as though I were headless. Then I walked to town, where I found a Filipino who took me in his car to Pismo Beach. The Filipino community was a small block near the sea—a block of poolrooms, gambling houses, and little green cottages where prostitutes were doing business. At first I did not know what the cottages were, but I saw many Filipinos going into them from the gambling houses near by. Then I guessed what they were, because cottages such as these were found in every Filipino community.

VISIONS OF AMERICA

I went into one of the cottages and sat in the warm little parlor where the Filipinos were waiting their turn to go upstairs. Some of the prostitutes were sitting awkwardly in the men's laps, wheedling them. Others were dancing cheek to cheek, swaying their hips suggestively. The Filipinos stood around whispering lustily in their dialects. The girls were scantily dressed, and one of them was nude. The nude girl put her arms around me and started cooing lasciviously.

I was extricated from her by the same Filipino who had taken me into his car in San Luis Obispo. He came into the house and immediately took the girl upstairs. In ten minutes he was down again and asked me if I would like to ride with him to Lompoc. I had heard of the place when I was in Seattle, so naturally I was interested. We started immediately and in about two hours had passed through Santa Maria.

Beyond the town, at a railroad crossing, highway patrolmen stopped our car. Speaking to me in our dialect, Doro, my companion, said:

"These bastards probably want to see if we have a white woman in the car."

"Why?" I asked him, becoming frightened.

"They think every Filipino is a pimp," he said. "But there are more pimps among them than among all the Filipinos in the world put together. I will kill one of these bastards someday!"

They questioned Doro curtly, peered into the car, and told us to go on.

I came to know afterward that in many ways it was a crime to be a Filipino in California. I came to know that the public streets were not free to my people: we were stopped each time these vigilant patrolmen saw us driving a car. We were suspect each time we were seen with a white woman. And perhaps it was this narrowing of our life into an island, into a filthy segment of American society, that had driven Filipinos like Doro inward, hating everyone and despising all positive urgencies toward freedom.

When we reached the mountains to the right of the highway, we turned toward them and started climbing slowly, following the road that winds around them like a taut ribbon. We had been driving for an hour when we reached the summit, and suddenly the town of Lompoc shone like a constellation of stars in the deep valley below. We started downward, hearing the strong wind from the sea beating against the car. Then we came to the edge of the town, and church bells began ringing somewhere near a forest.

It was the end of the flower season, so the Filipino workers were all in town. They stood on the sidewalks and in front of Japanese stores showing their fat rolls of money to the girls. Gambling was going on in one of the old buildings, in the Mexican district, and in a café across the street Mexican girls and Filipinos were dancing. I went inside the café and sat near the counter, watching the plump girls dancing drunkenly.

AMERICA IS IN THE HEART

I noticed a small Filipino sitting forlornly at one of the tables. He was smoking a cigar and spitting like a big man into an empty cigar box on the floor. When the juke box stopped playing he jumped to the counterman for some change. He put the nickels in the slot, waving graciously to the dancers although he never danced himself. Now and then a Filipino would go into the back room where the gamblers were playing cards and cursing loudly.

The forlorn Filipino went to the counter again and asked for change. He put all the nickels in the slot and bought several packages of cigarettes. He threw the cigarettes on the table near the juke box and then called to the old Mexican men who were sitting around the place. The Mexicans rushed for the table, grabbing the cigarettes. The Filipino went out lighting another big cigar.

I followed him immediately. He walked slowly and stopped now and then to see if I was following him. There was some mysterious force in him that attracted me. When he came to a large neon sign which said Landstrom Café, he stopped and peered through the wide front window. Then he entered a side door and climbed the long stairs.

I opened the door quietly and entered. I heard him talking to a man in one of the rooms upstairs. When I reached the landing a hard blow fell on my head. I rolled on the floor. Then I saw him with a gun in his hand, poised to strike at my head again. Standing behind him was my brother Amado, holding a long-bladed knife.

I scrambled to my feet screaming: "Brother, it is me! It is Allos! Remember?"

My brother told his friend to stop. He came near me, walking around me suspiciously. He stepped back and folded the blade of the knife. There was some doubt in his face.

"I am your brother," I said again, holding back the tears in my eyes. "I am Allos! Remember the village of Mangusmana? Remember when you beat our *carabao* in the rain? When you touched my head and then ran to Binalonan? Remember, Amado?" I was not only fighting for my life, but also for a childhood bond that was breaking. Frantically I searched in my mind for other remembrances of the past which might remind him of me, and re-establish a bridge between him and my childhood.

"Remember when I fell from the coconut tree and you were a janitor in the *presidencia?*" I said. "And you brought some magazines for me to read? Then you went away to work in the sugar plantations of Bulacan?"

"If you are really my brother tell me the name of our mother," he said casually.

"Our mother's name is Meteria," I said. "That is what the people call her. But her real name is Autilia Sampayan. We used to sell salted fish and salt in the villages. Remember?"

VISIONS OF AMERICA

My brother grabbed me affectionately and for a long time he could not say a word. I knew, then, that he had loved my mother although he had had no chance to show it to her. Yes, to him, and to me afterward, to know my mother's name was to know the password into the secrets of the past, into childhood and pleasant memories; but it was also a guiding star, a talisman, a charm that lights us to manhood and decency.

"It has been so long, Allos," Amado said at last. "I had almost forgotten you. Please forgive me, brother. . . ."

"My name is Alfredo," said his friend. "I nearly killed you!" He laughed guiltily, putting the gun in his pocket. "Yes, I almost killed you, Allos!"

My brother opened the door of their room. It was a small room, with one broken chair and a small window facing the street. Their clothes were hanging on a short rope that was strung between the door and a cracked mirror. I sat on the edge of the bed, waiting for my brother to speak. Alfredo started playing solitaire on the table, laughing whenever he cheated himself.

"Go out in the hall and wash your hands," said my brother. "Then we will go downstairs for something to eat. Where is your suitcase?"

"I don't have any—now," I said. "I lost it when I was in Seattle."

"Have you been in Seattle?" he asked.

"I have been in Alaska, too," I said. "And other places."

"You should have written to me," he said. "You shouldn't have come to America. But you can't go back now. You can never go back, Allos."

I could hear men shouting in a bar two blocks down the street. Then church bells started ringing again, and the wind from the sea carried their message to the farmhouses in the canyon near the river. I knew that as long as there was a hope for the future somewhere I would not stop trying to reach it. I looked at my brother and Alfredo and knew that I would never stay with them, to rot and perish in their world of brutality and despair. I knew that I wanted something which would ease my fear and stop my flight from dawn to dawn.

"Life is tough, Carlos," said my brother. "I had a good job for some time, but the depression came. I had to do something. I had to live, Carlos!"

I did not know what he was trying to tell me. But I noticed that he had started using my Christian name. I noticed, too, that he spoke to me in English. His English was perfect. Alfredo's English was perfect also, but his accent was still strong. Alfredo tried to speak the way my brother spoke, but his uncultured tongue twisted ridiculously about in his mouth and the words did not come out right.

"We are in the bootleg racket," said my brother. "Alfredo and I will make plenty of money. But it is dangerous."

"I like money," Alfredo said. "It is everything."

They spoke with cynicism, but there was a grain of wisdom in their words. We were driving a borrowed car toward a farmhouse, away from the flower fields that made Lompoc famous. We drove across a dry river and into a wide orchard, then Alfredo knocked on the door. An Italian came to the door and told us to follow him into the back yard.

"How many bottles do you want?" he asked my brother, starting to dig under a eucalyptus tree.

"I think I can sell two dozen," said Amado.

"The big size?" asked the Italian.

"The big size," Alfredo said.

The Italian looked at me suspiciously. When he had all the bottles ready, Amado paid him, and the Italian opened a small bottle and passed it around to us. I refused to drink, and Alfredo laughed. Then we went to the car and drove carefully to town.

They disappeared with the bottles, peddling their bootleg whisky in gambling houses and places of questionable reputation. They were boisterous when they entered the room, throwing their money on the bed and talking excitedly. They were disappointed when I told them that I wanted to go to Los Angeles.

"Don't you want to go into business with us?" Alfredo asked me.

"Maybe I will come back someday," I said.

"Well, I was hoping you would want to begin early," he said. There was a note of genuine disappointment in his voice. He put some money in my pocket. "Here is something for you to remember me by."

"If you would like to go to school," said my brother in parting, "just let me know. But whatever you do, Carlos, don't lose your head. Good-bye!"

I sat in the bus and watched them walking toward the Mexican district. I wanted to cry because my brother was no longer the person I had known in Binalonan. He was no longer the gentle, hard-working janitor in the *presidencia*. I remembered the time when he had gone to Lingayen to cook for my brother Macario! Now he had changed, and I could not understand him any more.

"Please, God, don't change me in America!" I said to myself, looking the other way so that I would not cry.

TO BEGIN WITH

Vivian Gornick

Vivian Gornick, essayist and feminist, was born, reared, and educated in New York City. Her essays and articles have been published in the *Village Voice,* the *New York Times,* the *Nation,* and other national periodicals. Her books include *In Search of Ali Mahmoud: An American Woman in Egypt* (1973), *Essays in Feminism* (1979), *Women in Science: Portraits from a World in Transition* (1983), and *Fierce Attachments* (1987). The following excerpt is from the first chapter of *The Romance of American Communism* (1978).

BEFORE I KNEW THAT I WAS JEWISH OR A GIRL I KNEW THAT I WAS a member of the working class. At a time when I had not yet grasped the significance of the fact that in my house English was a second language, or that I wore dresses while my brother wore pants, I knew—and I knew it was important to know—that Papa worked hard all day long. One of my strongest memories of early childhood is that no matter what we were doing, my mother and I, everything in our Bronx apartment stopped dead at four-thirty in the afternoon and she began cooking supper. If ever I questioned this practice, or complained, or demanded that we continue what we were doing, my mother—whose manner was generally frantic and uncontrolled—would answer with a sudden dignity that stopped me cold: "Papa works hard all day long. When he comes home his supper must be on the table."

TO BEGIN WITH

Papa works hard all day long. Those words, in my mother's mouth, spoke volumes, and from the age of reason on I absorbed their complex message. The words stirred in me, almost from the first time I heard them, an extraordinary resonance, one whose range was wide enough to compel my emotional attention throughout my subsequent life. To begin with, the words communicated pain and difficulty; my childish heart ached for my gentle father. The pain was frightening, and even as it began to flow inside me, like a liquid turning to a solid, I felt myself go numb. This emotion was awesome; it induced in me the sense of some mysterious force working on our lives, some force in which we were all caught: suspended, puzzled, moving blind. At the very same time, the mere articulation of the words in my mother's mouth produced a peculiar and relieving focus against the murkiness of that mysterious force, a focus which told me where and who I was: I was the daughter of Papa who worked hard all day long. Finally, the words said: We are all of us, here in this house, vitally connected to the fact that Papa works hard all day long. We pay attention to and respect that fact; we make common cause with it. This last, this oneness, this solidarity, produced in me pride and excitement; it dissolved the numbness and transformed the pain back into a moving, stirring, agitating element: something to be understood and responded to, something to be dealt with and struggled against.

My father stood upright on the floor of a dress factory on West Thirty-fifth Street in New York City with a steam iron in his hand for thirty years. My uncles owned the factory. My father was Labor, my uncles were Capital. My father was a Socialist, my uncles were Zionists. Therefore, Labor was Socialism and Capital was Nationalism. These equations were mother's milk to me, absorbed through flesh and bone almost before consciousness. Concomitantly, I knew also—and again, as though osmotically—who in this world were friends, who enemies, who neutrals. Friends were all those who thought like us: working-class socialists, the people whom my parents called "progressives." All others were "them"; and "them" were either engaged enemies like my uncles or passive neutrals like some of our neighbors. Years later, the "us" and "them" of my life would become Jews and Gentiles, and still later women and men, but for all of my growing-up years "us" and "them" were socialists and non-socialists; the "politically enlightened" and the politically *un*enlightened; those who were "struggling for a better world" and those who, like moral slugs, moved blind and unresponsive through this vast inequity that was our life under capitalism. Those, in short, who had class consciousness and those *lumpen* or bourgeois who did not.

This world of "us" was, of course, a many-layered one. I was thirteen or fourteen years old before I consciously understood the complex sociology of the progressive planet; understood that at the center of the globe stood those who were full-time organizing members of the Communist Party, at the outermost periphery stood those who were called "sympathizers," and at various points in between stood those who held Communist Party membership cards and those who were called "fellow travelers." In those early childhood years these distinctions did not exist for me; much less did I grasp that within this sociology my parents were merely "fellow travelers." The people who came to our house with the *Daily Worker* or the Yiddish newspaper *Der Freiheit* under their arms, the people at the "affairs" we attended, the people at the *shule* (the Yiddish school I was sent to after my public-school day was over), the people at the rallies we went to and the May Day parades we marched in, the people who belonged to the various "clubs" and were interminably collecting money for the latest cause or defense fund—they were all as one to me; they were simply "our people." Of a Saturday morning, the doorbell in our Bronx apartment would ring, my father would open the door, and standing there would be Hymie, a cutter in my father's shop, a small, thin man with gnarled hands and the face of an anxious bulldog. *"Nu,* Louie?" Hymie would say to my father. "Did you see the papers this morning? Did you see—a black year on all of them!—what they're saying about the Soviet Union *this* morning?" "Come in, Hymie, come in," my father would reply. "Have a cup of coffee, we'll discuss it." I did not know that there was a difference between Hymie, who was also only a "fellow traveler," and my cousins David and Selena, who were YCLers, or my uncle Sam, who was always off at "a meeting," or Bennie Grossman from across the street who had suddenly disappeared from the neighborhood ("unavailable" was the word for what Bennie had become, but it would be twenty years before I realized that was the word). It was, to begin with, all one country to me, one world, and the major characteristic of that world as I perceived it was this:

At the wooden table in our kitchen there were always gathered men named Max and Hymie, and women named Masha and Goldie. Their hands were work-blackened, their eyes intelligent and anxious, their voices loud and insistent. They drank tea, ate black bread and herring, and talked "issues." Endlessly, they talked issues. I sat on the kitchen bench beside my father, nestled in the crook of his arm, and I listened, wide-eyed, to the talk. Oh, that talk! That passionate, transforming talk! I understood nothing of what they were saying, but I was excited beyond words by the richness of their rhetoric, the intensity of their arguments, the urgency and longing behind that hot river of words that came ceaselessly pouring out of all of them. Something important was happening here, I always felt, something that had to do with understanding things. And "to understand things," I already knew, was the most exciting, the most important thing in life.

It was characteristic of that world that during those hours at the kitchen table with my father and his socialist friends I didn't know we were poor. I didn't know that in those places beyond the streets of my neighborhood we were without power, position, material or social existence. I only knew that tea and black bread were the most delicious food and drink in the world, that political talk filled the room with a terrible excitement and a richness of expectation, that here in the kitchen I felt the same electric thrill I felt when Rouben, my Yiddish teacher, pressed my upper arm between two bony fingers and, his eyes shining behind thick glasses, said to me: "Ideas, dolly, ideas. Without them, life is nothing. With them, life is *everything.*"

Sometimes I would slip off the bench and catch my mother somewhere between the stove and the table (she was forever bringing something to the table). I would point to one or another at the table and whisper to her: Who is this one? Who is that one? My mother would reply in Yiddish: "He is a writer. She is a poet. He is a thinker." Oh, I would nod, perfectly satisfied with these identifications, and return to my place on the bench. *He,* of course, drove a bakery truck. *She* was a sewing-machine operator. That other one over there was a plumber, and the one next to him stood pressing dresses all day long beside my father.

But Rouben was right. Ideas were everything. So powerful was the life inside their minds that sitting there, drinking tea and talking issues, these people ceased to be what they objectively were—immigrant Jews, disenfranchised workers—and, indeed, they became thinkers, writers, poets.

Every one of them read the *Daily Worker,* the *Freiheit,* and the *New York Times* religiously each morning. Every one of them had an opinion on everything he or she read. Every one of them was forever pushing, pulling, yanking, mauling those opinions into shape within the framework of a single question. The question was: Is it good for the workers? That river of words was continually flowing toward an ocean called *farshtand,* within whose elusive depths lay the answer to this question.

They were voyagers on that river, these plumbers, pressers, and sewing-machine operators. Disciplined voyagers with a course to steer, a destination to arrive at. When one of them yelled at another (as one of them regularly did) "Id-yot! What has *that* to do with anything? Use your brains! God gave you brains, yes or no? Well, use them!" he was, in effect, saying: Where will that question take us? Nowhere. Get back on course. We're going somewhere, aren't we? Well, then, let's go there.

They took with them on this journey not only their own narrow, impoverished experience but a set of abstractions as well, abstractions with the power to transform. When these people sat down at the kitchen table to talk, Politics sat down with them, Ideas sat down with them, above all, History sat down with them. They spoke and thought within a context that had world-making properties. This context lifted them out of the nameless, faceless obscurity of the soul into which they had been born and gave them, for the first time in their lives, a sense of rights as well as of obligations. They had rights because they now knew who and what they were. They were not simply the disinherited of the earth, they were proletarians. They were not a people without a history, they had the Russian Revolution. They were not without a civilizing world view, they had Marxism.

Within such a context the people at my father's kitchen table could place themselves; and if they could place themselves—compelling insight!—they could *become* themselves. For, in order to become one must first have some civilizing referent, some social boundary, some idea of nationhood. These people had no external nationhood; nothing in the cultures they had left, or the one to which they had come, had given them anything but a humiliating sense of outsidedness. The only nationhood to which they had attained was the nationhood inside their minds: the nationhood of the international working class. And indeed, a nation it was—complete with a sense of family, culture, religion, social mores, political institutions. The people in that kitchen had remade the family in the image of workers all over the world, political institutions in the image of the Communist Party, social mores in the image of Marxist allegiance, religion in the image of the new socialized man, Utopia in the image of the Soviet Union. They sat at the kitchen table and they felt themselves linked up to America, Russia, Europe, the world. Their people were everywhere, their power was the revolution around the corner, their empire "a better world."

To see themselves as part of an identifiable mass of human beings with a place and a destiny in the scheme of civilized life was suddenly to "see" themselves. Thus, paradoxically, the more each one identified himself or herself with the working-class movement, the more each one came individually alive. The more each one acknowledged his or her condition as one of binding connectedness, the more each one pushed back the darkness and experienced the life within. In this sense, that kitchen ceased to be a room in a shabby tenement apartment in the Bronx and became, for all intents and purposes, the center of the world as that center has ever been described since the time of the ancient Greeks. For, here in the turmoil and excitation of their urgent talk, the men and women at the kitchen table were involved in nothing less than an act of self-creation: the creation of the self through increased consciousness. The instrument of consciousness for them was Marx. Marx and the Communist Party and world socialism. Marx was their Socrates, the Party was their Plato, world socialism their Athens.

Few things in life equal the power and joy of experiencing oneself. Rousseau said there is nothing in life *but* the experiencing of oneself. Gorky said he loved his friends because in their presence he felt himself. "How important it is," he wrote, "how glorious it is—to feel oneself!" Indeed, how impossible it is not to love ardently those people, that atmosphere, those events and ideas in whose presence one feels the life within oneself stirring. How impossible, in fact, not to feel passionately in the presence of such stirrings. For the people among whom I grew this intensity of feeling was transmitted through Marxism as interpreted by the Communist Party.

At the indisputable center of the progressive world stood the Communist Party. It was the Party whose awesome structure harnessed that inchoate emotion which, with the force of a tidal wave, drove millions of people around the globe toward Marxism. It was the Party whose moral authority gave shape and substance to an abstraction. It was the Party that brought to astonishing life the kind of comradeship that makes swell in men and women the sense of their own humanness. For, of this party it could rightly be said, as Richard Wright in his bitterest moment did, nonetheless, say: "There was no agency in the world so capable of making men feel the earth and the people upon it as the Communist Party."

Who, who came out of that world could fail to remember the extraordinary quality these experiences embodied for all those living through them? You were, if you were there, in the presence of that process whereby one emerges by merging; whereby one becomes free, whole, and separate through the mysterious agency of a disciplining context; the control of the shared, irreducible self.

To all this the Communist Party spoke. From all this it drew its formidable strength.

I was twenty years old in April of 1956 when Khrushchev addressed the Twentieth Congress of the Soviet Union and "revealed" to the world the incalculable despair of Stalin's rule. I say "revealed" because Khrushchev's report compelled millions of people to know consciously that which many of them had known subconsciously for a very long time. The Twentieth Congress Report brought with it political devastation for the organized Left-wing. Coming as it did in the midst of one of the most repressive periods in American history—a period when Communists were hunted like criminals, suffered trial and imprisonment, endured social isolation and loss of work, had their professional lives destroyed and, in the case of the Rosenbergs, were put to death—the Khrushchev Report was the final instrument of annihilation for the American Left. Thousands of men and women in the Left walked about feeling as Ignazio Silone twenty-five years before them had felt: "Like someone who has had a tremendous blow on the head and keeps on his feet, walking, talking, gesticulating, but without fully realizing what has happened." And like Silone they, too, said to themselves: "For this? Have we sunk to this? Those who are dead, those who are dying in prison, have sacrificed themselves for this? The vagabond, lonely, perilous lives that we ourselves are leading, strangers in our own countries—is it all for this?" Overnight, the affective life of the Communist Party in this country came to an end. Within weeks of the Report's publication, thirty thousand people left the Party.

VISIONS OF AMERICA

Within a year the Party was as it had been in its 1919 beginnings: a small sect, off the American political map.

For me, at twenty, the Khrushchev Report snapped the last thread in a fabric of belief that was already worn to near disintegration. In the previous three or four years I had often been in a state of dismay as I felt the weight of simplistic socialist explanation pressing upon my growing inner life. At fifteen I had been a member of the Labor Youth League (the Party's last incarnation of the Young Communist League), attending meetings in a loft on New York's Prince Street where the walls were covered with huge poster pictures of Lenin, Stalin, and Mao, and where the Party organizer came weekly to deliver exhortations and assignments in a language that, increasingly, began to sound foreign to my ears: remote, very remote from the language of the kitchen which, itself, was beginning to be replaced by the language of Melville, Mann, Wolfe and Dostoevsky now sounding within me. As my interior language altered, and new kinds of thought challenged the once unquestioned, now vulnerable socialist ideology, shadows and confusions filled my mind. The logic of the "progressive" world began to break down; injustices began to loom; discrepancies in behavior nagged at me; questions arose for which there were no longer ready answers. I found myself arguing with my relatives and my father's friends; the arguments produced anger and divisions instead of explanations and unity. It was no longer sufficient to be told "The Party knows what it's doing" or "Do you know better than the Soviet Union what is good for the workers?" or "They know better than we do what's going on. If they do thus-and-so there's a very good reason for it. Who are *you* to question those in a position to know what's going on?"

Now, in 1956, we sat in the kitchen: my mother, my aunt, and I. My brother was married and long gone from the house (not to mention the progressive world). My father was dead, and so was my uncle Sam. We alone remained—we three women—in this crumbling house to face the crumbling world outside the kitchen. Our men, our race, our politics: dead and dying, lost and gone, smashed and murdered. Hitler had destroyed half of our world, now Stalin had destroyed the other half. I was beside myself with youthful rage. My mother was desperately confused. My aunt remained adamantly Stalinist. Night after night we quarreled violently.

"Lies!" I screamed at my aunt. "Lies and treachery and murder. A maniac has been sitting there in Moscow! A maniac has been sitting there in the name of socialism. In the name of *socialism!* And all of you—all these years—have undone yourselves over and over again in the service of this maniac. Millions of Russians have been destroyed! Millions of Communists have betrayed themselves and each other!"

"A Red-baiter!" my aunt yelled back. "A lousy little Red-baiter you've become! Louie Gornick must be turning over in his grave, that his daughter has become a Red-baiter!"

And we stared at each other, each of us trapped in her own anguish. I, in the grip of that pain and fury that I can feel to this day (waking suddenly in the night now, twenty years later, having just read or heard some new report of inhumanity from the Soviet Union, I often find myself very nearly saying out loud: "All this done in the name of socialism. In the *name* of socialism"), and she, my aunt, her strong peasant face ashen with grief and survival, the world inside her and all around her dissolving in a horror of confusion too great to bear, too annihilating to take in.

And all the while, in the back of my head—even as my aunt and I were turning and turning, locked together inside this waking nightmare of human disintegration—I was hearing the felt sound of Ignazio Silone's voice saying: "The truth is this: the day I left the Communist Party was a very sad one for me, it was like a day of deep mourning, the mourning I felt for my lost youth. And I come from a district where mourning is worn longer than elsewhere."

THE MAKING OF A WRITER:
FROM THE POETS IN THE KITCHEN

Paule Marshall

Paule Marshall was born in Barbados and grew up in Brooklyn, New York. She is the author of two collections of short stories and three novels, including *Brown Girl, Brownstones* (1959) and *Daughters* (1991). Ms. Marshall was a 1992 recipient of a MacArthur Foundation grant. She is presently working on a memoir.

SOME YEARS AGO, WHEN I WAS TEACHING A GRADUATE SEMINAR IN fiction at Columbia University, a well-known male novelist visited my class to speak on his development as a writer. In discussing his formative years, he didn't realize it but he seriously endangered his life by remarking that women writers are luckier than those of his sex because they usually spend so much time as children around their mothers and their mothers' friends in the kitchen.

What did he say that for? The women students immediately forgot about being in awe of him and began readying their attack for the question and answer period later on. Even I bristled. There again was that awful image of women locked away from the world in the kitchen with only each other to talk to, and their daughters locked in with them.

But my guest wasn't really being sexist or trying to be provocative or even spoiling for a fight. What he meant—when he got around to explaining himself more fully—was that, given the way children are (or were) raised in our society, with little girls kept closer to home and their mothers, the woman writer stands a better chance of being exposed, while growing up, to the kind of talk that goes on among women, more often than not in the kitchen; and that this experience gives her an edge over her male counterpart by instilling in her an appreciation for ordinary speech.

It was clear that my guest lecturer attached great importance to this, which is understandable. Common speech and the plain, workaday words that make it up are, after all, the stock in trade of some of the best fiction writers. They are the principal means by which characters in a novel or story reveal themselves and give voice sometimes to profound feelings and complex ideas about themselves and the world. Perhaps the proper measure of a writer's talent is skill in rendering everyday speech—when it is appropriate to the story—as well as the ability to tap, to exploit, the beauty, poetry and wisdom it often contains.

"If you say what's on your mind in the language that comes to you from your parents and your street and friends you'll probably say something beautiful." Grace Paley tells this, she says, to her students at the beginning of every writing course.

It's all a matter of exposure and a training of the ear for the would-be writer in those early years of apprenticeship. And, according to my guest lecturer, this training, the best of it, often takes place in as unglamorous a setting as the kitchen.

He didn't know it, but he was essentially describing my experience as a little girl. I grew up among poets. Now they didn't look like poets—whatever that breed is supposed to look like. Nothing about them suggested that poetry was their calling. They were just a group of ordinary housewives and mothers, my mother included, who dressed in a way (shapeless housedresses, dowdy felt hats and long, dark, solemn coats) that made it impossible for me to imagine they had ever been young.

Nor did they do what poets were supposed to do—spend their days in an attic room writing verses. They never put pen to paper except to write occasionally to their relatives in Barbados. "I take my pen in hand hoping these few lines will find you in health as they leave me fair for the time being," was the way their letters invariably began. Rather, their day was spent "scrubbing floor," as they described the work they did.

Several mornings a week these unknown bards would put an apron and a pair of old house shoes in a shopping bag and take the train or streetcar from our section of Brooklyn out to Flatbush. There, those who didn't have steady jobs would wait on certain designated corners for the white housewives in the neighborhood to come along and bargain with them over pay for a day's work cleaning their houses. This was the ritual even in the winter.

Later, armed with the few dollars they had earned, which in their vocabulary became "a few raw-mouth pennies," they made their way back to our neighborhood, where they would sometimes stop off to have a cup of tea or cocoa together before going home to cook dinner for their husbands and children.

The basement kitchen of the brownstone house where my family lived was the usual gathering place. Once inside the warm safety of its walls the women threw off the drab coats and hats, seated themselves at the large center table, drank their cups of tea or cocoa, and talked. While my sister and I sat at a smaller table over in a corner doing our homework, they talked—endlessly, passionately, poetically, and with impressive range. No subject was beyond them. True, they would indulge in the usual gossip: whose husband was running with whom, whose daughter looked slightly "in the way" (pregnant) under her bridal gown as she walked down the aisle. That sort of thing. But they also tackled the great issues of the time. They were always, for example, discussing the state of the economy. It was the mid and late thirties then, and the aftershock of the Depression, with its soup lines and suicides on Wall Street, was still being felt.

Some people, they declared, didn't know how to deal with adversity. They didn't know that you had to "tie up your belly" (hold in the pain, that is) when things got rough and go on with life. They took their image from the belly band that is tied around the stomach of a newborn baby to keep the navel pressed in.

They talked politics. Roosevelt was their hero. He had come along and rescued the country with relief and jobs, and in gratitude they christened their sons Franklin and Delano and hoped they would live up to the names.

If F.D.R. was their hero, Marcus Garvey was their God. The name of the fiery, Jamaican-born black nationalist of the twenties was constantly invoked around the table. For he had been their leader when they first came to the United States from the West Indies shortly after World War I. They had contributed to his organization, the United Negro Improvement Association (UNIA), out of their meager salaries, bought shares in his ill-fated Black Star Shipping Line, and at the height of the movement they had marched as members of his "nurses' brigade" in their white uniforms up Seventh Avenue in Harlem during the great Garvey Day parades. Garvey: He lived on through the power of their memories.

And their talk was of war and rumors of wars. They raged against World War II when it broke out in Europe, blaming it on the politicians. "It's these politicians. They're the ones always starting up all this lot of war. But what they care? It's the poor people got to suffer and mothers with their sons." If it was *their* sons, they swore they would keep them out of the Army by giving them soap to eat each day to make their hearts sound defective. Hitler? He was for them "the devil incarnate."

Then there was home. They reminisced often and at length about home. The old country. Barbados—or Bimshire, as they affectionately called it. The little Caribbean island in the sun they loved but had to leave. "Poor—poor but sweet" was the way they remembered it.

And naturally they discussed their adopted home. America came in for both good and bad marks. They lashed out at it for the racism they encountered. They took to task some of the people they worked for, especially those who gave them only a hard-boiled egg and a few spoonfuls of cottage cheese for lunch. "As if anybody can scrub floor on an egg and some cheese that don't have no taste to it!"

Yet although they caught H in "this man country," as they called America, it was nonetheless a place where "you could at least see your way to make a dollar." That much they acknowledged. They might even one day accumulate enough dollars, with both them and their husbands working, to buy the brown-stone houses which, like my family, they were only leasing at that period. This was their consuming ambition: to "buy house" and to see the children through.

There was no way for me to understand it at the time, but the talk that filled the kitchen those afternoons was highly functional. It served as therapy, the cheapest kind available to my mother and her friends. Not only did it help them recover from the long wait on the corner that morning and the bargaining over their labor, it restored them to a sense of themselves and reaffirmed their self-worth. Through language they were able to overcome the humiliations of the work-day.

But more than therapy, that freewheeling, wide-ranging, exuberant talk functioned as an outlet for the tremendous creative energy they possessed. They were women in whom the need for self-expression was strong, and since language was the only vehicle readily available to them they made of it an art form that—in keeping with the African tradition in which art and life are one—was an integral part of their lives.

And their talk was a refuge. They never really ceased being baffled and overwhelmed by America—its vastness, complexity and power. Its strange customs and laws. At a level beyond words they remained fearful and in awe. Their uneasiness and fear were even reflected in their attitude toward the children they had given birth to in this country. They referred to those like myself, the little Brooklyn-born Bajans (Barbadians), as "these New York children" and complained that they couldn't discipline us properly because of the laws here. "You can't beat these children as you would like, you know, because the authorities in this place will dash you in jail for them. After all, these is New York children." Not only were we different, American, we had, as they saw it, escaped their ultimate authority.

Confronted therefore by a world they could not encompass, which even limited their rights as parents, and at the same time finding themselves permanently separated from the world they had known, they took refuge in language. "Language is the only homeland," Czeslaw Milosz, the emigré Polish writer and Nobel Laureate, has said. This is what it became for the women at the kitchen table.

It served another purpose also, I suspect. My mother and her friends were after all the female counterpart of Ralph Ellison's invisible man. Indeed, you might say they suffered a triple invisibility, being black, female and foreigners. They really didn't count in American society except as a source of cheap labor. But given the kind of women they were, they couldn't tolerate the fact of their invisibility, their powerlessness. And they fought back, using the only weapon at their command: the spoken word.

Those late afternoon conversations on a wide range of topics were a way for them to feel they exercised some measure of control over their lives and the events that shaped them. "Soully-gal, talk yuh talk!" they were always exhorting each other. "In this man world you got to take yuh mouth and make a gun!" They were in control, if only verbally and if only for the two hours or so that they remained in our house.

For me, sitting over in the corner, being seen but not heard, which was the rule for children in those days, it wasn't only what the women talked about—the content—but the way they put things—their style. The insight, irony, wit and humor they brought to their stories and discussions and their poet's inventiveness and daring with language—which of course I could only sense but not define back then.

They had taken the standard English taught them in the primary schools of Barbados and transformed it into an idiom, an instrument that more adequately described them—changing around the syntax and imposing their own rhythm and accent so that the sentences were more pleasing to their ears. They added the few African sounds and words that had survived, such as the derisive suck-teeth sound and the word "yam," meaning to eat. And to make it more vivid, more in keeping with their expressive quality, they brought to bear a raft of metaphors, parables, Biblical quotations, sayings and the like:

"The sea ain' got no back door," they would say, meaning that it wasn't like a house where if there was a fire you could run out the back. Meaning that it was not to be trifled with. And meaning perhaps in a larger sense that man should treat all of nature with caution and respect.

"I has read hell by heart and called every generation blessed!" They sometimes went in for hyperbole.

A woman expecting a baby was never said to be pregnant. They never used that word. Rather, she was "in the way" or, better yet, "tumbling big." "Guess who I butt up on in the market the other day tumbling big again!"

THE MAKING OF A WRITER

And a woman with a reputation of being too free with her sexual favors was known in their book as a "thoroughfare"—the sense of men like a steady stream of cars moving up and down the road of her life. Or she might be dubbed "a free-bee," which was my favorite of the two. I liked the image it conjured up of a woman scandalous perhaps but independent, who flitted from one flower to another in a garden of male beauties, sampling their nectar, taking her pleasure at will, the roles reversed.

And nothing, no matter how beautiful, was ever described as simply beautiful. It was always "beautiful-ugly": the beautiful-ugly dress, the beautiful-ugly house, the beautiful-ugly car. Why the word "ugly," I used to wonder, when the thing they were referring to was beautiful, and they knew it. Why the antonym, the contradiction, the linking of opposites? It used to puzzle me greatly as a child.

There is the theory in linguistics which states that the idiom of a people, the way they use language, reflects not only the most fundamental views they hold of themselves and the world but their very conception of reality. Perhaps in using the term "beautiful-ugly" to describe nearly everything, my mother and her friends were expressing what they believed to be a fundamental dualism in life: the idea that a thing is at the same time its opposite, and that these opposites, these contradictions make up the whole. But theirs was not a Manichaean brand of dualism that sees matter, flesh, the body, as inherently evil, because they constantly addressed each other as "soully-gal"—soul: spirit; gal: the body, flesh, the visible self. And it was clear from their tone that they gave one as much weight and importance as the other. They had never heard of the mind/body split.

As for God, they summed up His essential attitude in a phrase. "God," they would say, "don' love ugly and He ain' stuck on pretty."

Using everyday speech, the simple commonplace words—but always with imagination and skill—they gave voice to the most complex ideas. Flannery O'Connor would have approved of how they made ordinary language work, as she put it, "double-time," stretching, shading, deepening its meaning. Like Joseph Conrad they were always trying to infuse new life in the "old old words worn thin . . . by . . . careless usage." And the goals of their oral art were the same as his: "to make you hear, to make you feel . . . to make you *see.*" This was their guiding esthetic.

By the time I was eight or nine, I graduated from the corner of the kitchen to the neighborhood library, and thus from the spoken to the written word. The Macon Street Branch of the Brooklyn Public Library was an imposing half-block-long edifice of heavy gray masonry, with glass-paneled doors at the front and two tall metal torches symbolizing the light that comes of learning flanking the wide steps outside.

The inside was just as impressive. More steps—of pale marble with gleaming brass railings at the center and sides—led up to the circulation desk, and a great pendulum clock gazed down from the balcony stacks that faced the entrance. Usually stationed at the top of the steps like the guards outside Buckingham Palace was the custodian, a stern-faced West Indian type who for years, until I was old enough to obtain an adult card, would immediately shoo me with one hand into the Children's Room and with the other threaten me into silence, a finger to his lips. You would have thought he was the chief librarian and not just someone whose job it was to keep the brass polished and the clock wound. I put him in a story called "Barbados" years later and had terrible things happen to him at the end.

I sheltered from the storm of adolescence in the Macon Street library, reading voraciously, indiscriminately, everything from Jane Austen to Zane Grey, but with a special passion for the long, full-blown, richly detailed eighteenth- and nineteenth-century picaresque tales: *Tom Jones, Great Expectations, Vanity Fair.*

But although I loved nearly everything I read and would enter fully into the lives of the characters—indeed, would cease being myself and become them—I sensed a lack after a time. Something I couldn't quite define was missing. And then one day, browsing in the poetry section, I came across a book by someone called Paul Laurence Dunbar, and opening it I found the photograph of a wistful, sad-eyed poet who to my surprise was black. I turned to a poem at random. "Little brown-baby wif spa'klin' / eyes / Come to yo' pappy an' set on his knee." Although I had a little difficulty at first with the words in dialect, the poem spoke to me as nothing I had read before of the closeness, the special relationship I had had with my father, who by then had become an ardent believer in Father Divine and gone to live in Father's "kingdom" in Harlem. Reading it helped to ease somewhat the tight knot of sorrow and longing I carried around in my chest that refused to go away. I read another poem. " 'Lias! 'Lias! Bless de Lawd! / Don' you know de day's / erbroad? / Ef you don' get up, you scamp / Dey'll be trouble in dis camp." I laughed. It reminded me of the way my mother sometimes yelled at my sister and me to get out of bed in the mornings.

And another: "Seen my lady home las' night / Jump back, honey, jump back. / Hel' huh han' an' sque'z it tight . . ." About love between a black man and a black woman. I had never seen that written about before and it roused in me all kinds of delicious feelings and hopes.

And I began to search then for books and stories and poems about "The Race" (as it was put back then), about my people. While not abandoning Thackeray, Fielding, Dickens and the others, I started asking the reference librarian, who was white, for books by Negro writers, although I must admit I did so at first with a feeling of shame—the shame I and many others used to experience in those days whenever the word "Negro" or "colored" came up.

No grade school literature teacher of mine had ever mentioned Dunbar or

THE MAKING OF A WRITER

James Weldon Johnson or Langston Hughes. I didn't know that Zora Neale Hurston existed and was busy writing and being published during those years. Nor was I made aware of people like Frederick Douglass and Harriet Tubman—their spirit and example—or the great nineteenth-century abolitionist and feminist Sojourner Truth. There wasn't even Negro History Week when I attended P.S. 35 on Decatur Street!

What I needed, what all the kids—West Indian and native black American alike—with whom I grew up needed, was an equivalent of the Jewish shul, someplace where we could go after school—the schools that were shortchanging us—and read works by those like ourselves and learn about our history.

It was around that time also that I began harboring the dangerous thought of someday trying to write myself. Perhaps a poem about an apple tree, although I had never seen one. Or the story of a girl who could magically transplant herself to wherever she wanted to be in the world—such as Father Divine's kingdom in Harlem. Dunbar—his dark, eloquent face, his large volume of poems—permitted me to dream that I might some day write, and with something of the power with words my mother and her friends possessed.

When people at readings and writers' conferences ask me who my major influences were, they are sometimes a little disappointed when I don't immediately name the usual literary giants. True, I am indebted to those writers, white and black, whom I read during my formative years and still read for instruction and pleasure. But they were preceded in my life by another set of giants whom I always acknowledge before all others: the group of women around the table long ago. They taught me my first lessons in the narrative art. They trained my ear. They set a standard of excellence. This is why the best of my work must be attributed to them; it stands as testimony to the rich legacy of language and culture they so freely passed on to me in the wordshop of the kitchen.

SPLIT AT THE ROOT:
AN ESSAY ON JEWISH IDENTITY

Adrienne Rich

Adrienne Rich was born in Baltimore, Maryland and graduated from Radcliffe College. In 1951 she won the Yale Younger Poets Award for her first book of poetry, *A Change of World*. Winner of numerous awards, Rich has published fifteen books of poetry, which include the National Book Award Winner, *Diving Into the Wreck* (1973), *The Dream of Common Language* (1978), and *An Atlas of the Difficult World* (1991). She has also published three books of prose: *Of Woman Born: Motherhood as Experience and Institution* (1976), *On Lies, Secrets and Silence* (1978), and *Blood, Bread, and Poetry* (1985).

FOR ABOUT FIFTEEN MINUTES I HAVE BEEN SITTING CHIN IN HAND in front of the typewriter, staring out at the snow. Trying to be honest with myself, trying to figure out why writing this seems to me so dangerous an act, filled with fear and shame, and why it seems so necessary. It comes to me that in order to write this I have to be willing to do two things: I have to claim my father, for I have my Jewishness from him and not from my gentile mother; and I have to break his silence, his taboos; in order to claim him I have in a sense to expose him.

And there is of course the third thing: I have to face the sources and the flickering presence of my own ambivalence as a Jew; the daily, mundane anti-Semitisms of my entire life.

These are stories I have never tried to tell before. Why now? Why, I asked myself sometime last year, does this question of Jewish identity float so impalpably, so ungraspably, around me, a cloud I can't quite see the outlines of, which feels to me without definition?

And yet I've been on the track of this longer than I think.

In a long poem written in 1960, when I was thirty-one years old. I described myself as "Split at the root, neither Gentile nor Jew, Yankee nor Rebel."* I was still trying to have it both ways: to be neither/nor, trying to live (with my Jewish husband and three children more Jewish in ancestry than I) in the predominantly gentile Yankee academic world of Cambridge, Massachusetts.

But this begins, for me, in Baltimore, where I was born in a hospital in the Black ghetto, whose lobby contained an immense, white marble statue of Christ.

My father was then a young teacher and researcher in the department of pathology at the Johns Hopkins Medical School, one of the very few Jews to attend or teach at that institution. He was from Birmingham, Alabama; his father, Samuel, was an immigrant from Austria-Hungary and his mother, Hattie Rice, a Sephardic Jew from Vicksburg, Mississippi. My grandfather had had a shoe store in Birmingham, which did well enough to allow him to retire comfortably, and to leave my grandmother, on his death, a small income. The only souvenirs of my grandfather, Samuel Rich, were his ivory flute, which lay on our living-room mantel and was not to be played with; his thin gold pocket-watch, which my father wore; and his Hebrew prayer book, which I discovered among my father's books in the course of reading my way through his library. In this prayer book there was a newspaper clipping about my grandparents' wedding, which took place in a synagogue.

My father, Arnold, was sent in adolescence to a military school in the Tennessee mountains, a place for training white Southern Christian gentlemen. I suspect that there were few if any other Jewish boys at Colonel Bingham's. Or at "Mr. Jefferson's university," in Charlottesville, where he studied as an undergraduate. With whatever conscious forethought, Samuel and Hattie sent their son into the dominant Southern WASP culture, to become an "exception," to enter the professional class. Never, in describing these experiences, did he ever speak of having suffered—from loneliness, cultural alienation, or outsiderhood. I never heard him use the word "anti-Semitism."

It was only in college, when I read a poem by Karl Shapiro beginning: "To hate the Negro and avoid the Jew / is the curriculum" that it flashed on me that there was an untold side to my father's story of his student years. He looked recogniz-

*"Readings of History" in Adrienne Rich, *Snapshots of a Daughter-in-Law*. W. W. Norton, New York, 1967, pp. 36–40.

ably Jewish, was short and slender in build with dark wiry hair and deepset eyes, high forehead, and curved nose.

My mother is a gentile. In Jewish law I cannot count myself a Jew. If it is true that "We think back through our mothers if we are women" (Virginia Woolf)—and I myself have affirmed this—then even according to lesbian theory, I cannot (or need not?) count myself a Jew.

The white Southern Protestant woman, the gentile, has always been there for me to peel back into. That's a whole piece of history in itself, for my gentile grandmother and my mother were also frustrated artists and intellectuals, a lost writer and a lost composer between them. Readers and annotators of books, note-takers, my mother a good pianist still, in her eighties. But there was also the obsession with ancestry, with "background," the Southern talk of family, not as people you would necessarily know and depend on, but as heritage, the guarantee of "good breeding." There was the inveterate romantic heterosexual fantasy, the mother telling the daughter how to attract men (my mother often used the word "fascinate"); the assumption that relations between the sexes could only be romantic, that it was in the woman's interest to cultivate "mystery," conceal her actual feelings. Survival tactics, of a kind, I think today, knowing what I know about the white woman's sexual role in the Southern racist scenario. Heterosexuality as protection, but also drawing white women deeper into collusion with white men.

It would be easy to push away and deny the gentile in me: that white Southern woman, that social Christian. At different times in my life, I suppose, I have wanted to push away one or the other burden of inheritance, to say merely, *I am a woman; I am a lesbian.* If I call myself a Jewish lesbian do I thereby try to shed some of my Southern gentile guilt, my white woman's culpability? If I call myself only through my mother, is it because I pass more easily through a world where being a lesbian often seems like outsiderhood enough?

According to Nazi logic, my two Jewish grandparents would have made me a *Mischling, first-degree:* non-exempt from the Final Solution.

The social world in which I grew up was Christian virtually without needing to say so; Christian imagery, music, language, symbols, assumptions everywhere. It was also a genteel, white middle-class world in which "common" was a term of deep opprobrium. "Common" white people might speak of "niggers"; *we* were taught never to use that word; *we* said "Negroes" (even as we accepted segregation, the eating taboo, the assumption that Black people were simply of a separate species). Our language was more polite, distinguishing us from the "rednecks," or the lynch mob mentality. So charged with negative meaning was even the word "Negro" that as children we were taught never to use it in front of Black people. We were taught that any mention of skin color in the presence of colored people was treacherous forbidden ground. In a parallel way, the word "Jew" was not used by polite gentiles. I sometimes heard my best friend's father, a Presbyterian minister, allude to "the Hebrew people," or "people of the Jewish faith." The world of acceptable folk was white, gentile (christian, really) and had "ideals" (which colored people, white "common" people, were not supposed to have). "Ideals" and "manners" included not hurting someone's feelings by calling her or him a Negro or a Jew—naming the hated identity. This is the mental framework of the 1930s and 1940s in which I was raised.

(Writing this I feel, dimly, like the betrayer: of my father, who did not speak the word; of my mother, who must have trained me in the messages; of my caste and class; of my whiteness itself.)

Two memories: I am in a play-reading at school, of *The Merchant of Venice.* Whatever Jewish law says, I am quite sure I was *seen* as Jewish (with a reassuringly gentile mother) in that double-vision that bigotry allows. I am the only Jewish girl in the class and I am playing Portia. As always, I read my part aloud for my father the night before, and he tells me to convey, with my voice, more scorn and contempt with the word "Jew": "Therefore, Jew. . . ." I have to say the word out, and say it loudly. I was encouraged to pretend to be a non-Jewish child acting a non-Jewish character who has to speak the word "Jew" emphatically. Such a child would not have had trouble with the part. But *I* must have had trouble with the part, if only because the word itself was really taboo. I can see that there was a kind of terrible, bitter bravado about my father's way of handling this. And who would not dissociate from Shylock in order to identify with Portia? As a Jewish child who was also a female I loved Portia—and, like every other Shakespearean heroine, she proved a treacherous role model.

A year or so later I am in another play, *The School for Scandal,* in which a notorious spendthrift is described as having "many excellent friends . . . among the Jews." In neither case was anything explained, either to me or to the class at large about this scorn for Jews and the disgust surrounding Jews and money. Money, when Jews wanted it, had it, or lent it to others, seemed to take on a peculiar nastiness, and Jews and money had some peculiar and unspeakable relation.

At this same school—in which we had christian hymns and prayers, and read aloud through the Bible morning after morning—I gained the impression that Jews were in the Bible and mentioned in English literature, had been persecuted centuries ago by the wicked Inquisition, but that they seemed not to exist in everyday life. These were the 1940s and we were told a great deal about the Battle of Britain, the noble French Resistance fighters, the brave, starving Dutch—but I did not learn of the resistance of the Warsaw Ghetto until I left home.

VISIONS OF AMERICA

I was sent to the Episcopal church, baptized, and confirmed, and attended it for about five years, though without belief. That religion seemed to have little to do with belief or commitment; it was liturgy that mattered, not moral passion. Neither of my parents ever entered that church, and my father would not enter *any* church for any reason—wedding or funeral. Nor did I enter a synagogue until I left Baltimore. When I came home from church, for a while, my father insisted on reading aloud to me from Thomas Paine's *The Age of Reason*—a diatribe against institutional religion. Thus, he explained, I would have a balanced view of these things, a choice. He—they—did not give me the choice to be a Jew. My mother explained to me when I was filling out forms for college that if any question was asked about "religion" I should put down "Episcopalian" rather than "none"—to seem to have no religion was, she implied, dangerous.

But it was white social christianity, rather than any particular christian sect, that the world was founded on. The very word "christian" was used as a synonym for virtuous, just, peaceloving, generous, etc. etc.* The norm was christian: "religion: none" was indeed not acceptable. Anti-Semitism was so intrinsic as not to have a name. I don't recall exactly being taught that the Jews killed Jesus; "Christ-killer" seems too strong a term for the bland Episcopal vocabulary; but certainly we got the impression that the Jews had been caught out in a terrible mistake, failing to recognize the true Messiah, and were thereby less advanced in moral and spiritual sensibility. The Jews had actually allowed *moneylenders in the Temple* (again, the unexplained obsession with Jews and money). They were of the past, archaic, primitive as older (and darker) cultures are supposed to be primitive: Christianity was lightness, fairness, peace on earth, and combined the feminine appeal of "the meek shall inherit the earth" with the masculine stride of "Onward, Christian Soldiers."

Sometime in 1946, while still in high school, I read in the newspaper that a theatre in Baltimore was showing films of the Allied liberation of the Nazi concentration camps. Alone, I went downtown after school one afternoon and watched the stark, blurry but unmistakable newsreels. When I try to go back and touch the pulse of that girl of sixteen, growing up in many ways so precocious and so ignorant, I am overwhelmed by a memory of despair, a sense of inevitability, more enveloping than any I had ever known. Anne Frank's diary and many other personal narratives of the Holocaust were still unknown or unwritten. But it came to me that every one of those piles of corpses, mountains of shoes and clothing, had contained, simply, individuals, who had believed, as I now believed of myself, that they were meant to live out a life of some kind of meaning, that

*In a similar way the phrase "that's white of you" implied that you were behaving with the superior decency and morality expected of white, but not of Black people.

the world possessed some kind of sense and order; yet *this* had happened to them. And I, who believed my life was intended to be so interesting and meaningful, was connected to those dead by something—not just mortality but a taboo name, a hated identity. Or was I—did I really have to be? Writing this now, I feel belated rage, that I was so impoverished by the family and social worlds I lived in, that I had to try to figure out by myself what this did indeed mean for me. That I had never been taught about resistance, only about passing. That I had no language for anti-Semitism itself.

When I went home and told my parents where I had been, they were not pleased. I felt accused of being morbidly curious, not healthy, sniffing around death for the thrill of it. And since, at sixteen, I was often not sure of the sources of my feelings or of my motives for doing what I did, I probably accused myself as well. One thing was clear: there was nobody in my world with whom I could discuss those films. Probably at the same time I was reading accounts of the camps in magazines and newspapers; what I remember was the films, and having questions that I could not even phrase: such as, are those men and women "them" or "us"?

To be able to ask even the child's astonished question *Why do they hate us so?* means knowing how to say "we." The guilt of not knowing, the guilt of perhaps having betrayed my parents, or even those victims, those survivors, through mere curiosity—these also froze in me for years the impulse to find out more about the Holocaust.

1947: I left Baltimore to go to college in Cambridge, Massachusetts, left (I thought) the backward, enervating South for the intellectual, vital North. New England also had for me some vibration of higher moral rectitude, of moral passion even, with its seventeenth-century Puritan inner scrutiny, its Abolitionist righteousness, Colonel Shaw and his Black Civil War regiment depicted in granite on Boston Common, its nineteenth-century literary "flowering." At the same time, I found myself, at Radcliffe, among Jewish women. I used to sit for hours over coffee with what I thought of as the "real" Jewish students, who told me about middle-class Jewish culture in America. I described my background—for the first time to strangers—and they took me on, some with amusement at my illiteracy, some arguing that I could never marry into a strict Jewish family, some convinced I didn't "look Jewish," others that I did. I learned the names of holidays and foods, which surnames are Jewish and which are "changed names"; about girls who had had their noses "fixed," their hair straightened. For these young Jewish women, students in the late 1940s, it was acceptable, perhaps even necessary, to strive to look as gentile as possible, but they stuck proudly to being Jewish; expected to marry a Jew, have children, keep the holidays, carry on the culture.

VISIONS OF AMERICA

I felt I was testing a forbidden current, that there was danger in these revelations. I bought a reproduction of a Chagall portrait of a rabbi in striped prayer-shawl and hung it on the wall of my room. I was admittedly young and trying to educate myself, but I was also doing something that *is* dangerous: I was flirting with identity.

One day that year I was in a small shop where I had bought a dress with a too-long skirt. The shop employed a seamstress who did alterations, and she came in to pin up the skirt on me. I am sure that she was a recent immigrant, a survivor. I remember a short, dark woman wearing heavy glasses, with an accent so foreign I could not understand her words. Something about her presence was very powerful and disturbing to me. After marking and pinning up the skirt she sat back on her knees, looked up at me, and asked in a hurried whisper: "You Jewish?" Eighteen years of training in assimilation sprang into the reflex by which I shook my head, rejecting her, and muttered, "No."

What was I actually saying "no" to? She was poor, older, struggling with a foreign tongue, anxious; she had escaped the death that had been intended for her, but I had no imagination of her possible courage and foresight, her resistance; I did not see in her a heroine who had perhaps saved many lives including her own. I saw the frightened immigrant, the seamstress hemming the skirts of college girls, the wandering Jew. But I was an American college girl, having her skirt hemmed. And I was frightened myself, I think, because she had recognized me ("It takes one to know one," my friend Edie at Radcliffe had said) even if I refused to recognize myself or her; even if her recognition was sharpened by loneliness, or the need to feel safe with me.

But why should she have felt safe with me? I myself was living in a false sense of safety.

There are betrayals in my life that I have known at the very moment were betrayals: this was one of them. There are other betrayals committed so repeatedly, so mundanely, that they leave no memory trace behind: only a growing residue of misery, of dull, accreted self-hatred. Often these take the form not of words but of silence. Silence before the joke at which everyone is laughing: the anti-woman joke, the racist joke, the anti-Semitic joke. Silence and then amnesia. Blocking it out when the oppressor's language starts coming from the lips of one we admire, whose courage and eloquence have touched us: *She didn't really mean that: he didn't really say that.* But the accretions build up out of sight, like scale inside a kettle.

1948: I come home from my freshman year at college flaming with new insights, new information. I am the daughter who has gone out into the world, to the pinnacle of intellectual prestige, Harvard, fulfilling my father's hopes for me, but

SPLIT AT THE ROOT

also exposed to dangerous influences. I have already been reproved for attending a rally for Henry Wallace and the Progressive Party. I challenge my father: "Why haven't you told me that I am Jewish? Why do you never talk about being a Jew?" He answered measuredly, "You know that I have never denied that I am a Jew. But it's not important to me. I am a scientist, a Deist. I have no use for organized religion. I choose to live in a world of many kinds of people. There are Jews I admire and others whom I despise. I am a person, not simply a Jew." The words are as I remember them, not perhaps exactly as spoken. But that was the message. And it contained enough truth—as all denial drugs itself on partial truth—so that it remained for the time being unanswerable, even though it left me high and dry, split at the root, gasping for clarity, for air.

At that time Arnold Rich was living in suspension, waiting to be appointed to the professorship of pathology at Johns Hopkins. The appointment was delayed for years, no Jew ever having held a professorial chair in that medical school. And he wanted it badly. It must have been a very bitter time for him, since he had believed so greatly in the redeeming power of excellence, of being the most brilliant, inspired man for the job. With enough excellence, you could presumably make it stop mattering that you were Jewish; you could become the *only* Jew in the gentile world, a Jew so "civilized," so far from "common," so attractively combining Southern gentility with European cultural values that no one would ever confuse you with the raw, "pushy" Jews of New York, the "loud, hysterical" refugees from Eastern Europe, the "overdressed" Jews of the urban South.

We—my sister, mother, and I—were constantly urged to speak quietly in public, to dress without ostentation, to repress all vividness or spontaneity, to assimilate with a world which might see us as too flamboyant. I suppose that my mother, pure gentile though she was, could be seen as acting "common" or "Jewish" if she laughed too loudly or spoke aggressively. My father's mother, who lived with us half the year, was a model of circumspect behavior, dressed in dark blue or lavender, retiring in company, ladylike to an extreme, wearing no jewelry except a good gold chain, a narrow brooch, a string of pearls. A few times, within the family, I saw her anger flare, felt the passion she was repressing. But when Arnold took us out to a restaurant, or on a trip, the Rich women were always tuned down to some WASP level my father believed, surely, would protect us all—maybe also make us unrecognizable to the "real Jews" who wanted to seize us, drag us back to the *shtetl*, the ghetto, in its many manifestations.

For, yes: that *was* a message—that some Jews would be after you, once they "knew," to rejoin them, to re-enter a world that was messy, noisy, unpredictable, maybe poor—"even though," as my mother once wrote me, criticizing my largely Jewish choice of friends in college: "some of them will be the most brilliant, fascinating people you'll ever meet." I wonder if that isn't one message of assimilation—of America—that the unlucky or the unachieving want to pull you backward, that to identify with them is to court downward mobility, lose the precious chance of passing, of token existence. There was always, within this sense of Jewish identity, a strong class discrimination. Jews might be "fascinating" as individuals but came with huge unruly families who "poured chicken soup over everyone's head" (in the phrase of a white Southern male poet). Anti-Semitism could thus be justified by the bad behavior of certain Jews; and if you did not effectively deny family and community, there would always be a cousin claiming kinship with you, who was the "wrong kind" of Jew.

I have always believed his attitude toward other Jews depended on who they were. . . . It was my impression that Jews of this background looked down on Eastern European Jews, including Polish Jews and Russian Jews, who generally were not as well educated. This from a letter written to me recently by a gentile who had worked in my father's department, whom I had asked about anti-Semitism there and in particular regarding my father. This informant also wrote me that it was hard to perceive anti-Semitism in Baltimore because the racism made so much more intense an impression: *I would almost have to think that Blacks went to a different heaven than the whites, because the bodies were kept in a separate morgue, and some white persons did not even want blood transfusions from Black donors.* My father's mind was racist and misogynist, yet as a medical student he noted in his journal that Southern male chivalry stopped at the point of any white man in a streetcar giving his seat to an old, weary, Black woman standing in the aisle. Was this a Jewish insight—an outsider's insight, even though the outsider was striving to be on the inside?

Because what isn't named is often more permeating than what is, I believe that my father's Jewishness profoundly shaped my own identity, and our family existence. They were shaped both by external anti-Semitism and my father's self-hatred, and by his Jewish pride. What Arnold did, I think, was call his Jewish pride something else: achievement, aspiration, genius, idealism. Whatever was unacceptable got left back under the rubric of Jewishness, or the "wrong kind" of Jews: uneducated, aggressive, loud. The message I got was that we were really superior: nobody else's father had collected so many books, had traveled so far, knew so many languages. Baltimore was a musical city, but for the most part, in the families of my school friends, culture was for women. My father was an amateur musician, read poetry, adored encyclopaedic knowledge. He prowled and pounced over my school papers, insisting I use "grown-up" sources; he criticized my poems for faulty technique and gave me books on rhyme and metre and form. His investment in my intellect and talent was egotistical, tyrannical, opinionated and terribly wearing. He taught me nevertheless to believe in hard work, to mistrust easy inspiration, to write and rewrite; to feel that I *was* a person of the book, even though a woman; to take ideas seriously. He made me feel, at a very young age, the power of language, and that I could share in it.

The Riches were proud, but we also had to be very careful. Our behavior had to be more impeccable than other people's. Strangers were not to be trusted, nor even friends; family issues must never go beyond the family; the world was full of potential slanderers, betrayers, *people who could not understand.* Even within the family, I realize that I never in my whole life knew what he was really feeling. Yet he spoke—monologued—with driving intensity. You could grow up in such a house mesmerized by the local electricity, the crucial meanings assumed by the merest things. This used to seem to me a sign that we were all living on some high emotional plane. It was a difficult force-field for a favored daughter to disengage from.

Easy to call that intensity Jewish; and I have no doubt that passion is one of the qualities required for survival over generations of persecution. But what happens when passion is rent from its original base, when the white gentile world is softly saying: "Be more like us and you can be almost one of us"? What happens when survival seems to mean closing off one emotional artery after another? His forebears in Europe had been forbidden to travel, or expelled from one country after another, had special taxes levied on them if they left the city walls, had been forced to wear special clothes and badges, restricted to the poorest neighborhoods. He had wanted to be a "free spirit," to travel widely among "all kinds of people." Yet in his prime of life he lived in an increasingly withdrawn world, in his house up on a hill in a neighborhood where Jews were not supposed to be able to buy property, depending almost exclusively on interactions with his wife and daughters to provide emotional connectedness. In his home, he created a private defense system so elaborate that even as he was dying my mother felt unable to talk freely with his colleagues, or others who might have helped her.

I imagine that the loneliness of the "only," the token, often doesn't feel like loneliness but like a kind of dead echo chamber. Certain things that ought to, don't resonate. Somewhere Beverly Smith writes of women of color "inspiring the behavior" in each other. When there's nobody to "inspire the behavior," act out of the culture, there is an atrophy, a dwindling, which is partly invisible.

I was married in 1953, in the Hillel House at Harvard, under a portrait of Albert Einstein. My parents refused to come. I was marrying a Jew, of the "wrong kind" from an Orthodox Eastern European background. Brooklyn-born, he had gone to Harvard, changed his name, was both indissolubly connected to his childhood world, and terribly ambivalent about it. My father saw this marriage as my having fallen prey to the Jewish family, Eastern European division.

Like many women I knew in the fifties, living under a then-unquestioned heterosexual imperative, I married in part because I knew no better way to disconnect from my first family. I married a "real Jew" who was himself almost equally divided between a troubled yet ingrained Jewish identity, and the pull toward Yankee approval, assimilation. But at least he was not adrift as a single token in a gentile world. We lived in a world where there was much intermarriage, where a certain "Jewish flavor" was accepted within the dominant gentile culture. People talked glibly of "Jewish self-hatred" but anti-Semitism was rarely identified. It was as if you could have it both ways, identity and assimilation, without having to think about it very much.

I was moved and gratefully amazed by the affection and kindliness my husband's parents showed me, the half-*shiksa*. I longed to embrace that family, that new and mysterious Jewish world. It was never a question of conversion— my husband had long since ceased being observant—but of a burning desire to do well, please these new parents, heal the split-consciousness in which I had been raised, and, of course, to belong. In the big sunny apartment on Eastern Parkway, the table would be spread on Saturday afternoons with a white or embroidered cloth and plates of coffee-cake, sponge-cake, *mohn*-cake, cookies, for a family gathering where everyone ate and drank—coffee, milk, cake—and later the talk eddied among the women still around the table or in the kitchen, while the men ended up in the living-room watching the ball-game. I had never known this kind of family, in which mock insults were cheerfully exchanged, secrets whispered in corners among two or three, children and grandchildren boasted about, and the new daughter-in-law openly inspected. I was profoundly attracted by all this, including the punctilious observance of *kashruth,* the symbolism lurking behind daily kitchen tasks. I saw it all as quintessentially and authentically Jewish, and thus I objectified both the people and the culture. My unexamined anti-Semitism allowed me to do this. But also, I had not yet recognized that as a woman I stood in a particular and equally unexamined relationship to the Jewish family and to Jewish culture.

There were several years during which I did not see, and barely communicated with my parents. At the same time, my father's personality haunted my life. Such had been the force of his will in our household that for a long time I felt I would have to pay in some terrible way for having disobeyed him. When finally we were reconciled, and my husband and I and our children began to have some minimal formal contact with my parents, the obsessional power of Arnold's voice or handwriting had given way to a dull sense of useless anger and pain. I wanted him to cherish and approve of me not as he had when I was a child, but as the woman I was, who had her own mind and had made her own choices. This, I finally realized, was not to be; Arnold demanded absolute loyalty, absolute submission to his will. In my separation from him, in my realization at what a price that once-intoxicating approval had been bought, I was learning in concrete

SPLIT AT THE ROOT

ways a great deal about patriarchy, in particular how the "special" woman, the favored daughter, is controlled and rewarded.

Arnold Rich died in 1968 after a long deteriorating illness; his mind had gone and he had been losing his sight for years. It was a year of intensifying political awareness for me, the Martin Luther King and Robert Kennedy assassinations, the Columbia University strike. But it was not that these events and the meetings and demonstrations that surrounded them, pre-empted the time of mourning for my father; I had been mourning a long time for an early, primary, and intense relationship, by no means always benign, but in which I had been ceaselessly made to feel that what I did with my life, the choices I made, the attitudes I held, were of the utmost consequence.

Sometimes in my thirties, on visits to Brooklyn, I sat on Eastern Parkway, a baby-stroller at my feet: one of many rows of young Jewish women on benches with children in that neighborhood. I used to see the Lubavitcher Hassidim—then beginning to move into the Crown Heights neighborhood—walking out on shabbas, the women in their *sheitels* a little behind the men. My father-in-law pointed them out as rather exotic—too old-country, perhaps, too unassimilated even for his devout sense of Jewish identity. It took many years for me to understand—partly because I understood so little about class in America—how in my own family, and in the very different family of my in-laws, there were degrees and hierarchies of assimilation which looked askance upon each other—and also geographic lines of difference, as between Southern Jews and New York Jews, whose manners and customs varied along class as well as regional lines.

I had three sons before I was thirty, and during those years I often felt that to be a Jewish woman, a Jewish mother, was to be perceived in the Jewish family as an entirely physical being, a producer and nourisher of children. The experience of motherhood was eventually to radicalize me; but before that I was encountering the institution of motherhood most directly in a Jewish cultural version; and I felt rebellious, moody, defensive, unable to sort out what was Jewish from what was simply motherhood, or female destiny. (I lived in Cambridge, not Brooklyn, but there, too, restless, educated women sat on benches with baby-strollers, half-stunned, not by Jewish cultural expectations, but by the American cultural expectations of the 1950s.)

My children were taken irregularly to Seders, to Bar Mitzvahs, and to special services in their grandfather's temple. Their father lit Hanukkah candles while I stood by, having relearned each year the English meaning of the Hebrew blessing. We all celebrated a secular, liberal Christmas. I read aloud from books about Esther and the Maccabees and Moses, and also from books about Norse goblins and Chinese grandmothers and Celtic dragon-slayers. Their father told stories of his boyhood in Brooklyn, his grandmother in the Bronx who had to be visited on the subway every week, of misdeeds in Hebrew school, of being a bright Jewish kid at Boys' High. In the permissive liberalism of academic Cambridge, you could raise your children to be vaguely or distinctly Jewish as you would, but Christian myth and calendar organized the year. My sons grew up knowing far more about the existence and concrete meaning of Jewish culture than I had. But I don't recall sitting down with them and telling them that millions of people like themselves, many of them children, had been rounded up and murdered in Europe in their parents' lifetime. Nor was I able to tell them that they came in part out of the rich, thousand-year-old, Ashkenazic culture of Eastern Europe, which the Holocaust destroyed; or that they came from a people whose secular tradition had included a hatred of oppression and a willingness to fight for justice—an anti-racist, a socialist, and even sometimes a feminist vision. I could not tell them these things because they were still too blurred in outline in my own mind.

The emergence of the Civil Rights movement in the sixties I remember as lifting me out of a sense of personal frustration and hopelessness. Reading James Baldwin's early essays, in the fifties, had stirred me with a sense that apparently "given" situations like racism could be analyzed and described and that this could lead to action, to change. Racism had been so utter and implicit a fact of my childhood and adolescence, had felt so central among the silences, negations, cruelties, fears, superstitions of my early life, that somewhere among my feelings must have been the hope that if Black people could become free, of the immense political and social burdens they were forced to bear, I too could become free, of all the ghosts and shadows of my childhood, named and unnamed. When "the Movement" began, it felt extremely personal to me. And it was often Jews who spoke up for the justice of the cause, Jewish civil rights lawyers who were traveling South; it was two young Jews who were found murdered with a young Black man in Mississippi. Schwerner, Goodman, Chaney.

Moving to New York in the mid-sixties meant almost immediately being plunged into the debate over community control of public schools, in which Black and Jewish teachers and parents were often on opposite sides of extremely militant barricades. It was easy as a white liberal to deplore and condemn the racism of middle-class Jewish parents or angry Jewish schoolteachers, many of them older women; to displace our own racism onto them; or to feel it as too painful to think about. The struggle for Black civil rights had such clarity about it for me: I knew that segregation was wrong, that unequal opportunity was wrong, I knew that segregation in particular was more than a set of social and legal rules, it meant that even "decent" white people lived in a network of lies and arrogance and moral collusion. In the world of Jewish assimilationist and liberal politics which I knew best, however, things were far less clear to me, and anti-Semitism went almost unmentioned. It was even possible to view anti-Semitism as a reactionary agenda, a concern of *Commentary* magazine or, later, the Jewish Defense League. Most of the political work I was doing in the late 1960s was on racial issues, in particular as a teacher in the City University during the struggle for Open Admissions. The white colleagues I thought of as allies were, I think, mostly Jewish. Yet it was easy to see other New York Jews, who had climbed out of poverty and exploitation through the public school system and the free city colleges, as now trying to block Black and Puerto Rican students trying to do likewise. I didn't understand then that I was living between two strains of Jewish social identity: the Jew as radical visionary and activist who understands oppression firsthand; and the Jew as part of America's devouring plan in which the persecuted, called to assimilation, learn that the price is to engage in persecution.

And indeed, there *was* intense racism among Jews as well as white gentiles in the City University, part of the bitter history of Jews and Blacks which James Baldwin had described much earlier, in his 1948 essay on "The Harlem Ghetto";* part of the divide-and-conquer script still being rehearsed by those of us who have the least to gain from it.

By the time I left my marriage, after seventeen years and three children, I had become identified with the women's liberation movement. It was an astonishing time to be a woman of my age. In the 1950s, seeking a way to grasp the pain I seemed to be feeling most of the time, to set it in some larger context, I had read all kinds of things, but it was James Baldwin and Simone de Beauvoir who had described the world—though differently—in terms that made the most sense to me. By the end of the sixties there were two political movements, one already meeting severe repression, one just emerging—which addressed those descriptions of the world.

And there was, of course, a third movement, or a movement-within-a-movement—the early lesbian manifestos, the new visibility and activism of lesbians everywhere. I had known very early on that the women's movement was not going to be a simple walk across an open field; that it would pull on every fibre of my existence; that it would mean going back and searching the shadows of my consciousness. Reading *The Second Sex* in 1950s isolation as an academic housewife had felt less dangerous than reading "The Myth of Vaginal Orgasm" or "Woman-Identified Woman" in a world where I was in constant debate and discussion with women over every aspect of our lives that we could as yet name.

Notes of A Native Son, Beacon Press, 1955.

De Beauvoir had placed "The Lesbian" on the margins, and there was little in her book to suggest the power of woman-bonding. But the passion of debating ideas with women was an erotic passion for me, and the risking of self with women that was necessary in order to win some truth out of the lies of the past was also erotic. The suppressed lesbian I had been carrying in me since adolescence began to stretch her limbs and her first full-fledged act was to fall in love with a Jewish woman.

Some time during the early months of that relationship, I dreamed that I was arguing feminist politics with my lover. *Of course,* I said to her in this dream, *if you're going to bring up the Holocaust against me, there's nothing I can do.* If, as I believe, I was both myself and her in this dream, it spoke of the split in my consciousness. I had been, more or less, a Jewish heterosexual woman; but what did it mean to be a Jewish lesbian? What did it mean to feel myself, as I did, both anti-Semite and Jew? And, as a feminist, how was I charting for myself the oppressions within oppression?

The earliest feminist papers on Jewish identity that I read were critiques of the patriarchal and misogynist elements in Judaism, or of the caricaturing of Jewish women in literature by Jewish men. I remember hearing Judith Plaskow give a paper called "Can a Woman Be a Jew?" (her conclusion was, "yes, but . . ."). I was soon after in correspondence with a former student who had emigrated to Israel, was a passionate feminist, and wrote me at length of the legal and social constraints on women there, the stirrings of contemporary Israeli feminism, and the contradictions she felt in her daily life. With the new politics, activism, literature of a tumultuous feminist movement around me, a movement which claimed universality though it had not yet acknowledged its own racial, class, and ethnic perspectives, or its fears of the differences among women—I pushed aside for one last time thinking further about myself as a Jewish woman. I saw Judaism, simply, as yet another strand of patriarchy; if asked to choose I might have said (as my father had said in other language): *I am a woman, not a Jew.* (But, I always added mentally, if Jews had to wear yellow stars again, I too would wear one. As if I would have the choice to wear it or not.)

Sometimes I feel I have seen too long from too many disconnected angles: white, Jewish, anti-Semite, racist, anti-racist, once-married, lesbian, middle-class, feminist, exmatriate Southerner, *split at the root:* that I will never bring them whole. I would have liked, in this essay, to bring together the meanings of anti-Semitism and racism as I have experienced them and as I believe they intersect in the world beyond my life. But I'm not able to do this yet. I feel the tension as I think, make notes: *if you really look at the one reality, the other will waver and disperse.* Trying in one week to read Angela Davis and Lucy Dawidowicz;* trying to hold throughout a feminist, a lesbian, perspective—what does this mean? Nothing has trained me for this. And sometimes I feel inadequate to make any statement as a Jew: I feel the history of denial within me like an injury, a scar—for assimilation has affected *my* perceptions, those early lapses in meaning, those blanks, are with me still. My ignorance can be dangerous to me, and to others.

Yet we can't wait for the undamaged to make our connections for us; we can't wait to speak until we are wholly clear and righteous. There is no purity, and, in our lifetimes, no end to this process.

This essay, then, has no conclusions: it is another beginning, for me. Not just a way of saying, in 1982 Right-wing America, *I too will wear the yellow star.* It's a moving into accountability, enlarging the range of accountability. I know that in the rest of my life, the next half-century or so, every aspect of my identity will have to be engaged. The middle-class white girl taught to trade obedience for privilege. The Jewish lesbian raised to be a heterosexual gentile. The woman who first heard oppression named and analyzed in the Black civil rights struggle. The woman with three sons, the feminist who hates male violence. The woman limping with a cane, the woman who has stopped bleeding, are also accountable. The poet who knows that beautiful language can lie, that the oppressor's language sometimes sounds beautiful. The woman trying, as part of her resistance, to clean up her act.

*Angela Y. Davis, *Women, Race and Class.* Random House, 1981; Lucy S. Dawidowicz, *The War Against the Jews 1933–1945* (1975), Bantam Books, 1979.

My gratitude to Michelle Cliff, whose work forced me to examine my own "passing"; to Elly Bulkin and Gloria Z. Greenfield, for the Jewish women's workshop at Storrs, Connecticut, June 1981: to Evi Beck, Maureen Brady, Michelle Cliff, Gloria Z. Greenfield, Irena Klepfisz, Judith McDaniel, for criticism of the first draft: and to Elana Dykewomon and Melanie Kaye, for their words.

from A NATIVE HILL

Wendell Berry

Wendell Berry was born in Kentucky, and is the author of several volumes of poetry, including *The Collected Poems of Wendell Berry 1957–1982*; novels (*A Broken Ground, Openings, The Country of Marriage*); and collections of essays, including *The Long-Legged House, The Hidden Wound,* and *The Unforeseen Wilderness.* The following excerpt is from *Recollected Essays (1965–1980)*.

I BEGAN MY LIFE AS THE OLD TIMES AND THE LAST OF THE OLD-time people were dying out. The Depression and World War II delayed the mechanization of the farms here, and one of the first disciplines imposed on me was that of a teamster. Perhaps I first stood in the role of student before my father's father, who, halting a team in front of me, would demand to know which mule had the best head, which the best shoulder or rump, which was the lead mule, were they hitched right. And there came a time when I knew, and took a considerable pride in knowing. Having a boy's usual desire to play at what he sees men working at, I learned to harness and hitch and work a team. I felt distinguished by that, and took the same pride in it that other boys my age took in their knowledge of automobiles. I seem to have been born with an aptitude for a way of life that was doomed, although I did not understand that at the time.

Free of any intuition of its doom, I delighted in it, and learned all I could about it.

That knowledge, and the men who gave it to me, influenced me deeply. It entered my imagination, and gave its substance and tone to my mind. It fashioned in me possibilities and limits, desires and frustrations, that I do not expect to live to the end of. And it is strange to think how barely in the nick of time it came to me. If I had been born five years later I would have begun in a different world, and would no doubt have become a different man.

Those five years made a critical difference in my life, and it is a historical difference. One of the results is that in my generation I am something of an anachronism. I am less a child of my time than the people of my age who grew up in the cities, or than the people who grew up here in my own place five years after I did. In my acceptance of twentieth-century realities there has had to be a certain deliberateness, whereas most of my contemporaries had them simply by being born to them.

In my teens, when I was away at school, I could comfort myself by recalling in intricate detail the fields I had worked and played in, and hunted over, and ridden through on horseback—and that were richly associated in my mind with people and with stories. I could recall even the casual locations of certain small rocks. I could recall the look of a hundred different kinds of daylight on all those places, the look of animals grazing over them, the postures and attitudes and movements of the men who worked in them, the quality of the grass and the crops that had grown on them. I had come to be aware of it as one is aware of one's body; it was present to me whether I thought of it or not.

When I have thought of the welfare of the earth, the problems of its health and preservation, the care of its life, I have had this place before me, the part representing the whole more vividly and accurately, making clearer and more pressing demands, than any *idea* of the whole. When I have thought of kindness or cruelty, weariness or exuberance, devotion or betrayal, carelessness or care, doggedness or awkwardness or grace, I have had in my mind's eye the men and women of this place, their faces and gestures and movements.

I have pondered a great deal over a conversation I took part in a number of years ago in one of the offices of New York University. I had lived away from Kentucky for several years—in California, in Europe, in New York City. And now I had decided to go back and take a teaching job at the University of Kentucky, giving up the position I then held on the New York University faculty. That day I had been summoned by one of my superiors at the university, whose intention, I had already learned, was to persuade me to stay on in New York "for my own good."

The decision to leave had cost me considerable difficulty and doubt and hard thought—for hadn't I achieved what had become one of the almost traditional goals of American writers? I had reached the greatest city in the nation; I had a good job; I was meeting other writers and talking with them and learning from them; I had reason to hope that I might take a still larger part in the literary life of that place. On the other hand, I knew I had not escaped Kentucky, and had never really wanted to. I was still writing about it, and had recognized that I would probably need to write about it for the rest of my life. Kentucky was my fate—not an altogether pleasant fate, though it had much that was pleasing in it, but one that I could not leave behind simply by going to another place, and that I therefore felt more and more obligated to meet directly and to understand. Perhaps even more important, I still had a deep love for the place I had been born in, and liked the idea of going back to be part of it again. And that, too, I felt obligated to try to understand. Why should I love one place so much more than any other? What could be the meaning or use of such love?

The elder of the faculty began the conversation by alluding to Thomas Wolfe, who once taught at the same institution. "Young man," he said, "don't you know you can't go home again?" And he went on to speak of the advantages, for a young writer, of living in New York among the writers and the editors and the publishers.

The conversation that followed was a persistence of politeness in the face of impossibility. I knew as well as Wolfe that there is a certain *metaphorical* sense in which you can't go home again—that is, the past is lost to the extent that it cannot be lived in again. I knew perfectly well that I could not return home and be a child, or recover the secure pleasures of childhood. But I knew also that as the sentence was spoken to me it bore a self-dramatizing sentimentality that was absurd. Home—the place, the countryside—was still there, still pretty much as I left it, and there was no reason I could not go back to it if I wanted to.

As for the literary world, I had ventured some distance into that, and liked it well enough. I knew that because I was a writer the literary world would always have an importance for me and would always attract my interest. But I never doubted that the world was more important to me than the literary world; and the world would always be most fully and clearly present to me in the place I was fated by birth to know better than any other.

And so I had already chosen according to the most intimate and necessary inclinations of my own life. But what keeps me thinking of that conversation is the feeling that it was a confrontation of two radically different minds, and that it was a confrontation with significant historical overtones.

I do not pretend to know all about the other man's mind, but it was clear that he wished to speak to me as a representative of the literary world—the world he assumed that I aspired to above all others. His argument was based on the belief that once one had attained the metropolis, the literary capital, the worth of one's origins was canceled out; there simply could be nothing *worth* going back to. What lay behind one had ceased to be a part of life, and had become "subject matter." And there was the belief, long honored among American intellectuals and artists and writers, that a place such as I came from could be returned to only at the price of intellectual death; cut off from the cultural springs of the metropolis, the American countryside is Circe and Mammon. Finally, there was the assumption that the life of the metropolis is *the* experience, the *modern* experience, and that the life of the rural towns, the farms, the wilderness places is not only irrelevant to our time, but archaic as well because unknown or unconsidered by the people who really matter—that is, the urban intellectuals.

I was to realize during the next few years how false and destructive and silly those ideas are. But even then I was aware that life outside the literary world was not without honorable precedent: if there was Wolfe, there was also Faulkner; if there was James, there was also Thoreau. But what I had in my mind that made the greatest difference was the knowledge of the few square miles in Kentucky that were mine by inheritance and by birth and by the intimacy the mind makes with the place it awakens in.

What finally freed me from these doubts and suspicions was the insistence in what was happening to me that, far from being bored and diminished and obscured to myself by my life here, I had grown more alive and more conscious than I had ever been.

I had made a significant change in my relation to the place: before, it had been mine by coincidence or accident; now it was mine by choice. My return, which at first had been hesitant and tentative, grew wholehearted and sure. I had come back to stay. I hoped to live here the rest of my life. And once that was settled I began to *see* the place with a new clarity and a new understanding and a new seriousness. Before coming back I had been willing to allow the possibility—which one of my friends insisted on—that I already knew this place as well as I ever would. But now I began to see the real abundance and richness of it. It is, I saw, inexhaustible in its history, in the details of its life, in its possibilities. I walked over it, looking, listening, smelling, touching, alive to it as never before. I listened to the talk of my kinsmen and neighbors as I never had done, alert to their knowledge of the place, and to the qualities and energies of their speech. I began more seriously than ever to learn the names of things—the wild plants and animals, the natural processes, the local places—and to articulate my observations and memories. My language increased and strengthened, and sent my mind into the place like a live root system. And so what has become the usual order of things reversed itself with me; my mind became the root of my life rather than its sublimation. I came to see myself as growing out of the earth like the other native animals and plants. I saw my body and my daily motions as brief coherences and articulations of the energy of the place, which would fall back into it like leaves in the autumn.

In this awakening there has been a good deal of pain. When I lived in other places I looked on their evils with the curious eye of a traveler; I was not responsible for them; it cost me nothing to be a critic, for I had not been there long, and I did not feel that I would stay. But here, now that I am both native and citizen, there is no immunity to what is wrong. It is impossible to escape the sense that I am involved in history. What I am has been to a considerable extent determined by what my forebears were, by how they chose to treat this place while they lived in it; the lives of most of them diminished it, and limited its possibilities, and narrowed its future. And every day I am confronted by the question of what inheritance I will leave. What do I have that I am using up? For it has been our history that each generation in this place has been less welcome to it than the last. There has been less here for them. At each arrival there has been less fertility in the soil, and a larger inheritance of destructive precedent and shameful history.

I am forever being crept up on and newly startled by the realization that my people established themselves here by killing or driving out the original possessors, by the awareness that people were once bought and sold here by my people, by the sense of the violence they have done to their own kind and to each other and to the earth, by the evidence of their persistent failure to serve either the place or their own community in it. I am forced, against all my hopes and inclinations, to regard the history of my people here as the progress of the doom of what I value most in the world: the life and health of the earth, the peacefulness of human communities and households.

And so here, in the place I love more than any other and where I have chosen among all other places to live my life, I am more painfully divided within myself than I could be in any other place.

I know of no better key to what is adverse in our heritage in this place than the account of "The Battle of the Fire-Brands," quoted in Collins' *History of Kentucky* "from the autobiography of Rev. Jacob Young, a Methodist minister." The "Newcastle" referred to is the present-day New Castle, the county seat of Henry County. I give the quote in full:

> The costume of the Kentuckians was a hunting shirt, buckskin pantaloons, a leathern belt around their middle, a scabbard, and a big knife fastened to their belt; some of them wore hats and some caps. Their feet were covered with moccasins, made of dressed deer skins. They did not think themselves dressed without their powder-horn and shot-pouch, or the gun and the

tomahawk. They were ready, then, for all alarms. They knew but little. They could clear ground, raise corn, and kill turkeys, deer, bears, and buffalo; and, when it became necessary, they understood the art of fighting the Indians as well as any men in the United States.

Shortly after we had taken up our residence, I was called upon to assist in opening a road from the place where Newcastle now stands, to the mouth of Kentucky river. That country, then, was an unbroken forest; there was nothing but an Indian trail passing the wilderness. I met the company early in the morning, with my axe, three days' provisions, and my knapsack. Here I found a captain, with about 100 men, all prepared to labor; about as jovial a company as I ever saw, all good-natured and civil. This was about the last of November, 1797. The day was cold and clear. The country through which the company passed was delightful; it was not a flat country, but, what the Kentuckians called, rolling ground—was quite well stored with lofty timber, and the undergrowth was very pretty. The beautiful canebrakes gave it a peculiar charm. What rendered it most interesting was the great abundance of wild turkeys, deer, bears, and other wild animals. The company worked hard all day, in quiet, and every man obeyed the captain's orders punctually.

About sundown, the captain, after a short address, told us the night was going to be very cold, and we must make very large fires. We felled the hickory trees in great abundance; made great log-heaps, mixing the dry wood with the green hickory; and, laying down a kind of sleepers under the pile, elevated the heap and caused it to burn rapidly. Every man had a water vessel in his knapsack; we searched for and found a stream of water. By this time, the fires were showing to great advantage; so we warmed our cold victuals, ate our suppers, and spent the evening in hearing the hunter's stories relative to the bloody scenes of the Indian war. We then heard some pretty fine singing, considering the circumstances.

Thus far, well; but a change began to take place. They became very rude, and raised the war-whoop. Their shrill shrieks made me tremble. They chose two captains, divided the men into two companies, and commenced fighting with the firebrands—the log heaps having burned down. The only law for their government was, that no man should throw a brand without fire on it—so that they might know how to dodge. They fought, for two or three hours, in perfect good nature; till brands became scarce, and they began to violate the law. Some were severely wounded, blood began to flow freely, and they were in a fair way of commencing a fight in earnest. At this moment, the loud voice of the captain rang out above the din, ordering every man to retire to rest. They dropped their weapons of warfare, rekindled the fires, and laid down to sleep. We finished our road according to directions, and returned home in health and peace.

The significance of this bit of history is in its utter violence. The work of clearing the road was itself violent. And from the orderly violence of that labor, these men turned for amusement to disorderly violence. They were men whose element was violence; the only alternatives they were aware of were those within the comprehension of main strength. And let us acknowledge that these were the truly influential men in the history of Kentucky, as well as in the history of most of the rest of America. In comparison to the fatherhood of such as these, the so-called "founding fathers" who established our political ideals are but distant cousins. It is not John Adams or Thomas Jefferson whom we see night after night in the magic mirror of the television set; we see these builders of the road from New Castle to the mouth of the Kentucky River. Their reckless violence has glamorized all our trivialities and evils. Their aggressions have simplified our complexities and problems. They have cut all our Gordian knots. They have appeared in all our disguises and costumes. They have worn all our uniforms. Their war whoop has sanctified our inhumanity and ratified our blunders of policy.

To testify to the persistence of their influence, it is only necessary for me to confess that I read the Reverend Young's account of them with delight; I yield a considerable admiration to the exuberance and extravagance of their fight with the firebrands; I take a certain pride in belonging to the same history and the same place that they belong to—though I know that they represent the worst that is in us, and in me, and that their presence in our history has been ruinous, and that their survival among us promises ruin.

"They knew but little," the observant Reverend says of them, and this is the most suggestive thing he says. It is surely understandable and pardonable, under the circumstances, that these men were ignorant by the standards of formal schooling. But one immediately reflects that the American Indian, who was ignorant by the same standards, nevertheless knew how to live in the country without making violence the invariable mode of his relation to it; in fact, from the ecologist's or the conservationist's point of view, he did it *no* violence. This is because he had, in place of what we would call education, a fully integrated culture, the content of which was a highly complex sense of his dependence on the earth. The same, I believe, was generally true of the peasants of certain old agricultural societies, particularly in the Orient. They belonged by an intricate awareness to the earth they lived on and by, which meant that they respected it, which meant that they practiced strict economies in the use of it.

The abilities of those Kentucky road builders of 1797 were far more primitive and rudimentary than those of the Stone Age people they had driven out. They could clear the ground, grow corn, kill game, and make war. In the minds and hands of men who "know but little"—or little else—all of these abilities are certain to be destructive, even of those values and benefits their use may be intended to serve.

On such a night as the Reverend Young describes, an Indian would have made do with a small shelter and a small fire. But these road builders, veterans of the Indian War, "felled the hickory trees in great abundance; made great log-heaps . . . and caused [them] to burn rapidly." Far from making a small shelter that could be adequately heated by a small fire, their way was to make no shelter at all, and heat instead a sizable area of the landscape. The idea was that when faced with abundance one should consume abundantly—an idea that has survived to become the basis of our present economy. It is neither natural nor civilized, and even from a "practical" point of view it is to the last degree brutalizing and stupid.

I think that the comparison of these road builders with the Indians, on the one hand, and with Old World peasants on the other, is a most suggestive one. The Indians and the peasants were people who belonged deeply and intricately to their places. Their ways of life had evolved slowly in accordance with their knowledge of their land, of its needs, of their own relation of dependence and responsibility to it. The road builders, on the contrary, were *placeless* people. That is why they "knew but little." Having left Europe far behind, they had not yet in any meaningful sense arrived in America, not yet having *devoted* themselves to any part of it in a way that would produce the intricate knowledge of it necessary to live in it without destroying it. Because they belonged to no place, it was almost inevitable that they should behave violently toward the places they came to. We *still* have not, in any meaningful way, arrived in America. And in spite of our great reservoir of facts and methods, in comparison to the deep earthly wisdom of established peoples we still know but little.

But my understanding of this curiously parabolic fragment of history will not be complete until I have considered more directly that the occasion of this particular violence was the building of a road. It is obvious that one who values the idea of community cannot speak against roads without risking all sorts of absurdity. It must be noticed, nevertheless, that the predecessor to this first road was "nothing but an Indian trail passing the wilderness"—a path. The Indians, then, who had the wisdom and the grace to live in this country for perhaps ten thousand years without destroying or damaging any of it, needed for their travels no more than a footpath; but their successors, who in a century and a half plundered the area of at least half its topsoil and virtually all of its forest, felt immediately that they had to have a road. My interest is not in the question of whether or not they *needed* the road, but in the fact that the road was then, and is now, the most characteristic form of their relation to the country.

The difference between a path and a road is not only the obvious one. A path is little more than a habit that comes with knowledge of a place. It is a sort of ritual of familiarity. As a form, it is a form of contact with a known landscape. It is not destructive. It is the perfect adaptation, through experience and familiarity, of movement to place; it obeys the natural contours; such obstacles as it meets it goes around. A road, on the other hand, even the most primitive road, embodies a resistance against the landscape. Its reason is not simply the necessity for movement, but haste. Its wish is to *avoid* contact with the landscape; it seeks so far as possible to go over the country, rather than through it; its aspiration, as we see clearly in the example of our modern freeways, is to be a bridge; its tendency is to translate place into space in order to traverse it with the least effort. It is destructive, seeking to remove or destroy all obstacles in its way. The primitive road advanced by the destruction of the forest; modern roads advance by the destruction of topography.

That first road from the site of New Castle to the mouth of the Kentucky River—lost now either by obsolescence or metamorphosis—is now being crossed and to some extent replaced by its modern descendant known as I–71, and I have no wish to disturb the question of whether or not *this* road was needed. I only want to observe that it bears no relation whatever to the country it passes through. It is a pure abstraction, built to serve the two abstractions that are the poles of our national life: commerce and expensive pleasure. It was built, not according to the lay of the land, but according to a blueprint. Such homes and farmlands and woodlands as happened to be in its way are now buried under it. A part of a hill near here that would have caused it to turn aside was simply cut down and disposed of as thoughtlessly as the pioneer road builders would have disposed of a tree. Its form is the form of speed, dissatisfaction, and anxiety. It represents the ultimate in engineering sophistication, but the crudest possible valuation of life in this world. It is as adequate a symbol of our relation to our country now as that first road was of our relation to it in 1797.

But the sense of the past also gives a deep richness and resonance to nearly everything I see here. It is partly the sense that what I now see, other men that I have known once saw, and partly that this knowledge provides an imaginative access to what I do not know. I think of the country as a kind of palimpsest scrawled over with the comings and goings of people, the erasure of time already in process even as the marks of passage are put down. There are the ritual marks of neighborhood—roads, paths between houses. There are the domestic paths from house to barns and outbuildings and gardens, farm roads threading the pasture gates. There are the wanderings of hunters and searchers after lost stock, and the speculative or meditative or inquisitive "walking around" of farmers on wet days and Sundays. There is the spiraling geometry of the rounds of implements in fields, and the passing and returning scratches of plows across croplands. Often these have filled an interval, an opening, between the retreat of the forest from the virgin ground and the forest's return to ground that has been worn out and given up. In the woods here one often finds cairns of stones picked up out of furrows, gullies left by bad farming, forgotten roads, stone chimneys of houses long rotted away or burned.

Occasionally one stumbles into a coincidence that, like an unexpected alignment of windows, momentarily cancels out the sense of historical whereabouts, giving with an overwhelming immediacy an awareness of the reality of the past.

The possibility of this awareness is always immanent in old homesites. It may suddenly bear in upon one at the sight of old orchard trees standing in the dooryard of a house now filled with baled hay. It came to me when I looked out the attic window of a disintegrating log house and saw a far view of the cleared ridges with wooded hollows in between, and nothing in sight to reveal the date. Who was I, leaning to the window? When?

It broke upon me one afternoon when, walking in the woods on one of my family places, I came upon a gap in a fence, wired shut, but with deep-cut wagon tracks still passing through it under the weed growth and the fallen leaves. Where that thicket stands there was crop ground, maybe as late as my own time. I knew some of the men who tended it; their names and faces were instantly alive in my mind. I knew how it had been with them—how they would harness their mule teams in the early mornings in my grandfather's big barn and come to the woods-rimmed tobacco patches, the mules' feet wet with the dew. And in the solitude and silence that came upon them they would set to work, their water jugs left in the shade of bushes in the fencerows.

As a child I learned the early mornings in these places for myself, riding out in the wagons with the tobacco-cutting crews to those steep fields in the dew-wet shadow of the woods. As the day went on the shadow would draw back under the feet of the trees, and it would get hot. Little whirlwinds would cross the opening, picking up the dust and the dry "ground leaves" of the tobacco. We made a game of running with my grandfather to stand, shoulders scrunched and eyes squinched, in their middles.

Having such memories, I can acknowledge only with reluctance and sorrow that those slopes should never have been broken. Rich as they were, they were too steep. The humus stood dark and heavy over them once; the plow was its doom.

from THE NAMES

N. Scott Momaday

THE JEMEZ DAY SCHOOL WAS BUILT IN 1929. IT STOOD FOR LESS than fifty years, not a long life for a building. In the last few years—since my time there—the character of the school changed remarkably. Other buildings grew up around it. The old storerooms, the coalbin, and the garage in which stood the Kohler engine that generated our light and heat, were converted into gleaming modern compartments—a cafeteria, a clinic, bathrooms. The old porch, where my parents and I sat talking or listening to the sounds of the village on summer evenings, became an administrative office, and a kindergarten now stands on the sandy beach where I pastured my horses. No, not a long time. But in that span and in that place were invested many days of my life, and many of the very best, I believe.

My parents hankered after the old, sacred world from which we had come to Hobbs, as I did, too, without clearly knowing it. If you have ever been to the hogans in Canyon de Chelly, or to a squaw dance near Lukachukai—if you have ever heard the riding songs in the dusk, or the music of the *yei bichai*—you will never come away entirely, but a part of you will remain there always; you will have found an old home of the spirit.

It happened that a teaching job opened up at the Cañoncito Day School on the Navajo reservation between Albuquerque and Gallup, and my mother decided to take it. Sooner or later there would be two positions somewhere, my mother was assured, and my father and I would join her. And so it came about, sooner than could have been expected. In a matter of days my parents were offered the two-teacher day school at Jemez Pueblo, some fifty miles north and west of Albuquerque, due west of Santa Fe, in the canyon country beneath the Jemez Mountains. None of us had ever been there before. My mother went there directly from Cañoncito, and my father and I collected our things and set out from Hobbs with a man whom my father had hired to move us in his truck. That was in September, 1946. We arrived late at night, having got lost and gone nearly to Cuba, New Mexico, on the Farmington road. I can still see that dirt and gravel road in the light of the headlamps, white, with the black night on either side, the blue, black-dotted dunes in the moonlight beyond, and the bright stars. Rabbits and coyotes crossed the road. There was no pavement then on our way beyond Bernalillo, and for the last thirty miles or so the little truck bounced and rattled into the wild country. I could remember having, years before, when I was small, driven with my father across Snake Flats, on the Navajo. In heavy rain or snow the road was impassable, and we had had to wait until late at night, when it was frozen hard, in order to drive upon it.

The next morning I woke up, and there was a great excitement in me, as if something strange and wonderful had happened in the night: I had somehow got myself deep into the world, deeper than ever before. Perhaps I really expected nothing, and so I could not have been disappointed, but I do not believe that. Anyway, no expectation could possibly have been equal to the brilliance and exhilaration of that autumn New Mexican morning. Outside I caught my breath on the cold, delicious air of the Jemez Valley, lying out at six thousand feet. Around me were all the colors of the earth that I have ever seen. As I think back to that morning, there comes to my mind a sentence in Isak Dinesen: "In the highlands you woke up in the morning and thought: Here I am, where I ought to be."

The valley slopes down from north to south, and the pueblo lies down in the depth of it, on the east bank of the shallow Jemez River. Some four miles to the north is the little settlement of Cañon, nestled in sheer formations of red rock, and beyond is the long, deep San Diego Canyon, rising sharply up to the dark-timbered walls of the Jemez Range, to the Valle Grande, which is the largest caldera in the world, and to the summit above eleven thousand feet, from which you can look across the distance eastward to the Sangre de Cristos. Five miles to the south is the village of San Ysidro, where the valley loses its definition and the earth fans out in wide reaches of white, semi-arid plains. The junction at San Ysidro is as close as you can come to Jemez Pueblo in a Trailways bus; State Road 44 runs south and east to Bernalillo, north and west to Cuba, Bloomfield, and Farmington, near my old home of Shiprock. The east side of the valley is a long blue mesa, which from the pueblo seems far away, and in my years there I never covered the whole distance between, though I rode around for a thousand miles, it may be, on horseback. The conformation of that mesa is the rule of a solar calendar; for as long as anyone knows the Jemez people have lived their lives according to the ranging of the sun as it appears every day on that long, level skyline. Closer on the west, across the river, the valley is sharp-edged, given up abruptly to a high, broken wall—to walls beyond walls—of many colors. There is the red mesa upon which are still to be found the ancient ruins of Zia, there the white sandstone cliffs in which is carved the old sacred cave of the Jemez Snake Clan, and there are pink and purple hills, ascending to the lone blue mountain in the northwest, where there are bears and mountain lions as well as deer and where once, in living memory, there were wolves.

The character of the landscape changed from hour to hour in the day, and from day to day, season to season. Nothing there of the earth could be taken for granted; you felt that Creation was going on in your sight. You see things in the high air that you do not see farther down in the lowlands. In the plains you can see farther than you have ever seen, and that is to gain a great freedom. But in the high country all objects bear upon you, and you touch hard upon the earth. The air of the mountains is itself an element in which vision is made acute; eagles bear me out. From my home of Jemez I could see the huge, billowing clouds above the Valle Grande, how, even motionless, they drew close upon me and merged with my life.

At that time the pueblo numbered about a thousand inhabitants. It was then a very close, integrated community, concentrated upon the plaza, with narrow streets and a number of buildings, in each of which several families lived. The population thinned out in proportion as you moved away from the plaza, though there were many *ranchitos,* especially on the north and west, where the fields were numerous. A few families kept houses across the river in order to be near the farthest fields, and in the summer they journeyed there in wagons and set themselves up, but when the harvest was in they returned to the village. It is a principle of their lives that the pueblo people move ever towards the center. Their sacred ceremonies are performed in the plaza, and in the kiva there. On the surrounding edge of the pueblo were numerous corrals, orchards, and little gardens of corn, chili, melons, and squash. In the autumn, and most of all in the late afternoons, the sun set a wonderful glow upon the adobe walls, in the colors of copper and gold, and brilliant red strings of chilies hung from the vigas. There was no electricity at Jemez in 1946, and no water in the village, other than that which was pumped from the ground by means of windmills, three or four in all. The men diverted water from the river for their fields; all about the farmlands was an intricate network of irrigation ditches. And of course much depended upon the rains, and the snowfalls in the mountains. Water is a holy thing in the pueblos; you come to understand there how the heart yearns for it. You learn to watch the level of the river, and when the rain comes, you hold your face and your hands up to it. There were perhaps three pickup trucks in the pueblo then, and no automobiles that I can remember. Everyone went abroad in wagons and on horseback, or else they walked; and frequently the boys and men, even the very young and the very old, ran about on their feet. The pueblo men have always been very good long-distance runners.

By car, unless you happened to come on the old road from San Ysidro, which was by and large a horse-and-wagon path, you entered the pueblo on the east side, on a street (that word is not entirely appropriate—"street," as Americans in cities and suburbs think of that word, does not truly indicate any of the ancient ways of that place, but it will have to do) which curved around the front of the Pueblo Church. The church was a large adobe building with three old Spanish bells in the façade and a burial ground in the yard. The Roman Catholic churches of the pueblos are so old, many of them, that they seem scarcely to impose an alien aspect upon the native culture; rather, they seem themselves almost to have been appropriated by that culture and to express it in its own terms. The church at Jemez has not the rich, rude beauty of the ruin at Acoma, or of even the church at Zia, say; nonetheless there is considerable strength and dignity in it. The extant parish records go back to 1720.

There you came to a fork. If you continued on around the church you were on the way to the San Diego Mission, which lay out on the west side of the village; there was the mission school, which went through the first eight grades, the residence house of the nuns who taught there, the rectory with its adjoining chapel, where lived the Franciscan parish priest and his assistants, and the United States Post Office. If you bore to the left you were on the way to the Jemez Day School, on the southwestern corner of the pueblo, and on the old wagon road to San Ysidro.

The day school was a large stucco building in the pueblo style, not unlike the Pueblo Church in certain respects, especially that part of it which was officially the "school"; it had vigas, a dozen large windows along the south wall, admitting light into the classrooms, and a belfry in front. The two classrooms, situated end to end, were of about the same size; each could accommodate about thirty pupils comfortably. The highest enrollment during my parents' tenure there was sixty-eight. The front classroom was my mother's; she taught the beginners (who comprised a kind of kindergarten class, and most of whom could not speak English when they came), the first, the second, and the third graders. In the other classroom my father, who was the principal, taught the fourth, fifth, and sixth graders. My parents were assisted by a "housekeeper," a Jemez woman whose job it was to clean the classrooms, supervise the playground, and prepare the noon meal for the children. Frequently she assisted as an interpreter as well. On the opposite side of the building were the teachers' quarters, roughly equivalent in size to one of the classrooms. There were a living room, a kitchen, two bedrooms, and a bath. There was also a screened porch in front, where it was comfortable to sit in the good weather, and another, much smaller, in back; the latter we used largely for storage; there was our woodbox, convenient to the living room, in which there was a fireplace, and to the kitchen, in which, when we moved there, there was an old wood-burning range. In the living room there was a door which opened upon my mother's classroom, and beside this door a wall telephone with two bells and a crank. We shared a party line with the San Diego Mission and the Jemez Trading Post; there were no other telephones in the pueblo; we answered to two long rings and one short.

There were two other buildings on the school grounds. In one of these was the garage, a storeroom, the coalbin, and a makeshift clinic to which Government Service doctors and nurses came periodically to treat the ailing people of the village; in the other there lived at various times chickens, ducks, and turkeys—and for some months the meanest rooster I have ever known; perhaps his name was Oliver Blount, or Thaddeus Waring. Once, after he had attacked me viciously, I knocked him unconscious with a stone. It was a lucky throw, through the fence, and the cowardice of it lay heavy on me for days afterwards. Oh, you are a mean one, Blount, but you are not so mean as I.

A white fence encircled the school. We had in back a windmill and a water tank, and beyond the white fence there was a large field where later my father and I built a corral and shelter for Pecos, my strawberry roan quarter horse, my darling, my delight. The grounds were bare at first, except for five elms which shaded the teacherage, but later my mother planted tamaracks and Russian olives along the fence; they flourished. Along the north side of the day school ran the road to the river, which was about a half mile west, and upon that road we saw much of the commerce of the village from our kitchen windows. And just across that road lived our closest neighbors, the Tosa family.

I resumed my seventh-grade studies at the mission school. I loved to walk there in the morning, for on the way there were interesting and beautiful things to see. The old man Francisco Tosa kept a flock of sheep, and as I passed by his corrals I often saw him there, tending them. He always greeted me heartily in Spanish, and there was much good humor in him. There are certain people whom you are simply glad to see at any moment, anywhere, for they hold themselves to their lives very peacefully and know who they are, and Francisco Tosa was one of these. He wore a red kerchief around his head, his long white hair tied with a finely woven band in a queue, and over this a big straw hat. He cut a very handsome figure, I thought, and he was a medicine man. It is the part of a medicine man to be inscrutable, if not austere—or so it has always seemed to me—but Francisco did not live up to such an image; he was jovial and serene, and he personified some old, preeminent ethic of pueblo life. I crossed over a little stream bed, where sometimes there was water, sometimes not; when it was there, animals came to drink, and the women washed corn in their yucca baskets. I passed through a lovely orchard near a house in which I liked to imagine there lived a witch; it strikes me that I never saw anyone there, and yet it was a fine old house and well kept; everything about it was in place. And I bent down through strands of barbed wire and was then in the yard of the mission school.

I was in that position of great advantage again, that of being alone among my classmates at home in the English language. From another and more valid point of view, it was a position of disadvantage. I had no real benefit of instruction at the mission school, and consequently I remember very little of what happened during those hours when I sat at my desk, listening to the nuns. One day Sister Mary Teresa put us the question "Which country is larger, the United States or the Soviet Union?" Child's play. Called upon, I replied confidently that the Soviet Union was certainly the larger country. "No," said Sister Mary Teresa, "the United States is quite a lot bigger than the Soviet Union." And to prove her point she held up two maps, one of each country, which bore no relation to each other in terms of scale; but the two countries were there irrefutably juxtaposed in our sight, and sure enough, the United States appeared to be larger by a third than the Soviet Union. The force of this logic made a great impression on me, and I have not forgotten it. There was a little parable on the nature of faith, I believe; it was as if I had been witness to a miracle.

PEARL HARBOR ECHOES IN SEATTLE

Monica Sone

Monica Sone was born in Seattle, Washington. Sone's studies at the University of Washington were interrupted by Executive Order 9066, which sent her and her family initially to Camp Harmony in Puyallup, Washington and finally to Camp Minidoka in Idaho. She eventually earned a B.A. from Hanover College and a M.A. in clinical psychology from Case Western Reserve University. *Nisei Daughter* (1953) is Sone's only book and for many years was the only first-hand account of the relocation experience by a Japanese American.

ON A PEACEFUL SUNDAY MORNING, DECEMBER 7, 1941, HENRY, SUMI, and I were at choir rehearsal singing ourselves hoarse in preparation for the annual Christmas recital of Handel's "Messiah." Suddenly Chuck Mizuno, a young University of Washington student, burst into the chapel, gasping as if he had sprinted all the way up the stairs.

"Listen, everybody!" he shouted. "Japan just bombed Pearl Harbor . . . in Hawaii! It's war!"

The terrible words hit like a blockbuster, paralyzing us. Then we smiled feebly at each other, hoping this was one of Chuck's practical jokes. Miss Hara, our music director, rapped her baton impatiently on the music stand and chided him, "Now Chuck, fun's fun, but we have work to do. Please take your place. You're already half an hour late."

PEARL HARBOR ECHOES IN SEATTLE

But Chuck strode vehemently back to the door, "I mean it, folks, honest! I just heard the news over my car radio. Reporters are talking a blue streak. Come on down and hear it for yourselves."

With that, Chuck swept out of the room, a swirl of young men following in his wake. Henry was one of them. The rest of us stayed, rooted to our places like a row of marionettes. I felt as if a fist had smashed my pleasant little existence, breaking it into jigsaw puzzle pieces. An old wound opened up again, and I found myself shrinking inwardly from my Japanese blood, the blood of an enemy. I knew instinctively that the fact that I was an American by birthright was not going to help me escape the consequences of this unhappy war.

One girl mumbled over and over again, "It can't be, God, it can't be!" Someone else was saying, "What a spot to be in! Do you think we'll be considered Japanese or Americans?"

A boy replied quietly, "We'll be Japs, same as always. But our parents are enemy aliens now, you know."

A shocked silence followed. Henry came for Sumi and me. "Come on, let's go home," he said.

We ran trembling to our car. Usually Henry was a careful driver, but that morning he bore down savagely on the accelerator. Boiling angry, he shot us up Twelfth Avenue, rammed through the busy Jackson Street intersection, and rocketed up the Beacon Hill bridge. We swung violently around to the left of the Marine Hospital and swooped to the top of the hill. Then Henry slammed on the brakes and we rushed helter-skelter up to the house to get to the radio. Asthma skidded away from under our trampling feet.

Mother was sitting limp in the huge armchair as if she had collapsed there, listening dazedly to the turbulent radio. Her face was frozen still, and the only words she could utter were, *"Komatta neh, komatta neh.* How dreadful, how dreadful."

Henry put his arms around her. She told him she first heard about the attack on Pearl Harbor when one of her friends phoned her and told her to turn on the radio.

We pressed close against the radio, listening stiffly to the staccato outbursts of an excited reporter: "The early morning sky of Honolulu was filled with the furious buzzing of Jap Zero planes for nearly three hours, raining death and destruction on the airfields below. . . . A warship anchored beyond the Harbor was sunk. . . ."

We were switched to the White House. The fierce clack of teletype machines and the babble of voices surging in and out from the background almost drowned out the speaker's terse announcements.

With every fiber of my being I resented this war. I felt as if I were on fire.

"Mama, they should never have done it," I cried. "Why did they do it? Why? Why?"

Mother's face turned paper white. "What do you know about it? Right or wrong, the Japanese have been chafing with resentment for years. It was bound to happen, one time or another. You're young, Ka-chan, you know very little about the ways of nations. It's not as simple as you think, but this is hardly the time to be quarreling about it, is it?"

"No, it's too late, too late!" and I let the tears pour down my face.

Father rushed home from the hotel. He was deceptively calm as he joined us in the living room. Father was a born skeptic, and he believed nothing unless he could see, feel and smell it. He regarded all newspapers and radio news with deep suspicion. He shook his head doubtfully, "It must be propaganda. With the way things are going now between America and Japan, we should expect the most fantastic rumors, and this is one of the wildest I've heard yet." But we noticed that he was firmly glued to the radio. It seemed as if the regular Sunday programs, sounding off relentlessly hour after hour on schedule, were trying to blunt the catastrophe of the morning.

The telephone pealed nervously all day as people searched for comfort from each other. Chris called, and I told her how miserable and confused I felt about the war. Understanding as always, Chris said, "You know how I feel about you and your family, Kaz. Don't, for heaven's sake, feel the war is going to make any difference in our relationship. It's not your fault, nor mine! I wish to God it could have been prevented." Minnie called off her Sunday date with Henry. Her family was upset and they thought she should stay close to home instead of wandering downtown.

Late that night Father got a shortwave broadcast from Japan. Static sputtered, then we caught a faint voice, speaking rapidly in Japanese. Father sat unmoving as a rock, his head cocked. The man was talking about the war between Japan and America. Father bit his lips and Mother whispered to him anxiously, "It's true then, isn't it, Papa? It's true?"

Father was muttering to himself, "So they really did it!" Now having heard the news in their native tongue, the war had become a reality to Father and Mother.

"I suppose from now on, we'll hear about nothing but the humiliating defeats of Japan in the papers here," Mother said, resignedly.

Henry and I glared indignantly at Mother, then Henry shrugged his shoulders and decided to say nothing. Discussion of politics, especially Japan versus America, had become taboo in our family for it sent tempers skyrocketing. Henry and I used to criticize Japan's aggressions in China and Manchuria while Father and Mother condemned Great Britain and America's superior attitude toward Asiatics and their interference with Japan's economic growth. During these arguments, we had eyed each other like strangers, parents against children. They left us with a hollow feeling at the pit of the stomach.

Just then the shrill peel of the telephone cut off the possibility of a family argument. When I answered, a young girl's voice fluttered through breathily, "Hello, this is Taeko Tanabe. Is my mother there?"

"No, she isn't, Taeko."

"Thank you," and Taeko hung up before I could say another word. Her voice sounded strange. Mrs. Tanabe was one of Mother's poet friends. Taeko called three more times, and each time before I could ask her if anything was wrong, she quickly hung up. The next day we learned that Taeko was trying desperately to locate her mother because FBI agents had swept into their home and arrested Mr. Tanabe, a newspaper editor. The FBI had permitted Taeko to try to locate her mother before they took Mr. Tanabe away while they searched the house for contraband and subversive material, but she was not to let anyone else know what was happening.

Next morning the newspapers fairly exploded in our faces with stories about the Japanese raids on the chain of Pacific islands. We were shocked to read Attorney General Biddle's announcement that 736 Japanese had been picked up in the United States and Hawaii. Then Mrs. Tanabe called Mother about her husband's arrest, and she said at least a hundred others had been taken from our community. Messrs. Okayama, Higashi, Sughira, Mori, Okada—we knew them all.

"But why were they arrested, Papa? They weren't spies, were they?"

Father replied almost curtly, "Of course not! They were probably taken for questioning."

The pressure of war moved in on our little community. The Chinese consul announced that all the Chinese would carry identification cards and wear "China" badges to distinguish them from the Japanese. Then I really felt left standing out in the cold. The government ordered the bank funds of all Japanese nationals frozen. Father could no longer handle financial transactions through his bank accounts, but Henry, fortunately, was of legal age so that business could be negotiated in his name.

In the afternoon President Roosevelt's formal declaration of war against Japan was broadcast throughout the nation. In grave, measured words, he described the attack on Pearl Harbor as shameful, infamous. I writhed involuntarily. I could no more have escaped the stab of self-consciousness than I could have changed my Oriental features.

Monday night a complete blackout was ordered against a possible Japanese air raid on the Puget Sound area. Mother assembled black cloths to cover the windows and set up candles in every room. All radio stations were silenced from seven in the evening till morning, but we gathered around the dead radio anyway, out of sheer habit. We whiled away the evening reading instructions in the newspapers on how to put out incendiary bombs and learning about the best hiding places during bombardments. When the city pulled its switches at blackout hour and plunged us into an ominous dark silence, we went to bed shivering and wondering what tomorrow would bring. All of a sudden there was a wild screech of brakes, followed by the resounding crash of metal slamming into metal. We rushed out on the balcony. In the street below we saw dim shapes of cars piled grotesquely on top of each other, their soft blue headlights staring helplessly up into the sky. Angry men's voices floated up to the house. The men were wearing uniforms and their metal buttons gleamed in the blue lights. Apparently two police cars had collided in the blackout.

Clutching at our bathrobes we lingered there. The damp winter night hung heavy and inert like a wet black veil, and at the bottom of Beacon Hill, we could barely make out the undulating length of Rainier Valley, lying quietly in the somber, brooding silence like a hunted python. A few pinpoints of light pricked the darkness here and there like winking bits of diamonds, betraying the uneasy vigil of a tense city.

It made me positively hivey the way the FBI agents continued their raids into Japanese homes and business places and marched the Issei men away into the old red brick immigration building, systematically and efficiently, as if they were stocking a cellarful of choice bottles of wine. At first we noted that the men arrested were those who had been prominent in community affairs, like Mr. Kato, many times president of the Seattle Japanese Chamber of Commerce, and Mr. Ohashi, the principal of our Japanese language school, or individuals whose business was directly connected with firms in Japan; but as time went on, it became less and less apparent why the others were included in these raids.

We wondered when Father's time would come. We expected momentarily to hear strange footsteps on the porch and the sudden demanding ring of the front doorbell. Our ears became attuned like the sensitive antennas of moths, translating every soft swish of passing cars into the arrival of the FBI squad.

Once when our doorbell rang after curfew hour, I completely lost my Oriental stoicism which I had believed would serve me well under the most trying circumstances. No friend of ours paid visits at night anymore, and I was sure that Father's hour had come. As if hypnotized, I walked woodenly to the door. A mass of black figures stood before me, filling the doorway. I let out a magnificent shriek. Then pandemonium broke loose. The solid rank fell apart into a dozen separate figures which stumbled and leaped pell-mell away from the porch. Watching the mad scramble, I thought I had routed the FBI agents with my cry of distress. Father, Mother, Henry, and Sumi rushed out to support my wilting body. When Henry snapped on the porch light, one lone figure crept out from behind the front hedge. It was a newsboy who, standing at a safe distance, called in a quavering voice, "I . . . I came to collect for . . . for the *Times.*"

Shaking with laughter, Henry paid him and gave him an extra large tip for the terrible fright he and his bodyguards had suffered at the hands of the Japanese. As he hurried down the walk, boys of all shapes and sizes crawled out from behind trees and bushes and scurried after him.

We heard all kinds of stories about the FBI, most of them from Mr. Yorita, the grocer, who now took twice as long to make his deliveries. The war seemed to have brought out his personality. At least he talked more, and he glowed, in a sinister way. Before the war Mr. Yorita had been uncommunicative. He used to stagger silently through the back door with a huge sack of rice over his shoulders, dump it on the kitchen floor and silently flow out of the door as if he were bored and disgusted with food and the people who ate it. But now Mr. Yorita swaggered in, sent a gallon jug of soy sauce spinning into a corner, and launched into a comprehensive report of the latest rumors he had picked up on his route, all in chronological order. Mr. Yorita looked like an Oriental Dracula, with his triangular eyes and yellow-fanged teeth. He had a mournfully long sallow face and in his excitement his gold-rimmed glasses constantly slipped to the tip of his long nose. He would describe in detail how some man had been awakened in the dead of night, swiftly handcuffed, and dragged from out of his bed by a squad of brutal, tight-lipped men. Mr. Yorita bared his teeth menacingly in his most dramatic moments, and we shrank from him instinctively. As he backed out of the kitchen door, he would shake his bony finger at us with a warning of dire things to come. When Mother said, "Yorita-san, you must worry about getting a call from the FBI, too," Mr. Yorita laughed modestly, pushing his glasses back up into place. "They wouldn't be interested in anyone as insignificant as myself!" he assured her.

But he was wrong. The following week a new delivery boy appeared at the back door with an airy explanation, "Yep, they got the old man, too, and don't ask me why! The way I see it, it's subversive to sell soy sauce now."

The Matsuis were visited, too. Shortly after Dick had gone to Japan. Mr. Matsui had died and Mrs. Matsui had sold her house. Now she and her daughter and youngest son lived in the back of their little dry goods store on Jackson Street. One day when Mrs. Matsui was busy with the family laundry, three men entered the shop, nearly ripping off the tiny bell hanging over the door. She hurried out, wiping sudsy, reddened hands on her apron. At best Mrs. Matsui's English was rudimentary, and when she became excited, it deteriorated into Japanese. She hovered on her toes, delighted to see new customers in her humble shop. "Yes, yes, something you want?"

"Where's Mr. Matsui?" a steely-eyed man snapped at her.

Startled, Mrs. Matsui jerked her thumb toward the rear of the store and said, "He not home."

"What? Oh, in there, eh? Come on!" The men tore the faded print curtain aside and rushed into the back room. "Don't see him. Must be hiding."

They jerked open bedroom doors, leaped into the tiny bathroom, flung windows open and peered down into the alley. Tiny birdlike Mrs. Matsui rushed around after them. "No, no! Whatsamalla, whatsamalla!"

"Where's your husband! Where is he?" one man demanded angrily, flinging clothes out of the closet.

"Why you mix 'em all up? He not home, not home." She clawed at the back of the burly men like an angry little sparrow, trying to stop the holocaust in her little home. One man brought his face down close to hers, shouting slowly and clearly, "WHERE IS YOUR HUSBAND? YOU SAID HE WAS IN HERE A MINUTE AGO!"

"Yes, yes, not here. *Mah, wakara nai hito da neh.* Such stupid men."

Mrs. Matsui dived under a table, dragged out a huge album, and pointed at a large photograph. She jabbed her gnarled finger up toward the ceiling saying, "Heben! Heben!"

The men gathered around and looked at a picture of Mr. Matsui's funeral. Mrs. Matsui and her two children were standing by a coffin, their eyes cast down, surrounded by all their friends, all of whom were looking down. The three men's lips formed an "Oh." One of them said, "We're sorry to have disturbed you. Thank you, Mrs. Matsui, and good-bye." They departed quickly and quietly.

Having passed through this baptism, Mrs. Matsui became an expert on the FBI, and she stood by us, rallying and coaching us on how to deal with them. She said to Mother, "You must destroy everything and anything Japanese which may incriminate your husband. It doesn't matter what it is, if it's printed or made in Japan, destroy it because the FBI always carries off those items for evidence."

In fact all the women whose husbands had been spirited away said the same thing. Gradually we became uncomfortable with our Japanese books, magazines, wall scrolls, and knickknacks. When Father's hotel friends, Messrs. Sakaguchi, Horiuchi, Nishibue, and a few others vanished, and their wives called Mother weeping and warning her again about having too many Japanese objects around the house, we finally decided to get rid of some of ours. We knew it was impossible to destroy everything. The FBI would certainly think it strange if they found us sitting in a bare house, totally purged of things Japanese. But it was as if we could no longer stand the tension of waiting, and we just had to do something against the black day. We worked all night, feverishly combing through bookshelves, closets, drawers, and furtively creeping down to the basement furnace for the burning. I gathered together my well-worn Japanese language schoolbooks which I had been saving over a period of ten years with the thought that they might come in handy when I wanted to teach Japanese to my own children. I threw them into the fire and watched them flame and shrivel into

PEARL HARBOR ECHOES IN SEATTLE

black ashes. But when I came face to face with my Japanese doll which Grandmother Nagashima had sent me from Japan, I rebelled. It was a gorgeously costumed Miyazukai figure, typical of the lady in waiting who lived in the royal palace during the feudal era. The doll was gowned in an elegant purple silk kimono with the long, sweeping hemline of its period and sashed with rich-embroidered gold and silver brocade. With its black, shining coiffed head bent a little to one side, its delicate pink-tipped ivory hand holding a red lacquer message box, the doll had an appealing, almost human charm. I decided to ask Chris if she would keep it for me. Chris loved and appreciated beauty in every form and shape, and I knew that in her hands, the doll would be safe and enjoyed.

Henry pulled down from his bedroom wall the toy samurai sword he had brought from Japan and tossed it into the flames. Sumi's contributions to the furnace were books of fairy tales and magazines sent to her by her young cousins in Japan. We sorted out Japanese classic and popular music from a stack of records, shattered them over our knees and fed the pieces to the furnace. Father piked up his translated Japanese volumes of philosophy and religion and carted them reluctantly to the basement. Mother had the most to eliminate, with her scrapbooks of poems cut out from newspapers and magazines, and her private collection of old Japanese classic literature.

It was past midnight when we finally climbed upstairs to bed. Wearily we closed our eyes, filled with an indescribable sense of guilt for having destroyed the things we loved. This night of ravage was to haunt us for years. As I lay struggling to fall asleep, I realized that we hadn't freed ourselves at all from fear. We still lay stiff in our beds, waiting.

Mrs. Matsui kept assuring us that the FBI would get around to us yet. It was just a matter of time and the least Mother could do for Father was to pack a suitcase for him. She said that the men captured who hadn't been prepared had grown long beards, lived and slept in the same clothes for days before they were permitted visits from their families. So Mother dutifully packed a suitcase for Father with toilet articles, warm flannel pajamas, and extra clothes, and placed it in the front hall by the door. It was a personal affront, the way it stood there so frank and unabashedly. Henry and I said that it was practically a confession that Papa was a spy, "So please help yourself to him, Mr. FBI, and God speed you."

Mother was equally loud and firm, "No, don't anyone move it! No one thought that Mr. Kato or the others would be taken, but they're gone now. Why should we think Papa's going to be an exception."

Henry threw his hands up in the air and muttered about the odd ways of the Japanese.

Every day Mrs. Matsui called Mother to check Father in; then we caught the habit and started calling him at the hotel every hour on the hour until he finally exploded, "Stop this nonsense! I don't know which is more nerve-wracking, being watched by the FBI or by my family!"

When Father returned home from work, a solicitous family eased him into his favorite armchair, arranged pillows behind his back, and brought the evening paper and slippers to him. Mother cooked Father's favorite dishes frenziedly, night after night. It all made Father very uneasy.

We had a family conference to discuss the possibility of Father and Mother's internment. Henry was in graduate school and I was beginning my second year at the university. We agreed to drop out should they be taken and we would manage the hotel during our parents' absence. Every weekend Henry and I accompanied Father to the hotel and learned how to keep the hotel books, how to open the office safe, and what kind of linen, paper towels, and soap to order.

Then a new menace appeared on the scene. Cries began to sound up and down the coast that everyone of Japanese ancestry should be taken into custody. For years the professional guardians of the Golden West had wanted to rid their land of the Yellow Peril, and the war provided an opportunity for them to push their program through. As the chain of Pacific islands fell to the Japanese, patriots shrieked for protection from us. A Californian sounded the alarm: "The Japanese are dangerous and they must leave. Remember the destruction and the sabotage perpetrated at Pearl Harbor. Notice how they have infiltrated into the harbor towns and taken our best land."

He and his kind refused to be comforted by Edgar Hoover's special report to the War Department stating that there had not been a single case of sabotage committed by a Japanese living in Hawaii or on the mainland during the Pearl Harbor attack or after. I began to feel acutely uncomfortable for living on Beacon Hill. The Marine Hospital rose tall and handsome on our hill, and if I stood on the west shoulder of the Hill, I could not help but get an easily photographed view of the Puget Sound Harbor with its ships snuggled against the docks. And Boeing airfield, a few miles south of us, which had never bothered me before, suddenly seemed to have moved right up into my back yard, daring me to take just one spying glance at it.

In February, Executive Order No. 9066 came out, authorizing the War Department to remove the Japanese from such military areas as it saw fit, aliens and citizens alike. Even if a person had a fraction of Japanese blood in him, he must leave on demand.

A pall of gloom settled upon our home. We couldn't believe that the government meant that the Japanese-Americans must go, too. We had heard the clamoring of superpatriots who insisted loudly, "Throw the whole kaboodle out. A Jap's a Jap, no matter how you slice him. You can't make an American out of little Jap

Junior just by handing him an American birth certificate." But we had dismissed these remarks as just hot blasts of air from an overheated patriot. We were quite sure that our rights as American citizens would not be violated, and we would not be marched out of our homes on the same basis as enemy aliens.

In anger, Henry and I read and reread the Executive Order. Henry crumpled the newspaper in his hand and threw it against the wall. "Doesn't my citizenship mean a single blessed thing to anyone? Why doesn't somebody make up my mind for me. First they want me in the army. Now they're going to slap an alien 4-C on me because of my ancestry. What the hell!"

Once more I felt like a despised, pathetic two-headed freak, a Japanese and an American, neither of which seemed to be doing me any good. The Nisei leaders in the community rose above their personal feelings and stated that they would cooperate and comply with the decision of the government as their sacrifice in keeping with the country's war effort, thus proving themselves loyal American citizens. I was too jealous of my recently acquired voting privilege to be gracious about giving in, and I felt most uncooperative. I noticed wryly that the feelings about the Japanese on the Hawaiian Islands were quite different from those on the West Coast. In Hawaii, a strategic military outpost, the Japanese were regarded as essential to the economy of the island and powerful economic forces fought against their removal. General Delos Emmons, in command of Hawaii at the time, lent his authoritative voice to calm the fears of the people on the island and to prevent chaos and upheaval. General Emmons established martial law, but he did not consider evacuation essential for the security of the island.

On the West Coast, General J. L. DeWitt of the Western Defense Command did not think martial law necessary, but he favored mass evacuation of the Japanese and Nisei. We suspected that pressures from economic and political interests who would profit from such a wholesale evacuation influenced this decision.

Events moved rapidly. General DeWitt marked off western Washington, Oregon, and all of California, and the southern half of Arizona as Military Area No. 1, hallowed ground from which we must remove ourselves as rapidly as possible. Unfortunately we could not simply vanish into thin air, and we had no place to go. We had no relatives in the east we could move in on. All our relatives were sitting with us in the forbidden area, themselves wondering where to go. The neighboring states in the line of exit for the Japanese protested violently at the prospect of any mass invasion. They said, very sensibly, that if the coast didn't want the Japanese hanging around, they didn't either.

A few hardy families in the community liquidated their property, tied suitcases all around their cars, and sallied eastward. They were greeted by signs in front of store windows, "Open season for Japs!" and "We kill rats and Japs here." On state lines, highway troopers swarmed around the objectionable migrants and turned them back under governor's orders.

General DeWitt must have finally realized that if he insisted on voluntary mass evacuation, hundreds and thousands of us would have wandered back and forth, clogging the highways and pitching tents along the roadside, eating and sleeping in colossal disorder. He suddenly called a halt to voluntary movement, although most of the Japanese were not budging an inch. He issued a new order, stating that no Japanese could leave the city, under penalty of arrest. The command had hatched another plan, a better one. The army would move us out as only the army could do it, and march us in neat, orderly fashion into assembly centers. We would stay in these centers only until permanent camps were set up inland to isolate us.

The orders were simple:

Dispose of your homes and property. Wind up your business. Register the family. One seabag of bedding, two suitcases of clothing allowed per person. People in District #1 must report at 8th and Lane Street, 8 P.M. on April 28.

I wanted no part of this new order. I had read in the paper that the Japanese from the state of Washington would be taken to a camp in Puyallup, on the state fairgrounds. The article apologetically assured the public that the camp would be temporary and that the Japanese would be removed from the fairgrounds and parking lots in time for the opening of the annual State Fair. It neglected to say where we might be at the time when those fine breeds of Holstein cattle and Yorkshire hogs would be proudly wearing their blue satin ribbons.

We were advised to pack warm, durable clothes. In my mind, I saw our permanent camp sprawled out somewhere deep in a snow-bound forest, an American Siberia. I saw myself plunging chest deep in the snow, hunting for small game to keep us alive. I decided that one of my suitcases was going to hold nothing but vitamins from A to Z. I thought of sewing fur-lined hoods and parkas for the family. I was certain this was going to be a case of sheer animal survival.

One evening Father told us that he would lose the management of the hotel unless he could find someone to operate it for the duration, someone intelligent and efficient enough to impress Bentley Agent and Company. Father said, "Sam, Joe, Peter, they all promised to stay on their jobs, but none of them can read or write well enough to manage the business. I've got to find a responsible party with experience in hotel management, but where?"

Sumi asked, "What happens if we can't find anyone?"

"I lose my business and my livelihood. I'll be saying good-bye to a lifetime of labor and all the hopes and plans I had for the family."

We sagged. Father looked at us thoughtfully, "I've never talked much about the hotel business to you children, mainly because so much of it has been an uphill climb of work and waiting for better times. Only recently I was able to clear up the loans I took out years ago to expand the business. I was sure that in the next five or ten years I would be getting returns on my long-range investments, and I would have been able to do a lot of things eventually. . . . Send you through medical school," Father nodded to Henry, "and let Kazu and Sumi study anything they liked." Father laughed a bit self-consciously as he looked at Mother, "And when all the children had gone off on their own, I had planned to take Mama on her first real vacation, to Europe as well as Japan."

We listened to Father wide-eyed and wistful. It had been a wonderful, wonderful dream.

Mother suddenly hit upon a brilliant idea. She said maybe the Olsens, our old friends who had once managed the Camden Apartments might be willing to run a hotel. The Olsens had sold the apartment and moved to Aberdeen. Mother thought that perhaps Marta's oldest brother, the bachelor of the family, might be available. If he refused, perhaps Marta and her husband might consider the offer. We rushed excitedly to the telephone to make a long-distance call to the Olsens. After four wrong Olsens, we finally reached Marta.

"Marta? Is this Marta?"

"Yes, this is Marta."

I nearly dove into the mouthpiece, I was so glad to hear her voice. Marta remembered us well and we exchanged news about our families. Marta and her husband had bought a small chicken farm and were doing well. Marta said, "I come from the farm ven I vas young and I like it fine. I feel more like home here. How's everybody over there?"

I told her that we and all the rest of the Japanese were leaving Seattle soon under government order on account of the war. Marta gasped, "Everybody? You mean the Saitos, the Fujinos, Watanabes, and all the rest who were living at the Camden Apartments, too?"

"Yes, they and everyone else on the West Coast."

Bewildered, Marta asked where we were going, what we were going to do, would we ever return to Seattle, and what about Father's hotel. I told her about our business situation and that Father needed a hotel manager for the duration. Would she or any of her brothers be willing to accept such a job? There was a silence at the other end of the line and I said hastily, "This is a very sudden call, Marta. I'm sorry I had to surprise you like this, but we felt this was an emergency and . . ."

Marta was full of regrets. "Oh, I vish we could do something to help you folks, but my husband and I can't leave the farm at all. We don't have anyone here to help. We do all the work ourselves. Magnus went to Alaska last year. He has a goot job up there, some kind of war work. My other two brothers have business in town and they have children so they can't help you much."

My heart sank like a broken elevator. When I said, "Oh . . ." I felt the family sitting behind me sink into a gloomy silence. Our last hope was gone. We finally said good-bye, Marta distressed at not being able to help, and I apologizing for trying to hoist our problem on them.

The next weekend Marta and Karl paid us a surprise visit. We had not seen them for nearly two years. Marta explained shyly, "It was such a nice day and we don't go novair for a long time, so I tole Karl, 'Let's take a bus into Seattle and visit the Itois.' "

We spent a delightful Sunday afternoon talking about old times. Mother served our guests her best green tea and, as we relaxed, the irritating presence of war vanished. When it was time for them to return home, Marta's sparkling blue eyes suddenly filled, "Karl and I, we feel so bad about the whole ting, the war and everything, we joost had to come out to see you, and say 'good-bye.' God bless you. Maybe we vill see you again back home here. Anyvay, we pray for it."

Marta and Karl's warmth and sincerity restored a sense of peace into our home, an atmosphere which had disappeared ever since Pearl Harbor. They served to remind us that in spite of the bitterness war had brought into our lives, we were still bound to our hometown. Bit by bit, I remembered our happy past, the fun we had growing up along the colorful brash waterfront, swimming through the white-laced waves of Puget Sound, and lolling luxuriously on the tender green carpet of grass around Lake Washington from where we could see the slick, blue-frosted shoulders of Mount Rainier. There was too much beauty surrounding us. Above all, we must keep friends like Marta and Karl, Christine, Sam, Peter and Joe, all sterling products of many years of associations. We could never turn our faces away and remain aloof forever from Seattle.

THE MESSENGER OF THE LOST
BATTALION

Gregory Orfalea

Gregory Orfalea was born in Los Angeles, California. After earning degrees from Georgetown University and the University of Alaska, he taught at several schools, including Miramonte Elementary in south central Los Angeles. He is the author of *Before the Flames: A Quest for the History of Arab Americans* (1988) and a collection of poetry, *The Capital of Solitude* (1988).

"The Messenger of the Lost Battalion" is part of a work-in-progress about the 551st Parachute Infantry Battalion in the Second World War.

Was it for this the clay grew tall?
—WILFRED OWEN

I

IN THE DARK PERIOD MY FATHER WAS OUT OF WORK AFTER HE HAD closed his twenty-five-year-old garment manufacturing business, he gave in to the suggestion of a friend that he take his frustration to a shooting range. He was not a lover of guns and, unlike many in the San Fernando Valley who assure intruders of an "armed response," did not own a firearm. I wouldn't say he was without fear; but he was without that kind of fear.

Nevertheless, from boredom or loneliness, he accompanied his friend—

whose dress firm was still puttering along—to shoot. It was a fateful decision. It's possible that Dad hadn't shot a gun since the Second World War and, aiming at the target with a pistol, the several explosions of an afternoon bent his eardrum. From that day forward he complained of a ringing in his ears—tinnitus, it's called. No doctor or friend could help.

As he struggled to get his work bearings, I would on occasion see him put his hand up to his ear. His own voice, and the voices of others, began to echo. I thought of him in those hard days as some kind of Beethoven trying to make music as the bustle of the world slowly ebbed out of him. Seven years after the factory closing he lay dead on the floor of his new photocopy store, a smile on his face. The ringing had stopped, the symphony begun.

In the many nights I have stayed awake thinking about him, I have wondered whether he heard that bullet coming for forty years without knowing it, and that the ringing from the shooting range was only the last warning. I mean forty years after a bad winter in Belgium in which he, like tens of thousands of men, had dropped.

My father repeated only two things about his life as a paratrooper in World War II: "I ate my K-rations on a silver platter at the Hotel Negresco in Nice," and "All my friends were killed around me." That last referred to the Battle of the Bulge. Though in retrospect I see him as the freest man I ever knew, for him the war was too painful an event to dwell on. And at sixty he was dead, the secrets of a most jarring event in his life, it would seem, buried with him.

Full of questions I had barely begun to formulate about my father, in August 1989 I was given a luminous chance to recover something of him. Members of his old battalion—a courageous and ill-fated unit—were returning to France and Belgium; my brother Mark and I didn't resist their invitation. Would we find someone who knew Aref Orfalea? What really had been his war experience and how had it shaped the unusual man he was? His driven life and tragic death? Would something in the men themselves recall him? At the last minute his seventy-nine-year-old eldest sister Jeannette, who at age five had sung "Over There!" for a World War I war bond drive, joined us, too.

Soon we were hustling down the Promenade d'Anglais in Nice, halted momentarily by a visionary sight of a man in parachute tugged out to sea by speedboat, para-sailing. The carmine dome of the whitewashed grand old Negresco loomed. We ducked in over the plush red carpet and under a giant chandelier. Our mission was belied by our attire—bathing suits.

The floor manager's mouth pursed cynically at our story of traveling with American veterans who had run the Nazis out of Nice long ago, "Oh yes, we were captured by Italy, then Germany, and we were lib-er-a-ted by you Americans." It was like the salad Niçoise—sour and cold.

But when I wondered aloud if the Negresco still served K-rations warm on silver plates, and mentioned my dead father had sure liked them that way, the man's face visibly changed.

"Go into the bar, please, and order whatever drink you would like—on the house."

Jean-Paul Marro later joined us, shaking his head at our gin-and-tonics. "What, no champagne?" He motioned for a mint drink himself and told us of his war experience in Algeria. His wife and he had toured the United States recently for their twentieth anniversary; Marro had found himself most moved by Arlington National Cemetery. "I realized there how many lives had been given by America for us," he bowed his head.

Seeing us off at the front of the Negresco, Marro took a green package from behind his back: "This is for your mother. Tell her France appreciates what her husband did for our freedom." It was a bottle of French perfume.

That was a moment of beauty and linkage across time, continents, and generations I will never forget, brought by joining our search with that of the few survivors of one of the most unusual units in U.S. military history—the 551st Parachute Infantry Battalion.

Why, exactly, was the 551st unique? One of only two independent U.S. parachute battalions which fought in the war, it evolved into a highly individualistic, cantankerous band of outsiders, some of whom comprised the original Test Platoon which first jumped out of planes at Fort Benning, Georgia, in 1940. On August 15, 1944 the 551st executed a near perfect jump into the foothills behind Nice as part of Operation Dragoon. It was the first daylight combat drop in U.S. history. Two months after D-Day in Normandy, General Eisenhower had overruled Churchill, who wanted an invasion of the Balkans, by opening up a second front in southern France.

The 551st had other distinctions. It was the first Allied unit to capture a Nazi general (in Draguignan), the first to reach Cannes and Nice. For a job that normally would have required a regiment (three times its size), the 551st patroled a forty-mile stretch of the France-Italy border in harsh winter conditions under Nazi shelling in the Maritime Alps. Finally, on December 27, 1944, Gen. James Gavin of the 82nd Airborne gave the 551st the "signal honor," as he called it, of spearheading the Allied counterattack against the terrifying German "Bulge" in Belgium. Its heroic push came at great cost—on January 7 only 110 of its 793 men walked out of the decisive battle at Rochelinval. Other than the wipeout at Anzio, Italy, of the 509th—the other independent parachute battalion—the 551st had sustained the worst casualties of any U.S. battalion on the European front.

Strangely, shortly after Rochelinval, the 551st was disbanded, its records destroyed, its valor undecorated, and its existence forgotten—a fate more akin to Vietnam, it would seem, than the so-called good war.

It didn't take long to realize the reunion in Europe carried a great deal of emotional weight for all. There was familial weight, as well. With the twenty returning veterans were twelve spouses, thirteen children, and seven grandchildren. Phil Hand of Georgia, who had first begun to piece the few survivors of the 551st together in the late seventies, brought a son whose mind, he said, had been destroyed by glue-sniffing in the sixties. "He thinks he's a paratrooper," "Bubbles" Hand, a pink-faced man with sad, Irish setter eyes, said to me one afternoon on a veranda in Nice. Ralph Burns of Lake View Terrace, California— no youngster at sixty-nine with a Parkinson's shake—did not leave behind his crippled wife Ruth, but wheeled her everywhere we went, up and down war memorial steps, over the lawns of the graves at Henri Chapelle. A wealthy California developer with a taste for alcohol had brought his two feisty daughters—or they had brought him. (He took sick in Nice and would be confined much of the trip to his hotel room.) Jack Leaf was no deadbeat, though. Early on in the trip I asked if he had married a French girl. "Everytime I met one," he dropped.

Even Aunt Jeannette, to whom Dad had sent most of his war correspondence, would not let a black-and-blue knee bashed the week of our departure stop her. The flame of war is terrible and magnetic, especially for those whose youth was brought to a climax in it. For our journey Aunt Jeannette became the older sister many of the men had written to during the war.

I never asked my mother to accompany us. I knew what her answer would be—silence. Dad had promised her such a trip someday, too, to Europe. But the vagaries of raising three children, the crazy fashion industry, and his subsequent financial decline forestalled it. When she finally went to Europe it was with her brother and his wife on their invitation. Dad minded the store. It was given to me to reach her that dim August night; she was in London. I instructed my uncle not to tell her husband had been shot, nor by whom. I had to get her home, after all, so I concocted a lie. "Car accident, bad shape" was all I said.

For her I am sure as she flew home the whole continent of Europe sank to a bottomless Sargasso Sea.

II

In addition to the about-face at the Negresco, three moments stood out in our twelve-day journey: the visit to the Dragoon drop-zone at La Motte, a troubled vet's hike to a machine-gun nest site at La Turbie, and Rochelinval itself, the site of the destruction of the 551st.

The men seemed in a trance as they moved out—now in their sixties and seventies—across the vineyards of the Valbourges estate at La Motte, trying to remember just which bush or plot of earth took their falling bodies forty-five

THE MESSENGER OF THE LOST BATTALION

years ago. Their maroon berets, navy blue blazers, white shirts and hair flickered among the grape vines, raspberries, apple and pear trees.

"There it is!" Will Marks of Pennsylvania pointed to a lone poplar in the distance fronting a pond. "All my life I dreamt of falling into a tree by itself. You guys have been telling me we fell in the woods. And there it is—my tree!"

Harry Renick, a retired machinist from Detroit who now makes, of all things, wishing wells, commented drily, "I made a three-point landing here: feet, butt, and helmet."

Others were seriously injured, impaled on stakes in the vineyard.

Approaching Valbourges to dedicate a plaque at the Stevens family chapel, Otto Schultz of West Virginia spied the tiled roof of a barn and remembered banging down on the tiles, riding his still-inflated chute to the ground. One of the Stevens family joked, "The broken tiles—they are still there. You may fix them!"

In the courtyard of the old, worn chateau like an apparition in a wheelchair sat ninety-one-year-old Mrs. Stevens, who had bound up the first wounds of the 551st. The men spoke to her in low, hoarse English; she followed their eyes, hugged them. As I approached someone said, "But you are too young to be one of the paratroopers, no?" I looked at Mrs. Stevens—she resembled my father's irascible Lebanese immigrant mother who had peddled on the streets of New York at the turn of the century. "I am here for my father, Madame," I said in basic French, tipping my beret. "He is dead now, but I give you his thanks." She clasped my hand in two of hers.

I wore that maroon beret the whole trip, some admission for an old Vietnam War protester. Col. (Ret.) Doug Dillard, then president of the 551st Association, had given the beret to me earlier in the day for a wreath-laying ceremony at the U.S. Rhone cemetery at Draguignan. It was cocked correctly for me by one of the *veilles suspentes* ("old attics," what the surviving French resistance paratroopers call themselves) who'd come all the way from Paris for the ceremony. When I heard the "Star Spangled Banner," the "Marseillaise," and "Taps," my hand instinctively moved from heart to forehead to join the men.

On our bus that night back to Nice I asked Harry Renick what the 551st motto—GOYA—meant. "Get Off Your Ass," Harry said mildly. That smacked of Dad's favorite "Go get 'em!" cried out whenever he was happy, challenged, or off on his beloved motorcycle into the Mojave Desert. My brother's Freebird restaurant in Santa Barbara, in fact, commemorates both the motto and the motorcycle, which hangs from the ceiling above the diners. Listening to this, Otto ventured, "You know, we requisitioned a motorcycle from the Germans at Cannes. One guy was fond as hell of that thing. It could have been your father." Indeed, he and Otto shared the same company (Headquarters), and Dad had been a courier for the battalion.

Slowly the gray canvas of my father's life in the war gained an oval of color here, there, and the anger and gaiety we knew as he was raising us began to dovetail with the verve in darkness that got him through the war, or indeed, was caused by it. My father was a life-messenger. He always seemed to want to urge life along; left to its own means, life could atrophy or destroy or worst of all reveal itself meaningless. GOYA! "Go get 'em!" "Rise and shine!" "Up and at 'em!" "We're off and running!" "Zing 'em!" For Dad, reveille was a constant requirement in civilian life—at all hours, I might add.

How many childhood car trips to the Sierras began with his lusty version of "Blood on the Risers" (sung to the tune of "The Battle Hymn of the Republic" with all the irony toward Paul Fussell's "chickenshit" intact):

> "Is everybody happy?" cried the sergeant looking up,
> Our Hero feebly answered, "Yes," and then they stood him up,
> He leaped right out into the blast, his static line unhooked,
> AND HE AIN'T GONNA JUMP NO MORE!
> GORY, GORY, WHAT A HELLUVA WAY TO DIE!

I had a last curiosity about the La Motte drop. Dad once vaguely mentioned his most fearful moment in the service being a night jump. But the 551st had dropped in southern France on a late summer afternoon. Fear of the night was replaced by the fear of German guns which could sight them. When was the night jump? The men figured it wasn't in Europe but in training at Camp Mackall, North Carolina, where they participated in dangerous, innovative airborne tests, such as the first live parachute jumps from gliders. There on the foggy night of February 16, 1944, eight GIs were misdropped in lakes; they parachuted with eighty pounds of equipment straight to the bottom and drowned. The disaster jolted the bereaved relatives of drop victim Benjamin Preziotti of Brooklyn to contact columnist Drew Pearson. An angry piece by Pearson prompted the Army to adopt the British "quick release" harness.

The only quick release the horrific event engendered in the men was of jets of anxiety. Restless by nature (their first mission to drop on a Vichy-leaning Martinique was aborted), the 551st rebelled. At one point, two hundred of their men were in the guardhouse. I remember Dad once telling me, only half-jokingly, that he spent more time jumping in between two warring servicemen than in combat against the Nazis. When one is pumped up for war and the climax is withdrawn, or worse, one's own men are wasted in training, something in the muscles either goes limp or very taut. To blur training and combat, as Paul Fussell has noted in *Wartime*, is "so wrong as to be unmentionable."

Only the return of their charismatic, youthful commander, Col. Wood Joerg, calmed them somewhat. After a hearing, an older Col. Rupert Graves, who had overseen the tragic Mackall night jump, was transferred, but not before shouting

THE MESSENGER OF THE LOST BATTALION

at the 551st from his balcony, "You're not going to ruin my career! You're not soldiers! You're all rabble!"

In one of the ironies of war Colonel Graves ended up alongside the 551st at the Battle of the Bulge as commander of the 517th Parachute Infantry Regiment. And it was the 551st which got the nod to enter the meat grinder. Colonel Dillard points out that the 551st was ordered to attack Rochelinval by the 504th Parachute Regiment, not the 517th, and that the survivors of the 517th have been avid to see the 551st receive a late justice. Still, not a few of the men of the 551st wonder if they were the victims of a clash of personalities at the top, if not outright vengefulness, that traced itself to their training days.

III

Maybe the rebellion was inbred.

What, in fact, makes a man want to jump out of a plane? And not just that—but be one of the first to do it in battle? It's a bit like running away to the circus, but worse—no one shoots at the acrobat on the high wire.

I can't imagine doing it myself. I am a born acrophobe. My wife, who thinks nothing of waterskiing in the ninth month of pregnancy, was ordered to grip my hand when, on our honeymoon, we ascended to the apex of the Eiffel Tower. I distracted myself by focusing on the stripes of her sweater. There is something about *terra firma* that is very dear to me, and I am being literal.

I queried the men about being "airborne." Otto Schultz, retired from Union Carbide (he had worked on the Bhopal project and shook his head about it) thought back to childhood, "I'd run along a wall to leap into sand as a kid—always the farthest one back." Charles Fairlamb, the oldest of our group at seventy-four and retired from Boeing in Seattle, joined the 551st in Panama where he was working with the phone company repairing lines. "I figured I liked to keep climbing poles!" he grinned. There seemed in the men an excess of energy, a critical mass of sorts, that had made them a chancy bunch. There was an almost cherished restlessness about them. "Most people who became paratroopers were dissatisfied where they were," Phil Hand put it bluntly.

Parachuting attracted the romantic, no doubt. Lt. Col. (Ret.) Dan Morgan, the unit's historian, joined the 551st after being disappointed to discover that there was no horse cavalry mounted to fight the Japanese: "They had replaced horses with halftracks." Perhaps more than most, they wanted to be unique. "If you could see it lightning and hear it thunder you could get into the Army," said Charles Austin of Texas. "Not everyone could be a paratrooper." It wasn't so much a question of being fearless. "After jumping thirteen times, I had never landed in a plane in my life, so the first time I landed it was like a screw propeller going into the ground—I was scared as hell," admitted a grizzled, trim

VISIONS OF AMERICA

Max Bryan from Yorktown, Virginia. "But you say to yourself—I was a man."

As for Dad, I can only guess the motive. He was the last of six children, after four sisters and a brother already stationed in Burma. He certainly had had plenty of babying and something to prove. As for heights it is known that he once fell out of a tree and broke his leg. The restlessness is harder to pinpoint, though I am sure it was there at an early age. It may have been that, unlike his siblings who had grown up in wealth, by the time Aref was coming of age in Cleveland, Ohio, his millionaire linen merchant father had lost it all in the Depression. He watched his father move from being a gent with a gold fob at the cash register to operating a lathe. There was plenty of rancor between my grandmother and grandfather at that time. Grandmother took up work in a cafeteria. In fact, in the mid-thirties the family had split apart—some going to Los Angeles and some holding the fort in Cleveland. A life of grandeur and wealth slipping into penury— what else to do but jump? A good war is a good place to jump.

Like all rebels, the men of the 551st seemed to be acutely skeptical of authority—not the best attitude for those involved in that hierarchical penulti- mate, the U.S. Army. (The murderous blunder at Camp Mackall only reinforced this.) Their very "551" was out of whack with the normal paratroop battalion sequence numbered 501 to 517 in order to dupe the Germans into thinking there were more U.S. paratroopers than actually existed. They savored their indepen- dent status, and relished it when their beloved commanding officer, Col. Wood Joerg, told them, "Each of you is worth five other men."

If one person appears to have epitomized the spirit of the 551st, it was Joerg himself. Ebullient, charming, a unreconstructed rebel "Jaw-Jaw" boy at West Point, he was not a great student. The 1937 Point yearbook lists him as 230th out of 298 in class ranking. But it also credits him as a "Rabble Rouser" who pumped up the stands during ball games and had "a heart a yard long and a smile a mile wide." By the time of the offensive at the Bulge, that smile and that heart would have to change places.

He liked to root, work his deep southern accent on the girls in a way that was both shy and confident, and dance. He was not, according to one classmate, "a hive (bookworm)" but a "hopoid." Joerg was hop manager for the Point. He was not a "make" (cadet officer) but a "clean sleeve" (no chevrons to denote rank or authority). He was also an "area bird"—someone who spent many hours walking punishment tours around the Point with a rifle because of his horsing around.

A classmate who outlived him enough to become a brigadier general said Joerg was "full of the milk of human kindness." He had a weakness for plebes who took a terrible beating as he had from upperclassmen, a sympathy he later felt—to reprimand—for men under his command.

The men of the 551st loved him, it seems, and he returned it; some remember him on the phone in a frenzy to get the suicidal mission at Rochelinval canceled. It appears the man from Jaw-Jaw saw death at an early age, and it made him dance. Joerg's first roommate at West Point died as a cadet, sending Joerg into great inner turmoil. The first Pointer killed in World War II was from Joerg's cadet company.

It fit the dark irony surrounding the 551st like a hard chute that one Maj. Gen. C. S. O'Malley would remember Wood Joerg's "heroic death at Bastogne," for when the hot shrapnel pierced his helmet and killed him, Joerg and the men who fell around him in the snow were twenty-five miles north of McAuliffe, his famous "Nuts!" and rescue by Patton, with no rescue at a snow-clamped, anonymous knoll called Rochelinval.

IV

My father was not a physical fitness nut. His generation as a whole found nothing particularly worshipful in the body—the generation that fought World War II worked like dogs to land on a circular drive or in a kidney-shaped pool, daily ate bacon and eggs, drank coffee before it was decaffeinated, smoked Lucky Strikes or Marlboros before the Surgeon General got tough, had affairs instead of relationships, and took up, if anything, bowling, or the somnolent game of golf. Dad vehemently was *not* a golfer.

As a teenager in Cleveland he played football and ice hockey. A split end for a rather accomplished neighborhood football team, the Cleveland Olympics, just before he entered the war he hit a peak when the Olympics copped a citywide championship during a warm-up game for the pro Cleveland Rams at Shaw Stadium.

His quarterback friend, Bud Lank, and he were the only two fellows who played on both first- and second-string teams. They were never out of the Olympics lineup. Muscular in a lean way, about five foot ten, Aref was pound-for-pound the best tackler and blocker on the team, Lank thought. He recalled fondly, "Your father was a contact kind of guy."

That he was. He would hold your shoulder to make a point, touch a finger to knee to underscore it, bear hug with a grip that was not afraid to last. Lank said Aref was always slapping the players on the back in the huddle, spiriting them to a faster stop-and-go, a blunter block. He was, in short, a Wood Joerg type.

Los Angeles was not the best place for an excellent ice skater to bring up a family. As much as he loved Mother it was clearly a disappointment to him that she never learned to skate (and abhorred his motorcycle). I became his partner on ice as a boy, as did my sister, Leslie. But most of the time he skated alone with the slight crouch of a speed-skater, crossing over smoothly on turns, weaving gently, swiftly, in and out of the fumbling Angelenos, an anonymous messenger of grace. He loved skating music; if he heard "Frenesi" or anything by Glenn Miller, he immediately took off. An eve at the small Valley rink would end with him unlacing our boots, wistfully blowing over his hot chocolate as he confided that that ultimate female skating partner had eluded him.

If he had found her, earlier, would any of us children have existed? Perhaps a son would not have been afraid of heights.

I tried. I skated pretty well for a native Los Angeleno—I had a good teacher. But I never learned to stop on a dime as my father, who barreled toward the wall, pivoted at the last second, bit his blades sideways into the ice with a shuusssh, ice shavings sprayed on my sister and me. I suppose if you know how to stop you're not so afraid of speed. If I speed-skate anywhere it's on the page, or parachute to its bottom. It's not a bad substitute for innate, physical grace, which my father—unconscious of his own body—had in spades.

The jogging-and-health mania that began with my generation and Jane Fonda'd into a billion-dollar industry over the past decade seemed stupid and pointless to him even when he discovered, as did everyone, cholesterol. "I'm going puffing," he would announce to my mother's exhortations, exhaling smoke. He smoked seriously—inhales and exhales were dramatic billowing caesuras, smoke signals of dilemma or pain. Strangely enough, smoke for him was a life force. Toward the end he tried to quit for Mom, even adopted lower-tar cigarettes. But his heart wasn't in it.

I say all this to note the paradox of that generation of Americans which spent its childhood in the Depression, fought the Second World War as teenagers, and built as adults the country we are today, for better or worse, richer or polluted, in plutonium and in health. That paradox is one of excess and selflessness. It was a generation which acted first, thought later. Ours, on the other hand, thinks most everything into oblivion. Ours projects all, yet seems at a loss to do anything that will substantially alter what we so brilliantly project, most of which is payment for forty-five years of excess since the war—chemical water, dying forests, soaring deficits, clogged arteries, rockets and bombs like hardened foam from a million panting mouths.

I can't blame my father or his generation for the Age of Excess anymore than I blame my own for its Age of Informed Narcissism. History and time create us more than we fathom. I only note the ironies—Dad's excess was generous, selfless, and dealt the future some mortal blows. Our touted social consciousness seems drained to a pittance of the grand protest era that gave us "our" war crucible. We are late, curiously cranky parents. And we are not so hot with the future, either, sinking in the mire of the present, saving nothing but the bills from our credit cards.

Our sin is presbyopia; his generation's—myopia. Even then by the day we escape from the immediate, from *contact.* We are all learning to draw in our wagons quite well from the teeming hordes of the ghetto, crack wars, the homeless. We become kinder, gentler Republicans at a fair remove from what needs our kindness and gentleness less than our ability to act. To *act*? That might entail uncertainty, even heartache.

Perfectly healthy as I was in my twenties—a bicycler, basketball player, swimmer—I once prodded Dad that he needed exercise. He snapped, "I got my exercise hauling fifty dresses at a clip over my shoulders up and down Ninth and Los Angeles streets. I got my exercise lugging an eighty-pound radio over the Maritime Alps." It was the closest he ever came to bravado. It was as out of character as it was for him to be out of work.

I used to dream about the Maritime Alps, unable ever to find them on the map. They held a lofty, Tibetan image in my mind. After the 551st came down from the Provence foothills of their parachute drop, taking Cannes, Nice and other towns of the Cote d'Azur, it was ordered to go up into the high mountains separating France from Italy, where the retreating Germans fled. This was September 1944. These were the Maritime Alps. (Three months after serving the longest uninterrupted combat stint in Europe, the 551st was relieved in the Alps by the heralded Japanese-American unit, the 442nd.)

In 1989 on some bright August days we veterans and family ascended the Maritimes. I had my eye out for old Army radios. His had probably been an SCR–300 backpack version, good practice for hauling a garment bag stuffed with samples. German pillboxes still squatted in the crags of the mountain. Chuck Fairlamb remembered boulders the Germans had rolled into the dry riverbed of the Var River so that gliders couldn't land there. As the road narrowed and steepened, and the clear green Var flowed in lazy late summer falls past islets and cottonwoods, Harry Renick seemed dreamy.

"What a place to come at night with a girl!" he mused, his dull blue eyes brightening at the sight. "You lie down on a towel with the rocks and the water rushing by. And boy, the wind over you! After you're done, you go dip it in the cold water. Downstream it gets warmer!"

I asked Harry, a tall man who looked like he might hunt, if the 551st ever saw bears or other animals in the Alps.

"Animals?" he dropped. "We were too concerned with the two-legged animals."

At St. Martin-Vesubie, we embarked to a good-sized crowd which swarmed us in the town square where, *tilleuls* rippling in a mountain breeze, we had a wreath-laying ceremony with the mayor and town council and *vin d'honneur.* One gap-toothed woman, eyes sparkling in a leathery face, insisted I translate for her that she had done the men's laundry during the war. Another with eyeglasses had given them gum, she nodded shyly. Everywhere we went were townspeople clutching forty-year-old photos, trying to compare the burnished boyish GI faces with the men whose skin had turned to many dry rivers, but whose eyes were searching, too, for that one person who knew them then, who bound a bullet wound or even sold them *baguettes*.

Swerving up the steep, narrow mountain road to the next village of their Alpine duty—tiny Isola—I could just imagine Dad in his glory on the motorcycle bending to the precipice as he distributed messages to the battalion. A chapel from the Middle Ages jutted above the green valley.

"Helluva nice place to live—I wouldn't want to fight a war here," Max Bryan mused.

Phil Hand recalled that after the war his insomnia and bad nerves from the Bulge were relieved only by imagining the period the 551st had spent in the snow-covered Alps, "one of the most beautiful and peaceful things I'd ever known." It was arduous duty, as well. Many of the men had to learn cross-country skiing for their patrols; some were picked off in the snow by German snipers. Some did the picking.

In November 1944 Dad wrote his sister Jeannette that he helped "serve Mass," avoiding in the V-mail tradition saying where he was. It was the Alps period. Attending Mass in a little chapel in Isola, Mark and I lit a candle and thought of him pouring the cruets as an nineteen-year-old in fatigues. For all his passion, he had a deep well of humility and faith that began to ebb only with the onset of my sister's mental illness in the late 1970s. A rosary taken from a bombed shrine in 1944 by scout Joe Cicchinelli of Arizona—miraculously unhurt—was worn by a statue of the Blessed Mother at Isola chapel. Outside the chapel, Bob Van Horssen of Grand Haven, Michigan—father of ten—gave his wings to a crippled girl.

Before having lunch at the Hotel de France (which had been badly shelled during the war) we found ourselves made part of a procession for St. Roch, the local patron, through whose intercession the Black Plague of the Middle Ages bypassed Isola. Down the cobblestones we walked behind a wooden statue of St. Roch. Someone pointed up a wall. Bullet holes from the war still peppered it. St. Roch had not prevented that. And some mute collective protest bone in Isola had kept that evidence from being erased.

Higher we went, up to seven thousand feet and the last Alpine town patrolled by the 551st—St. Etienne de Tinée. We were mobbed. It seemed the entire town of one thousand turned out to greet us. There was another French Army band and a company of French troops for the ceremonies. A gaggle of French generals and an admiral stood pointing, nodding.

Chuck Miller of Rancho Cucamonga, California, remembered the long, arduous hikes up and down the mountain slope, playing a kind of hide-and-seek with the Germans above: "At St. Etienne we'd switch places with the Germans. We'd look up with our binoculars at them, and then they would go down and look up at us." I thought of a line from Melville on the American Civil War: "All wars are boyish, and are fought by boys."

By midnight we were beautifully beat and traveling down the mountain. In the dark Glenn Miller tunes bathed us in memory, like a warm tide. Doug Dillard had put on a tape. "Oh K-A-L-A-M-A-Z-O-Oh what a gal! In Kalamazoo! I'll make my bid for that freckle-faced kid I'm hurrying to. I'm going to Michigan to see the sweetest gal in Kalamazoo-zoo-zoo."

Wishing-well Harry, who really had taken to the willowy brunette waitress in St. Etienne ("Tell her she's got class. Tell her she's beautiful"), saw in the dimness Aunt Jeannette drink some spring water from a bottle.

"Don't drink that water, it'll rust your pipes," Harry said, having a last beer.

"I'm not going to worry about that now!" squawked almost-octogenarian Aunt Jen.

Harry leaned over and flicked on my reading light as I was taking out my notebook. "You gotta put a little life in this life," he made us laugh, garbling "life" for "light." Considering the 551st, perhaps that was not a garble.

At La Turbie, Joe Cicchinelli took me on a forced march up a hillside to a disturbing memory. In advance of the battalion and with the help of French civilian Charles Calori, Cicchinelli and two other GIs had lobbed grenades into the machine-gun nest in a shack, killing three young, blond Germans. Cicchinelli still has the ID photos taken off their bodies forty-five years ago.

But it was at the shadowy hutch out back—where two more Germans were surprised with bullets—that Cicchinelli jumped back and forth in the underbrush, squeezing his jaw. "One of them didn't die," he shook his head. It was that one, Joe said lowering his voice, that he shot in the head and watched, agog, the youth's brains spill in a stream on the floor.

"What could I do?" Joe raised his head up to the sky. There was no answer—not from the bracken he was breaking as he paced, not from the bleached wood of the shack, not from us.

A shorter version of our father with his weathered tan, mustache, taut strength, and share of ghosts—Cicchinelli had spent three years in psychotherapy working on that moment in La Turbie, a bayonet attack at the Bulge, and months as a German POW. Today Joe counsels Vietnam veterans.

That shack. That hutch. It was the first time he had faced it again since the war. And though Cicchinelli had returned three times to Europe and was staying with a maquis veteran rather than at our hotel, he admitted, "The reason I come back—I hope by coming I can forget it," looking at me with sincere, wood-colored eyes that were somehow burning.

On the dirt path back I came upon the incongruous rusted guts of a piano. It made me think about Dad, who had met Mother while playing his patented single piano tune at a party. Had he ever killed someone face-to-face in the war? Mark said he had asked him that question once, and that Dad had said, no, he hadn't.

He lied.

Some months after we returned from Europe, his old football-playing buddy Bud Lank sent me a revealing tape of his childhood memories of my father.

After the war, and after some months' stay at various Army hospitals for his frozen feet, my father came back to Cleveland. One night he, Lank, and two other ex-GIs (including Tommy Stampfl of the 551st) went out drinking. By midnight, they were fairly well loosened up in a bar and began to tell what many GIs would never tell again—their darkest moment in the war.

Danny Polomski's moment was his body, or what was left of it—he'd lost both legs and an arm to a mine. Lank had broken his leg in a jeep accident. Dad's dark moment was not his injury, however.

He said about forty German soldiers had holed up in a bakery. The 551st opened up with machine guns and rifles. As two Germans tried to escape out the side window, my father shot them both. Later, walking with a squad along a hedgerow some Germans jumped up, and at pointblank range he shot one of them.

At the Battle of the Bulge the 551st fought through farmland, for the most part. The towns they went through were barely a cluster of stone houses— Dairomont, Odrimont. It's probable that the hedgerow incident was in Belgium. But the bakery?

One day I took a close look at an old photo of Joe Cicchinelli crouching with townspeople in Draguignan just after he had helped capture the Nazi general there and torn down the Nazi flag from the mayor's office. I squinted at the store window behind him. There it said: *Patisserie.*

It is likely my father had to kill two men whose faces he could see all too well only a day into battle, a day after the jump into France. It must have stunned him. After 1945, he told no one about it.

In childhood games of cowboy and Indian, Aref was the only kid who always played the Indian, Lank said.

I think of Joe Cicchinelli now holding his jaw in anguish at La Turbie, and I think of my father holding his ear from the gunshot ringing at the range and at the bakery. What it must have cost one who had always been the Indian to have the upper, lethal hand, even for a few seconds.

Phil Hand spoke of "emptying into" a German soldier at La Motte. "Fifty others emptied into him," Hand thought—pure fear of first day in battle. The idea of killing being an emptying of self—a draining of one, violently, into another— there is something pathetically sexual about it, something utterly forlorn. You are emptying more than bullets. Your soul is switched in the kill. You become the dead one. In killing him, in "emptying into" him, his deadness, by implication, invades you. In death he is full of you; in life you are a vacuum.

The day before we left Nice for Belgium I sat with Cicchinelli on the roof of the Hotel Pullman. The sun glared off the mirror sunglasses of some women lounging topless by the rooftop pool. Around us the great bowl of Nice sparkled—its steeples, clay-tiled roofs, mottled, hazy hills. California by another name.

After a while we stopped talking. Joe fingered a napkin and looked up at me. "How did your father die?"

"He was shot." I startled myself. Few who ask get the truth, and no one else in the 551st asked.

"Who shot him?"

"My sister."

He clamped my hand. His grip was hard, as if he were squeezing the handle of an elevator cut loose in a shaft. His head bent, ticking slightly.

"Oh, ooh."

There was less oxygen in Nice that afternoon, and much less sun, and no topless women. That languid roof shrank into a lonely hutch in back of a photocopy store—a place where people are put out of their misery.

V

"I know him."

Phil Hand held up a black-and-white photo of my father—the dashing GI home from the war, his Airborne patch captured on his shoulder, his thick black hair pleasantly awry at the widow's peak, "ears lowered." A slight mustache. He looks like Richard Gere. There's a gal tucked behind his ear, someone who didn't become my mother.

His feet are unfrozen, healed, and though they hurt in the cold, tonight is not cold, the liquor is flowing. He's at a club in Cleveland or some family shindig. He's manly, confident. But not too confident. He isn't smiling. His eyes are tree-bark in snow.

"I know him."

Phil Hand didn't nod, looking at the photo as we sat on the veranda of our Nice hotel. He was staring steadily through thick glasses. No histrionics here. He knows the man's soul, I think, but not the man. That may be better than the man, but that is not what I want. I want damn physical recognition.

I'd been showing the photo to the men of the 551st from the day we began the journey. No one knew him or recognized him. Most wanted to, no doubt, for our sake. But recognition of buddies they knew then takes a while for the old vets, even with flesh-and-blood partners before them.

VISIONS OF AMERICA

I began to realize that no one really remembered my father from the war. Perhaps my hopes were unrealistic. A battalion is 800 men; a company is 200 men; a platoon, 40. Of the four members of Dad's Headquarters Company on the trip (Hand, Fairlamb, Schultz, and Church Bernard of Cleveland, Ohio), Phil Hand was the only one in Demolitions platoon—in fact, he was its lieutenant (Hand was the only wartime officer on the trip). My father had trained in demolitions. Perhaps, I wanted to believe badly, Phil did know Aref Orfalea.

But in all Hand's wartime photo albums, Father is in not one picture. In only one of hundreds shown me is there a face so darkened, so inscrutable, I can pour my hope of recognition into it, one among fifteen grease-smeared men waiting to take off from Italy for the drop into southern France.

"It's yours. Take it." Phil gave the shade-man to me. I had thought the trip might lessen, not lengthen, the shadows I have come with live with.

Our Nice farewell speaker that night at dinner was Rear Adm. H. G. "Hank" Chiles, Jr., commander of a submarine group with the U.S. Sixth Fleet. Only about fifty people, we were hardly a big enough group to draw an admiral, not to mention one on active duty in the midst of another hostage-crisis (Colonel Higgins of the United Nations Truce Supervision Organization had just been hanged on videotape in south Lebanon). Chiles himself was substituting for the commander of the entire Sixth Fleet—Vice Adm. J. D. Williams.

"I and many of my generation stand in awe of you and the sacrifice of your generation during World War II," Chiles told the men. "You must know it's a humbling experience for a fifty-one-year-old rear admiral to stand here. I've asked myself over the past few days what I could possibly say that would be meaningful to people such as you. You see, you are *legends.*"

The men looked stunned. They were, after all, mostly privates during the war. To be praised by an admiral in such an intimate setting for a feat long ago forgotten by the high brass—it was disorienting, to say the least. But very pleasing, too.

Chiles pointed with interest to "recent progress with the Soviets" and thought that *"glasnost/perestroika* give us hope for a more open, less militant Soviet stance." He cited the first cathedral opened in forty years in Lithuania (a year later Lithuania was a free country, and at the end of 1991 the great Soviet Union itself broke up into fifteen free-market states with hardly a shot fired). Chiles called recent fleet exchange visits to Norfolk and Sebastopol "very successful."

"There are signs of a more peaceful world, signs that perhaps future generations of Americans might know a world less disposed to violence than what you saw and fought for," he told the vets.

Who of us doesn't want to believe that? Yet I saw in my mind's eye the hot muzzle of my sister's gun—the hell it wreaked in a few seconds. That had nothing to do with Communism, foreign policy. If all the wars in the world suddenly stopped, the impossible time bomb of our waste would have to be dismantled; 200 million guns, 70 million of them handguns, would remain marking time in their American drawers, closets, beds, hands. And 2 million as sick as my sister was sick. No. There is another war. It is in front of us everyday. It stems from who we are, what we are—it is a war of being, of being fractured. Drugs, AIDS, the homeless, the insane—as they grow the war grows. As do the guns. We are at war with ourselves. We very much need—in the midst of our tenuous plenty— an American *perestroika.*

A poet of Russia's Silver Age, Valerie Bruysov, noted that there are those who are freedom's "captives." Precisely.

Chiles ended with a surprisingly pacifistic reference to a soldier at Verdun, tipped his cap once again to the 551st for its "great contribution to freedom," and asked the men and their families to pray "for an America strong in peace so we don't have to be strong in war."

I couldn't have agreed more. Two hundred million guns on our streets is not strength.

VI

"I didn't want to live it—I didn't have to relive it. Maybe it's better to keep it cloudy. But I seem strong-willed enough not to be torn up by the past. I've been called cold-hearted. I knew we'd taken a horrible beating. But until I went to my first 551st reunion in 1988 in Chicago, I was under the impression we only had three people left."

It was Chuck Miller, an un-cold retired air conditioner repairman, looking out from a porch on the silent green hills of the Ardennes where, in a bitter two weeks at the turn of 1945, the 551st came to its end. Miller was talking about memory, the dread of it and its strange allure. There were few of the returning veterans who approached the killing field "with tranquil restoration," as Wordsworth would have it.

Memory. Drawn like moths to the flame of it, worried as to what it might contain, avid to share it with loved ones who might believe the otherwise unbelievable, or in Cicchinelli's case, to burn it so hot in the soul it would finally cool and come off like a scab. Something awe-full and awful to confront. What else but memory makes us human? As if preparing for the original battle, however difficult, the old men seemed to say: *We are what we remember.* Not the half of it we nurse or suppress, but the all of it we find, usually, with others.

The community of memory—the only community that lasts—quickened in the men when by train and bus following the route the 551st took in December 1944 as it rushed to the Ardennes to help stop Hitler's last onslaught, we arrived in Belgium.

Five facts: Ardennes horses, more nervous and quick than most, are exported to the United States. Belgians are the largest per capita drinkers of beer in the world. The towns of eastern Belgium in the Ardennes have been crushed three times this century by invading Germans. The world's largest mushroom industry based here uses the cool, damp, old Nazi bunkers for growth. And lastly, according to our host and former Belgian resistance leader Leo Carlier, Belgians are obstinately independent, each wanting "his house to be different." This sounded like 551st territory. It was also the scene of Hitler's last stand.

Over a million men in uniform fought in the month after December 16, 1944, the fiercest clash of the war in Europe—the Battle of the Bulge. Well over half those men were Americans, who took most of the 81,000 Allied casualties in that period. Begun with the Nazi SS massacre of eighty U.S. POWs near Malmedy, the Battle of the Bulge was Hitler's last desperate, and nearly successful, attempt to throw back the Allies who had been advancing steadily towards Germany since D-Day. No one thought he would attack in the dense Ardennes forest, or increase the attack in the midst of the worst European winter recorded in the century. He did both.

Pine shadows riddled the men on the bus while Carlier related, "You have been the Unknown Soldiers, the 551st. I met Colonel Dillard in 1984 and heard for the first time about your story and your destruction. I promised him we would make a memorial and I vowed you would never be forgotten. Tomorrow you will be invaded."

He wasn't kidding. Hundreds of people, some from as far as Brussels, showed up for the dedication. Their fervor was moving, even for one as skeptical of American foreign policy as I am. A poster inside the town hall at Liernaux still warned children not to touch live bullets and shells in the fields—destructive relics of two world wars. (A united Germany is for eastern Belgians at least as nervous a condition as for Silesians and other Poles.)

Now in the village of Rochelinval a monument to the 551st exists. Not the Americans, not the U.S. Army, but the Belgians themselves built the stone memorial; it took them two years. A young architect, Claude Orban, did much of the spade work. We watched in hushed silence Heide and Bo Wilson, grandchildren of Col. Wood Joerg killed in an artillery treeburst nearby, unveil the memorial.

The next day, our last, the men roamed the fields and the woods. "Can you imagine the enormous sound then, and how quiet it is now?" mused Chuck Miller as he hiked, shaking off a question about his heart condition.

I stood with the man who fired the first mortar of that historic December 27 raid on Noirefontaine ordered by General Gavin that commenced the Allied rollback of the Bulge. He was Chuck Fairlamb, seventy-four, of Seattle. He remembered Colonel Joerg pointing out a sniper and ordering him to "Go get that apple!"

But the worst was the foggy, freezing, delirious stretch January 3–7, 1945, when over a snow-filled, forested area near Trois Ponts the 551st pushed the Germans back five miles in five days—very slow, agonized fighting, often hand-to-hand combat. "It's always easier to defend, as at Bastogne, than to attack, as we did toward Rochelinval," explained Phil Hand. "We had to swing over the area like a gate."

"By God, did we take that many casualties in that small area?" wondered Doug Dillard, who feels closer to the 551st than to battalions he himself commanded in Korea and Vietnam. Dillard pointed out a creek where the men soaked their boots, the beginning of their battle with frostbitten feet and trench foot in the subzero weather. Dad's feet froze up; he was evacuated to Liège. When I leapt over a barbed wire fence to photograph the creek, the men smiled. Airborne, if for a second.

Hard to conceive in the green, silent farmland, but many froze to death, too. No overshoes were issued. The men were given a merciless order not to wear overcoats so that they would be distinguishable from Germans. Cicchinelli remembered firing ("We were so pissed") at overcoat-clad 517th GIs. Hand recalled soldiers "circling a little sapling which they gripped," trying to stay both awake and warm. Sleep was death. After three days of no sleep or food, some slept.

On January 4, 1945, the only platoon-sized fixed bayonet attack in the European theater occurred—yes, it was Company A of the 551st.

They lurched forward together, the repressed and the haunted, remembering Lt. Dick Durkee of Maryland's order to fix bayonets so that they would not shoot their own people in the fog. It's an order given in a desparate situation to strike up a soldier's adrenalin. The Germans stood up in their gun depressions, stunned. Sixty-four of them were killed by gun butts and blades. "I could very well have blocked it all out because of this day," Miller admitted. "And you know I'm German. It's such a dirty shame that someone like Hitler could change people's psyches the way he did."

"We were going a little mad, you know," Cicchinelli confessed. Company A stabbed and mutilated corpses until Durkee stopped them. They were breaking the stocks of their rifles off on the dead bodies. Durkee named it cruelty. But few of Company A survived, either. When Durkee ordered Pvt. Pat Casanova to get the rest of the men, Casanova of New Jersey shouted, "I can't, sir." "Why not?" Durkee yelled. "Because they're all dead, sir," was the reply.

Shortly after the bayonet attack Cicchinelli was taken prisoner by a Nazi patrol probably as lost in the snow as he was. Seventeen years later, working as a mail carrier he came to a wooded area near Flagstaff, Arizona, that resembled the Ardennes of Belgium. "I relived it all," he said, and had to rearrange his route before quitting altogether.

Finally we faced the mile-grade of hill below Rochelinval, now green, covered on January 7, 1945 with a foot and a half of snow. The day before, 1,262 rounds of artillery had been promised to the 551st for its attack on Rochelinval. But by dawn nothing had arrived, and nothing would arrive. Joerg tried to get the half-crazed unit relieved, to get the attack called off. He got neither. Only an order to take the hill, which was topped by dug-in Germans and their machine guns.

"He saved my life by giving me an order," Joe Thibault of Massachusetts said in choked voice, recalling Joerg's last moments. " 'Go get the self-propelled [gun]!' I saw it in his eyes. He knew." Charles Fairlamb also saw Joerg rise out of the protection of his foxhole and say, "Isn't the smell of mortars sweet, Chuck?" Fairlamb opined, "I think he knew he was doomed and we all were doomed. He just sort of stood up to take his fate."

Incredibly, their commander dead, down to less than a hundred men and a dozen officers, the 551st crested the hill and took Rochelinval, pushing the Germans behind the Salm River.

The 551st should have been one of the most decorated units in U.S. military history. Instead it became one of its most forgotten. In late January 1945, General Gavin told the 551st that they had been disbanded by the Department of the Army. Survivors filtered elsewhere. As Harry Renick put it, "I was disintegrated into the 82nd Airborne."

For all the "firsts" they notched, the 551st lost not only its existence, but its history. Dan Morgan of Washington (one of the first GIs to enter Dachau), in researching his self-published account of the unit, *The Left Corner of My Heart,* found twelve cubic feet of official records for the other independent parachute battalion—also disbanded—the heavily decorated 509th. For the 551st he found papers in a folder less than one-quarter of a inch thick. When Morgan visited Fort Benning in 1981, every parachute unit had a plaque on the wall—except for the 551st.

What explains this? The men chew on several theories: that Gavin was embarrassed enough by the losses as to wipe out all records and the remnant of the 551st; that the men were so heartbroken at their disbandment after Rochelinval they burned the records in the fields themselves; that the 551st was just snake-bitten from the beginning; that the death of their commander deprived them of their most credible pleading voice for honors; that their impossible objective at Rochelinval was punishment for being an oddball, maverick unit. But they have no answers.

THE MESSENGER OF THE LOST BATTALION

Neither, apparently, does Gen. Matthew Ridgway, who commanded the XVIII Airborne Corps for the Bulge campaign and was Gavin's immediate superior. Declassified in 1981, the Corps' March 1945 "Operation Report Ardennes" carries no mention either of the 551's historic attack on the Noirefontaine garrison, or of its capture in spite of terrible casualties of Rochelinval. Some of the men think the unit's final humiliation lies with Ridgway, who apparently disliked the independent paratroop units and was on the verge of disbanding them anyway before the Bulge hit. Yet Ridgway, now ninty-four, wrote Colonel Dillard on July 29, 1989, that the blotting out of the 551st was "a grave error and injustice to as gallant a combat battalion as any in World War II in Europe." Declining an interview due to illness, Ridgway also wrote me on February 8, 1990, "I have an abiding admiration for the members of the 551st Parachute Battalion's record of gallantry in the Battle of the Bulge, but as far as I can remember, I had no personal contact with it. At one time I had a 65–mile front to cover with only a handful of troops, though there were no finer ones." Ridgway also noted that he was aware of "serious efforts" underway to bring the "full record" of the 551's heroism and tragic fate to public light.

After the few survivors were broken apart and stripped of their history together, thirty years went by. In 1977, Phil Hand determined "to find whatever buddies I had left before I died." He used telephone directories, ads in *Static Line,* the airborne newsletter, his wife's government WATS line. The first reunion in August 1977 brought eighteen members. Now there are about one hundred forty found, though many are in ill health.

How strange it is that these precious men could receive the French Croix de Guerre personally from General Charles DeGaulle and many years after see a monument erected to their sacrifice in Belgium but be completely ignored by their own country. The men talk about the Presidential Unit citation received by the 509th, but they do not hold their diminishing breath.

Lt. Gen. (Ret.) William Yarborough, then commander of the 509th, their brother unit laden with honors denied the 551st, calls the independent units' disbandment "a crime of the first order." Speaking of the extraordinary intangibles that go into making an elite unit, he said, "For the Army as a whole to forget this, or to sublimate it to the degree that it is considered less important than bullets and bayonets, is to break faith with the real meaning of what it portends to be a soldier."

Or a man.

VII

One night in Liège, Fred Hilgardner of Missouri made me realize my brother Mark and I were not alone in our own search.

"I'm retracing my father's steps, just like you," he said, taking a good pull of his cigarette. The elder Hilgardner had lost a leg during the First World War at the nearby Meuse-Argonne, dying when his son was barely a year old. "Everybody loved him," Fred crushed his cigarette, and in the furl of smoke I saw emerge one last time in Belgium the phoenix-genie of our father. How a father can pull the wagon of a son's life, even from the grave!

The trip had shaken Fred Hilgardner: "I broke down at a lot of our ceremonies." He went on bitterly, "What is the Fourth of July? Firecrackers. We used to learn the history of the flag. The kids today don't even know the capitals of the states. They'll play the national anthem at a ballgame—ball players will scratch their nuts, chew gum. Men in the stands sucking their beer, not taking off their caps. Flags on the Fourth—some drag the ground. The flag means more to me than a piece of cloth. It represents men's lives."

Whether or not flag-burning should be unlawful, sentiments such as Fred Hilgardner's should never be taken lightly. There is no blind patriotism in the 551st—quite the contrary. Becoming "a shadow battalion," as Dan Morgan calls it, ensured that—discarded in the war by history, by the Army itself. Medals is not what the 551st is after or impressed with.

Truth is medal enough. "Setting the record straight" for a handful of children and grandchildren as to what their fathers did in history's near-suicide was really the purpose of going back, as Doug Dillard intimated one night. It uncovered the depths of the men's sadness and their sacrifice, not a small one.

Suddenly Hilgardner had a vision, and tapped me on the shoulder, "You get around these guys and you don't seem so damn old. You know, there were two guys that last night in Nice who'd swing a gal around so well. They topped everybody. They danced jitterbug. Maybe your Dad was one of 'em."

Did he love to dance! *That* my mother handled well, to the point that when they danced they seemed to fuse. They never looked at each other, but a quick touch at fingertip would trigger a whirl, a twist, a sidestep, a clinch. Different as they were, they were rhythm personified, *In the Mood*. And they taught us children to dance, plugging in the phonograph, scattering sand on the garage floor.

Maybe one of those hopoids was Dad, Fred. Maybe Wood Joerg was clapping. That last night before Belgium . . .

It became clear to me. From the first day of the trip when Joe Thibault, whose son died of a drug overdose at thirty-nine, came over with tears in his eyes, gripping me on the shoulder, to Otto's sequestered motorcycle, to Phil Hand's shadowy photo, to Hilgardner's last dancer, that the men of the 551st were looking for their messenger. He was unknown. That made him all the more sought after. He was their youth. He was the cipher of their strange, long-delayed coming together. He had something to say to them in the form of two sons. Just as we sought our father in them, they sought him in us.

Mark said it best with a spontaneous toast at our Liège farewell dinner, palpable in candlelight: "It's been painful to realize that none of you knew Dad personally. But I must tell you extraordinary men that in these short days I found a piece of my father in every one of you. Here's to the men of the 551st! May their memory live forever!"

From the troubled exuberance of Joe Cicchinelli to the stoic avoidance of Chuck Miller that spared others pain—these had our father stamped on them. Each was the kind of man in whose care you would place your life. And they evoked something of that in you—in their gracious, wry, self-abnegating way.

My sister placed her life in my father's hands. He did not drop it, though it killed him. During her sometimes frightening ten-year struggle with schizophrenia, my sister was not abandoned by Mother or Father.

In his old factory Dad gave employ to a Black with a cleft palate, a French dress designer with a hunchback, a Jewish bookkeeper who, at seventy, supported an invalid brother. At home he brought in for help with housekeeping a magnificent human being named Margarita Cruz, whose son was killed by death squads in El Salvador. He was the Indian. He dropped from planes for others.

That inkling he had during the war intensified toward the end in his ear's ringing—of a war closer to home. He didn't see a way out of it. For one of his disposition, there wasn't any. Maybe this is why he clung so to life, with such abandon, knowing what a lucky gift a moment of joy was, knowing its duration, knowing how a landscape could be green with friends and too soon snow-covered with their bodies.

A few months before he died, he sat in front of me and said softly, looking up, "Life is hell."

I suppose I will think about that statement till I die. How out of character it was.

But maybe not. Maybe, for a GOYA, it was a compliment. I have come to see my father's fate as akin to the fate of the men with whom he served in battle so long ago. They became in their sacrifice what he became: anonymous, lost, but a messenger of life at all costs.

Remember that line of Hickey's from Eugene O'Neill's *The Iceman Cometh* about his doomed wife? "I could see disgust having a battle in her eyes with love. Love always won." Staring down the barrel of the past I think the 551st saw the same thing my father saw that terrible day in Belgium and in Los Angeles: ultimate love.

GOING HOME: BROOKLYN REVISITED

Barbara Grizzuti Harrison

Barbara Grizzuti Harrison was born in Brooklyn, New York. She is the author of several books, including *Learning the Lie: Sexism in Schools* (1970), *Visions of Glory* (1978), *Off Center* (1980), *Italian Days* (1989), and *The Astonishing World* (1992).

November, 1974

DURING WORLD WAR II MY GRANDFATHER HAD A VICTORY GARDEN in Bensonhurst, a small plot of city-owned land on which, as his contribution to the war effort, he planted hot and sweet peppers, zucchini, tomatoes, oregano (without which the Allies must surely lose the war), mint, and sweet basil. To be able, with the blessing and under the patronage of the American government, to do the noble work of farming the good earth made glad his lyrical Italian heart; he sang aloud with happiness. The song he sang aloud (*very* loud), as he harvested and hoed, was the Italian Fascist Youth Anthem. Grandpa was unable to see any irony in this; attempts to persuade him that the work of his hands contradicted the words of his mouth merely reinforced his conviction that all

158

GOING HOME: BROOKLYN REVISITED

American-Americans were simpletons, *pazzi* (crazy). Wasn't he Italian, after all? And wasn't he American, after all? And weren't all American-Americans perverse—unable and unwilling to understand the first thing about Italian-Americans, who in any case had no wish to be understood by people so *pazzi* that they couldn't even pronounce Il Duce's name correctly? Till the day he died, Grandpa persisted in pronouncing Mussolini *Mussolino,* arguing with awesome circuitous logic that if FDR called him Mussolini, then—since all Americans were *pazzi* and perverse and had never cared enough to get the final vowel of any Italian name right—it must of necessity be Mussolin*o.* Toward the end of his life, Grandpa, as fierce in senility as he had been in full-blooded vigor, regaled visitors with the story of his flight across the Atlantic with Charles Lindbergh. He had been denied recognition, he claimed, because *they* wouldn't let it be known that an Italian had shared the controls with "an American boy." Italians were always deprived of their just rewards. (My grandfather, a carpenter, had once worked with Bruno Hauptmann, the kidnapper of the Lindbergh baby; even his most baroque fictions usually had some remote link to an esoteric truth.)

I grew up in Bensonhurst among people who, if they had little else, had the courage of their contradictions. I grew up trying to sort truth from fiction (which was almost always more picturesque and more compelling than truth) among proud, stubborn, Italian-Americans who were convinced that they were doomed to be misunderstood . . . a conviction that paradoxically was a source of stoic pride. To compound the paradox, these same people—who were eloquent in their belief that they would be forever deprived, by the *pazzi* Americans, of what was rightfully theirs—managed also to believe absolutely in the American Dream: when Grandpa wasn't singing hymns to the Brownshirts, he was singing Frank Sinatra's *What Is America to Me? The house I live in . . . the street, the house, the road . . . the church, the school, the clubhouse . . . the little corner newsstand . . . the dream that's been agrowin' for about two hundred years.*

Bensonhurst is still Sinatra territory. Some say it is Mafia territory. It is still peopled by proud, stubborn, first-, second-, and third-generation southern Italians for whom the ownership of a little bit of land represents not just material success but the attainment of the highest moral and ethical ideal. The church, the school, the clubhouse—especially the neighborhood school—are regarded now, as they were then, as theirs to love and theirs to defend. Now, more than ever, Bensonhurst's Italian-Americans are convinced that *they* are trying to take away the just rewards—especially the neighborhood schoolhouse—that by right should have accrued to decent, hardworking patriots.

What is no longer certain is that anyone in Bensonhurst believes, any more, in the American Dream. The dreams of Bensonhurst's Italian-Americans are blood-colored now; and the stink of fear is in the air.

On Monday, October 7, racial tension exploded into racial violence at New Utrecht High School (*my* old high school).

During the nine-thirty A.M. third period, a white male student jumped a black male student in a hallway. As news of the attack spread, enraged black students, outnumbered at Utrecht four to one, fled from their classrooms and stormed through the lunchroom and out of the school building. Teachers barricaded their classroom doors and locked white students inside. The following day, racial fights on the nearby BMT "el" and outside the school building resulted in several injuries to both white and black students (some serious enough to require hospitalization) and in the suspension of eighteen students and the arrest of six others. On Wednesday, school was shut down. On Thursday, New Utrecht, heavily guarded by police from four precincts, opened only for Regents exams. On Friday, October 11, school reopened. No serious incidents were reported that day to the more than two hundred policemen who were there to be sure that there would be no repetition of bloody Tuesday. On that tense Friday, however, twenty-one blacks, reputed to be carrying meat cleavers, pipes, and chains, were arrested at the BMT station. None of them was a New Utrecht student.

Those are the facts on which everybody—black students and white students, neighborhood hang-out goons, teachers, school administrators, and community people—seem to agree. Those are the *only* facts on which everybody agrees. From there on in, trying to sort truth from fiction is as onerous a proposition as trying to convince Grandpa that the name of the man who made the trains run on time was Mussoli*ni*.

There is one other point of consensus; that is the fact that no one from the press cares enough even to try to sort truth from fiction. The population of Bensonhurst and New Utrecht is vociferously contemptuous of media people and, in particular, of televsion journalists, who are seen as predatory, manipulative trouble-mongerers with scant regard for fact or sensibility. I heard from too many sources not to give credence to the story that television cameramen "posed" and instructed kids ("All right, let's have fists up in the air . . . let's hear 'kill the niggers' " . . . or " 'kill whitey' ") for maximum-impact footage. (The first call alerting anybody to the troubles at Utrecht was made [by a student] not to the cops but to Channel 5 TV.)

I returned to Bensonhurst in the aftermath of the riots, and in permawood-paneled, chandeliered, plastic-and-velvet living rooms that I could feel my way blindfolded around, I found myself once again in that familiar territory where cynicism and sanguinity, pragmatism and rococo fantasies, fight for psychic space in the complex personalities of insular, ghettoized Italian-Americans who, like my grandfather, defend the very contradictions that confound them, and who, like him, seldom manage to coordinate their emotional/political reflexes. There was

GOING HOME: BROOKLYN REVISITED

one added ingredient in the familiar volatile brew; it pervades the working- and lower-middle-class community of Bensonhurst as it pervades New Utrecht High School: that ingredient is despair.

One of the more bizarre aspects of that post-riot evening, which I shared with my brother ex-Utrechtites and former schoolmates, is that almost every conversation wrapped itself around a central myth: "The blacks don't want to be here anyway. Wouldn't they rather be jiving with their own kind in their own neighborhood the way we did when we were kids?"

It is inconceivable to most Bensonhurst Italians—who, when they get married, usually move "down the stoop" from their mother's house—that anybody would not want to stay "with his own kind." If anyone leaves his own kind to come to New Utrecht, it is (1) because he's looking for trouble; or (2) because there's no discipline in his home; or (3) because "outside agitators," including parents, have put him in Utrecht against his will. The fact is, of course, that under the Board of Education's Open Enrollment Program every one of the 1,100 black students at NUHS has *chosen* to be there. Black kids from East New York, Crown Heights, and Bed-Stuy (all of which areas Bensonhurst residents tend to lump together under one generic name—*Harlem*) travel up to three and a half hours every day on public transportation to get to the school of their choice. You have to be pretty highly motivated to do that for three years when everybody around is cold-nosing you. Nevertheless, almost without exception, the Italian-Americans I spoke to truly believe that "the coloreds don't want to be bussed in from Harlem in the first place, so why are *they* taking away our pride by putting them here?" People who point defensively—"Am I a bigot?"—to framed pictures of Hank Aaron on their walls "swear to God" they wouldn't mind if the blacks who went to New Utrecht were neighborhood kids; it's the feeling of being invaded by outsiders and tricked by *them* that they can't tolerate. (But, on the other hand, what would they do if blacks moved into Bensonhurst? "Move.")

I graduated from New Utrecht in January, 1952. The student body then, reflecting the composition of the neighborhood, was fifty percent Jewish and fifty percent Italian. (There were a few exceptions, among whom was Fatima Ouida, a magnificently endowed Egyptian girl who charmed snakes, and nice Jewish boys, in her bedroom, while her father—universally known as "the guy who prays to the West End train"—made his ritual prayers to Mecca facing the window in the living room that was six inches away from the BMT "el.") It was taken for granted by students and teachers alike that Jews were smart (they took academic courses) and Italians were dumb (we took commercial and general courses). I was once asked by a teacher why I had an Italian last name. He wasn't being hostile or precious; he was, quite simply, puzzled: how could an Italian girl be smart? When, miracle of miracles, my friend Angela made Senior Arista and won a scholarship to Radcliffe, her grandmother, draped in funereal black, accompanied her to Cambridge on the bus, making novenas to Saint Jude, patron saint of Lost Causes, all the way. While Angela was at Radcliffe, Harold Brodkey wrote his famous *New Yorker* short story about a love affair between a Harvard boy and a Radcliffe girl. Angela came back to Brooklyn in a very large hurry and assembled all her friends; together we bought every copy of that *New Yorker* we could find from Bay Parkway to Bath Avenue on the off-chance that Angela's grandmother might come across Brodkey's story, realize that college kids actually *did it,* and yank Angela back to Bensonhurst and the safety of her virginal pink-and-white bedroom forever.

Utrecht in the fifties had a reputation for being a school for "gees"—"hard guys," or "hoods." (While nearby Erasmus Hall High School was nurturing Beverly Sills, we were getting ready to give the world John Saxon and Buddy Hackett.) If you didn't bother the gees, they didn't bother you. You minded your business, you stayed out of trouble. Arnold Horowitz, a lovely, nurturing English teacher, was forever sending packages of pepperoni off to Utrecht gees who'd wound up in jail and forever imploring us to believe in the possibility of redemption and the basic goodness of human nature. We believed.

In my senior class at Utrecht there were 468 whites and one black girl, Joan Smith. No one ever spoke to Joan Smith, and Joan Smith never spoke to anybody. At the end of the senior year, she was voted "Most Friendly."

My brother remembers what it was like to have one black classmate in 1955: "That kid was lucky. He was bright and good-looking. If he was just a regular black kid, he'd have had bad trouble. . . . Every time teachers talked about black history or slavery, my word of honor, I felt sorry for the kid. If they'd have talked about Italian history, there'd have been thirty of us Italians, we wouldn't be embarrassed . . . not that they ever talked about Italian history."

When Jimmie D.—an auto mechanic who still lives, with his wife and three kids, in his mother's two-family house in Bensonhurst—went to Utrecht from '58 to '60, there was one black kid, too; he *wasn't* extraordinarily bright and good-looking. "He never opened his mouth; nobody ever bothered with him. If there'd have been twenty of them, though, we'd have killed them just on general principle. . . .

"Remember when Bay Fifteen in Coney Island was ours? We beat the shit out of any black kid who put a foot past Bay Thirteen, even if he was just an eight-year-old snot who got lost from his mother. Once a colored guy came in and stabbed one of ours with an ice pick," Jimmie said. "We smashed his head against a pier and we never saw black skin for the rest of that summer. That was *our* Bop House." "And the younger Italian kids," my brother said. "We taught them respect. They had to call us 'Uncle.' If they didn't behave good, we'd make them shine our shoes with their spit—just on general principle."

GOING HOME: BROOKLYN REVISITED

I know those stories don't make Jimmie D. or my brother sound altogether lovable. They rehearsed them because they wanted desperately to believe, for one evening at least, that we all still have a chance, that things are better now, not worse. Perhaps we still believe what Arnold Horowitz told us—that human nature is basically good, that redemption is possible.

"My kids want to know why all this is happening. What can I tell them? I know I got some prejudice left. If one of my kids got mugged I'd take it out on the first colored I saw. But I don't want my prejudice to slip out in front of my kids. I want them to be better than me," Jimmie D. said.

But, he also said, "If one of my daughters dated a black guy, it'd be Bay Fifteen all over again."

And: "I tell the guys on the job people ought to live together—I'm not better than him, he's not better than me. And they call me a nigger-lover. I don't want my kids bussed—and they call me a racist. So what am I?"

What am I? And who is my enemy? . . . contradiction and pain. Confusion and alarm. . . . Years ago, I saw *Dr. Strangelove* at the Bensonhurst Eighty-sixth Street Loews. All through the movie the woman behind me kept saying, "But I don't understand. *Who's the enemy?*" . . . Sitting in a Bensonhurst living room, we tried, once again, to identify the enemy.

"It ain't the kids. It's the politicians—the Communists who send their kids to private schools. Democrats and Republicans, all those creeps, those *giabronis* are all the same. . . . Listen, I'd be demonstrating in front of those schools in South Boston with the Irish. I move out of a ghetto to do good for my kids, how can I have any pride if I gotta send my kids back to the jungle for school? I had to sweat to buy my house. Am I a racist?

"Who cares about us? Does the Board of Education care? Three o'clock and the teachers don't want to know nothin'. Nobody cares. The teachers don't get no support, nobody wants to be bothered."

Fifteen years ago, Diane was a Booster and a Twirler at NUHS. "Look," she said, "this is a safe neighborhood. They used to laugh at Bensonhurst, right? You were a cornball if you lived here. Now they're going to have to put a wall around it, it's so safe. . . . My cousin plays *bocci* in a cottage that a colored lady owns in Long Island. Blacks go there. She plays Scrabble with them. We're colorblind if they're our equal. But tough teenagers aren't my equal. It's not like the gees—you could ignore them. I know all teenagers are wild, but if they look familiar, they don't scare me. Blacks scare me because they don't look familiar. I *know* the tough white kids that hang out on the corners drinking. And it's okay because I *know* them. I'm not saying the blacks are wilder. I'm saying they don't look familiar. So why don't they stay in their own schools and in their own neighborhoods where they're familiar? Why are they sending them here to scare us?"

Richy, an ex-Utrechtite who brings secondhand shoes and clothes and used record albums to the poor black kids bussed into the neighborhood junior high school his kids go to: "It's not the Utrecht kids who are making the trouble. It's the dropouts, the big shots, the candy-store hang-out kids, it's them. Their IQ and their foot size is the same number. They could've been somebody—they could've gotten athletic scholarships. But they're twenty and they're still hanging out in the schoolyard. Fifteen years old, and they think it's glamorous to get drunk on boilermakers and get busted for drugs and have flashy cars and hard-looking girls. They're all playing James Caan playing Sonny. When they're twenty-five they'll look up to the decent people, but then it'll be too late."

"It's the Mafia."

"Yeah, but the Mafia keeps the neighborhood safe."

Jimmie D. adds to the Enemy List the "geeps" from the other side: "We got this big influx of Italians from the old country. They're not like us. They got a chip on their shoulder. Mouth-y. They say, Blacks have been here for a hundred years and they couldn't make it; now it's our turn. It was a geep who beat up on a black kid at Utrecht. The geeps are here three years and they got money to buy a four-family house. That's all they think of is money. They never heard of going to the movies. They never heard of anisette. They never even heard of *coffee.* You go to their house, they don't give you anything to eat. What kind of Italian is that? They work two jobs, and they eat macaroni every night—*pasta lenticci, pasta fazool,* that's it. We're here eating pork chops and drinking highballs and we hear them every night cracking macaroni into the pot—unbelievable."

Diane's cousin, who plays *bocci* in the colored lady's house on Long Island, comes in from an evening class at Bernard Baruch College. "As long as there are blacks and whites there's going to be trouble," she says. "We're all victims of the system."

"You know what," my brother says wryly. "It isn't hip to be racist any more. Aside from it isn't decent."

So what's the solution? "Do something in their own neighborhoods?" "Make their local schools better?"

"There is no solution," everybody says.

"Clockwork Orange is just around the corner," Richy says. "It's too late."

As we drive away, my brother says, "Most people are decent. And that's the sin. Are those bad people? Did you ever meet more sincere people?"

Most people need to believe they're decent. Italian-Americans are—it is bred in the bone and marrow of a people who for centuries have had to defend themselves against alien invaders—suspicious and insular, guarded and, now, bitter. But their own hatred terrifies them. Lacking any real political analysis, they can't identify the enemy—the *They* who are taking away everything they've fought for. . . . And that's the tragedy.

All I could think of, as I approached New Utrecht High School with its hundreds of cops, were the cupcakes we used to buy for a nickel in the school lunchroom. Confronted with spiritual crises, I make grocery lists and compose menus. Confronted with that prisonlike building in which I learned for the first time to value myself—because Arnold Horowitz valued me; confronted with that bleak edifice in which I first fell in love—with Arnold Horowitz; confronted with that gothic grotesquerie in which Arnold taught me to question and to doubt the fundamentalist religion that had straitjacketed me in a claustrophobic simplicity, I used my press card to get past the police, past the teachers with their newly issued ID tags—and into my old school lunchroom. To think about cupcakes. To try not to think about Arnold, who died before Bensonhurst's world shattered.

I am an imposter: to be the bearer of a press card is—one is given to understand—proof that one is a reporter. I am here to report the facts; but the essential fact is that this fortress was my womb. I grew up in this building; it is not an exaggeration to say I was born here. I love this place. I try, nevertheless, to get the facts. I don't really want the facts; I want a blessing. I want Arnold again—his charity, his clarity, his love. I was born here—Arnold gave birth to me here—and now it smells like death here.

There are no more cupcakes in the school lunchroom. New Utrecht was built to accommodate 2,600 pupils. There are 4,300 students enrolled here now. Cupcakes are a luxury New Utrecht cannot afford. And charity is in short supply.

The air in the lunchroom is thick with rumors. It is rumored that the violence was timed to coincide with the threatened strike of Utrecht's eight security guards, and that everybody knew it was coming. It is rumored that on Halloween trouble will explode again; Nair and eggs and hair spray are being stockpiled as defensive weapons. There is the rumor of the Missing Ear. A white ear, some kids say. A black ear, some kids say. Knifed off, some kids say. Bitten off, some kids say.

"Grossly exaggerated, tragic nonsense," the principal, Michael Russo, says. Handsome, all dapper solicitousness, Russo effusively greets smiling matriarchs from the black community as he nods to the priests who mingle with the cops who mingle with the teachers, many of whom hate Russo's guts—or lack of them. "He doesn't even know our names. All he's got is charm. The first year he was here, the Italian kids loved him. President Ford should have had the honeymoon he had. He was as cute as Anna Maria Alberghetti doing an Italian-salad-dressing commercial. The second year he was here, we never saw his face—except when he came into the auditorium to throw kisses and say a couple of words in Italian. Now he wears his best suit every day for the television cameras. The entire Board and this whole administration care about appearances, period. Russo will tell you we have a wonderful school—he'll tell you all about the Boosters, the football team, the pep rallies, the Twirlers, the Sings. When everybody else knew trouble was coming, he was planning a fiftieth anniversary alumni dance. All the rottenness is kept under covers. Nobody wants to face the fact that the system is failing."

In the teachers' lunchroom, the air is heavy with bitterness: *"The New York Times* said we were 'overrun with three hundred blacks.' We were *not* overrun with blacks. You can expect to hear that version from some of the kids, too—'A coupla kids gave one black kid a hard time, and then the coloreds came in by the busload from Bed-Stuy.' No black kids came *in* from anywhere. Our black students ran through the lunchroom on Monday because they were scared. I don't want to hear that they looked like Amazons—you could practically taste their fear. On Tuesday, the black kids all arranged to meet at the Pacific Street subway station and come to Utrecht in a group, that's your 'three hundred blacks.' Sure, they looked like a terrifying mob. You should have seen what the white kids throwing bottles out of the windows looked like."

Some of the white kids are eager indeed to advance the busload-of-outsiders-from-Bed-Stuy version of the riots: "After the black guy got jumped, the blacks called all their friends in from Lincoln High School and Jefferson High School and FDR High School—troops, man. They had pipes and chains. So naturally we threw bottles. . . . It was like Attica. Exciting."

The official line, as advanced by Herbert Potell, Assistant Principal, is that "black and white students work and play beautifully together. There are undesirable characters, black and white outsiders, who hang around the school and incite trouble. And up till now we have not been too successful in communicating with black parents, because they live out of the community. Eighty percent of the neighborhood people have never even heard of the 'fifty-four Supreme Court decision. But this year got off to an unbelievably good start. There was nothing we could have seen below the surface to alert us to trouble. We were taken unaware." He adds, in an unofficial aside, "You know, the black girls are tough, they're harder than the boys . . . they come from a seamier part of life. Don't get me wrong. Some of them are sweet. But the white girls are always scared." (I remember Mr. Potell when he was an English teacher at Utrecht. In my senior yearbook there is a Last-Will-and-Testament inscription to him: "And to Mr. Potell, we leave an Academy Award for the Most Touching Performance of the Year as Lady Macbeth.")

Student leaders, presenting a united front, agree that it was outsiders—white outsiders, the goons who hang out on the street corners, the ones whose IQ and foot size are the same number—who provoked the riots. They are eager

GOING HOME: BROOKLYN REVISITED

to disabuse interrogators of the notion that blacks and whites at Utrecht are perpetually prepped for battle in separate armed camps. But when they discuss among themselves the viability of black-and-white friendships at Utrecht, their bravado rapidly crumbles into ambivalence and pathos.

Cheryl Walker, fifteen, of the Black Student Coalition: "We have friends. When we have games, we're all together, united against other schools. Last year we had a basketball playoff against Charles Evans Hughes, a black high school. Hughes lost, and they started a riot. The black students protected the white students, male and female. . . . We do good at games. We might not get along too good, but we don't fight. Ordinarily. But a white girl who has a black girl to her house is called a nigger-lover. . . . Maybe I don't have friends. It's hard to know any more. . . . It's always been hard." Toni Napoli, secretary of the G.O.: "I have black friends. But they can't come to my house, they live too far away. . . . And what's going to happen to me if I go to them against my side? You feel bad if you talk to another color against your own kind."

Most of the white students I spoke with had rather odd notions of friendship. (Most of the black students slipped home too fast to be interviewed.)

"Sure, I got black friends. I shake their hands on the handball courts. I play track with them. . . . They're my friends till trouble starts. Now I think we ought to kill 'em all."

"I treat the coloreds just like they were as good as whites. But what are they doing in my school?"

"Alone, a colored can be nice. In a group, we're more civilized."

"We have niggers on all the teams—we're friends."

But I am giving these kids less than their due. Taken alone, one by one, they are not unlikable. They want an education, they want security and familiar fun and familiar faces. Taken in a group—and, by and large, that's how I took them on Friday, October 11—they are tribal and defiant and frighteningly silly, drawing courage from one another's hard-ass talk. They are also—I was occasionally, stunningly reminded, by their sudden excursions into giggles or their uncontrolled, breaking voices, or their ridiculous attempts to be grown-up, back-slapping oracles—children, victims, if you will, of manipulation and polarization, of carefully nurtured ignorance and insularity and paranoia. They are victims; but they are also potential murderers.

At New Utrecht High School, the outline of a simple equation begins to present itself. When inflation and the specter of depression—the corrosive fear that *they* are going to take away everything your people have fought for—tears at your guts, you go for the easy and immediate solution: you "rip a nigger's heart out." With your tribal instincts and your adolescent lust for excitement providing the adrenaline, you collectively go for the jugular of the person you suppose to be the enemy—the jugular of a black. ("They'd kill us if we went into their neighborhood. What do they expect in ours?") Your resentments find the nearest target. ("I can't even get a dumb train pass 'cause I live less than two miles away—so how come they can get in?") You don't shout *Kill Rockefeller*—even if you did perceive any connection between Rockefeller and your pain, Rockefeller is too remote. You shout *Kill a nigger*—a nigger is real to you, present, seen, felt . . . and feared.

And you have the outsiders—the white-agitator hang-out "goons" to egg you on.

It ought to be easy to hate and to despise the hang-out goons. They are bigots hot with bloodlust. They are dangerous children on a murderous rampage; and they scared the hell out of me. But I could not hate them. I hated their words, I abominated their deeds . . . and out of some spiritual left field, I felt in myself feelings that, on the face of it, were totally inappropriate to the situation: I felt pity for them. And—it was hard for me to acknowledge that I was feeling this, and it is harder still to write it—I felt protective of them. Mostly I felt impotent rage . . . which is exactly what they were feeling.

Murderers . . . and victims. They are both.

What can you feel about a twenty-three-year-old man-child who hangs out at Utrecht because "things bother me. I used to drive a car for the *Daily News* and now I only work three days a week because one of them animals got half my job. They're taking my job away. I never had no opportunity; why should they have an opportunity? When my wife got pregnant I was bringing home seventy-four dollars a week. And I asked for Medicaid and they said, Forget it. And you know if I was a nigger or a spic I'd have got it. . . . Things bother me. They take away our jobs from us and now they're taking our school and pretty soon they'll take our neighborhood; and I'm staying here when there's trouble. This is my place. What other place do I got?"

Can you hate him? He can drive you wild with anger—and inspire a lunatic urge to deliver a lecture on political science and economy, or a diatribe against politicians who give their cronies $500,000 handouts while a hang-out/goon/slob can't get his wife adequate medical care (the baby died). But can you hate him?

It is wonderful, though, and terrible, how hate answers hate. On that Friday, I wanted somebody to hate. Not "the system" or Nelson Rockefeller—nothing, nobody remote—somebody present and real I could decently, cathartically hate.

I thought I'd found him in Johnny G. Johnny G., who put a *No Niggers Allowed* sign in the window of the Utrecht Avenue pizzeria. Johnny G., who snapped his fingers and yelled, "Everybody out of the pizza parlor, I'm talking to this here lady reporter." (Everybody cleared out—fast . . . but not before Johnny G. commanded one freshman to buy his cigarettes, another freshman to get some batteries, and a third to wax his red TR 6 sports car.) Johnny G., who said, exposing beautiful muscled arms, "See these scars? I got them from a

GOING HOME: BROOKLYN REVISITED

nigger. But what I done to him, I broke his jaw—it's hard to break African noses—and I broke his jaw, and I gave him six stitches over his eye. Beautiful." Johnny G., Big Man, who says he's been "shit on" all his life. "They kicked me out of school. Why? Because three colored kids jumped a small white kid, so naturally I wiped the schoolyard with one I caught." Johnny G., twenty years old, half-Italian, half-Arab, whose mouth smilingly issues forth venom, whose face is so broodingly beautiful, so sensitive, I see images of Terry Malloy superimposed on it. Johnny G., whose half-sister was knifed. Johnny G., who says, "Sometimes I get so mad I smash walls, I break things." Incongruously he smiles, that dazzling, heartbreaking, unexpected smile. "Arabs aren't Africans," he says. (Is it a non sequitur?) Johnny G., who has a job: "I deliver teeth." *You deliver teeth?* "Yeah, I work for a creative dental caterer, and I deliver false teeth." The Triumph doesn't belong to Johnny G. It belongs to his boss. It doesn't belong to the Big Man who delivers false teeth. "My sister," Johnny G. says, "ain't half-Arab. She's smart. Once she sang Maria in *West Side Story*—you know, one of them spics. I take care of her."

Take care of yourself, I hear myself say. And I mean it. He takes umbrage. I say, stupidly (but because I'm feeling protective—*protective*—of Johnny G., whom I can't hate): "Why don't you take a screen test and do your fighting in the movies?" (Because some day, Johnny G., a victim with a heart full of murder and a face like an angel's, is going to kill or get killed.) His chest swells. "You gotta be crazy. You think I could *be* somebody?"

I go home and read the Principal's Message in my high school senior yearbook, Class of '52 (Arnie Goldfedder and Anne Bosco, Most Likely to Succeed, where are you now?).

". . . in America, the future belongs to you. That is the way it has always been. That is America's promise to you. The dreams you dream, the hopes you have for yourself and for others, will be realized. . . . They will be yours if you want them hard enough and if you think, work, and plan for them. This kind of fulfillment has come to millions of young Americans before you. It will be yours, too."

Tell it to Bensonhurst.

SUBURBS

Geoffrey O'Brien

Geoffrey O'Brien is a poet whose essays on poetry, fiction, and film appear regularly in the *New York Review of Books* and the *Village Voice.* His nonfiction books include *Hard-boiled America, Dream Time: Chapters from the Sixties* (1988), and *A Book of Maps* (1989).

ONCE UPON A TIME IN THE SUBURBS THE NINE-YEAR-OLDS STOOD on the playground talking about Hiroshima. As their ice cream dripped on the asphalt they felt their way toward the enormous structures of the grown-up world. Like little adults, they huddled together exchanging serious information. The acrid fumes of a cap pistol were incense to evoke visions of blood and battle smoke and armored battalions.

"My daddy fought in Germany in the war." "My uncle has a Japanese sword." A torn flag or the loading clip from a Luger were relics of a chaos outside the playground and its blue sky. The choas had been the world. It happened just before their memories began. On long sheets of brown paper they crayoned their imaginations of it: red and orange and yellow bursts of flame.

To their senses the school building and the driveway and the network of

170

suburban lanes had always existed. In that unwobbling geography of rectangular lawns and sliding picture windows the seasons revolved on schedule. The death of summer was calmly succeeded by Halloween, Thanksgiving, and Christmas.

In the classroom they sat through film strips of hungry faces and diseased bodies. These were the people of other lands. The teacher once wrote on the blackboard the word *refugee* and asked: Does anybody know what this means? Is the corridor it turned out that somebody's mother had been a refugee once, in Vienna, in the other world.

Among the boys on the playground—for pleasure, to educate one another, out of a sense of the fitness of things—an oral epic came into being, incorporating garbled fragments of Munich and Pearl Harbor and Stalingrad, of Rommel forced to suicide and Mussolini strung up in an Italian square. This was History, like in the *Landmark Book of Alexander the Great,* the *Golden Stamp Album of Napoleon,* or Jimmy Stewart in *The F.B.I. Story.* Everything was part of History. They would grow up to be part of it, too. It was something that happened in public, a kind of display. It was big and final. It had something to do with the awesome sleek shapes that filled the skies of *Strategic Air Command* or the arsenal of missiles poised to launch at the slightest tremor of the DEW-Line. They had seen the four-color diagrams in Junior Scholastic. Somewhere down at the end of every road of thought were the brave blue jets lined up on the runway for eventual takeoff toward dimly imagined Soviet mountains.

And that was called World War Three. It would happen, unquestionably. The label itself ordained it, because where there is a one and a two there must be a three, for completion. A child's logic is invincible.

They lived in a civilization that brought them things. They could count on a new crop of toys each Christmas, always a little more technologically advanced than last year's models: tin robots that spoke and walked, plastic rockets with a range of up to thirty feet. New television programs were provided each September to set the tone for that autumn's play, whether the props were Davy Crockett hats or Zorro capes or a rifle like Chuck Connors used. Life was to be a succession of surprise presents from the entertainment companies. With the same regularity that the world produced new snow, new tulips, or new calendar years, there would always be new games, new dress-up disguises, new launchers, and new wired tracks; new jokes, new adventure stories, exciting new designs on packages of bubble gum.

Life in the future was going to be fun, and American kids were going to have the most fun of all. There would be telephones with picture screens. People would live on the moon under bubble domes. Electronic ramps would glide noiselessly into vast silos. Everything would be shiny and in bright colors.

The future had a style all its own. That style was foreshadowed by the glassy houses that were coming to birth around them, new gleaming homes emerging out of empty lots with their disorder of thickets and vines, out of leftover chunks of forest littered with wire and rusted cans and torn bedding. The last tangled corners were annihilated. Dawn rose on leveled ground that was now a hard-edged lawn of unvarying green, in whose exact center a clean and seamless structure had poked up.

Older houses—the ones that still predominated—were elaborate forms full of hiding places. Darkness gathered in their winding corridors and tall cupboards, basement labryinths and tiny dormer-windowed attics. But in the new houses light was everywhere. It streamed across the patio, glistened on the chlorinated water of the aquamarine pool, lit up every corner of the airy living room. All the heavy furniture of the old architecture, the armory of plasterwork and banisters, had been flattened out and translated into broad sweeps of color, empty spaces of undefined function, rooms that seemed to open into one another. Here there was nothing to be afraid of. It was a bright world of light and space and calm water.

In the world of the old houses, no space was free of some reminder of its use. You always had to think about what you were supposed to do. But in the new houses there was space which you could make into whatever you wanted it to be. There were wide areas where you could roll back and forth and around. On the walls there were paintings that were not pictures of anything. If the old houses seemed repositories of secrets, the new houses were glass-bottomed boats in which the distinction between inside and outside began to blur. People wore swimsuits all summer and slung towels across the armless couch. When they bathed, sunlight enveloped them.

There was a succession of big green lawns. And in the sky above them hung the little dots that were Mars and Jupiter and points beyond. Space: and how passionately they longed (aged seven and nine and eleven) to go there. Somewhere out in the grown-up world the launching pads were being readied. In their lifetime men would walk on Mars. They could hardly wait.

First of all there will be the weightlessness, the ability to float within the capsule. The space vehicle's snug dimensions somehow contain freedom. Matter is lighter and you almost move beyond the body. In here you have all you need: a book to look at, a floating jug of space drink, an earphone through which distant earth sounds are piped. Out there, on the other side of the porthole, is infinite nothingness.

Stretching their minds to try to encompass the notion of "light-year," an odd thrill shot through them. Lying in bed, they could almost imagine the lone astronaut's consciousness, enduring that nothingness—ten years, twenty years of nothingness—waiting for the rings of Saturn, or for the mouth of the time warp that would carry him into the heart of the Andromeda Galaxy.

The mere thought of intergalactic spaces could create a sensation of swimming through air. Behind closed eyelids, patterns of revolving light emerged from a black background, transforming themselves endlessly. That was a kind of sky, too. But if that was a sky, then what was the earth of that sky? It was too difficult. It was something to ask your father about in the morning, if you could remember to. Is it true that that place exists? Is it true you can be someplace else just by thinking about being someplace else? It almost seemed you could be everywhere at the same time. But then you wouldn't really exist, would you?

It was fun, it was very exciting, to have thoughts like that. Even if it was a little scary, too. You would go back to those thoughts, if you could, and feel grateful for wherever it was they were coming from.

To be able to sneak out of your own body like that was like the freedom of Aquaman to breathe underwater or of John Jones (Jahnn Jonzz), Manhunter from Mars, to become invisible or assume someone else's form. In storybooks people were always stretching and shrinking, sliding through keyholes, or finding a door hidden under a hedge and opening it and walking down the steps until the boat was reached, and the sea under the land, and the other land on the far shore of the sea.

The storybook world—an environment of water, marshland, meadow, forest, mountain—was perfect. Everything was inside it. It knew (there was a knowledge in its center) how to have the right thing happen at every turning of the road, as the ragged soldier or starving animal or terrified child moved forward into unknown land. An old woman with a tinderbox materialized because she *had* to.

Because there is a danger, insurmountable, the horror of every storybook. Death, at the hands of ogres or by imperial edict, has already been ordained. The reader of the story is a prisoner of the same law. And yet (and this is a miracle, the one and only miracle) the horror is deception, after all. Hidden in nature there is a formula, an herb, a magic packet that will dissolve it. The old woman knows. And in the end it will seem as if the only reason the giants or the bad king existed was to allow this magic packet to come into play. The world of tests and risks has been an opportunity for a charm to fulfill its role, by revealing the illusory nature of all that threatens.

In the morning of the magical act, the hero's eyes are washed clean. The real world begins: the never-to-be-chronicled eternity of his marriage to the princess.

But this, no matter how real, was not what happened now, although it had happened once and would surely somehow happen again. What happened now was more history all the time: a gangster shot dead in a barbershop, a boy's body chopped up and distributed among various suitcases, an airplane crashing into a city.

A radio voice told the time with urgency. They had never heard anybody talk like that. No matter what he said, the news man (they saw him with black mustache, gaunt cheeks, serious piercing eyes) was saying something important: this *happened*. It happened in a way that was different from the noise the crickets made outside the house. Different from the bucket of paint that was knocked over one day. It happened not just in one place but in every place, at once. It was something above them, outside them, bigger than them, happening in unseen rooms full of machines clicking.

The room with the television, after the television came, was big, and what was beyond its window—thick branches, spots of sky, sloping grassy hill—was much bigger even. As the light faded, the outside slipped away and the glowing screen in the corner became more definite and dominating. The whole room fell into darkness and the burning light inside the television silhouetted the black-and-white figures moving on the screen. The figures did not become rounder or take on color. It was more as if the room gradually got flat and monochrome.

The television was an open funnel, with its other end stuck in the middle of everything. Dots and sounds were feeding through it. One day the dots reassembled to become a newsreel of Portland, Oregon. The piercing sound was the red alert signaling the evacuation of the city. The prolonged siren had an invading effect even on television. Civil defense teams commandeered vehicles and frightened crowds pressed past the bank and the diner and the bus depot toward the city limits. That they were more of the fuzzy washed-out television figures gave them the raw appearance of being there.

At the bottom of the screen a white word flashed: SIMULATION. It flashed as they crowded the air-raid shelters and again when Portland went up in a thermonuclear cloud at the end of the program. A voice explained that it had been a necessary dramatization. The cloud at least was real, borrowed from one of the images they had already seen so many times, in a 1945 photograph or a spread in *Life* about Bikini Atoll. Later some footage from a testing ground in Utah would be spliced into the opening moments of a low-budget monster movie, where it functioned as a device to get the plot moving. It was not difficult to be aware of the Atomic Age. Everybody got the word sooner or later.

Important things usually weren't said out loud. Out loud was for the ordinary acts of passing a fork or talking about the bank or reciting a television joke. There was no tone of voice that could carry a large thing like the shape of the world. It came out as a squeak.

But things that were never said were sometimes written down in obscure places. The end of the world was announced in red letters in a four-page tract found tucked between bus seats. Line drawings of expressionless people— father, mother, child, businessman, farmer, soldier—were slotted in between prophecies in bold italics. This whisper of catastrophe came from some scary sect outside the community. It could certainly not have come from the cozy well-appointed nondenominational church by the shopping plaza, whose most extreme pamphlets tended to deal with the sexual conduct of teenagers and how to control it. Apocalypse, for that tastefully attired congregation, was precisely a pale-lipped woman in black—maybe she lived across the highway, near the truck stop, in a barely furnished shanty—thrusting the literature of terror through a suburban doorway.

There has to be, in response, a literature of comfort where you can go, whose words would affirm as durable the sunlight sweeping across hedge and patio. But the heaviest fears are sown by words that mean to reassure. The cherry red, white, and blue of a Bantam paperback called *How to Survive an Atomic Bomb* told you it was there to help you: "This fact-filled, easy-to-read book . . . will tell you how to protect yourself and your family in case of atomic attack. There is no 'scare talk' in this book. Reading it will actually make you *feel better.*"

It was the tone of the doctor or dentist on the verge of inflicting pain, trying to still the patient's jerking muscles. And it never did work, no matter how calm or sonorous his voice. "There is one fact [the spokesman for the National Security Resources Board was speaking] you *must remember*—and it definitely is a *fact.* Not one person in Hiroshima or Nagasaki was killed or injured by lingering radioactivity. That is a *fact.*" Thus italicized, the word "fact" itself became ominous, as if an anguished voice were screaming "Why won't you believe me?" like the witness in a Perry Mason show who always turned out to be guilty.

At school they were periodically marched into the hall, lined up, and in-structed to lie down until the all clear sounded, exactly the way it said in that Bantam book: "Lie down full length on your stomach. . . . *That's the single most important safety rule in this whole book. . . . Everyone must always lie down full-length on his stomach with his face buried in his arms.* (Right now is the best time to practice this. Get off in your own room where you won't be laughed at and try it a few times.)" Some of the neighbors were starting to dig survival shelters in their backyards, little underground playhouses full of canned food and rifles. The rifles were for shooting the other neighbors who hadn't been smart enough to build one. The nuclear family would gather around the shortwave radio and wait. There would still be house chores to be done, and some schoolbooks so they wouldn't fall too far behind in their studies.

By now they knew that the pamphlets lied. The orderly typesetting, the stolid blocks of questions and answers were a screen to keep things from slipping through. There were so many other, more generous sources of information to fill them in on the other side of the screen. Rod Serling knew a lot more than President Eisenhower. "The Twilight Zone" was a weekly bulletin of the new, updating the earlier data of *Five* (1951), *The Day the World Ended* (1956), *World Without End* (1956), *The World, the Flesh and the Devil* (1959), or *On the Beach* (1959). If you liked to read, there were all the science fiction novels that explained things, the stories of Ray Bradbury, and the adaptations of those stories for E.C. Comics. There were even jokes about the atom bomb in *Mad,* a gallows humor commenting on its own ghastliness: "The last example of this nauseating, busted-crutch type humor is to show an atom-bomb explosion! However, this routine, we feel, is giving way to the even more hilarious picture of the hydrogen bomb!"

The jittery aftertaste of that joke clarified. It was a splinter driven through the carefully measured prose on the back of some Mentor book about Man and His Destiny. In the world of serious thought—they were just about old enough to have gotten to the edges of it—Man was always approaching the crossroads, or evaluating the long road he had traveled, or weighing his future in the balance. It never sounded so bad, especially since Man had done such remarkable things in the past. He had forged myths and symbols to express his relationship to the cosmos. He had made tools that had gotten ever more complex. He had expanded the boundaries of his mind and created a coherent body of scientific knowledge. He had written encyclopedias and dictionaries and the Great Books of the Western World, and now they were all being put on microfilm to make room for more. This Man was quite a serious character, serious enough to have invented *The Saturday Review* and *The New York Times* and long shelves of impenetrable technical journals. He was bound to find a way to squeeze out of this present dilemma. Edward R. Murrow or Albert Schweitzer or Pablo Casals would come up with something. And there would be a moment of silence at the United Nations, and then a resounding organ chorale, while sunlight streamed through the modernistic stained glass. And everywhere children of all races would gather in a ring and beam.

But in the night, lights out, Hitler and Al Capone crept up and hit Albert Schweitzer over the head. Furies were uncorked until the redeeming words of the generalizers snapped shut and ceased to exist as anything but black marks on white paper. The bed was solid and finite. It was located in a particular place. The weight of the body itself made the body shudder in the dark. The thought that "it's all *real,* throat and veins and iris," heaved up out of something that seemed to know something. As if there were a spaceman inside you.

A spaceman posted there to listen in, to gather data. A spaceman who had learned to glide through the interstices of time and space, probing for fault lines. In the remote galaxy of the coolly intelligent immortals, was an alarm going off?

At least this much was clear (who was thinking this?). The world has opened up. All the hidden caves and mountains and secret valleys are staked out, exposed. The warm dark places toward which one would have crawled, into which a whole nation of silent fugitives (guided by a rainbow or an oracle) would have crept hauling baskets and infants, are turned inside out. To be here is to be a target. Why walk into the house? Why go to the basement?

The machines have really taken over. It has already happened. Whatever horizon once existed already recoils on itself. The places constrict. Future time falters and recedes. An odor of metal interpenetrates the air molecules.

A man (they were twelve now) must have been born to do something. There must have been a book in which these things were written down. All the events, every single one, happened as though they had already been completed from the start, the way the whole tulip was in the bulb.

The tulip was in the bulb and the bulb was in the tulip and it went on like that forever. Except it didn't. It ended brutally and there was nothing. By accident.

Like a joke. By not fitting in, a joke momentarily interrupted the world. That was what made it funny. But after the joke you recognized it was a joke and went back to the integral world that the joke broke. But what if it never came back again, and the little gap stayed there and became everything?

They didn't know and they would never know. You would have to be a spaceman to know something like that. A spaceman had a different type of mind that could contain everything. It could even contain more than everything. And a spaceman didn't even have to try: that was important. A spaceman was calm and had a faintly sardonic smile, like Basil Rathbone playing Sherlock Holmes. A spaceman might be kind, but in an offhand way as if he were humoring you. Talking to you like a kid, with your trivial concept of what was real and what wasn't.

And he is not a man, really, even if he looks like Michael Rennie in *The Day the Earth Stood Still*, the benign superintelligence Klaatu with weathered face and penetrant eyes. His body itself is perhaps a force field adapting itself to human concepts. He projects images because that is all the earthlings understand. His harshness and kindness are merely ploys to manipulate the humans' behavior.

He doesn't really care about people. If they had continued to die quietly, nothing would have stirred him from his corner of the universe.

He cares only about balance. The whole thing is kept together by the balance of its parts. That's what he loves, that little oscillation when all the fields of gravity are hanging right. He can detect the smallest slackening of tension. And having detected it, he must once again ride out in the tiresome saucer, to zero in on the source of the imbalance. He had been so happy doing nothing at all. Being nothing at all, and humming at the same time. Converting energy to matter and matter to energy, back and forth, inside himself, forever. And loving it!

They had remembered all that, or invented it. It had begun to get dark. Sitting on the rug with the television glowing (the sound turned off) they had begun to forget names and years. A marble glittered at the foot of the couch by the drape, like a moon of Neptune. Now the table lamp clicked on and they were back. There was still some twilight out in the yard, enough to play by. It was a new cycle, a quicker cycle. They ran out and raced around on the grass until supper.

SILENT DANCING

Judith Ortiz Cofer

Judith Ortiz Cofer was born in Puerto Rico and came to the United States at the age of three. She is the author of seven books of poetry, including *Latin Women Pray* (1980) and *The Line of the Sun* (1989). Her personal essays have been collected in the volume *Silent Dancing: A Partial Remembrance of a Puerto Rican Childhood* (1989), from which the following essay is taken.

We have a home movie of this party. Several times my mother and I have watched it together, and I have asked questions about the silent revelers coming in and out of focus. It is grainy and of short duration, but it's a great visual aid to my memory of life at that time. And it is in color—the only complete scene in color I can recall from those years.

WE LIVED IN PUERTO RICO UNTIL MY BROTHER WAS BORN IN 1954. Soon after, because of economic pressures on our growing family, my father joined the United States Navy. He was assigned to duty on a ship in Brooklyn Yard—a place of cement and steel that was to be his home base in the States until his retirement more than twenty years later. He left the Island first, alone,

179

going to New York City and tracking down his uncle who lived with his family across the Hudson River in Paterson, New Jersey. There my father found a tiny apartment in a huge tenement that had once housed Jewish families but was just being taken over and transformed by Puerto Ricans, overflowing from New York City. In 1955 he sent for us. My mother was only twenty years old, I was not quite three, and my brother was a toddler when we arrived at El Building, as the place had been christened by its newest residents.

My memories of life in Paterson during those first few years are all in shades of gray. Maybe I was too young to absorb vivid colors and details, or to discriminate between the slate blue of the winter sky and the darker hues of the snow-bearing clouds, but that single color washes over the whole period. The building we lived in was gray, as were the streets, filled with slush the first few months of my life there. The coat my father had bought for me was similar in color and too big; it sat heavily on my thin frame.

I do remember the way the heater pipes banged and rattled, startling all of us out of sleep until we got so used to the sound that we automatically shut it out or raised our voices above the racket. The hiss from the valve punctuated my sleep (which has always been fitful) like a nonhuman presence in the room—a dragon sleeping at the entrance of my childhood. But the pipes were also a connection to all the other lives being lived around us. Having come from a house designed for a single family back in Puerto Rico—my mother's extended-family home—it was curious to know that strangers lived under our floor and above our heads, and that the heater pipe went through everyone's apartment. (My first spanking in Paterson came as a result of playing tunes on the pipes in my room to see if there would be an answer.) My mother was as new to this concept of beehive life as I was, but she had been given strict orders by my father to keep the doors locked, the noise down, ourselves to ourselves.

It seems that Father had learned some painful lessons about prejudice while searching for an apartment in Paterson. Not until years later did I hear how much resistance he had encountered with landlords who were panicking at the influx of Latinos into a neighborhood that had been Jewish for a couple of generations. It made no difference that it was the American phenomenon of ethnic turnover which was changing the urban core of Paterson, and that the human flood could not be held back with an accusing finger.

"You Cuban?" one man had asked my father, pointing at his name tag on the navy uniform—even though my father had the fair skin and light brown hair of his northern Spanish background, and the name Ortiz is as common in Puerto Rico as Johnson is in the United States.

"No," my father had answered, looking past the finger into his adversary's angry eyes. "I'm Puerto Rican."

SILENT DANCING

"Same shit." And the door closed.

My father could have passed as European, but we couldn't. My brother and I both have our mother's black hair and olive skin, and so we lived in El Building and visited our great-uncle and his fair children on the next block. It was their private joke that they were the German branch of the family. Not many years later that area too would be mainly Puerto Rican. It was as if the heart of the city map were being gradually colored brown—*café con leche* brown. Our color.

The movie opens with a sweep of the living room. It is "typical" immigrant Puerto Rican decor for the time: the sofa and chairs are square and hard-looking, uphol-stered in bright colors (blue and yellow in this instance) and covered with the transparent plastic that furniture salesmen then were so adept at convincing women to buy. The linoleum on the floor is light blue; where it had been subjected to spike heels, as it was in most places, there were dime-size indentations all over it that cannot be seen in this movie. The room is full of people dressed up: dark suits for the men, red dresses for the women. When I have asked my mother why most of the women are in red that night, she has shrugged and said, "I don't remember. Just a coincidence." She doesn't have my obsession for assigning sym-bolism to everything.

The three women in red sitting on the couch are my mother, my eighteen-year-old cousin, and her brother's girlfriend. The novia *is just up from the Island, which is apparent in her body language. She sits up formally, her dress pulled over her knees. She is a pretty girl, but her posture makes her look insecure, lost in her full-skirted dress, which she has carefully tucked around her to make room for my gorgeous cousin, her future sister-in-law. My cousin has grown up in Paterson and is in her last year of high school. She doesn't have a trace of what Puerto Ricans call* la mancha *(literally, the stain: the mark of the new immigrant—something about the posture, the voice, or the humble demeanor that makes it obvious to everyone the person has just arrived on the mainland). My cousin is wearing a tight, sequined cocktail dress. Her brown hair has been lightened with peroxide around the bangs, and she is holding a cigarette expertly between her fingers, bringing it up to her mouth in a sensuous arc of her arm as she talks animatedly. My mother, who has come up to sit between the two women, both only a few years younger than herself, is somewhere between the poles they represent in our culture.*

It became my father's obsession to get out of the barrio, and thus we were never permitted to form bonds with the place or with the people who lived there. Yet El Building was a comfort to my mother, who never got over yearning for *la isla*. She felt surrounded by her language: the walls were thin, and voices speaking and arguing in Spanish could be heard all day. *Salsas* blasted out of radios, turned on early in the morning and left on for company. Women seemed to cook rice and beans perpetually—the strong aroma of boiling red kidney beans permeated the hallways.

Though Father preferred that we do our grocery shopping at the supermarket when he came home on weekend leaves, my mother insisted that she could cook only with products whose labels she could read. Consequently, during the week I accompanied her and my little brother to La Bodega—a hole-in-the-wall grocery store across the street from El Building. There we squeezed down three narrow aisles jammed with various products. Goya and Libby's—those were the trademarks that were trusted by her *mamá,* so my mother bought many cans of Goya beans, soups, and condiments, as well as little cans of Libby's fruit juices for us. And she also bought Colgate toothpaste and Palmolive soap. (The final *e* is pronounced in both these products in Spanish, so for many years I believed that they were manufactured on the Island. I remember my surprise at first hearing a commercial on television in which "Colgate" rhymed with "ate.") We always lingered at La Bodega, for it was there that Mother breathed best, talking in the familiar aromas of the foods she knew from Mamá's kitchen. It was also there that she got to speak to the other women of El Building without violating outright Father's dictates against fraternizing with our neighbors.

Yet Father did his best to make our "assimilation" painless. I can still see him carrying a real Christmas tree up several flights of stairs to our apartment, leaving a trail of aromatic pine. He carried it formally, as if it were a flag in a parade. We were the only ones in El Building that I knew of who got presents on both Christmas and *día de Reyes,* the day when the Three Kings brought gifts to Christ and to Hispanic children.

Our supreme luxury in El Building was having our own television set. It must have been a result of Father's guilt feelings over the isolation he had imposed on us, but we were among the first in the barrio to have one. My brother quickly became an avid watcher of Captain Kangaroo and Jungle Jim, while I loved all the series showing families. By the time I started first grade, I could have drawn a map of Middle America as exemplified by the lives of characters in *Father Knows Best, The Donna Reed Show, Leave It to Beaver, My Three Sons,* and (my favorite) *Bachelor Father,* where John Forsythe treated his adopted teenage daughter like a princess because he was rich and had a Chinese houseboy to do everything for him. In truth, compared to our neighbors in El Building, *we* were rich. My father's navy check provided us with financial security and a standard of living that the factory workers envied. The only thing his money could not buy us was a place to live away from the barrio—his greatest wish, Mother's greatest fear.

·   ·   ·

SILENT DANCING

In the home movie the men are shown next, sitting around a card table set up in one corner of the living room, playing dominoes. The clack of the ivory pieces was a familiar sound. I heard it in many houses on the Island and in many apartments in Paterson. In Leave It to Beaver, *the Cleavers played bridge in every other episode; in my childhood, the men started every social occasion with a hotly debated round of dominoes. The women would sit around and watch, but they never participated in the games.*

Here and there you can see a small child. Children were always brought to parties and, whenever they got sleepy, were put to bed in the host's bedroom. Babysitting was a concept unrecognized by the Puerto Rican women I knew: a responsible mother did not leave her children with any stranger. And in a culture where children are not considered intrusive, there was no need to leave the children at home. We went where our mothers went.

Of my preschool years I have only impressions: the sharp bite of the wind in December as we walked with our parents toward the brightly lit stores downtown; how I felt like a stuffed doll in my heavy coat, boots, and mittens; how good it was to walk into the five-and-dime and sit at the counter drinking hot chocolate. On Saturdays our whole family would walk downtown to shop at the big department stores on Broadway. Mother bought all our clothes at Penney's and Sears, and she liked to buy her dresses at the women's specialty shops like Lerner's and Diana's. At some point we'd go into Woolworth's and sit at the soda fountain to eat.

We never ran into other Latinos at these stores or when eating out, and it became clear to me only years later that the women from El Building shopped mainly in other places—stores owned by other Puerto Ricans or by Jewish merchants who had philosophically accepted our presence in the city and decided to make us their good customers, if not real neighbors and friends. These establishments were located not downtown but in the blocks around our street, and they were referred to generically as La Tienda, El Bazar, La Bodega, La Botánica. Everyone knew what was meant. These were the stores where your face did not turn a clerk to stone, where your money was as green as anyone else's.

One New Year's Eve we were dressed up like child models in the Sears catalogue: my brother in a miniature man's suit and bow tie, and I in black patent-leather shoes and a frilly dress with several layers of crinoline underneath. My mother wore a bright red dress that night, I remember, and spike heels; her long black hair hung to her waist. Father, who usually wore his navy uniform during his short visits home, had put on a dark civilian suit for the occasion: we had been invited to his uncle's house for a big celebration. Everyone was excited because my mother's brother Hernan—a bachelor who could indulge himself with luxuries—had bought a home movie camera, which he would be trying out that night.

Even the home movie cannot fill in the sensory details such a gathering left imprinted in a child's brain. The thick sweetness of women's perfumes mixing with the ever-present smells of food cooking in the kitchen: meat and plantain *pasteles,* as well as the ubiquitous rice dish made special with pigeon peas— *gandules*—and seasoned with precious *sofrito*— sent up from the Island by somebody's mother or smuggled in by a recent traveler. *Sofrito* was one of the items that women hoarded, since it was hardly ever in stock at La Bodega. It was the flavor of the Puerto Rico.

The men drank Palo Viejo rum, and some of the younger ones got weepy. The first time I saw a grown man cry was at a New Year's Eve party: he had been reminded of his mother by the smells in the kitchen. But what I remember most were the boiled *pasteles,* plaintain or yucca rectangles stuffed with corned beef or other meats, olives, and many other savory ingredients, all wrapped in banana leaves. Everybody had to fish one out with a fork. There was always a "trick" *pastel*—one without stuffing—and whoever got that one was the "New Year's Fool."

There was also the music. Long-playing albums were treated like precious china in these homes. Mexican recordings were popular, but the songs that brought tears to my mother's eyes were sung by the melancholy Daniel Santos, whose life as a drug addict was the stuff of legend. Felipe Rodríguez was a particular favorite of couples, since he sang about faithless women and broken-hearted men. There is a snatch of one lyric that has stuck in my mind like a needle on a worn groove: *De piedra ha de ser mi cama, de piedra la cabezera . . . la mujer que a mi me quiera . . . ha de quererme de veras. Ay, Ay, Ay, corazón, porque no amas . . .* I must have heard it a thousand times since the idea of a bed made of stone, and its connection to love, first troubled me with its disturbing images.

The five-minute home movie ends with people dancing in a circle—the creative filmmaker must have set it up, so that all of them could file past him. It is both comical and sad to watch silent dancing. Since there is no justification for the absurd movements that music provides for some of us, people appear frantic, their faces embarrassingly intense. It's as if you were watching sex. Yet for years, I've had dreams in the form of this home movie. In a recurring scene, familiar faces push themselves forward into my mind's eye, plastering their features into distorted close-ups. And I'm asking them: "Who is *she?* Who is the old woman I don't recognize? Is she an aunt? Somebody's wife? Tell me who she is."

SILENT DANCING

"See the beauty mark on her cheek as big as a hill on the lunar landscape of her face—well, that runs in the family. The women on your father's side of the family wrinkle early; it's the price they pay for that fair skin. The young girl with the green stain on her wedding dress is *la novia*—just up from the Island. See, she lowers her eyes when she approaches the camera, as she's supposed to. Decent girls never look at you directly in the face. *Humilde,* humble, a girl should express humility in all her actions. She will make a good wife for your cousin. He should consider himself lucky to have met her only weeks after she arrived here. If he marries her quickly, she will make him a good Puerto Rican-style wife; but if he waits too long, she will be corrupted by the city, just like your cousin there."

"She means me. I do what I want. This is not some primitive island I live on. Do they expect me to wear a black mantilla on my head and go to mass every day? Not me. I'm an American woman, and I will do as I please. I can type faster than anyone in my senior class at Central High, and I'm going to be a secretary to a lawyer when I graduate. I can pass for an American girl anywhere—I've tried it. At least for Italian, anyway—I never speak Spanish in public. I hate these parties, but I wanted the dress. I look better than any of these *humildes* here. *My* life is going to be different. I have an American boyfriend. He is older and has a car. My parents don't know it, but I sneak out of the house late at night sometimes to be with him. If I marry him, even my name will be American. I hate rice and beans—that's what makes these women fat."

"Your *prima* is pregnant by that man she's been sneaking around with. Would I lie to you? I'm your *tiá política,* your great-uncle's common-law wife—the one he abandoned on the Island to go marry your cousin's mother. *I* was not invited to this party, of course, but I came anyway. I came to tell you that story about your cousin that you've always wanted to hear. Do you remember the comment your mother made to a neighbor that has always haunted you? The only thing you heard was your cousin's name, and then you saw your mother pick up your doll from the couch and say: 'It was as big as this doll when they flushed it down the toilet.' This image has bothered you for years, hasn't it? You had nightmares about babies being flushed down the toilet, and you wondered why anyone would do such a terrible thing. You didn't dare ask your mother about it. She would only tell you that you had not heard her right, and yell at you for listening to adult conversations. But later, when you were old enough to know about abortions, you suspected.

"I am here to tell you that you were right. Your cousin was growing an *americanito* in her belly when this movie was made. Soon after, she put something long and pointy into her pretty self, thinking maybe she could get rid of the problems before breakfast and still make it to her first class at the high school. Well, *niña,* her screams could be heard downtown. Your aunt, her *mamá,* who had been a midwife on the Island, managed to pull the little thing out. Yes, they probably flushed it down the toilet. What else could they do with it—give it a Christian burial in a little white casket with blue bows and ribbons? Nobody wanted that baby—least of all the father, a teacher at her school with a house in West Paterson that he was filling with real children, and a wife who was a natural blonde.

"Girl, the scandal sent your uncle back to the bottle. And guess where your cousin ended up? Irony of ironies. She was sent to a village in Puerto Rico to live with a relative on her mother's side: a place so far away from civilization that you have to ride a mule to reach it. A real change in scenery. She found a man there—women like that cannot live without male company—but believe me, the men in Puerto Rico know how to put a saddle on a woman like her. *La gringa,* they call her. Ha, ha, ha. *La gringa* is what she always wanted to be . . ."

The old woman's mouth becomes a cavernous black hole I fall into. And as I fall, I can feel the reverberations of her laughter. I hear the echoes of her last mocking words: *la gringa, la gringa!* And the conga line keeps moving silently past me. There is no music in my dream for the dancers.

When Odysseus visits Hades to see the spirit of his mother, he makes an offering of sacrificial blood, but since all the souls crave an audience with the living, he has to listen to many of them before he can ask questions. I, too, have to hear the dead and the forgotten speak in my dream. Those who are still part of my life remain silent, going around and around in their dance. The others keep pressing their faces forward to say things about the past.

My father's uncle is last in line. He is dying of alcoholism, shrunken and shriveled like a monkey, his face a mass of wrinkles and broken arteries. As he comes closer I realize that in his features I can see my whole family. If you were to stretch that rubbery flesh, you could find my father's face, and deep within *that* face—my own. I don't want to look into those eyes ringed in purple. In a few years he will retreat into silence, and take a long, long time to die. *Move back, Tío,* I tell him. *I don't want to hear what you have to say. Give the dancers room to move. Soon it will be midnight. Who is the New Year's Fool this time?*

LOVE ME OR LEAVE ME

Bharati Mukherjee

Bharati Mukherjee was born in Calcutta and earned graduate and postgraduate degrees in English in India before enrolling at the University of Iowa Writing Workshop. She has lived in the United States since 1980. Her novels include *The Tiger's Daughter* (1972), *Wife* (1975), and *Jasmine* (1989). Mukherjee has also written two collections of short stories, *Darkness* (1985) and *The Middleman and Other Stories* (1988), which won the National Book Critics Circle Award. With her husband, Clark Blaise, she is the co-author of two nonfiction books, *Days and Nights in Calcutta* (1977) and *The Sorrow and the Terror: The Haunting Legacy of the Air India Tragedy* (1987).

I FIRST SAW AMERICA WHEN I WAS TWENTY. OUTDOORS, EVEN IN New York City, the air must have been lambent with summertime the day that my seventeen-year-old sister and I flew into Idlewild, but inside the terminal, waiting in a long, nervous line of foreign students and tourists to be questioned by suspicious Immigration and Naturalization Service officials, the light felt interrogation-harsh.

"Let's go back home," my sister said. She was a veteran shuttler betwen India and the United States, having already put in a fall semester as a sophomore at Vassar College, and having rushed back, homesick, at Christmas.

We didn't turn around and get on an Air India plane that summer afternoon because we didn't want to disappoint our father. Coming to school in the States had been his idea, not ours. We stayed in line and had our visas and chest X-rays checked by an official who was amused that I was headed for the University of Iowa.

"Know how to find Iowa on the map?" the man asked me. And when I lied, yes, he laughed, "Hell, I don't," and wished me good luck.

My sister got homesick again that winter, desperately enough to be sent back to India.

"It must be hard for you, too," my father wrote in each of his thrice-weekly letters. "But be brave. And before you know it, the program will be over." Meanwhile, he was interviewing Bengali Brahmin bachelors in order to find me the perfect groom.

The truth, which I couldn't share with my family, was that I was happier in Iowa City than in Calcutta. It was that time in my life when every song and film about love seemed to speak directly to me. I fell in love with, and married, a man who happened to be an American citizen, and scrapped all plans for ever going back to live in India.

If I had gone to graduate school in Paris or London, I might just as easily have fallen in love with a Frenchman or a Briton and made my life over very differently than I have in America. But in my family, my father, a very successful businessman, a devout Brahmin, and a benevolent patriarch who made all decisions, was also a contradictory man. He had no son; thus his financial empire could not be passed on. He wanted education and independence for his three daughters. (When would-be husbands later demanded dowries, he answered, "My daughters are all educated women. That is worth more than all the gold I could give them.") He was a progressive man in a traditional context; he saw in Doris Day an empowered woman.

He sent us to America, a country he himself had not seen, instead of to Europe, where he had been a happy graduate student, because he was in love with the world of Doris Day and all MGM musicals. He never spoke of "the United States." It was always "America." To him America was a realistic-looking facade on an MGM backlot, where fantasies about young women achieving fulfillment and power could be acted out as they couldn't in tradition-bound Calcutta.

My father never missed Doris Day at the Metro Cinema on Chowringhee Avenue. He would call my sisters and me from his office on Thursdays—which was our day off from school, a neo-colonial establishment run by Irish nuns for Calcutta's most proper girls—to say that he had rearranged his schedule so that he could accompany us to the matinee show.

Though he savored every Doris Day film, even *Please Don't Eat the Daisies* and *Pillow Talk,* his favorite was *The Man Who Knew Too Much.* On jerky drives through the crowded city, in between yelling at the chauffeur to be more cautious and at the two bodyguards cramped in the back of our conspicuously large Dodge station wagon to be more alert for bomb-tossing, acid-splashing, communism-inspired thugs, he would sing "Que Será, Será." "What Will Be, Will Be" became for him more a mantra than a song; it synthesized a New World pleasure in risk taking with a fatalistic Hindu acceptance of disastrous outcomes.

The marvel that was my father's love for Doris Day will become clearer if I tell you that the neighborhoods we had to drive through to get from our home or from my father's pharmaceutical factory on the outskirts of the city to the Metro Cinema in midtown roiled with the fecund despair of the destitute and the permanently displaced. The Calcutta of the fifties—the Calcutta of my child-hood—should have been heady with post-Independence hope and vitality. Certainly politicians promised every Indian boom times. But what choked the streets was the human debris from famines and religious riots. Even an oversheltered, overprivileged child like me was toughened enough by Old World cynicism (which, in those days, I accepted as a synonym for wisdom) to cut through jingoistic nation-building slogans. Though at school the nuns assured us that prayer would quickly bring Mr. Stalin and his Calcutta admirers to their senses, we could see and smell the "blood-dimmed tide" surging at our horizon. In that transitional decade, when preparations to flee the city seemed cowardly and prayer little more than escapism, Doris Day was an abstraction for democracy. A person with gumption—any person, even a ten-cents-a-dance taxi dancer like Ruth Etting—could turn her grim life around. The handicaps of caste, class, and gender could be overcome.

Doris Day was a physical curiosity. I don't think I'd ever come across a woman so tall, so big. And in those days, the only blond hair I expected to see was the Technicolor-bright cap of it on her Cinemascope-sized head. Most en-forcers of the Raj—people who might have had natural or bleached yellow hair, British corporate executives and civil servants, for instance, the lighter-skinned Eurasians, even many of the Iraqi and Syrian Jews whom we'd thought of as "Europeans"—had left just before or just after 1947, when India became a sovereign nation. The bedtime stories my mother told me had been about teen-age Bengali freedom fighters rather than the traditional ones about gods fighting shape-changing demons.

I had thrilled to my mother's stories about schoolgirls raiding police arsenals or hiding pistols in dormitories. Fan worship of a British film star would have seemed to me treasonous regression. Doris Day, with her mighty shoulders and toothy smile, a woman who said exactly what was on her mind and said it in a nearly incomprehensible American accent with stereophonic loudness, was all right to love precisely because she was American. (In my neo-colonial school I had been forced to study British and European history, not the history of the United States and its various involvements, and so was slow to catch the ironies of undeclared imperialism.)

Brought up as I was to accept rather than to protest decisions made for me, Doris Day grew into an icon of spunk.

My father may have been in Europe on a business trip when *Love Me or Leave Me* finally came to Calcutta. Or perhaps he had seen the trailer for it the week before and decided that the Doris Day who sang "Que Será, Será"—*his* Doris Day—had to be kept separate from the gritty Doris Day who cocked a hip in a black sheath dress and burned the screen with "Ten Cents a Dance." Perhaps he saw the film on his own and decided that he had to protect us from the sex and sleaze it revealed about adult life just ahead. In any case, this was the only Doris Day film I didn't see or talk over with him.

Ten of us convent-school friends went to see it the evening our Overseas Cambridge School Leaving Certificate Examinations were over. I was fifteen. In three weeks I would start college as a sophomore. That I should be sneaking into my first "adults only" film that evening seemed deliciously symbolic.

I try not to think now how we must have appeared to the street people and beggars outside the Metro Cinema or how we might have appeared to Charles Vidor, the director, if he had seen us being chaperoned by servants from cars to the movie theater. We were ten adventurous but shockable young ladies dressed in our mothers' evening saris, with hair pinned up in elaborate chignons and smelling of sandalwood soap and jasmine. I remember I wore a peach-colored French chiffon sparkling with sequins.

I also remember that I walked into the theater (which always smelled of musty velvet drapes) expecting to be titillated, and that I walked out convinced I'd been uplifted.

What *could* I have discovered in a story about an obscure chorine in Chicago who meets a crooked nightclub owner and allows him to help her become a singing star even though it means denying or delaying true love? That the world was a rough place in which to be a poor woman with talent but without protection.

Early in the film, when Ruth Etting had to wear skimpy, spangled chorus-line costumes and put up with the teasing of less ambitious chorus girls ("Oh, I forgot. You're different. You're going places"), I identified with her totally. I, too, intended to go places, be somebody.

"You don't have to do a thing!" I mimicked her telling off Marty Snyder, played by James Cagney, my second-most-favorite screen villain. (James Mason was the first.) "I'll get it for myself!"

"It" was my own desire to be a writer and touch people with my novels.

I'd started my first novel at age nine and had published several first-person stories about Roman gladiators and Napoleon in local English-language magazines. But I was careful to hide from the nuns and from relatives and friends the forcefulness of my need for self-expression. They tolerated my "gift for the pen" (the mother superior's phrase) only because they regarded fiction writing as a womanly accomplishment, on a par with flower arranging or playing a musical instrument.

The Doris Day of *Love Me or Leave Me* sent me subliminal messages. When she pleaded with James Cagney to let her sing in bigger clubs in cities out of his reach, she pleaded for me. And when she begged, "I have to work. Don't you understand? I've got to. It's all I've got," I substituted "write" for "work." In Marty's admonition, "You're going to work here so you don't get so big," I heard my own community's censure of women who didn't accept their place.

Though my world was silken with privilege, I would have to choose, like Ruth Etting, between paralysis and ambition, between protection and pain.

My parents and the parents of my friends were nominally patrons of the arts in that they bought or were given tickets to events such as the premiere of Jean Renoir's *The River* (set in Bengal) or charity performances by the Moral Rearmament Society, but they knew no writers or filmmakers. They didn't attend screenings at the foreign-film club founded by Satyajit Ray. Like them, I hadn't heard of *film noir* at the time, and I certainly hadn't known of screenwriter Daniel Fuchs, let alone read his proletariat novels about Brooklyn Jews. I must have missed the neo-*noir* significance of the first shot of Marty "The Gimp" Snyder standing in shadow outside a garishly lit dance hall, lusting after a spirited blond goddess. I had to have missed the odd resonance of Marty's mumbled "Mazel tov!" as Ruth, "Chicago's Sweetheart," went off to give her first star performance. How could I have caught the ethnic ambiguity of Snyder as a last name? Or that Fuchs's Chicago was not that different from Brooklyn? What I did instead was to Bengalize Fuchs's Chicago-Brooklyn, just as I had, before the age of ten, Bengalized the alien societies of my favorite Tolstoy, Dostoyevsky, and Gorky novels.

I accepted, more readily perhaps than I should have, that Charles Vidor's film was about Ruth Etting. Ruth was its hero, Marty its villain. But even the huge and wholesome Doris Day couldn't quite sanitize her character's moral ambiguities. For a decade the nuns had forced on us an annual course titled "Moral Science" in which they presented right and wrong with absolute clarity. But there on the Metro Cinema screen (from which I learned more about the world outside than from the school-approved Victorian and Edwardian novels) was virtuous Doris Day assuring me through song that "I can be good, I can be bad/It all depends on you . . . ," that it was not at all unethical for the Woman as Artist to lie and cheat and use men on the way to stardom.

With one song she reduced the stern, solid truths of Moral Science to fictions. She guaranteed us women who fancied ourselves talented extraordinary absolution.

"I've tried it without help," she explains to Johnny, her piano-playing faithful admirer, as she breaks a date. "I didn't mind it being hard. I just minded that it didn't work." And off she goes for a night of salacious fun with corrupt and ill-mannered Marty, who can pack her shows with his applauding friends.

The nuns had taught us that what mattered was how we played the game and not whether we won or lost. And my Hindu parents had taught us that after the householder phase of material comforts and family devotions we must prepare for phases of self-abnegation. But Doris Day, the oracle of the silver screen, busted those old truths in one evening. The end justified the means.

Doris Day's Ruth Etting was a woman whose virtue was not assailed by her manipulativeness with men. (I think now that if Rita Hayworth had played the role I might have been totally unsettled by Etting's self-justifications; I didn't see a Rita Hayworth film until years later.) The trouble was that I couldn't stop worrying about the walk-on chorines, the fatigued women in soiled leotards and snagged stockings. They may have had more talent than Ruth, but they were less calculating. The first time Marty Snyder visited her in her dressing room, Ruth had pegged him as a powerful man and seized rather promptly his offer of protection. She'd rejected a lifetime of cheap pick-ups. She was, as Marty might say, a smart cookie.

I did believe her when she declared, "I'm not a tramp!" Marty was accustomed to picking up whores, not artists who were having to pay the bills with taxi dancing, women he could get his faithful buddy, Georgie, to throw back into mean streets with a tip or a pat on the rump. Her sense of self-worth had been established within the first few minutes of screen time; even as a starving rookie taxi dancer, she'd kicked the letch who for his ten cents had groped when he should only have danced.

The woman artist combined smart-cookie-ness with integrity and innocence. I watched, amazed, as Ruth's self-righteous morality triumphed over Marty's street codes on the larger-than-life screen.

Marty himself was an ambiguous villain. In fact, he was more a raw force than a villain. In his crooked, dog-eat-dog world, his crook's-eye view made sense.

"I couldn't handle those people with kid gloves." That was Marty's convincing self-defense. "It's push or get pushed."

How could I fault him for initially assuming that Ruth shared his moral environment? When Ruth refused to weekend with him in Florida as payment for his having gotten her a big singing gig in his Chicago nightclub, he sized her up as a smart cookie holding out for more. "Ah, I get it," he rationalized. "She thinks it's a line . . . I say Miami, and she thinks it'll be Atlantic City."

I just couldn't summon up hate for him.

LOVE ME OR LEAVE ME

So he was a crook; so what? My schoolfriends and I—Calcutta's small, elite band of missionary-educated postcolonial adolescents, brought up on too much Oscar Wilde and Somerset Maugham—confused mordant wit and cynicism with sophistication. I persuaded myself that Marty was, in fact, an incompetent in the world of serious crime.

Marty won me over with his enthusiasm. How could I dislike a man who used "You've got a very excellent personality" as his line to a dancer in a dingy dressing room?

Like my father, an optimist, Marty could say lines like "You want to know what your trouble is, girlie? You got no faith in human nature," and mean it.

Marty trying to control his wife didn't shock me. In traditional, patriarchal Hindu families like mine, men commanded and women obeyed; to love was to protect. I understood that Marty slapping Ruth was Hollywood—not Hindu— shorthand for deplorable behavior and that Hollywood would deliver Marty his comeuppance.

To me, Marty was a bewildered, lovesick fool; a man of strength brought low by bravado or hubris. (At fifteen I could declaim soliloquies from Shake-speare, Racine, and Sophocles, and regularly used words like "hubris" and "catharsis.") Marty was a man who bullied and bossed because he lacked self-confidence. Without Ruth's total dependence on him, he became nothing. He was the guy from the wrong side of the tracks, the thug, the loner, who had built himself a fortune but not an identity and confidence. In his life the question "Who *are* you?" and the answer "They think I'm nothing" recurred with sinister regularity.

How could I know then—coming from an overdetermined, confident hierar-chical culture in which everyone knew the most minute detail of everyone else's life, in which a family name revealed caste and region—that the ambiguously named, mysteriously unrooted Marty Snyder was, in his splendor, his power, his pathetic hollowness, an American archetype? And that the reading of such ambi-guity, from the stagnant steadiness of the Calcutta upper classes, could be alluring?

Marty's crime was love, the kind of monstrously possessive, Othello-like love that turned the beloved into chattel. It was not that different and no more overwhelming than the love I both cherished and hoped to escape. In Marty's "Didn't I do wonders for her?" guilt made me imagine I was hearing a patriarch's lament.

By the time Doris Day finally sang "Love Me or Leave Me," I knew what the future held. Things would work out for me as a writer as long as I rejected both the Johnnys and the Martys. The Martys, the tiny tough guys with limps, were all trouble; they charged you up with unseemly passion and got you to break rules, take calamitous risks. The patient, long-suffering Johnnys appealed to your modesty and goodness; they shamed you into working hard, following rules, and waiting for a payoff that was more likely to be self-righteous liberty than stardom.

There was a cost. There was always a cost. Ruth didn't know or couldn't admit that cost to herself. She hadn't *asked* Marty for "breaks." Marty had sensed her wants. He'd given; she'd grabbed.

That cynical lesson cut deep. As I left the Metro Cinema that winter night and drove through a city awaiting Marxist revolution, I hoped that when I started my life over on an MGM backlot made up to look like America, I'd retain enough of the worldliness of my Calcutta youth to be more honest with myself than Ruth had been.

f r o m THE WOMAN WARRIOR

Maxine Hong Kingston

Maxine Hong Kingston was born in Stockton, California, lived nearly twenty years in Honolulu, and is now a resident of Oakland, California. Her first two books, *The Woman Warrior* (1976) and *China Men* (1980), were widely acclaimed, receiving the National Book Critics Circle Award and the American Book Award respectively. Kingston's technique of blending Chinese myths and stories with Chinese American contemporary concerns continues in her novel, *Trickmaster Monkey* (1989).

MY AMERICAN LIFE HAS BEEN SUCH A DISAPPOINTMENT.

"I got straight A's, Mama."

"Let me tell you a true story about a girl who saved her village."

I could not figure out what was my village. And it was important that I do something big and fine, or else my parents would sell me when we made our way back to China. In China there were solutions for what to do with little girls who ate up food and threw tantrums. You can't eat straight A's.

When one of my parents or the emigrant villagers said, " 'Feeding girls is feeding cowbirds,' " I would thrash on the floor and scream so hard I couldn't talk. I couldn't stop.

"What's the matter with her?"

"I don't know. Bad, I guess. You know how girls are. 'There's no profit in raising girls. Better to raise geese than girls.' "

"I would hit her if she were mine. But then there's no use wasting all that discipline on a girl. 'When you raise girls, you're raising children for strangers.' "

"Stop that crying!" my mother would yell. "I'm going to hit you if you don't stop. Bad girl! Stop!" I'm going to remember never to hit or to scold my children for crying, I thought, because then they will only cry more.

"I'm not a bad girl," I would scream. "I'm not a bad girl. I'm not a bad girl." I might as well have said, "I'm not a girl."

"When you were little, all you had to say was 'I'm not a bad girl,' and you could make yourself cry," my mother says, talking-story about my childhood.

I minded that the emigrant villagers shook their heads at my sister and me. "One girl—and another girl," they said, and made our parents ashamed to take us out together. The good part about my brothers being born was that people stopped saying, "All girls," but I learned new grievances. "Did you roll an egg on *my* face like that when *I* was born?" "Did you have a full-month party for *me?*" "Did you turn on all the lights?" "Did you send *my* picture to Grandmother?" "Why not? Because I'm a girl? Is that why not?" "Why didn't you teach me English?" "You like having me beaten up at school, don't you?"

"She is very mean, isn't she?" the emigrant villagers would say.

"Come, children. Hurry. Hurry. Who wants to go out with Great-Uncle?" On Saturday mornings my great-uncle, the ex-river pirate, did the shopping. "Get your coats, whoever's coming."

"I'm coming. I'm coming. Wait for me."

When he heard girls' voices, he turned on us and roared, "No girls!" and left my sisters and me hanging our coats back up, not looking at one another. The boys came back with candy and new toys. When they walked through Chinatown, the people must have said, "A boy—and another boy—and another boy!" At my great-uncle's funeral I secretly tested out feeling glad that he was dead—the six-foot bearish masculinity of him.

I went away to college—Berkeley in the sixties—and I studied, and I marched to change the world, but I did not turn into a boy. I would have liked to bring myself back as a boy for my parents to welcome with chickens and pigs. That was for my brother, who returned alive from Vietnam.

If I went to Vietnam, I would not come back; females desert families. It was said, "There is an outward tendency in females," which meant that I was getting straight A's for the good of my future husband's family, not my own. I did not plan ever to have a husband. I would show my mother and father and the nosey emigrant villagers that girls have no outward tendency. I stopped getting straight A's.

And all the time I was having to turn myself American-feminine, or no dates.

THE WOMAN WARRIOR

There is a Chinese word for the female *I*—which is "slave." Break the women with their own tongues!

I refused to cook. When I had to wash dishes, I would crack one or two. "Bad girl," my mother yelled, and sometimes that made me gloat rather than cry. Isn't a bad girl almost a boy?

"What do you want to be when you grow up, little girl?"

"A lumberjack in Oregon."

Even now, unless I'm happy, I burn the food when I cook. I do not feed people. I let the dirty dishes rot. I eat at other people's tables but won't invite them to mine, where the dishes are rotting.

If I could not-eat, perhaps I could make myself a warrior like the swordswoman who drives me. I will—I must—rise and plow the fields as soon as the baby comes out.

Once I get outside the house, what bird might call me; on what horse could I ride away? Marriage and childbirth strengthen the swordswoman, who is not a maid like Joan of Arc. Do the women's work; then do more work, which will become ours too. No husband of mine will say, "I could have been a drummer, but I had to think about the wife and kids. You know how it is." Nobody supports me at the expense of his own adventure. Then I get bitter: no one supports me; I am not loved enough to be supported. That I am not a burden has to compensate for the sad envy when I look at women loved enough to be supported. Even now China wraps double binds around my feet.

When urban renewal tore down my parents' laundry and paved over our slum for a parking lot, I only made up gun and knife fantasies and did nothing useful.

From the fairy tales, I've learned exactly who the enemy are. I easily recognize them—business-suited in their modern American executive guise, each boss two feet taller than I am and impossible to meet eye to eye.

I once worked at an art supply house that sold paints to artists. "Order more of that nigger yellow, willya?" the boss told me. "Bright, isn't it? Nigger yellow."

"I don't like that word," I had to say in my bad, small-person's voice that makes no impact. The boss never deigned to answer.

I also worked at a land developers' association. The building industry was planning a banquet for contractors, real estate dealers, and real estate editors. "Did you know the restaurant you chose for the banquet is being picketed by CORE and the NAACP?" I squeaked.

"Of course I know." The boss laughed. "That's why I chose it."

"I refuse to type these invitations," I whispered, voice unreliable.

He leaned back in his leather chair, his bossy stomach opulent. He picked up his calendar and slowly circled a date. "You will be paid up to here," he said. "We'll mail you the check."

VISIONS OF AMERICA

If I took the sword, which my hate must surely have forged out of the air, and gutted him, I would put color and wrinkles into his shirt.

It's not just the stupid racists that I have to do something about, but the tyrants who for whatever reason can deny my family food and work. My job is my own only land.

To avenge my family, I'd have to storm across China to take back our farm from the Communists; I'd have to rage across the United States to take back the laundry in New York and the one in California. Nobody in history has conquered and united both North America and Asia. A descendant of eighty pole fighters, I ought to be able to set out confidently, march straight down our street, get going right now. There's work to do, ground to cover. Surely, the eighty pole fighters, though unseen, would follow me and lead me and protect me, as is the wont of ancestors.

Or it may well be that they're resting happily in China, their spirits dispersed among the real Chinese, and not nudging me at all with their poles. I mustn't feel bad that I haven't done as well as the swordswoman did; after all, no bird called me, no wise old people tutored me. I have no magic beads, no water gourd sight, no rabbit that will jump in the fire when I'm hungry. I dislike armies.

I've looked for the bird. I've seen clouds make pointed angel wings that stream past the sunset, but they shred into clouds. Once at a beach after a long hike I saw a seagull, tiny as an insect. But when I jumped up to tell what miracle I saw, before I could get the words out I understood that the bird was insect-sized because it was far away. My brain had momentarily lost its depth perception. I was that eager to find an unusual bird.

The news from China has been confusing. It also had something to do with birds. I was nine years old when the letters made my parents, who are rocks, cry. My father screamed in his sleep. My mother wept and crumpled up the letters. She set fire to them page by page in the ashtray, but new letters came almost every day. The only letters they opened without fear were the ones with red borders, the holiday letters that mustn't carry bad news. The other letters said that my uncles were made to kneel on broken glass during their trials and had confessed to being landowners. They were all executed, and the aunt whose thumbs were twisted off drowned herself. Other aunts, mothers-in-law, and cousins disappeared; some suddenly began writing to us again from communes or from Hong Kong. They kept asking for money. The ones in communes got four ounces of fat and one cup of oil a week, they said, and had to work from 4 A.M. to 9 P.M. They had to learn to do dances waving red kerchiefs; they had to sing nonsense syllables. The Communists gave axes to the old ladies and said, "Go and kill yourself. You're useless." If we overseas Chinese would just send money to the Communist bank, our relatives said, they might get a percentage of it for themselves. The aunts in Hong Kong said to send money quickly; their children were begging on the sidewalks, and mean people put dirt in their bowls.

When I dream that I am wire without flesh, there is a letter on blue airmail paper that floats above the night ocean between here and China. It must arrive safely or else my grandmother and I will lose each other.

My parents felt bad whether or not they sent money. Sometimes they got angry at their brothers and sisters for asking. And thye would not simply ask but have to talk-story too. The revolutionaries had taken Fourth Aunt and Uncle's store, house, and lands. They attacked the house and killed the grandfather and oldest daughter. The grandmother escaped with the loose cash and did not return to help. Fourth Aunt picked up her sons, one under each arm, and hid in the pig house, where they slept that night in cotton clothes. The next day she found her husband, who had also miraculously escaped. The two of them collected twigs and yams to sell while their children begged. Each morning they tied the faggots on each other's back. Nobody bought from them. They ate the yams and some of the children's rice. Finally Fourth Aunt saw what was wrong. "We have to shout 'Fuel for sale' and 'Yams for sale,' " she said. "We can't just walk unobtrusively up and down the street." "You're right," said my uncle, but he was shy and walked in back of her. "Shout," my aunt ordered, but he could not. "They think we're carrying these sticks home for our own fire," she said. "Shout." They walked about miserably, silently, until sundown, neither of them able to advertise themselves. Fourth Aunt, an orphan since the age of ten, mean as my mother, threw her bundle down at his feet and scolded Fourth Uncle, "Starving to death, his wife and children starving to death, and he's too damned shy to raise his voice." She left him standing by himself and afraid to return empty-handed to her. He sat under a tree to think, when he spotted a pair of nesting doves. Dumping his bag of yams, he climbed up and caught the birds. That was where the Communists trapped him, in a tree. They criticized him for selfishly taking food for his own family and killed him, leaving his body in the tree as an example. They took the birds to a commune kitchen to be shared.

It is confusing that my family was not the poor to be championed. They were executed like the barons in the stories, when they were not barons. It is confusing that birds tricked us.

What fighting and killing I have seen have not been glorious but slum grubby. I fought the most during junior high school and always cried. Fights are confusing as to who has won. The corpses I've seen had been rolled and dumped, sad little dirty bodies covered with a police khaki blanket. My mother locked her children in the house so we couldn't look at dead slum people. But at news of a body, I would find a way to get out; I had to learn about dying if I wanted to become a swordswoman. Once there was an Asian man stabbed next door, words on cloth pinned to his corpse. When the police came around asking questions, my father said, "No read Japanese. Japanese words. Me Chinese."

I've also looked for old people who could be my gurus. A medium with red hair told me that a girl who died in a far country follows me wherever I go. This spirit can help me if I acknowledge her, she said. Between the head line and heart line in my right palm, she said, I have the mystic cross. I could become a medium myself. I don't want to be a medium. I don't want to be a crank taking "offerings" in a wicker plate from the frightened audience, who, one after another, asked the spirits how to raise rent money, how to cure their coughs and skin diseases, how to find a job. And martial arts are for unsure little boys kicking away under fluorescent lights.

I live now where there are Chinese and Japanese, but no emigrants from my own village looking at me as if I had failed them. Living among one's own emigrant villagers can give a good Chinese far from China glory and a place. "That old busboy is really a swordsman," we whisper when he goes by, "He's a swordsman who's killed fifty. He has a tong ax in his closet." But I am useless, one more girl who couldn't be sold. When I visit the family now, I wrap my American successes around me like a private shawl; I *am* worthy of eating the food. From afar I can believe my family loves me fundamentally. They only say, "When fishing for treasures in the flood, be careful not to pull in girls," because that is what one says about daugthers. But I watched such words come out of my own mother's and father's mouths; I looked at their ink drawing of poor people snagging their neighbors' flotage with long flood hooks and pushing the girl babies on down the river. And I had to get out of hating range. I read in an anthropology book that Chinese say, "Girls are necessary too"; I have never heard the Chinese I know make this concession. Perhaps it was a saying in another village. I refuse to shy my way anymore through our Chinatown, which tasks me with the old sayings and the stories.

The swordswoman and I are not so dissimilar. May my people understand the resemblance soon so that I can return to them. What we have in common are the words at our backs. The idioms for *revenge* are "report a crime" and "report to five families." The reporting is the vengeance—not the beheading, not the gutting, but the words. And I have so many words—"chink" words and "gook" words too—that they do not fit on my skin.

2 G

Sonia Pilcer

Sonia Pilcer was born in Landsberg, Germany and grew up in New York City.
Her published novels include *Teen Angel* (1978), *Maiden Rites,* (1982), and
I-Land: Manhattan in Monologue (1987), which has been produced as a play
in New York and Los Angeles.

> "Yours is a privileged generation: you remember things that you have
> not lived; but you remember them so well, so profoundly, that every one
> of your words, every one of your stories, every one of your silences
> comes to bear on our own. You are our justification."
>
> —ELIE WIESEL

I DON'T EVER REMEMBER NOT KNOWING. THE WORD *HOLOCAUST*
was not used in our home. "During the war" was how the stories began.
Everyone told them. In lieu of living family, my parents belonged to a large
network of Polish Jews. All were survivors. The women played canasta and the
men, poker. As they tossed bright plastic chips and picked up cards, blue numbers flashing on the insides of their arms, the stories multiplied.

"Pish posh. I knew Genia in the laager when she wasn't such a fancy lady. She cleaned toilets with the rest of us."

"If Yacob hadn't given me his piece of bread, I wouldn't be here. Lucky me, I was dealt two red threes!"

"I wouldn't give Uzek a broken cent. Now he's an important man in B'nai B'rith. During the war, he had a big mouth."

The delivery was usually offhand. Lineups, beatings, starvation were discussed as casually as yesterday's weather. Their voices rose with excitement as they regaled one another with tales of daredevil escapes, morsels of wartime gossip, teasing each other's memories as at a college reunion. After all, most of them had been in their teens when the war broke out. "You remember Yola. She was the not-bad-looking one with crooked teeth, who went with the German. He gave her crabs."

I understood Polish so none of it escaped me. None of the innuendos. And I knew the cast of characters from borsht belt summers spent in bungalow colonies. The survivors and children vacationed en masse, sometimes fifty families or more, at places with names like Kozy Kottages or Blue Paradise, *greener* pastures, where they organized theme parties, beauty pageants, and mock weddings in which the bride wore white as few of them ever did—usually played by the most hirsute man among them. I listened for hours as I changed Pier Angeli's cutout ensembles.

Few outsiders understand the survivor sensibility. It is profoundly and terrifyingly cynical about human nature. Yet funny. But the humor is definitely dark. "The streets of Piotrkow resembled Hollywood. You never saw so many stars." They had names for the Germans. My mother referred to the two women guards who tormented her as *Pietruszka,* "parsley," and *Marchevka,* "carrot," because of her hideous red hair. She imitated their graceless walk and cursed that they should die of cholera. When I was young, I took it for granted. I knew we weren't *Father Knows Best.* Americans, the survivors say, what do they know of life? But I thought all Jewish families were like mine.

I am named Sonia Hanna, after both of my parents' murdered mothers. I spent my first year with hundreds of Jewish refugees, orphans of large families and communities, in a displaced-persons camp in Landsberg, Germany. Polish and Yiddish swelled the air. America! Everyone chanted the magic word of passage. The children sat quiet as baggage.

The Displaced Persons Act of 1950 raised the ceiling for Jewish refugees from 205,000 to 341,000. We arrived via the ship *General Hersey* on Rosh Hashanah, our New Year. The Hebrew Immigrant Aid Society found us a room at the St. Marks Hotel, near its offices on Lafayette Street. The Rescue Information Bulletin featured a photograph of two women from Czestochowa, with the caption: "New land, new tastes—these H.I.A.S. protegees eat their first ice cream cones."

My parents learned to speak English, my father got a job in a factory, and my mother a large apartment in Brooklyn, which she kept spotless. They made new lives for themselves, had babies and bankbooks, covered couches in clear plastic.

I forgot my Polish. I was an American girl with no accent. I had friends, my own life, which I longed to grow into like a pair of oversize shoes. When I left home, I intended to create a self that had nothing to do with my parents' past. But I wanted to be a writer. A dangerous vocation.

It is our way to tell tales, bug-eyed people of the Book. We become writers and shrinks because we believe in the power of storytelling. As if the right arrangement of words could release us.

As a child, my parents' stories held me with the power of prehistoric myth. How my mother's mother had forced her to tie a white woolen kerchief around her head as they lined up at the *Umschlagplatz* during Selection. She had been sent to the right side along with her parents and brother. All of a sudden, a Polish policeman searched the line. *"Bialy szalik!* Where's the girl with the white kerchief?" She had tried to hide behind her mother. He spotted her, then shoved her into the other line, which was destined for a labor camp. Was it the white scarf that saved my mother's life while her whole family was sent to the gas chambers? She kept it through the war. Even when the kerchief was only a small square. She kept it until she was liberated by the Russians. "Then—I lost it," she told me. "Maybe Momma thought I didn't need her protection anymore."

After surviving until the Lodz ghetto was liquidated, then several months in Auschwitz, my father's laager was forced to march from Poland into Germany. When a guard turned his back to pee, my father ran into a forest near Gliwice. It had been raw impulse, as he didn't have the chance to warn his brother, who marched only several yards ahead of him. My father weighed less than 47 kilos when he was found by the Russians.

Such stories. Lives saved by split-second decisions, coincidences that strained credibility, amazing reversals. One of my parents' friends had been in the showers when the gas failed and her execution was postponed: Another had been dropped in a mass grave, pretended to be dead, and climbed out in the dark. Like the Ancient Mariner, my parents and their circle of refugee friends repeated the moments of their miraculous reprieves as if they still could not quite believe them. An implicit question haunted their stories: Why them? Why did they live and the others did not? If asked, they had no answer. "We were not any smarter, hardly better, human beings. The good people were killed."

Stories of the others were told too, of the unlucky one who lit a cigarette and was shot, of the young mother who was taken away. My mother and several women in the laager hid her little boy in a crack in the wall. Somehow he knew not to cry. They watched fearfully as he grew larger, knowing he would soon be discovered. The night my father escaped, his brother was locked in an airtight potato cellar; he couldn't get close enough to the crack under the cellar door to breathe.

I don't ever remember not knowing. I believe I sucked the knowledge in my mother's milk. It gave me a secret inner life that was as voluptuous as it was tortured. I supplemented my fantasies with movies. My mother was Ingrid Bergman and my father, Tyrone Power. I embellished his heroic escape into the woods. He fought the Germans and saved my mother's life. At the war's end, they locked in passionate embrace.

Then I saw my first documentary footage of the camps. I had walked in as my parents sat in front of our black-and-white Westinghouse. I watched hundreds of naked bodies, more bone than flesh, being dumped in the bottom of a huge cavity. The skeletons dropped like debris into the mass grave. I observed close-ups of faces with vacant, wide-eyed stares. My mother wept. My father peered intently at the television set as if he might spot someone he knew.

We call ourselves 2Gs. This is group shorthand for Second Generation, the survivors' children. There is a cabal of us. We have organizations with names like the Generation After, support groups and kinship meetings, well-attended conferences in the States and Israel. Scholarly books and articles are published. "There's no business like *shoah* business," one of my 2G friends quips. *Shoah* is the Hebrew word for "Holocaust."

The term *Second Generation* implies something that's passed on. Diabetes, blue eyes, twins, and—genocide? One even hears of 3G, referring to the Third Generation of transmission. Recently, when my son, Jacob, was born, the *Piotr-kov Trybunalski Relief Association Bulletin* ran an announcement: "God bless the Third Generation."

Many 2Gs become psychotherapists. The theory is that growing up, we nurture our parents and grow accustomed to intuiting their needs. Surviving the survivors. Thus, the natural career choice. Some become disturbed.

Dark-eyed Anny, anorexic before anyone knew the word, wrote short stories at CCNY about the stench of burning skin on Krakow streets, relations turned to bars of soap. "If God really loved us, would He have given us wrists?" On the anniversary of Anny's mother's incarceration and the incineration of her family, she committed herself to a Long Island hospital.

Benson, producer of TV commercials, craved coked excitement and told me he could only have sex with black prostitutes. "This is my Aunt Tessa," he said, pointing to a lampshade in his apartment. "She could always tan easily."

Randy emigrated from Westchester and joined the Israeli army. On Yom

Kippur, he ate pork chops, followed by an all-night poker game. "What's the difference between pizza and a Jew?" he asked. "A pizza doesn't scream when it's put into the oven."

I've often been struck by the irony that the survivors seem to have the ability to go on with their lives. The Bar Mitzvahs and weddings of their children are huge, festive affirmations of life. It is these same children who spend much of their time, not to mention money, talking to Ph.D.s, M.S.W.s, and therapists. In unaccented, well-reasoned English, we speak of anger and guilt, trying to separate ourselves from our parents and their Holocaust past.

The Holocaust is our scar, distinguishing us like stigmata. It gives our life gravity and we cling to it. We would be ordinary without it. Secretly, we believe that nothing we can ever do will be as important as our parents' suffering.

From the Statement of Purpose of the International Network of Children of Jewish Holocaust Survivors: "As the heirs of the six million Jews who perished during the Holocaust and as the sons and daughters of those who survived its horrors, we pledge ourselves to forging our future by remembering our past."

This April 22 is Yom Hashoah, the Day of Remembrance. Survivors light *Yortzeit* candles and say kaddish for the dead. In Israel, a siren goes off at eight A.M. It is an eerie sound, reminiscent of deportation wagons in war movies. All traffic stops except for Arab buses and cars. For a full minute, there is silence. On the street, people freeze as in a game of statue. The soldiers in fatigue uniforms, holding their guns and plastic bags of yogurt, hard-boiled eggs, and oranges. A gnarled old man bent over like an ancient tree. The peasant woman who sells buttons and thread closes her eyes and weeps. At the end of the day, one of my Israeli friends mutters, "God, I'm *shoah*-ed out."

Let us remember those who perished in the Nazi Holocaust. Join us in paying tribute to the six million Jewish martyrs. We will not forget, we will not forgive.

On the Day of Remembrance, an American flag flies full mast at the entrance to the Temple Emanu-El on Fifth Avenue. Inside, people wear black-and-white stickers on their lapels: "Remember 6,000,000." My mother is one of thirty women who march in a memorial candle-lighting. A black lace veil floats over her face as she lights a white candle for the dead from her city.

There is a hierarchy of suffering. Treblinka survivors feel superior to the ones who were in Terezin—summer camp in comparison—who are above those in labor camps, who supercede the escapees to Sweden, Russia, and South America. The key question is, Where did you spend the war? The more dire the circumstances, the more family murdered, the greater the starvation and disease, the higher the rung in this social register.

Suddenly, a nervous hush fills the sanctuary. The spotlight catches the dark, hollowed sockets of his eyes, the thin wisps of hair, his deeply lined face and gaunt body. In the realm of remembrance, Elie Wiesel is a superstar. "Let us tell tales . . ." he begins softly. Temple Emanu-El reverberates with his chilling voice. In 1983, the *Times* published his Auschwitz number, A-7713, as well as a photograph of his barrack with a dozen blank-eyed skulls, a white circle drawn around his recognizable face. Over the years, he has created the prototype of Holocaust writing. His key words: *Remember the unspeakable night darkness God six million suffering death nightmares survivor forsaken silence to bear witness legacy not forget.*

"Forgetfulness leads to exile. Remembrance is the secret of redemption." This quote from Baal Shem Tov proliferates. Most of my life I've been urged, goaded, and beseeched to remember. I receive letters that begin, "Dear Survivor," and end: "We serve notice to the world that the Holocaust can never be forgotten, must never be repeated. Your commitment to bear witness must go on. We are not a people who forget. Please check off: Male/Female/Survivor/Second Generation/Third Generation/Spouse."

Memory is our bogeyman. In spite of all the injunctions to remember, I am afflicted with selective amnesia when it comes to this "war business." The names of dead relatives, the dates and places of their internment, the cities and ghettos my parents lived in—seem to vanish into black holes. No matter how many times I hear these facts, I just can't hold onto them.

I once asked my father to help me draw a family tree. "A tree!" He laughed mirthlessly. "Without branches or leaves."

I used to feel ashamed of these memory lapses. I knew James Joyce's birthday, Malcolm X's death, and the places where Georgia O'Keeffe had lived. How could I care so little for my parents? And what of their relations who had perished during the war? I just couldn't understand my own forgetfulness.

At a meeting of 2Gs, the subject of memory came up. One young woman admitted that she couldn't remember the names of her family's dead relatives. She began to cry shamefully. Someone else confided his inability to remember where his parents were during the war. Soon everyone was confessing to one kind of amnesia or another. No one could keep the names and places straight.

Something snapped. I wanted to demand: Remember what? Lives extinguished? Privates mutilated? Dead grandparents? Uncles, aunts, cousins? Childhoods, entire countries and cultures lost? I knew no one. I had seen nothing.

Yes, I was *their* first seed of life after so much death. A living monument to their survival, a shrine to their mothers. But I wasn't a *survivor.* All that I had survived was my childhood and my parents' fierce, anxious love.

As their child, I find myself in limbo. I had no personal experience of the war. But I was born on the other side, lived my first year in a displaced-persons camp. My father had numbers, my mother nightmares, and me the legacy. The last act of the horror show of the century. I had almost not been born but for a whim, a white scarf, and an impulse to run into the forest.

A BOOK-WRITING VENTURE

Kim Yong Ik

Kim Yong Ik was born in Choongmoo, a seaport in South Korea, and came to the U.S. at the age of twenty-eight to study English literature at Florida Southern College and later creative writing at the Iowa Writers' Workshop. His short stories have been published in *Harper's Bazaar, The Atlantic, The New Yorker,* and *The Sewanee Review.* Kim's novels and stories for children and adults have won numerous awards and many translations; they include *The Happy Days* (1960), *The Diving Gourd* and *Love in Winter* (1962), *Blue in the Seed* (1964), and *Wedding Shoes* (1984).

IN 1948 WHEN I STARTED TO WRITE A NOVEL APART FROM MY REGU-
lar school work at Florida Southern College, Lakeland, Florida, my roommate in the dormitory told me, "If I were you, I wouldn't waste time in this country. I'll give you five hundred dollars if you publish one book in America. Breaking into that racket is nearly impossible even for an American writer who has mastered his own language." I was far from a master of English, but I didn't listen to him inside. I had studied English literature during the Second World War when it was a most unpopular subject to take up in the Orient, but I wanted to study it. Once in America, I wanted to write so much that I refused to accept the fact that my English was far from being adequate to write a novel. I put in three hours early every morning writing a book.

The language problem that I was attacking loomed larger and larger as I began to learn more. When I would describe in English certain concepts and objects enmeshed in Korean emotion and imagination, I became slowly aware of nuances, of differences between two languages even in simple expression. The remark "Kim entered the house" seems to be simple enough, yet, unless a reader has a clear visual image of a Korean house, his understanding of the sentence is not complete. When a Korean says he is "in the house," he may be in his courtyard, or on his porch, or in his small room! If I wanted to give a specific picture of entering the house in the Western sense, I had to say "room" instead of house—sometimes. I say "sometimes" because many Koreans entertain their guests on their porches and still are considered to be hospitable, and in the Korean sense, going into the "room" may be a more intimate act than it would be in the English sense. Such problems! That is merely an example. My Florida friends tried to help.

After three years in Florida, I moved to the University of Kentucky to continue my book-writing venture. During a holiday season when I was hired by the library to wax some leather-bound books, for fifty cents an hour, I often daydreamed that some day I would have my book published and bound in that shining, aromatic leather. I was all by myself in the Precious Books section upstairs. While working with the bindings with my hands full of grease and wax, I would read aloud from a book of poetry open before me. Reading poetry did not require me to turn pages often. I also loved the rhythmical voice in it. Each time my reading was interrupted because with dirty hands I could not turn the page immediately, I was frustrated, as though a phonograph record got stuck in a scratch on a recording of my favorite song. As I was reading Robert Frost's "The Road Not Taken," I saw the librarian in charge of the section standing right behind me. I knew that she would chide me or even dismiss me, for the library was strict about student workers reading during their work hours. I couldn't look up at her to say hello. I saw her dry hand reach for the book, as though she would take it away; instead, her fingers turned the page for me to go on, and she left the room without saying a word! I was deeply moved as I finished the poem— "And that has made all the difference."

I did go on to finish writing my book. In 1953 when I enrolled in the Writers Workshop of the University of Iowa, I had been writing fiction for six years and had completed one novel. I started to send it to various publishers in New York.

I had to send it by railway express and had to pay return postage. This amounted to nearly five dollars for each mailing. Since it took about a month for the rejected manuscript to reach me, this turned out to be a regular monthly expense. I would walk to the outskirts of Iowa City to the railroad station to save the bus fare that would help pay for mailing the manuscript. The railway express man was quite curious about the mysterious package that kept reappearing, and finally he asked me what was in it.

A BOOK-WRITING VENTURE

I explained to him, and he told me there was an old man in Iowa City who kept on mailing his manuscript about every month, just as I did.

Still I appeared so often that finally I was embarrassed whenever I met the express agent. We got to know each other rather well. By this time, he knew that Korean was my mother tongue; Japanese my second (I had learned this under the Japanese occupation); and English my third (I started to learn English during my high school days in Korea). One day I asked him what had become of the old man and his manuscript, and he said "That fellow's manuscript always came back but he is now dead."

I kept up the game of mailing and receiving my novel manuscript, as well as several short stories. I felt I was making some progress in mastering the English language even if my collection of rejection slips seemed to shout otherwise. As days and seasons passed, I became more desperate. I read and wrote harder than before. Even on the train on the way to Maine to work for a family for the summer, I kept up my morning ritual of three hours of writing. By day, I read stories for their children, enjoying the rhythm of the English language. At night, I stayed up late writing. Word got around that the Korean "liked to sleep with his light on."

I returned to school that fall only to write. My landlady in Iowa City would complain that I did not leave the room on the weekend so she could properly clean my room, and further remarked that she wouldn't like her boy to go abroad just to stay in a room always. I listened to her advice only to learn living language.

I would walk around with a night watchman or with janitors on night duty, and from them I would have free lessons of English—by listening. When I went to work at the University Hospital cafeteria across the Iowa River, I used to copy a poem or two on a slip of paper to read on the way. In the cafeteria I kept the slip of paper hidden under the counter and tried to memorize it while serving food. Of course, I was fired after two weeks.

I actually cared very little about a degree, so there was very small satisfaction in academic success. I wanted to have one story accepted. I was beginning to feel that perhaps this would never happen. I had only my many rejection slips to contemplate—after so many years of labor.

One Saturday it was snowing really hard outside. I was filled with self-doubt and wondered how in the world I had acquired the fantastic idea that I could write the drama of human emotion in fiction in a second language—no, in my third. I was feeling so dejected that I went out and spent nearly all my money on a record player. At least I could have music. Then I borrowed a record of Anthony Vivaldi's *Four Seasons* from the library and played it over and over that day, not even stopping to eat.

As I sat listening and watching the falling snow, I had a strange fantasy. I imagined that I saw a pair of Korean wedding shoes walking away from me in the snow. I followed the shoes in my mind, but I was always behind the figure who wore them, watching the back of the silk brocade shoes and the white muslin socks. The silken wedding shoes walked on and on toward the distant hills. I wanted to discover the person who wore the shoes, but she and her shoes wouldn't turn so I could see her. I heard my heart beat as I ran after the footmarks not to lose sight of the beautiful shoes, fearing that the snow might be wetting the finest silk.

I thought that if only I could see the elusive owner of these shoes, then I could write a real story! I came out of my reverie and got up determined to do just that. I went out.

By then I had begun to feel the effects of my day's fast, so my first stop was the corner grocery store. I went to the back to see the butcher who greeted me with a cheering "Merry Christmas" and a few words of encouragement.

I asked for a few slices of sandwich meat. (After my extravagances with my manuscripts and the impulsive purchase of the record player, there wasn't much left for food.)

I was surprised when the butcher took out a huge hunk of meat, and I reminded him "only a few slices, please." But he quickly wrapped it up and marked it twenty cents. I was sure that this was really about two dollars' worth of meat and I asked, "Is this really only twenty cents?"

He answered, "Yes, sir."

When I went to pay the cashier, she looked closely at package and then at me, but she accepted the twenty cents without comment.

After that, whenever I returned to the butcher, the package of meat seemed to grow even larger but the price was still twenty cents. Because of this kindness of the butcher, I had a high protein diet for the month and a half when I was writing my story of "The Wedding Shoes."

In my story, the butcher in a Korean valley is a very kind man who would give a very generous amount whenever a poor shoemaker's daughter came in with too little money. I wrote the story as if seen through the eyes of the butcher's son. While chasing the coveted shoes in my mind, I tried to capture the rhythm of my own language in English writing and tried not to take a chance of any misunderstanding by putting everything in concrete terms. Whenever I found it difficult to describe a certain scene, I had my usual temptation to delete it. But by this time I knew better than "to glide over" any scene or word that belonged in my work; more often than not, the thorny word or passage that does pose a language problem is the one that breathes pulsing life into the story.

When I completed "The Wedding Shoes," I gave it to Paul Eagle, the director of the Writers Workshop, but he was busy at the time and gave it to Margarette Young, author of *The Angel of the Forest.* She called me up and said with great enthusiasm, "This is wonderful. You must send this story to *Harper's Bazaar* right away." I did.

A few weeks later I found a letter in my mail box instead of the familiar ugly yellowed package. Alice Morris, the literary editor of *Harper's Bazaar,* wrote me that she wanted to print my story and would pay me $250. It was a time of great joy, but I had no one to share it with.

Soon after my story appeared, *London Bazaar* cabled me: "Offer twenty-five guineas for "The Wedding Shoes.' " About the same time, an amateur ballet group in Iowa City planned a ballet based on my story—so, on an electric light pole in front of the grocery store was posted an advertising poster: "A Ballet: The Silken Brocade Shoes."

After my stories had been accepted by the *Mademoiselle, Botteghe Oscure,* and *The New Yorker,* I returned to my homeland after spending ten years in America. Besides my teaching at a university, I continued to write in English as well as in my native tongue. In 1960 I revisited the United States to see my old friends. I was happy to find the librarian at the Precious Books section when I dropped in at the University of Kentucky. She remembered my reading poetry during my work hours and even the incident of turning the page for me. She asked me what I had been doing. When I mentioned what I had written for magazines, that I'd had juvenile books published by Little, Brown, and that an adult novel of mine was to be published by Alfred A. Knopf, she did not believe me until she looked them up in the publication index of the library. Then she was so happy for me that she invited me for dinner in a Chinese restaurant, and later we drove around in that bluegrass country.

That winter, I received a Christmas gift from Little, Brown—a copy of my first juvenile fiction book, written in Florida and Kentucky—*The Happy Days,* bound in beautiful leather.

"I CAN'T STAND YOUR BOOKS": A WRITER GOES HOME

Mary Gordon

Mary Gordon was born in Far Rockaway, New York, graduated from Barnard College, and has an M.A. from Syracuse University. She is the author of novels, stories, and essays. Among her published books are *Final Payments* (1978), *The Company of Women* (1981), *Men and Angels* (1986), *Temporary Shelter* (1988), *The Other Side* (1990), and *Good Boys and Dead Girls and Other Essays* (1991).

A FRIEND OF MINE WHO IS INTENSELY INTERESTED IN THE FULFILL-
ment of immigrant fantasies recently asked me if my family was proud of me. I was able to say with perfect frankness that they were not, that except for my mother, one cousin, and one aunt, they considered me an embarrassment or a lost soul. This led me to wonder about the connections among my family's reaction to me, the place of the writer in the Irish-American community, and the faintness of the Irish-American voice in the world of letters.

Let me begin with my uncle's funeral. My uncle was a lovable man, heroic even, in a way particularly Irish Catholic. He was the most nearly silent man I've ever known and perhaps the kindest. Like many Irishmen, he married late; he devoted his young manhood to family responsibilities. When he was forty, he met a young, beautiful, intelligent woman—a semiprofessional tennis player, a

Wellesley graduate who shared his passion for sports. In the early 1950s, she had done the daring thing of touring Europe alone on a motorcycle; she did the equally daring thing of wearing pants to our family gatherings. When my uncle announced to his mother that he was to marry this woman, my grandmother took to her bed for a week. Only with his wife's encouragement, my uncle finished his teaching degree and, at forty-five, got his first full-time job. But the real focus of his life was supporting her in her career as a tennis player; he coached her, accompanied her all over the country to tennis tournaments. They were perhaps the most happily married couple I have ever known, but I never saw them touch or even stand near each other, or address to each other an intimate word. My aunt became, in time, an ardent feminist, and my uncle accompanied her to ERA rallies. This shy, silent man stood in groups of women and carried signs saying ERA TODAY. When I went to his house the day after the funeral, attached to his refrigerator with a magnet was a list of members of Congress who needed to be written to in order to enlist their support for the ERA.

I loved my uncle very much; so did everyone else who stood before his coffin. We all wept. I held my baby son in my arms and wept, leaning my cheek against his for comfort. Who could imagine a situation in which an attack was less expected, less appropriate? Yet one of my uncles chose this time to say to me: "I just want to tell you I can't stand your books. None of us can. I tried the first one; I couldn't even get past the first chapter. The second one I couldn't even get into; I didn't even want to open it up. I didn't even buy it; I wouldn't waste the money."

Well, it would have been easy to laugh, but I didn't laugh; or easy to say, "A prophet is always without honor in his own family." But who is with honor in my family? Not my cousin the doctor. Not my cousin the businessman, with his million-dollar house. The honored person in the family is my cousin the nun. She walked into the funeral parlor; if the family could have carried her on their shoulders, they would have. She came up to me, after a while, and took my hand. "Mary," she said, "I just feel I need to tell you that I think your books are dreadful. I know that many people find them good, but I don't. They're just too worldly for me. Of course, I do understand that a lot of hard work went into them." Later, she said to one of my aunts, "She didn't really want to put all that sex in those books. The publishers made her."

They all thought my books were dirty. This brings out an aspect central and important to the Irish character: sexual puritanism. It is different in its flavor from Anglo-Saxon puritanism, and also from the French Jansenism that is its historical source. There is nothing thin-blooded about it and nothing of the merely finicky. Because it exists alongside a general sense of the enjoyableness of life, a love of liquor and horses, a sense of the importance of hospitality and of the beauty of the earth. And it lives side by side with a robust and lively wit.

VISIONS OF AMERICA

It would be easy to say that the source of it is the Roman Catholic Church; for certainly the folklore of the Celts abounds with heroes, male and female, who shy away from nothing in the body's life. Yet it is not only Catholicism that explains it. The Italians are Catholic, and the French, and the Spanish: these races are emblems in the popular mind for warm-bloodedness, for sexiness, and for romance. Of all Catholic countries, only Ireland came up with men who believed what the Church told them about sex. Only in Ireland are the churches filled with a near-even mix of male and female. Only in Ireland would a man married at thirty be thought of as marrying young.

I think that what is at the root of Irish puritanism is a profound fear of exposure, shared by both men and women in an oddly equal degree. "Silence, exile and cunning," said Stephen Dedalus, is the only route to survival. Cunning, of course, is understandable: it is the coin of exchange of any oppressed group. The wily slave, the tricky peasant, is a staple of every folklore in the world. Silence, too, is another form of protective coloration not unknown by the oppressed. But exile, the ultimate, most deeply willed concealment of identity, is the most singular part of Joyce's formula. To be an exile, to choose exile, is to put oneself among a group of people who will always have to struggle to understand one, is to put oneself in a situation where one's gestures are not readily legible, where one is not given away by a word, a look, a tone of voice. To be permanently in exile is to be permanently in disguise; it is an extreme form of self-protection. And self-protection is an Irish obsession.

Irish sexual puritanism is only a metaphor, as it is really in all of us, for an entire ontology. I am convinced that this desire to hide for self-protection is at the core of a great deal of Irish behavior—behavior that was shipped successfully from Ireland to America. This is, of course, another reason why the Irish, a people so imbued with the power of the Word, do not value writers in their midst. A writer speaks out loud; a writer reveals. And to reveal, for the Irish, is to put oneself and the people one loves in danger.

In *That Most Distressful Nation,* Andrew Greeley says of the Irish-American terror of standing out that "if brilliance and flair are counterproductive, the slightest risk-taking beyond the limits of approved career and personal behavior is unthinkable. Art, music, literature, poetry, theater, to some extent even academia, politics of any variety other than the traditional, are all too risky to be considered. The two most devastating things that can be said to the young . . . Irishman who attempts to move beyond these rigid norms are 'Who do you think you are?' and 'What will people say?' "

The second of these two questions, "What will people say?" is used by nearly all but the most courageous parents from every ethnic group. But the first question is, I think, a rarer one. It is, after all, *the* ontological question. "Who do you think you are?" The implied answer, or the implied right answer for the

American Irish, is "I'm not much." This answer contains the Augustinian world-view that so permeates the Irish; it isn't mere immigrant inferiority. "I'm not much" doesn't mean "I'm not much, but the WASPs are a lot." It means that the human condition isn't much, and anyone who thinks it is is merely a fool. And better, far better, to be invisible than to be a fool. And the proper response to the fool is ridicule.

Irish ridicule is different, for example, from its black counterpart. "Black ridicule," Andrew Greeley says, "is an exercise in verbal skill, designed to display virtuosity in the ability to be outrageous. Irish ridicule is intended to hurt, to give as much pain as is necessary to keep each other at a distance." I agree with Father Greeley that Irish ridicule is intended to hurt, but it is also a balked expression of love. It is also a desire to protect, or at least to urge self-protection upon the victim. It is the stick to beat in front of the stray member of the herd, to urge him or her back to his or her proper place, the place of hiding. It is a language whose purpose is two levels of concealment. It conceals the speaker's concern or his overt hostility, and it urges the victim to conceal himself or herself. The Irish are masters at the language of concealment.

Why this obsession with concealment? It is not simply the manifestation of the fear of an oppressed group. Certainly Jews have been at least as oppressed as the Irish, to say nothing of the blacks. Yet neither American Jews nor American blacks have shown the Irish reluctance for self-expression. One understands the factors that have enabled the Jews to turn their pain into literature. I spoke with Richard Fein, the Yiddish scholar and translator, who suggested some reasons for the extraordinary articulateness of the Jews. The Jews, he said, are a people brought up on critical commentary upon a text; it is natural that this process would transform itself to fiction. The high literacy rate among immigrant Jews, the Yiddish press's policy of translating and serializing the best of European fiction, the presence of intellectuals—all factors the Irish miss in their experience—can account for the audibility of the Jewish-American experience, the silence of the Irish. But blacks had none of the advantages of Jewish immigrants, and their advantages were far fewer than those of the Irish. Their literacy rate was much lower than among the Irish; they were even more cut off from ancient poetic traditions than the Irish, and intellectuals were certainly much rarer among them. Yet from the time of slavery onward, blacks have expressed their sense of pain and injustice in language: the poetry of spirituals, of the blues, nowhere has its counterpart in anything Irish. There is no Irish Langston Hughes, no Irish Jean Toomer, no Irish Richard Wright, no Irish James Baldwin, no Irish Toni Morrison. The great linguistic facility of the Irish restricted itself in this country to two forms: popular journalism and political speeches.

I have been for some time puzzled, unable to explain why the country of the bards, the country of Goldsmith and Swift, of Maria Edgeworth and Oscar

Wilde and George Bernard Shaw, above all the country of Yeats and Joyce, the country of O'Casey and Synge, of O'Connor and O'Faolain, produced so little in its American literary branch. It would make good sense to teach a course in the American Jewish Literary Experience, or in American Black Literature. But a course in American Irish Literature would take up barely half a semester. You could begin, if you were a loose constructionist, with O'Neill and Fitzgerald; but the majority of their work would have to be excluded. You could go then to James T. Farrell, whose *Studs Lonigan* recorded—with vigor but, to my mind, with sloppiness that borders on the dime novel—the experience of the Chicago Irish in the nineteen-twenties and thirties. You would have to jump, then, to J. F. Powers's brilliant tales of fifties priests. Then you could go on to William Alfred's *Hogan's Goat,* to Elizabeth Cullinan, to Maureen Howard and William Kennedy. After that, there would be nowhere to go.

What happened to make the Irish so comparatively silent? In part, it is the lack of an audience. Whereas American Jews and American blacks seem patently exotic, American Irish, seemingly more familiar, are less interesting to the book-buying American public—largely WASPs and Jews. And, I think, the silence of the American Irish is connected to the singular relationship the Irish have to the English language, a relationship heightened by the experience of immigration. The Irish have been, for hundreds of years, a colonized people. But they were colonized by a people who did not look so physically different from themselves. And the colonizers conquered the land, subjected the people, and imposed their own language without succeeding in eroding national identity. What an odd set of circumstances this is! As a working language, Irish was lost to the Irish by the nineteenth century. It ceased quickly to be the language of commerce and the language of government, but it ceased as well to be the family tongue. And so Irish poetry was lost to the majority of the Irish. But the memory of the figures embodied in the poetry was not.

The English could not conquer the racial identity of the Irish for the added reason of the strength of their Catholic faith. But in terms of language, the very strength of Catholicism in Ireland created another kind of colonization. For the sacred language, the language of ritual, was not Irish or even English: it was Latin. And by the time of the late Middle Ages, the Irish character of the liturgy was lost to the Irish; they had become successfully Romanized.

Despite this double linguistic colonization, the Irish maintained a lively oral tradition, of tales involving fantastical creatures, heroes and saints. All that was there for Yeats and the other Celtic twilighters to draw upon. But it was not what Joyce drew upon; it interested him no more than the price of potatoes and considerably less than the aesthetic theories of Flaubert. No one appreciates local color like a colonizer; to fix the colonized in a highly ornamental carapace of the past is to keep them from genuine contemporary power. So it is not surprising that the Irish-Americans, once they gained the necessary literacy, did not follow the path of Yeats. But why did none of them follow the path of Joyce—the Joyce, at least, of *Dubliners*—and draw upon the verbal facility so much a part of their culture to create a realistic picture of the contemporary urban life they and their kind were living?

The American Irish are a people who were doubly colonized linguistically and who arrived in America already knowing the language. Yet this knowledge of the language didn't spare them from the hatred and contempt of the natives. Sharing a tongue, and even physical characteristics, made no difference to the Yankees. And what did it do to the immigrants themselves? Did it make them resentful of their fellow immigrants, with whom they had to share menial, degrading jobs, even though they possessed the advantage of speaking the English language? Did it, perhaps, create in them the illusion that if they behaved, didn't make waves, didn't stand out, they might be accepted? The similarity of language between the Irish and the Yankees made problems of identity more complicated and less clear, a situation that echoed the earlier experience of oppression by the English. And the Irish-American solution once again was to keep out of the world of the dominant group, to create a parallel world in which success could be defined and measured, to ignore, insofar as possible, the inferior position in which they were placed.

All these factors—linguistic colonization occurring at the same time as a preservation of national identity, a self defined in highly local terms, the creation of parallel worlds—are some reasons why there have been so few Irish-American writers. To think of oneself as a writer of literature rather than a journalist or a popular writer, one must think of oneself as a citizen of a larger world. By this I do not mean that one necessarily defines oneself as outside the smaller community—my own prejudice is that to lose the identification with the small community is to lose irreplaceable riches. But if one is going to think of oneself as a writer-artist, one must think of oneself as in the company of other great artists. Artists who will not come from one's own community, who have lived in different ages, spoken different languages, written about people who exist only because these writers have preserved their lives. And if one is a writer whose early years were formed in a small, closed community, one must have the courage to understand that it is outside the community that one may very likely find the people who will be the audience for one's work.

I want to say, of course, that not everything about the Irish Catholics is harmful to a writer. For one thing, the Irish are always interesting. There is the wit and the refinement of language that the sense of the necessity for constant ridicule engenders. And the very hiddenness of the lives of Irish-Americans makes them an irresistible subject for fiction. One has the sense of breaking into a private treasure, kept from the eyes of most, and therefore a real piece of news.

VISIONS OF AMERICA

I once wrote that "Irish Catholics are always defending something—probably something indefensible: the CIA, the virginity of Mary—which is why their parties always end in fights." The problem is that the Irish-Americans are nearly always defending the wrong thing; nevertheless, most people find nothing worth defending, and the posture of the mistaken defender is compelling to the spirit, whether its bent is classical or romantic. The Irish have always in the back of their eye the vision of the ideal. Therefore, they must always be failures. For it is impossible to live up to the ideal; but to be attracted to it, to keep it in the back of one's eye, to know that one's endeavors are, however successful, inevitably failures, is to see the human condition in its clearest, most undiluted colors, to feel its starkest music in the bone.

There is the starkness of the Irish temperament; there is also its kindness. I go back to my uncle. The Irish-American experience has fed me because my uncle could have thriven in no soil but the Irish-American. And someone needs to tell about him. I have said it once; he was the kindest man I ever knew. He was capable of the deepest disappointment in people. He went to Communion every week of his life; his wife was an atheist. Although he never said a personal word to me, he had the capacity to make me feel immensely beloved and perfectly safe.

I had thought he was proud of my success. At his funeral, I talked about this to my favorite aunt, his sister. She, alone, defended me at my uncle's funeral. She didn't quite have the courage to confront the uncle who insulted me, but at least she directed her comments to the air around his head. "Imagine saying such a terrible thing at a funeral," she said, looking up at the ceiling.

My aunt and I were walking out of the funeral parlor to go to the cemetery. "They are awful, aren't they?" she said of the family who had insulted me. Well, I told her, they were awful, but they were so awful and so foolish that they couldn't hurt me. What mattered was that I knew my uncle who had just died was proud of me.

"Oh, he was proud of you," she said. "He always loved you very much. But he thought your books were very dirty. He couldn't read them, you know."

I walked with my infant son to the car that would drive us to the cemetery, and I thought how perfectly the experience of Irish-American Catholicism had been captured in my uncle's death and burial. And I wondered how much of it I would want to pass on to my children. That was a question to which I had no answer. But I knew one thing for certain: there was no doubt that I would write about it.

from LOST IN TRANSLATION:
A LIFE IN A NEW LANGUAGE

Eva Hoffman

Eva Hoffman was born in Cracow, Poland. She has taught literature and written on a variety of contemporary issues. She is currently an editor of *The New York Times Book Review* and the author of a memoir, *Lost in Translation: A Life in a New Language* (1989).

IT'S APRIL 1969, AND I'M WALKING, IDLY, ACROSS HARVARD YARD. MY first year at Harvard is coming to an end, I've just come out of a class on Victorian aesthetics, and I'm about to meet some friends in the cafeteria, where we'll exchange bits of literary gossip and personal analysis. Like so many events in my patchwork American existence, my being here is a sort of accident. In the middle of a year I spent at the Yale Music School—a year I gave myself to solve the music question—a friend drove me to Boston, and the city's hilly narrow streets, its brownstones rosy in the wintry light, an apothecary store with gleaming wooden fixtures, and a sudden, premature dusk so answered some deep desire in me that when I decided to follow the academic trail after all, I knew this was the place where I wanted to do it.

I get into Harvard itself on the last blaze of immigrant bravura. I had spent the previous summer in a paralysis of conflict about what to do next, so it's only in the early fall that I walk into the English Department office and tell the chairman that he must let me in. At this point, I'm decorated with enough honors and fellowships not to be an impostor, but the chairman, a gruff, affable man who looks at me with some interest once I present him with my clearly unreasonable request, tells me that even if John Donne himself showed up at this point, he couldn't do anything for him—or in any case, "they" wouldn't. "Who are they?" I ask, and the chairman informs me that they are the admissions office, which would surely refuse to process an application at this late date. "And if they agree to do it?" I say with a conspiratorial smile, and the chairman waves me out of the office with a gesture of mock exasperation. Once he gives me the opening, it's child's play, and I use the pressure of my need and my best Polish wiles to persuade all the parties concerned that they want to do their part; after a few days, I'm in.

After this outburst of willfulness, the last blaze of Polish *polot,* I go into a moping, glassy-eyed despondency. At this moment, when I should feel the muscular pleasure of success, my will deflates as if from overuse; just when I've gotten myself where I supposedly want to be, I feel as disoriented as a homing pigeon that has been blindfolded and turned around too many times, and now doesn't know the direction of home. "I'm Eva, I live in Cambridge, Mass., I go to Harvard University," I keep repeating to myself. I've been confounded by being too long a stranger.

And so, after I emerge from this hiatus, I begin walking around the crooked, cobblestoned streets of Cambridge as if I were tentatively trying on a new home. I'm pleased by its low wooden buildings, the ramshackle comfiness, the coffeehouses where I spend too many hours gossiping with friends, and the bursting bookstores—even though they also induce a kind of anxiety of plenitude in me, because so much has been already written, and so much needs to be known; I'm pleased by the New England modesty of Harvard Yard, and the wood-paneled rooms in which the English Department conducts its endless sherry parties, and the tweed-jacketed professors with their dry faces and perfectly professorial airs.

My friends assure me that, having come to the republic's eastern shore, I've landed in the real America at last. "Being American means that you feel like you're the norm," one of my friends tells me, "and the Northeast is the norm that sets the norm." An ironically timed statement, since we've entered a period during which these very friends of mine will try to unwrap, unravel, and demolish every norm passed on to them from their parents and the culture at large; for a while, they will use their inheritance and their sense of entitlement for that most luxurious of rights, the right to turn down one's privileges; for a while at least, they will refuse to inherit the earth.

As for me, I want to figure out, more urgently than before, where I belong

LOST IN TRANSLATION

in this America that's made up of so many sub-Americas. I want, somehow, to give up the condition of being a foreigner. I no longer want to tell people quaint stories from the Old Country, I don't want to be told that "exotic is erotic," or that I have Eastern European intensity, or brooding Galician eyes. I no longer want to be propelled by immigrant chutzpah or desperado energy or usurper's ambition. I no longer want to have the prickly, unrelenting consciousness that I'm living in the medium of a specific culture. It's time to roll down the scrim and see the world directly, as the world. I want to reenter, through whatever Looking Glass will take me there, a state of ordinary reality.

And that's when I begin fighting with my friends.

Although I've always thought of myself as a pliable, all-too-accommodating sort of person, I now get into fights all the time. Sitting with a friend over an afternoon coffee at the Pamplona, or walking with another along one of the more bucolic Cambridge streets, I suddenly find myself in the middle of an argument whose ferocity surprises us both. Anything can start it, any conversational route can suddenly take a swerve that'll lead us down a warpath. We fight about the most standard and the most unlikely subjects: the value of exercise and the proper diet, the implications of China's Cultural Revolution, whether photography is a form of violence, and whether all families are intrinsically repressive. In the conversation of my friends, I sniff out cultural clichés like a hound on the scent of hostile quarry. An innocent remark like "Well, I don't know what to tell you, it really depends on how you feel" provokes in me the most bitter reflections on American individualism, and how a laissez-faire tolerance can mask a callous indifference. Behind the phrase "You've got to stay in control," thrown in as a conversational filler, I vengefully detect an ironical repression on the part of those who hate repression most. In the counternorms my peers profess, I perceive the structure of the norms they ostensibly reject, inverted like an underwater reflection, but still recognizable.

Much of the time, I'm in a rage. Immigrant rage, I call it, and it can erupt at any moment, and at seemingly miniscule provocation. It's directed with equal force at "the Culture"—that weird artifice I'm imprisoned in—and at my closest friends. Or rather, it's directed at the culture-in-my-friends. My misfortune is to see the grid of general assumptions drawn all over particular personalities, to notice the subjection to collective ideology where I should only see the free play of subjectivity. In the most ordinary, interstitial gestures—secretiveness about money, or a reluctance to let sadness show—I sense the tyranny of subliminal conventions. Where my friends suppose they're voicing their deepest beliefs, I whiff the dogma of intellectual fashion; in the midst of a discussion, I cease seeing the face of one person, and start throwing myself against the wall of an invisible, impregnable, collective force.

In Peter Schneider's novel, *The Wall Jumper,* the West German narrator has an East German girlfriend named Lena. Lena has chosen to live on the Western side of the Berlin Wall, but she's severe about what she sees there. When her boyfriend happens to glance at a cover of *Playboy,* she accuses him of decadence, and when he cracks jokes with friends in a bar, she scowls at their triviality. She thinks the West Germans' politics are frivolous, and their pleasures vapid. Her boyfriend sees how much she suffers from this hypersensitivity; for a while, he admires her severity; but finally, it drives him away.

I know what I'm supposed to think of Lena, but I identify with her. I think she's in the right. I want more severe standards of seriousness to obtain. In other words, I'm a scourge.

I think I also know the cause of Lena's defensiveness and seeming arrogance: It's that her version of things is automatically under suspicion and at a discount. That's the real subtext of my fights, the piercing provocation behind the trivial ones. My sense of reality, powerful and vulnerable, is in danger of coming under native domination. My interlocutors in these collisions stare at me with incredulity or dismay; what am I getting so worked up about? They, after all, are only having a conversation. They don't want to question every sentence they speak, and they don't need to; the mass of shared conviction is so thick as to constitute an absoluteness, a reality of a kind. They explain politely and firmly where I'm wrong. Or they become goaded to anger themselves. At parties, my demurrals are often greeted with plain silence, as if they didn't need to be entertained. This increases my frustration, my ire, still more. Censorship in the living room, I mutter to myself bitterly, and after a while begin to censor myself.

"If you've never eaten a real tomato, you'll think that the plastic tomato is the real thing, and moreover, you'll be perfectly satisfied with it," I tell my friends. "It's only when you've tasted them both that you know there's a difference, even though it's almost impossible to describe." This turns out to be the most persuasive argument I have. My friends are moved by the parable of the plastic tomato. But when I try to apply it, by analogy, to the internal realm, they balk. Surely, inside our heads and souls things are more universal, the ocean of reality one and indivisible. No, I shout in every one of our arguments, no! There's a world out there; there are worlds. There are shapes of sensibility incommensurate with each other, topographies of experience one cannot guess from within one's own limited experience.

I think my friends often suspect me of a perverse refusal to play along, an unaccountable desire to provoke and disturb their comfortable consensus. I suspect that the consensus is trying to colonize me and rob me of my distinctive shape and flavor. Still, I have to come to terms with it somehow. Now that I'm no longer a visitor, I can no longer ignore the terms of reality prevailing here, or sit on the margins observing the curious habits of the natives. I have to learn how to live with them, find a common ground. It is my fear that I have to yield too much of my own ground that fills me with such a passionate energy of rage.

MY AMERICAN FRIEND: What did you think about that Hungarian movie last week?
I: I thought it was quite powerful.
M.A.F.: Me too. It was a very smart comment on how all of us can get co-opted by institutions.
I: But it wasn't about all of us. It was about the Communist party in Hungary circa 1948.
M.A.F.: Collaboration isn't the monopoly of the Communist party, you know. You can be bought and co-opted by Time, Inc., quite successfully.
I: I think there may be just the tiniest difference between those two organizations.
M.A.F.: You with your liberal quibbles. I don't think your eyes have been opened about this country.
I: For heaven's sake, don't you understand what went on over there? That people got imprisoned, tortured, hanged?
M.A.F.: Don't get so upset, this was a Hungarian movie. You don't have to be loyal to all of Eastern Europe.
I: I'm loyal to some notion of accuracy, which is more than I can say for you! The world isn't just a projection screen for your ideas, highly correct though they may be.
M.A.F.: I'm allowed to have my interpretation of the world. That's called theory, for your information.
I: That's called not thinking, as far as I can see. You're not allowed to let theory blind you to all distinctions.
M.A.F.: Spare me your sarcasm. Just because awful things happened over there doesn't mean that awful things don't happen here. You like to exaggerate these distinctions, as if you wanted to keep yourself apart.
I: This is not a psychological issue!
M.A.F.: On some level, everything is.
I: This makes me want to emigrate.
M.A.F.: Feel free.

I: How are things going with Doug?
M.A.F.: Terrible. We fuck each other blind, and then he won't tell his wife that we're involved.
I: I imagine that'd be hard to do.
M.A.F.: Why?
I: Why! Haven't you ever heard of possessiveness? Jealousy?

M.A.F.: Yes, I've heard about them. I just don't think they're natural instincts that we're supposed to accept as sacred. They may have served some purpose in the Paleozoic era, but we aren't running around being hunters and gatherers anymore, if you've noticed.

I: Yes, I've noticed. I've also noticed that we continue to be possessive and jealous.

M.A.F.: You know, you're becoming a perfect bourgeois.

I: And you're turning into a Stalinist of everyday life. You're not supposed to be jealous, you're not supposed to be guilty, you're supposed to get in touch with your anger. . . . What is this, some kind of internal morality squad?

M.A.F.: I'm beginning to suspect that you're threatened because I fuck a lot.

I: As far as I'm concerned, you're welcome to have as many affairs as you like.

M.A.F.: You see, you can't even say fuck.

I: I can say fuck very well, thank you.

M.A.F.: Why are you getting so hostile?

I: Because I believe you're attacking me.

M.A.F.: *I'm* attacking *you?*

I: I don't like being on trial for my vocabulary.

M.A.F.: You've been dripping disdain during this whole conversation. You've got me pegged as some naïve American country bumpkin.

I: I think you pretend to innocence. Some things are perfectly self-explanatory, you know.

M.A.F.: Nothing is, unless you're a reactionary.

I: I can't stand this!

M.A.F.: Believe me, the feeling is mutual.

The dialogues don't end, though, with our going off in a huff, or with whatever tentative resolutions we're willing to settle for. Afterward, as I walk down the street hardly conscious of my surroundings, or at night as I toss on my bed, the furious conflicts continue to rage within my own head. The opposing voices become mine, and each of them is ready to lacerate the other. In one of them, I'm ready to dismiss all of American Culture as a misconceived experiment. Scornfully, I think there's too much reinventing of the wheel going on around here. The wheel has already been invented, why bother again? There's too much surprise at the fact that the earth is round, and too much insistence the sun may be moving around us after all. My American Friends think privileged thoughts, I think bitterly, thoughts that cost nothing and that weren't produced by the labor of their own experience. Surplus thoughts that do not have to be paid for in consequences either. Do they, in their own private triangulations, in their night accountings with themselves, believe that a marital squabble has causes too deep for analysis, or that jealousy can be eliminated by ideological fiat, or that the revolution is just around the corner? It is in my incapacity to imagine my friends' private thoughts that the gap between us continues to exist. I can't enter sufficiently into their souls to know where conviction stops and self-presentation begins. Certainly, my American Friends do not deliberately say things they believe to be untrue in order to make themselves look better or somebody else look worse. Hypocrisy, that old-fashioned and un-American vice, requires a public ideal of virtue to pretend to; it also needs the certainty of ego to do the pretending effectively. For all their many certainties, my friends don't seem to have that toughness, or hiddenness, which would enable them to pay lip service to the proper pieties while keeping their true opinions to themselves. The dance of personality happens differently here, and the ideal of personal sincerity—supplanting common virtues, perhaps—is deeply ingrained. My friends want, sincerely, to believe what they would like to believe. But I wonder how much leeway that leaves for a willful self-deception—that subtle falseness that the self only half-knows. "We French lie to others. Americans lie to themselves," a Frenchman I know once remarks, and sometimes I think that my friends' desire to possess only the best ideas prevents them from knowing which ideas are really theirs.

But when the full force of my disapproval is spent, the dialogue with myself takes a U-turn, and I remember that my rage is an immigrant's rage, my suspiciousness the undignified, blinding suspiciousness of an outsider. Then I try, fairly, to think from the other point of view, to stand on the other end of the triangle's base. What's going on here, I think, is a new version of the grand Emersonian experiment, the perennial American experiment, which consists precisely of reinventing the wheel, of taking nothing for granted and beholding human nature with a primeval curiosity, as though nothing has ever been observed or thought before. This is the spirit that invented the cotton gin and Whitman's free verse, and the open marriage. My American Friends are just running a few theoretical experiments on themselves—but why should they do otherwise, since so little in their condition is given, and so little is forbidden either? They live in a culture which is still young, and in which the codes and conventions are still up for grabs. Since there are no rules for how to be a lover, they need to figure out the dynamics of an affair as if it were a complicated problem in physics, and their minds grow new muscles in the process. My American Friends have gained insights about the human mechanism they may never have come by if they had not needed to ask the most rudimentary questions about love and anger and sex. Their explorations are a road to a new, instead of an ancestral, wisdom—a wisdom that may be awkward and ungainly, as youthful wisdom is, but that is required in a world whose social, if not physical, frontiers are still fluid and open and incompletely charted.

Theodor Adorno, that most vitriolic of America's foreign critics, once warned his fellow refugees that if they lost their alienation, they'd lose their souls. A bracingly uncompromising idea of integrity: but I doubt that Adorno could have maintained it over a lifetime without the hope of returning home—without having a friendly audience back there for his dialectical satires. The soul can shrivel from an excess of critical distance, and if I don't want to remain in arid internal exile for the rest of my life, I have to find a way to lose my alienation without losing my self. But how does one bend toward another culture without falling over, how does one strike an elastic balance between rigidity and self-effacement? How does one stop reading the exterior signs of a foreign tribe and step into the inwardness, the viscera of their meanings? Every anthropologist understands the difficulty of such a feat; and so does every immigrant.

It is no wonder—in our time of mass migrations and culture collisions and easy jet travel, when the whole world lies below us every time we rise into the skies, when whole countries move by like bits of checkerboard, ours to play on—it's no wonder that in this time we've developed whole philosophies of cultural relativity, and learned to look at whole literatures, histories, and cultural formations as if they were toy blocks, ours to construct and deconstruct. It's no wonder, also, that we have devised a whole metaphysics for the subjects of difference and otherness. But for all our sophisticated deftness at cross-cultural encounters, fundamental difference, when it's staring at you across the table from within the close-up face of a fellow human being, always contains an element of violation. My American Friends and I find it an offense to our respective identities to touch within each other something alien, unfamiliar, in the very woof and warp of our inner lives. I suppose we could—following one kind of philosophy—adopt an attitude of benevolent openness to each other, and declare our differences interesting and beautiful; but such mellow tolerance is easier to maintain with, say, an Indian swami, who remains safely exotic, and doesn't intend to become our personal friend. Or, adhering to a later, and more skeptical philosophical fashion, we could accept each other's irreducible otherness and give up on our nettlesome and painful back and forth. We could declare each other products of different cultures—as we, of course, are—and leave it, respectfully, at that. But that would leave us separate and impermeable—something that is easier to accept with impersonal entities like class, or gender, or country than with a fellow human being clamoring to be understood.

My American Friends and I are forced to engage in an experiment that is relatively rare; we want to enter into the very textures, the motions and flavors of each other's vastly different subjectivities—and that requires feats of sympathy and even imagination in excess of either benign indifference or a remote respect.

Of course, in these entanglements, our positions are not exactly symmetrical. In the politics of daily perception, I'm at a distinct disadvantage. My American

LOST IN TRANSLATION

Friends are so many, and they share so many assumptions that are quite invisible to them, precisely because they're shared. These are assumptions about the most fundamental human transactions, subcutaneous beliefs, which lie just below the stratum of political opinion or overt ideology: about how much "space," physical or psychological, we need to give each other, about how much "control" is desirable, about what is private and what public, about how much interest in another person's affairs is sympathy and how much interference, about what's a pretty face or a handsome body, about what we're allowed to poke fun at and what we have to revere, about how much we need to hide in order to reveal ourselves. To remain outside such common agreements is to remain outside reality itself—and if I'm not to risk a mild cultural schizophrenia, I have to make a shift in the innermost ways. I have to translate myself. But if I'm to achieve this without becoming assimilated—that is, absorbed—by my new world, the translation has to be careful, the turns of the psyche unforced. To mouth foreign terms without incorporating their meanings is to risk becoming bowdlerized. A true translation proceeds by the motions of understanding and sympathy; it happens by slow increments, sentence by sentence, phrase by phrase.

Does it still matter, in these triangulations, that my version of reality was formed in Eastern Europe? It is well known that the System over there, by specializing in deceit, has bred in its citizens an avid hunger for what they still quaintly call the truth. Of course, the truth is easier to identify when it's simply the opposite of a lie. So much Eastern European thinking moves along the axis of bipolar ideas, still untouched by the peculiar edginess and fluidity created by a more decentered world. Perhaps I'm not quite equal to the challenge of postmodern uncertainty. But as I wrestle with the American Friend in my head, I am haunted not by a longing for certainty but by the idea, almost palpable, of the normal. The normal, in my mental ideogram, is associated with a face: Pani Ruta's face, perhaps, or Piotr Ostropov's. It's not an innocent, or a particularly cheerful face; it bespeaks, instead, both a quick perspicacity and an unforced seriousness. *"C'est normale,"* the expression on this face says. *"N'exagères pas."* It's a face that has seen a lot, and is not easily astonished. It knows, in its cultural memory, the limits of human ideals, and the limitations of human passions. Foibles, in its steady gaze, are just that: foibles. It's not apt to work itself up into moral heat or analytic anguish. It has a stored knowledge, passed on through generations, of the devious traceries of the human heart, and it has learned where the mean lies in the soul, and what's excess. The normal is derived not from a conventional norm but from this knowledge of proportion. The face expresses a skepticism that is a hair's breadth away from cynicism, but is also adjacent to an acceptance of things as they are, and not as they should be or might be in a more ideal, a nonhuman world.

I think if I could enter the subjectivity of that face, then I could encompass both myself and my American Friend within it. I could then see our polarities within some larger, more capacious terms, and resolve our antitheses within a wiser synthesis. I could see that we're both—as the phrase echoes from my childhood—just human. It's that face that I keep as a beacon in my furious mono-dialogues and my triangulations. I want a language that will express what that face knows, a calm and simple language that will subsume the clangor of specialized jargons and of partial visions, a language old enough to plow under the superficial differences between signs, to the deeper strata of significance.

from HUNGER OF MEMORY

Richard Rodriguez

Richard Rodriguez was born in San Francisco, educated at Stanford, Columbia, the University of California, Berkeley, London's Warburg Institute, and awarded a Fulbright scholarship to study English Renaissance literature in England. He is the author of two books, an autobiography, *Hunger of Memory* (1982), and *Children of Mexico* (forthcoming).

I GREW UP VICTIM TO A DISABLING CONFUSION. AS I GREW FLUENT in English, I no longer could speak Spanish with confidence. I continued to understand spoken Spanish. And in high school, I learned how to read and write Spanish. But for many years I could not pronounce it. A powerful guilt blocked my spoken words; an essential glue was missing whenever I'd try to connect words to form sentences. I would be unable to break a barrier of sound, to speak freely. I would speak, or try to speak, Spanish, and I would manage to utter halting, hiccuping sounds that betrayed my unease.

When relatives and Spanish-speaking friends of my parents came to the house, my brother and sisters seemed reticent to use Spanish, but at least they managed to say a few necessary words before being excused. I never managed so gracefully. I was cursed with guilt. Each time I'd hear myself addressed in

Spanish, I would be unable to respond with any success. I'd know the words I wanted to say, but I couldn't manage to say them. I would try to speak, but everything I said seemed to me horribly anglicized. My mouth would not form the words right. My jaw would tremble. After a phrase or two, I'd cough up a warm, silvery sound. And stop.

It surprised my listeners to hear me. They'd lower their heads, better to grasp what I was trying to say. They would repeat their questions in gentle, affectionate voices. But by then I would answer in English. No, no, they would say, we want you to speak to us in Spanish. (". . . en español.") But I couldn't do it. *Pocho* then they called me. Sometimes playfully, teasingly, using the tender diminutive—*mi pochito*. Sometimes not so playfully, mockingly, *Pocho*. (A Spanish dictionary defines that word as an adjective meaning "colorless" or "bland." But I heard it as a noun, naming the Mexican-American who, in becoming an American, forgets his native society.) *"¡Pocho!"* the lady in the Mexican food store muttered, shaking her head. I looked up to the counter where red and green peppers were strung like Christmas tree lights and saw the frowning face of the stranger. My mother laughed somewhere behind me. (She said that her children didn't want to practice "our Spanish" after they started going to school.) My mother's smiling voice made me suspect that the lady who faced me was not really angry at me. But, searching her face, I couldn't find the hint of a smile.

Embarrassed, my parents would regularly need to explain their children's inability to speak flowing Spanish during those years. My mother met the wrath of her brother, her only brother, when he came up from Mexico one summer with his family. He saw his nieces and nephews for the very first time. After listening to me, he looked away and said what a disgrace it was that I couldn't speak Spanish, *"su proprio idioma."* He made that remark to my mother; I noticed, however, that he stared at my father.

I clearly remember one other visitor from those years. A long-time friend of my father from San Francisco would come to stay with us for several days in late August. He took great interest in me after he realized that I couldn't answer his questions in Spanish. He would grab me as I started to leave the kitchen. He would ask me something. Usually he wouldn't bother to wait for my mumbled response. Knowingly, he'd murmur: *"¿Ay Pocho, Pocho, adónde vas?"* And he would press his thumbs into the upper part of my arms, making me squirm with currents of pain. Dumbly, I'd stand there, waiting for his wife to notice us, for her to call him off with a benign smile. I'd giggle, hoping to deflate the tension between us, pretending that I hadn't seen the glittering scorn in his glance.

I remember that man now, but seek no revenge in this telling. I recount such incidents only because they suggest the fierce power Spanish had for many people I met at home; the way Spanish was associated with closeness. Most of those people who called me a *pocho* could have spoken English to me. But they would not. They seemed to think that Spanish was the only language we could use, that Spanish alone permitted our close association. (Such persons are vulnerable always to the ghetto merchant and the politician who have learned the value of speaking their clients' family language to gain immediate trust.) For my part, I felt that I had somehow committed a sin of betrayal by learning English. But betrayal against whom? Not against visitors to the house exactly. No, I felt that I had betrayed my immediate family. I *knew* that my parents had encouraged me to learn English. I *knew* that I had turned to English only with angry reluctance. But once I spoke English with ease, I came to *feel* guilty. (This guilt defied logic.) I felt that I had shattered the intimate bond that had once held the family close. This original sin against my family told whenever anyone addressed me in Spanish and I responded, confounded.

But even during those years of guilt, I was coming to sense certain consoling truths about language and intimacy. I remember playing with a friend in the backyard one day, when my grandmother appeared at the window. Her face was stern with suspicion when she saw the boy (the *gringo*) I was with. In Spanish she called out to me, sounding the whistle of her ancient breath. My companion looked up and watched her intently as she lowered the window and moved, still visible, behind the light curtain, watching us both. He wanted to know what she had said. I started to tell him, to say—to translate her Spanish words into English. The problem was, however, that though I knew how to translate exactly *what* she had told me, I realized that any translation would distort the deepest meaning of her message: It had been directed only to me. This message of intimacy could never be translated because it was not *in* the words she had used but passed *through* them. So any translation would have seemed wrong; her words would have been stripped of an essential meaning. Finally, I decided not to tell my friend anything. I told him that I didn't hear all she had said.

This insight unfolded in time. Making more and more friends outside my house, I began to distinguish intimate voices speaking through *English.* I'd listen at times to a close friend's confidential tone or secretive whisper. Even more remarkable were those instances when, for no special reason apparently, I'd become conscious of the fact that my companion was speaking only to me. I'd marvel just hearing his voice. It was a stunning event: to be able to break through his words, to be able to hear this voice of the other, to realize that it was directed only to me. After such moments of intimacy outside the house, I began to trust hearing intimacy conveyed through my family's English. Voices at home at last punctured sad confusion. I'd hear myself addressed as an intimate at home once again. Such moments were never as raucous with sound as past times had been when we had had "private" Spanish to use. (Our English-sounding house was never to be as noisy as our Spanish-speaking house had been.) Intimate moments were usually soft moments of sound. My mother was in the dining room while I did my homework nearby. And she looked over at me. Smiled. Said something—her words said nothing very important. But her voice sounded to tell me *(We are together)* I was her son.

(Richard!)

Intimacy thus continued at home; intimacy was not stilled by English. It is true that I would never forget the great change of my life, the diminished occasions of intimacy. But there would also be times when I sensed the deépest truth about language and intimacy: *Intimacy is not created by a particular language; it is created by intimates.* The great change in my life was not linguistic but social. If, after becoming a successful student, I no longer heard intimate voices as often as I had earlier, it was not because I spoke English rather than Spanish. It was because I used public language for most of the day. I moved easily at last, a citizen in a crowded city of words.

————

This boy became a man. In private now, alone, I brood over language and intimacy—the great themes of my past. In public I expect most of the faces I meet to be the faces of strangers. (How do you do?) If meetings are quick and impersonal, they have been efficiently managed. I rush past the sounds of voices attending only to the words addressed to me. Voices seem planed to an even surface of sound, soundless. A business associate speaks in a deep baritone, but I pass through the timbre to attend to his words. The crazy man who sells me a newspaper every night mumbles something crazy, but I have time only to pretend that I have heard him say hello. Accented versions of English make little impression on me. In the rush-hour crowd a Japanese tourist asks me a question, and I inch past his accent to concentrate on what he is saying. The Eastern European immigrant in a neighborhood delicatessen speaks to me through a marinade of sounds, but I respond to his words. I note for only a second the Texas accent of the telephone operator or the Mississippi accent of the man who lives in the apartment below me.

My city seems silent until some ghetto black teenagers board the bus I am on. Because I do not take their presence for granted, I listen to the sounds of their voices. Of all the accented versions of English I hear in a day, I hear theirs most intently. They are *the* sounds of the outsider. They annoy me for being loud—so self-sufficient and unconcerned by my presence. Yet for the same reason they seem to me glamorous. (A romantic gesture against public acceptance.) Listening to their shouted laughter, I realize my own quiet. Their voices enclose my isolation. I feel envious, envious of their brazen intimacy.

I warn myself away from such envy, however. I remember the black political activists who have argued in favor of using black English in schools. (Their argument varies only slightly from that made by foreign-language bilingualists.) I have heard "radical" linguists make the point that black English is a complex and intricate version of English. And I do not doubt it. But neither do I think that black English should be a language of public instruction. What makes black English inappropriate in classrooms is not something *in* the language. It is rather what lower-class speakers make of it. Just as Spanish would have been a dangerous language for me to have used at the start of my education, so black English would be a dangerous language to use in the schooling of teenagers for whom it reenforces feelings of public separateness.

This seems to me an obvious point. But one that needs to be made. In recent years there have been attempts to make the language of the alien public language. "Bilingual education, two ways to understand . . . ," television and radio commercials glibly announce. Proponents of bilingual education are careful to say that they want students to acquire good schooling. Their argument goes something like this: Children permitted to use their family language in school will not be so alienated and will be better able to match the progress of English-speaking children in the crucial first months of instruction. (Increasingly confident of their abilities, such children will be more inclined to apply themselves to their studies in the future.) But then the bilingualists claim another, very different goal. They say that children who use their family language in school will retain a sense of their individuality—their ethnic heritage and cultural ties. Supporters of bilingual education thus want it both ways. They propose bilingual schooling as a way of helping students acquire the skills of the classroom crucial for public success. But they likewise insist that bilingual instruction will give students a sense of their identity apart from the public.

Behind this screen there gleams an astonishing promise: One can become a public person while still remaining a private person. At the very same time one can be both! There need be no tension between the self in the crowd and the self apart from the crowd! Who would not want to believe such an idea? Who can be surprised that the scheme has won the support of many middle-class Americans? If the barrio or ghetto child can retain his separateness even while being publicly educated, then it is almost possible to believe that there is no private cost to be paid for public success. Such is the consolation offered by any of the current bilingual schemes. Consider, for example, the bilingual voters' ballot. In some American cities one can cast a ballot printed in several languages. Such a document implies that a person can exercise that most public of rights— the right to vote—while still keeping apart, unassimilated from public life.

It is not enough to say that these schemes are foolish and certainly doomed. Middle-class supporters of public bilingualism toy with the confusion of those

Americans who cannot speak standard English as well as they can. Bilingual enthusiasts, moreover, sin against intimacy. An Hispanic-American writer tells me, "I will never give up my family language; I would as soon give up my soul." Thus he holds to his chest a skein of words, as though it were the source of his family ties. He credits to language what he should credit to family members. A convenient mistake. For as long as he holds on to words, he can ignore how much else has changed in his life.

It has happened before. In earlier decades, persons newly successful and ambitious for social mobility similarly seized upon certain "family words." Working-class men attempting political power took to calling one another "brother." By so doing they escaped oppressive public isolation and were able to unite with many others like themselves. But they paid a price for this union. It was a public union they forged. The word they coined to address one another could never be the sound *(brother)* exchanged by two in intimate greeting. In the union hall the word "brother" became a vague metaphor; with repetition a weak echo of the intimate sound. Context forced the change. Context could not be overruled. Context will always guard the realm of the intimate from public misuse.

Today nonwhite Americans call "brother" to strangers. And white feminists refer to their mass union of "sisters." And white middle-class teenagers continue to prove the importance of context as they try to ignore it. They seize upon the idioms of the black ghetto. But their attempts to appropriate such expressions invariably changes the words. As it becomes a public expression, the ghetto idiom loses its sound—its message of public separateness and strident intimacy. It becomes with public repetition a series of words, increasingly lifeless.

The mystery remains: intimate utterance. The communication of intimacy passes through the word to enliven its sound. But it cannot be held by the word. Cannot be clutched or ever quoted. It is too fluid. It depends not on word but on person.

My grandmother!

She stood among my other relations mocking me when I no longer spoke Spanish. *"Pocho,"* she said. But then it made no difference. (She'd laugh.) Our relationship continued. Language was never its source. She was a woman in her eighties during the first decade of my life. A mysterious woman to me, my only living grandparent. A woman of Mexico. The woman in long black dresses that reached down to her shoes. My one relative who spoke no word of English. She had no interest in *gringo* society. She remained completely aloof from the public. Protected by her daughters. Protected even by me when we went to Safeway together and I acted as her translator. Eccentric woman. Soft. Hard.

When my family visited my aunt's house in San Francisco, my grandmother searched for me among my many cousins. She'd chase them away. Pinching her granddaughters, she'd warn them all away from me. Then she'd take me to her room, where she had prepared for my coming. There would be a chair next to the bed. A dusty jellied candy nearby. And a copy of *Life en Español* for me to examine. "There," she'd say. I'd sit there content. A boy of eight. *Pocho.* Her favorite. I'd sift through the pictures of earthquake-destroyed Latin American cities and blond-wigged Mexican movie stars. And all the while I'd listen to the sound of my grandmother's voice. She'd pace round the room, searching through closets and drawers, telling me stories of her life. Her past. They were stories so familiar to me that I couldn't remember the first time I'd heard them. I'd look up sometimes to listen. Other times she'd look over at me. But she never seemed to expect a response. Sometimes I'd smile or nod. (I understood exactly what she was saying.) But it never seemed to matter to her one way or another. It was enough I was there. The words she spoke were almost irrelevant to that fact—the sounds she made. Content.

The mystery remained: intimate utterance.

"TOMORROW IS FOR OUR MARTYRS"

James Farmer

James Farmer was born in Marshall, Texas. He studied at Wiley College in Texas before pursuing graduate studies in religion at Howard University, where he earned a degree in divinity in 1941. Farmer was co-founder of the Congress of Racial Equality (CORE) in 1942, which was the first African American organization to adopt the methods of nonviolent resistance advocated by Gandhi. In 1961 CORE introduced the Freedom Ride to Alabama and Mississippi. James Farmer is the author of *Freedom When?* (1965) and *Lay Bare the Heart* (1986), his autobiography, from which " 'Tomorrow Is for Our Martyrs' " is taken.

IT HAD BEEN A CALM DAY IN THE OFFICE, IF ANY DAYS COULD BE considered calm in the frenetic atmosphere in which we functioned. There had been no major crises; no mass arrests or calls for immediate bail money; no libel suits had been filed against any of our chapters; no scandals were threatening to erupt in the press; the sky had not fallen that day. Such tranquility was rare, particularly in the freedom summer of 1964 when CORE and SNCC had drawn hundreds of young volunteers into Mississippi, blanketing the state with voter registration workers.

I went home the evening of June 21, 1964, with a sense of well-being, cherishing the night of easy sleep that lay ahead.

Gretchen, now an old dog, labored to get on the bed and snuggle in her favorite spot on the pillows between Lula's head and mine. ("I always knew some bitch would come between us," Lula had once said.) At 3:00 A.M., the bedside phone rang. Cursing the intrusion, I growled hello into the receiver.

CORE's Mississippi field secretary, George Raymond, spoke into the phone: "Jim, three of our guys, Schwerner, Goodman, and Chaney, are missing. They left Meridian yesterday afternoon to go over to the town of Philadelphia in Neshoba County to look at the ruins of the church where they had been teaching voter registration courses. You know that church was burned down a week ago. They were supposed to return by sundown, but they're not back yet. Can you come down right away?"

"Don't jump to conclusions, George," I said. "It's only been a few hours. Maybe they stopped to visit some friends for dinner and decided to take a nap before driving home."

"Face facts, Jim," Raymond shouted into the phone. "Our guys and gals don't just stop over and visit friends or take a nap without calling in. Those three are responsible guys; they wouldn't be nine hours late without calling us. That is, if they could call."

"Okay, I'll be on the next plane to Meridian," I said. "I'll call you back in a few minutes to let you know the time of arrival."

I wanted company going to Neshoba County, so I called Dick Gregory at his home in Chicago, waking him up. Before he answered the phone, I glanced at Lula and saw that she was wide awake, watching with no sign of emotion.

"Hey, big daddy," said Gregory. "What's happening?"

"Three of my guys are missing in Mississippi," I said.

After a brief silence, Gregory said, "Okay. I know you're going down there. I'll meet you there. What airport do I fly to?"

Meridian, though close to Neshoba County, was an island of relative sanity in Mississippi. At the airport when we arrived were a few dozen city policemen with rifles. They were there to ensure my safety. I was given a police escort to the small, unpretentious black hotel. Immediately, I was closeted with George Raymond; Mickey Schwerner's wife, Rita; and several other CORE people in Meridian.

It was early evening on the day after the disappearance, and still there was no word. We were certain our colleagues were dead. Rita, no more than five feet tall and less than a hundred pounds, was dry-eyed and rational. When Mickey had accepted the assignment, both of them were well aware of the risks. Mickey was a social worker from New York who had joined the CORE staff several months earlier. Rita intended to study law.

The local and state officials were showing no interest in locating the men or their bodies. We had alerted the FBI, but there was not yet any evidence of their involvement in the search. A nearby U.S. military unit had just been called in to search some of the swamps for bodies, but the results thus far were negative. The CORE car in which the men had been riding when last seen—a white Ford station wagon—had not been found.

As we discussed things that might be done to aid the search, Rita suggested that going through the ashes at the city dump where trash was burned might possibly yield some fragments of metal that could be identified as having belonged to one of the three men. Nothing more helpful than that came immediately to mind.

I told them that on the following morning, I intended to go into Philadelphia in Neshoba County to talk with Sheriff Lawrence Rainey and Deputy Sheriff Cecil Price about the disappearance of the men. Considering the racist reputation of the sheriff and his deputy, all agreed that one or both of them knew something about the disappearance of our friends.

George Raymond told us that Dick Gregory had called to say that he would be joining me in Meridian early the next morning.

"Good," I said. "Let's time my trip to Philadelphia so that Dick can go along with me."

Early the next morning, after Gregory's arrival, he and I sat in the small hotel office on the ground floor with Raymond and one or two other CORE staffers. There was also a lieutenant of the Meridian City Police. Outside the building were several uniformed policemen and two squad cars, with others ready if needed.

The police official asked me what our plans were and I told him of my intention to talk with Rainey and Price in their office. He let out a low whistle. "Farmer," he said, "you cain't go over there. That's Neshoba County. That's real red-neck territory. We cain't protect you outside of Meridian."

"Lieutenant, we do appreciate the protection the city police is giving us and we want to thank you for it. However, we're not asking for protection, and certainly not from the Meridian police, when we go into Neshoba to see the sheriff and his deputy. That is our right and our duty, and we intend to exercise it."

The lieutenant shook his head and then made a phone call to a Mr. Snodgrass, head of the Mississippi State Police. I knew Snodgrass and had always respected him. He was a conscientious law enforcement officer and, I felt, a humane one. At the various marches and demonstrations CORE had held in Mississippi, when Snodgrass personally was present, I had felt a little more at ease.

This time, I could hear Snodgrass shouting over the phone from ten feet away: "He can't go over there. They'll kill him in that place. We can't protect him."

The lieutenant handed me the phone. "Mr. Snodgrass wants to talk to you."

Still shouting, Snodgrass said, "Farmer, don't go over there. That's one of the worst red-neck areas in this state. They would just as soon kill you as look at you. We cannot protect you over there."

"Mr. Snodgrass, we have not asked for your protection. This is something we have to do, protection or not."

"Okay, okay," Snodgrass replied. "What time are you going?"

"We're leaving here in about an hour and a half," I said and hung up.

We left Meridian in a caravan of five cars, with an escort of city police cars. Dick Gregory and I were in the lead car. Our escort left us at the Meridian city limits.

At the Neshoba County line, there was a roadblock with two sheriff's cars and one unmarked vehicle. A hefty middle-aged man, stereotypical of the "Negro-hating" southern sheriff of that day—chewing either a wad of tobacco or the end of a cigar, I forget which—swaggered up to our lead car. He was closely followed by an equally large but younger deputy sheriff.

The middle-aged man spoke to me: "Whut's yo' name?"

"James Farmer, and this gentleman is Mr. Dick Gregory, the entertainer and social critic."

"Where yo' think you goin'?"

"Mr. Gregory and I are going to Philadelphia."

"Whut yo' gon' do there?"

"We are going to talk to Sheriff Rainey and Deputy Price."

"Whut you' wanna talk ta them 'bout?"

"We are going to talk with them about the disappearance of three of the staff members of the organization I head: Michael Schwerner, Andrew Goodman, and James Chaney."

"Well, Ah'm Sheriff Rainey and this heah's mah deputy, Deputy Price. Y'all wanna talk ta us heah?"

"No. We want to talk to you in your office."

"Awright, folla me."

"Just a moment," I said, "let me pass the word back down the line that we're all going to Philadelphia."

"Naw. Jus' you and this heah man can come," he said, pointing to Gregory. "The rest of them boys'll have to wait heah."

I glanced at the unmarked car and saw that leaning against it was Mr. Snodgrass, watching the scene closely.

Gregory and I followed Rainey and Price into town. Outside the courthouse were several hundred shirt-sleeved white men, standing with assorted weapons in hand. Surrounding the courthouse, though, were state police with rifles pointed at the crowd. State police also flanked the sidewalk leading to the steps of the building.

Gregory and I followed Rainey and Price up those steps and into the courthouse. We followed them to an elevator, and as the doors closed behind us, we thought of the same thing simultaneously. We never should have gotten into that box with those two men. They could have killed us and said that we had jumped them and that they had to shoot us in self-defense. And there would have been no witnesses. But it was too late now. We shrugged our shoulders.

To our relief, the door opened on the second floor without event, and we followed the two men down the hallway to an office at its end. Rainey introduced the three men seated in that office as the city attorney of Philadelphia, the county attorney of Neshoba, and Mr. Snodgrass of the state police. Snodgrass merely nodded at the introduction, and looked sharply at the faces of the other men in the room.

Rainey cleared his throat and rasped, "Ah've got laryngitis or somethin'. This heah man will talk fer me." He was pointing at the county attorney. I nodded, but thought it strange that I had not noticed the impaired throat during our conversation at the roadblock.

The county attorney squinted his eyes, and said to me, "Well, we're all heah. What was it you wanted to talk to the sheriff and his deputy about?"

I told him that, as national director of CORE, I was charged with responsibility for the supervision of all members of the CORE staff. Three members of that staff had been missing for thirty-six hours. Mr. Gregory and I were there, I said, to try to find out what had happened to them and whether they were alive or dead. Specifically, I indicated I wanted to ask Deputy Price a question.

Price then sat upright in his seat. Deputy Price had given conflicting stories to the press, I pointed out. First, he had said he never saw the men, then he said he had arrested them and released them in the evening. I wanted to know the true story.

The attorney looked at Price and the deputy spoke: "Ah'll tell ya the God's truth. Ah did see them boys. I arrested them for speedin' and took them ta jail—"

"What time did you arrest them?" I said.

"It was about three or three-thirty. yeah, closer to three-thirty when Ah arrested them. Ah kept them in jail till 'bout six-thirty or seven in the evenin'—"

"Why would you keep men in jail for three and a half hours for speeding?"

"Ah had to find out how much the justice of the peace was gonna fine them. The justice of the peace was not at home, so Ah had to wait till he got home. He fined them fifteen dollars. That colored boy, Chaney, who wuz drivin' the car, didn't have no fifteen dollars, but one of them Jew boys, Schwerner, had fifteen an' he paid the fine. Then, I took them boys out to the edge of town and put them in their car and they headed for Meridian. Ah sat in mah car and watched their taillights as long as Ah could see them. An' they were goin' toward Meridian. Then Ah turned around and came back into town, and that was the last Ah seen of them boys. Now, that's the God's truth."

''TOMORROW IS FOR OUR MARTYRS''

"At this moment," I said, "I have about fifteen young men waiting at the county line. They are friends and coworkers of Mickey Schwerner, Jim Chaney, and Andy Goodman. They want to join in the search for their missing colleagues."

"What would they do? Where would they look?" the county attorney asked, rather anxiously, I felt. Could it have been he thought we might have gotten some clue as to where the bodies could be found?

"They would look anywhere and everywhere that bodies could be hidden or disposed of—in the woods, the swamps, the rivers, whatever."

"No!" he said. "We can't let them go out there by themselves without any supervision."

"Oh, they'll be supervised," I replied. "I'll go with them."

"And I'll be with them, too," Gregory added.

"No, no! I can't let you do that. This is private property all around heah and the owners could shoot you for trespassing. We don't want anything to happen to you down here," he said.

"Something already *has* happened to three of our brothers. I'll take my chances," I said.

"No, these swamps around here are very dangerous," the attorney said. "They've got water moccasins, rattlesnakes, copperheads, and everything else in them. Like I said, we don't want anything to happen to you. We won't allow you to do it."

"Then," I said, "I have another question. We heard over the car radio coming here that the car in which the men were riding, that white Ford station wagon, has been found burned out on the other side of town, the opposite side from Meridian. That automobile belonged to the organization I serve as national director, and I want to look at what is left of it."

"No," said the county lawyer emphatically. "We can't let you do that either. You might destroy fingerprints or some other evidence that will be useful to Sheriff Rainey or Deputy Price in solving this crime—if there has been a crime. You know, those boys may have decided to go up north or someplace and have a short vacation. They'll probably be coming back shortly."

Dick Gregory, who had shown masterful restraint thus far, rose to his feet. He began speaking to the assembled men, pointing his finger at them, looking at each one with sharp eyes, and speaking with an even sharper tongue. He made it clear that he thought someone there knew much more about the disappearance of the three men than was being told. He said that we were not going to let this matter rest but were going to get to the bottom of it, and the guilty persons were going to pay for their crimes.

I felt that this was neither the time nor the place to have a showdown with Rainey and Price. Yet, I was struggling with my own feelings. I was not Christ.

I was not Gandhi. I was not King. I wanted to kill those men—not with bullets, but with my fingers around their throats, squeezing tighter as I watched life ebb from their eyes.

Back in Meridian, I called a meeting of the CORE staff and summer volunteers. Our embattled southern staff evidenced little of the black/white tension so prevalent in the North. At the meeting, I announced that I wanted two volunteers for an extraordinarily important and dangerous mission. The qualifications for the volunteers were that they had to be black, male, and young. I wanted them to slip into Philadelphia in Neshoba County in the dead of night, not going by the main highway but by side routes. They would very quietly disappear into the black community of Philadelphia, see a minister, and ask if he could find a family for them to stay with.

They would have to do all they could to keep the officials from knowing that they were there or of their mission. I believed that the black community would take them in, for that is an old tradition among blacks—the extended family. They would have to try not to be conspicuous, but to disappear into the woodwork, so to speak, until they were trusted by the blacks in Philadelphia.

In all probability, George Raymond and I believed, some person or persons in the black community knew what had happened to the three men. Someone in that community always does, but no one would tell the FBI or any city or state officials, for fear of retribution.

When accepted and trusted, our men were to begin asking discreet questions. When any information was secured, they were to communicate that to me. If they did so by phone, it was to be from a phone booth and not the same one each time. If by letter, the message should be mailed from another town, and without a return address on the envelope. If they had any reason to believe that Rainey or Price knew of their presence or mission, they were to contact me immediately by phone.

Practically all hands went up. Everyone wanted to go. When George Raymond and I selected two, most others felt let down and angry.

The two volunteers left the meeting, packed small suitcases, and surreptitiously moved into Philadelphia. It was about two weeks before I began getting reports. Those reports from eyewitnesses of various parts of the tragedy indicated a clear scenario, the stage for which had been set by an earlier report from another source.

A black maid in Meridian had told us of overhearing a phone call from a black Meridian man who was speaking in an open telephone booth. The man allegedly fingered the three young CORE men. The maid, of course, did not know to whom the call was made, but we suspected it was either to Sheriff Rainey or Deputy Price. The caller said that the three guys, two Jews and one colored, were in a white '62 Ford station wagon. He also gave the license number of the car. He said the three had just left Meridian, heading for Philadelphia.

The scenario as told to the CORE volunteers by various eyewitnesses was as follows: when Schwerner, Goodman, and Chaney entered Philadelphia, they were trailed by Deputy Price, who kept his distance. When they stopped at the charred ruins of the small black church on the other side of town, Price parked at a distance and watched them. As they got back into the car to drive on, Deputy Price, according to the witnesses, closed in on them.

James Chaney, who was driving the car, saw Price in his rearview mirror and, knowing Price's reputation as a "nigger killer," sped up.

Price then shot a tire on the Ford wagon and it came to a halt. The men were arrested and taken to jail, as Price had said. Also, as the deputy had told us, he took them out of jail about sundown, but there the similarity between the deputy's story and fact seemed to end.

He took them to the other side of town, not the Meridian side, and turned them over to a waiting mob in a vacant field. The three men were pulled into the field and pushed beneath a large tree. There, members of the mob held Schwerner and Goodman while the other mobsters beat Chaney without mercy. He was knocked down, stomped, kicked, and clubbed. Schwerner broke away from his captives and tried to help Chaney. He was then clubbed once on the head and knocked unconscious. Seconds later, he revived and was again held by members of the mob while the beating of Chaney continued.

By this time Chaney appeared dead, and the beating stopped. Members of the mob huddled, and then Deputy Price, who was also in the group, went back to his car and drove away. The mob remained there, holding Schwerner and Goodman and looking at the prone form of Chaney on the ground.

A little while later, Price returned and said something to the members of the mob. They then dragged Schwerner and Goodman and Chaney's body to a car and threw them into it. The car drove off.

The latter scene was allegedly witnessed by two blacks crossing different corners of the field at about the same time, on the way to church for a prayer meeting.

We turned this information over to the FBI.

It was weeks later—August fifth—when I received a call from Deke DeLoach, then assistant to the director at FBI headquarters in Washington, D.C.

DeLoach said, "Mr. Farmer, since Schwerner, Goodman, and Chaney were members of your staff, I wanted you to be the first to know. We have found the bodies. An informant told us to look under a fake dam. We drove in a bulldozer and with the first scoop of earth uncovered the three bodies. Though they were badly decomposed, there was every evidence that Chaney had received the most brutal beating imaginable. It seemed that every bone in his body was broken. He was beaten to death. Each of the other two was shot once in the heart."

Months later, on October 3, 1964, the FBI arrested a group of men and charged them with conspiracy to violate the civil rights of the dead trio—the only charge available to the federal government, since murder is a state charge. Mississippi never charged them with murder.

Among those arrested and convicted of conspiracy, in addition to Deputy Price, was a minister of the gospel. When he prayed to his God, did he feel remorse? Or had he silenced the still, small voice within his soul?

Evil societies always kill their consciences.

We, who are the living, possess the past. Tomorrow is for our martyrs.

THE WHITE ALBUM

Joan Didion

Joan Didion, novelist, essayist, and political journalist, was born in Sacramento, California. She graduated from the University of California, Berkeley. Among her novels are *Play It as It Lays,* a 1970 nominee for the National Book Award; *A Book of Common Prayer* (1977); and *Democracy: A Novel* (1984). Her nonfiction titles include *Slouching Towards Bethlehem* (1968), *The White Album* (1979), *Salvador* (1983), and *After Henry* (1992).

1.

WE TELL OURSELVES STORIES IN ORDER TO LIVE. THE PRINCESS IS caged in the consulate. The man with the candy will lead the children into the sea. The naked woman on the ledge outside the window on the sixteenth floor is a victim of accidie, or the naked woman is an exhibitionist, and it would be "interesting" to know which. We tell ourselves that it makes some difference whether the naked woman is about to commit a mortal sin or is about to register a political protest or is about to be, the Aristophanic view, snatched back to the human condition by the fireman in priest's clothing just visible in the window behind her, the one smiling at the telephoto lens. We look for the sermon in the suicide, for the social or moral lesson in the murder of five. We interpret what we see, select the most workable of the multiple choices. We live entirely, especially if we are writers, by the imposition of a narrative line upon disparate images, by the "ideas" with which we have learned to freeze the shifting phantasmagoria which is our actual experience.

Or at least we do for a while. I am talking here about a time when I began to doubt the premises of all the stories I had ever told myself, a common condition but one I found troubling. I suppose this period began around 1966 and continued until 1971. During those five years I appeared, on the face of it, a competent enough member of some community or another, a signer of contracts and Air Travel cards, a citizen: I wrote a couple of times a month for one magazine or another, published two books, worked on several motion pictures; participated in the paranoia of the time, in the raising of a small child, and in the entertainment of large numbers of people passing through my house; made gingham curtains for spare bedrooms, remembered to ask agents if any reduction of points would be *pari passu* with the financing studio, put lentils to soak on Saturday night for lentil soup on Sunday, made quarterly F.I.C.A. payments and renewed my driver's license on time, missing on the written examination only the question about the financial responsibility of California drivers. It was a time of my life when I was frequently "named." I was named godmother to children. I was named lecturer and panelist, colloquist and conferee. I was even named, in 1968, a *Los Angeles Times* "Woman of the Year," along with Mrs. Ronald Reagan, the Olympic swimmer Debbie Meyer, and ten other California women who seemed to keep in touch and do good works. I did no good works but I tried to keep in touch. I was responsible. I recognized my name when I saw it. Once in a while I even answered letters addressed to me, not exactly upon receipt but eventually, particularly if the letters had come from strangers. "During my absence from the country these past eighteen months," such replies would begin.

This was an adequate enough performance, as improvisations go. The only problem was that my entire education, everything I had ever been told or had told myself, insisted that the production was never meant to be improvised: I was supposed to have a script, and had mislaid it. I was supposed to hear cues, and no longer did. I was meant to know the plot, but all I knew was what I saw: flash pictures in variable sequence, images with no "meaning" beyond their temporary arrangement, not a movie but a cutting-room experience. In what would probably be the middle of my life I wanted still to believe in the narrative and in the narrative's intelligibility, but to know that one could change the sense with every cut was to begin to perceive the experience as rather more electrical than ethical.

During this period I spent what were for me the usual proportions of time in Los Angeles and New York and Sacramento. I spent what seemed to many people I knew an eccentric amount of time in Honolulu, the particular aspect of which lent the illusion that I could at any minute order from room service a revisionist theory of my own history, garnished with a vanda orchid. I watched Robert Kennedy's funeral on a verandah at the Royal Hawaiian Hotel in Honolulu, and also the first reports from My Lai. I reread all of George Orwell on the Royal Hawaiian Beach, and I also read, in the papers that came one day late from the mainland, the story of Betty Lansdown Fouquet, a twenty-six-year-old woman with faded blond hair who put her five-year-old daughter out to die on the center divider of Interstate 5 some miles south of the last Bakersfield exit. The child, whose fingers had to be pried loose from the Cyclone fence when she was rescued twelve hours later by the California Highway Patrol, reported that she had run after the car carrying her mother and stepfather and brother and sister for "a long time." Certain of these images did not fit into any narrative I knew.

Another flash cut:

In June of this year patient experienced an attack of vertigo, nausea, and a feeling that she was going to pass out. A thorough medical evaluation elicited no positive findings and she was placed on Elavil, Mg 20, tid. . . . The Rorschach record is interpreted as describing a personality in process of deterioration with abundant signs of failing defenses and increasing inability of the ego to mediate the world of reality and to cope with normal stress. . . . Emotionally, patient has alienated herself almost entirely from the world of other human beings. Her fantasy life appears to have been virtually completely preempted by primitive, regressive libidinal preoccupations many of which are distorted and bizarre. . . . In a technical sense basic affective controls appear to be intact but it is equally clear that they are insecurely and tenuously maintained for the present by a variety of defense mechanisms including intellectualization, obsessive-compulsive devices, projection, reaction-formation, and somatization, all of which now seem inadequate to their task of controlling or containing an underlying psychotic process and are therefore in process of failure. The content of patient's responses is highly unconventional and frequently bizarre, filled with sexual and anatomical preoccupations, and basic reality contact is obviously and seriously impaired at times. In quality and level of sophistication patient's responses are characteristic of those of individuals of high average or superior intelligence but she is now functioning intellectually in impaired fashion at barely average level. Patient's thematic productions on the Thematic Apperception Test emphasize her fundamentally pessimistic, fatalistic, and depressive view of the world around her. It is as though she feels deeply that all human effort is foredoomed to failure, a conviction which seems to push her further into a dependent, passive withdrawal. In her view

she lives in a world of people moved by strange, conflicted, poorly comprehended, and, above all, devious motivations which commit them inevitably to conflict and failure. . . .

The patient to whom this psychiatric report refers is me. The tests mentioned—the Rorschach, the Thematic Apperception Test, the Sentence Completion Test and the Minnesota Multiphasic Personality Index—were administered
privately, in the outpatient psychiatric clinic at St. John's Hospital in Santa
Monica, in the summer of 1968, shortly after I suffered the "attack of vertigo
and nausea" mentioned in the first sentence and shortly before I was named a
Los Angeles Times "Woman of the Year." By way of comment I offer only that
an attack of vertigo and nausea does not now seem to me an inappropriate
response to the summer of 1968.

2.

In the years I am talking about I was living in a large house in a part of Hollywood
that had once been expensive and was now described by one of my acquaintances
as a "senseless-killing neighborhood." This house on Franklin Avenue was
rented, and paint peeled inside and out, and pipes broke and window sashes
crumbled and the tennis court had not been rolled since 1933, but the rooms were
many and high-ceilinged and, during the five years that I lived there, even the
rather sinistral inertia of the neighborhood tended to suggest that I should live
in the house indefinitely.

In fact I could not, because the owners were waiting only for a zoning
change to tear the house down and build a high-rise apartment building, and for
that matter it was precisely this anticipation of imminent but not exactly immediate destruction that lent the neighborhood its particular character. The house
across the street had been built for one of the Talmadge sisters, had been the
Japanese consulate in 1941, and was now, although boarded up, occupied by a
number of unrelated adults who seemed to constitute some kind of therapy
group. The house next door was owned by Synanon. I recall looking at a house
around the corner with a rental sign on it: this house had once been the Canadian
consulate, had twenty-eight large rooms and two refrigerated fur closets, and
could be rented, in the spirit of the neighborhood, only on a month-to-month
basis, unfurnished. Since the inclination to rent an unfurnished twenty-eight-
room house for a month or two is a distinctly special one, the neighborhood was
peopled mainly by rock-and-roll bands, therapy groups, very old women wheeled
down the street by practical nurses in soiled uniforms, and by my husband, my
daughter and me.

THE WHITE ALBUM

Q. And what else happened, if anything. . . .

A. He said that he thought that I could be a star, like, you know, a young Burt Lancaster, you know, that kind of stuff.

Q. Did he mention any particular name?

A. Yes, sir.

Q. What name did he mention?

A. He mentioned a lot of names. He said Burt Lancaster. He said Clint Eastwood. He said Fess Parker. He mentioned a lot of names. . . .

Q. Did you talk after you ate?

A. While we were eating, after we ate. Mr. Novarro told our fortunes with some cards and he read our palms.

Q. Did he tell you you were going to have a lot of good luck or bad luck or what happened?

A. He wasn't a good palm reader.

These are excerpts from the testimony of Paul Robert Ferguson and Thomas Scott Ferguson, brothers, ages twenty-two and seventeen respectively, during their trial for the murder of Ramon Novarro, age sixty-nine, at his house in Laurel Canyon, not too far from my house in Hollywood, on the night of October 30, 1968. I followed this trial quite closely, clipping reports from the newspapers and later borrowing a transcript from one of the defense attorneys. The younger of the brothers, "Tommy Scott" Ferguson, whose girl friend testified that she had stopped being in love with him "about two weeks after Grand Jury," said that he had been unaware of Mr. Novarro's career as a silent film actor until he was shown, at some point during the night of the murder, a photograph of his host as Ben-Hur. The older brother, Paul Ferguson, who began working carnivals when he was twelve and described himself at twenty-two as having had "a fast life and a good one," gave the jury, upon request, his definition of a hustler: "A hustler is someone who can talk—not just to men, to women, too. Who can cook. Can keep company. Wash a car. Lots of things make up a hustler. There are a lot of lonely people in this town, man." During the course of the trial each of the brothers accused the other of the murder. Both were convicted. I read the transcript several times, trying to bring the picture into some focus which did not suggest that I lived, as my psychiatric report had put it, "in a world of people moved by strange, conflicted, poorly comprehended and, above all, devious motivations"; I never met the Ferguson brothers.

I did meet one of the principals in another Los Angeles County murder trial during those years: Linda Kasabian, star witness for the prosecution in what was commonly known as the Manson Trial. I once asked Linda what she thought about the apparently chance sequence of events which had brought her first to the Spahn Movie Ranch and then to the Sybil Brand Institute for Women on charges, later dropped, of murdering Sharon Tate Polanski, Abigail Folger, Jay Sebring, Voytek Frykowski, Steven Parent, and Rosemary and Leno LaBianca. "Everything was to teach me something," Linda said. Linda did not believe that chance was without pattern. Linda operated on what I later recognized as dice theory, and so, during the years I am talking about, did I.

It will perhaps suggest the mood of those years if I tell you that during them I could not visit my mother-in-law without averting my eyes from a framed verse, a "house blessing," which hung in a hallway of her house in West Hartford, Connecticut.

> *God bless the corners of this house,*
> *And be the lintel blest—*
> *And bless the hearth and bless the board*
> *And bless each place of rest—*
> *And bless the crystal windowpane that lets the starlight in*
> *And bless each door that opens wide, to stranger as to kin.*

This verse had on me the effect of a physical chill, so insistently did it seem the kind of "ironic" detail the reporters would seize upon, the morning the bodies were found. In my neighborhood in California we did not bless the door that opened wide to stranger as to kin. Paul and Tommy Scott Ferguson were the strangers at Ramon Novarro's door, up on Laurel Canyon. Charles Manson was the stranger at Rosemary and Leno LaBianca's door, over in Los Feliz. Some strangers at the door knocked, and invented a reason to come inside: a call, say, to the Triple A, about a car not in evidence. Others just opened the door and walked in, and I would come across them in the entrance hall. I recall asking one such stranger what he wanted. We looked at each other for what seemed a long time, and then he saw my husband on the stair landing. "Chicken Delight," he said finally, but we had ordered no Chicken Delight, nor was he carrying any. I took the license number of his panel truck. It seems to me now that during those years I was always writing down the license numbers of panel trucks, panel trucks circling the block, panel trucks parked across the street, panel trucks idling at the intersection. I put these license numbers in a dressing-table drawer where they could be found by the police when the time came.

That the time would come I never doubted, at least not in the inaccessible places of the mind where I seemed more and more to be living. So many encounters in those years were devoid of any logic save that of the dreamwork. In the big house on Franklin Avenue many people seemed to come and go without relation to what I did. I knew where the sheets and towels were kept but I did not always know who was sleeping in every bed. I had the keys but not the key. I remember taking a 25–mg. Compazine one Easter Sunday and making a large and elaborate lunch for a number of people, many of whom were still around on Monday. I remember walking barefoot all day on the worn hardwood floors of that house and I remember "Do You Wanna Dance" on the record player, "Do You Wanna Dance" and "Visions of Johanna" and a song called "Midnight Confessions." I remember a babysitter telling me that she saw death in my aura. I remember chatting with her about reasons why this might be so, paying her, opening all the French windows and going to sleep in the living room.

It was hard to surprise me in those years. It was hard to even get my attention. I was absorbed in my intellectualization, my obsessive-compulsive devices, my projection, my reaction-formation, my somatization, and in the transcript of the Ferguson trial. A musician I had met a few years before called from a Ramada Inn in Tuscaloosa to tell me how to save myself through Scientology. I had met him once in my life, had talked to him for maybe half an hour about brown rice and the charts, and now he was telling me from Alabama about E-meters, and how I might become a Clear. I received a telephone call from a stranger in Montreal who seemed to want to enlist me in a narcotics operation. "Is it cool to talk on this telephone?" he asked several times. "Big Brother isn't listening?"

I said that I doubted it, although increasingly I did not.

"Because what we're talking about, basically, is applying the Zen philosophy to money and business, dig? And if I say we are going to finance the underground, and if I mention major money, you know what I'm talking about because you know what's going down, right?"

Maybe he was not talking about narcotics. Maybe he was talking about turning a profit on M–1 rifles: I had stopped looking for the logic in such calls. Someone with whom I had gone to school in Sacramento and had last seen in 1952 turned up at my house in Hollywood in 1968 in the guise of a private detective from West Covina, one of very few licensed women private detectives in the State of California. "They call us Dickless Tracys," she said, idly but definitely fanning out the day's mail on the hall table. "I have a lot of very close friends in law enforcement," she said then. "You might want to meet them." We exchanged promises to keep in touch but never met again: a not atypical encounter of the period. The Sixties were over before it occurred to me that this visit might have been less than entirely social.

3.

It was six, seven o'clock of an early spring evening in 1968 and I was sitting on the cold vinyl floor of a sound studio on Sunset Boulevard, watching a band called The Doors record a rhythm track. On the whole my attention was only minimally engaged by the preoccupations of rock-and-roll bands (I had already heard about acid as a transitional stage and also about the Maharishi and even about Universal Love, and after a while it all sounded like marmalade skies to me), but The Doors were different, The Doors interested me. The Doors seemed unconvinced that love was brotherhood and the Kama Sutra. The Doors' music insisted that love was sex and sex was death and therein lay salvation. The Doors were the Norman Mailers of the Top Forty, missionaries of apocalyptic sex. *Break on through,* their lyrics urged, and *Light my fire,* and:

> *Come on baby, gonna take a little ride*
> *Goin' down by the ocean side*
> *Gonna get real close*
> *Get real tight*
> *Baby gonna drown tonight—*
> *Goin' down, down, down.*

On this evening in 1968 they were gathered together in uneasy symbiosis to make their third album, and the studio was too cold and the lights were too bright and there were masses of wires and banks of the ominous blinking electronic circuitry with which musicians live so easily. There were three of the four Doors. There was a bass player borrowed from a band called Clear Light. There were the producer and the engineer and the road manager and a couple of girls and a Siberian husky named Nikki with one gray eye and one gold. There were paper bags half filled with hard-boiled eggs and chicken livers and cheeseburgers and empty bottles of apple juice and California rosé. There was everything and everybody The Doors needed to cut the rest of this third album except one thing, the fourth Door, the lead singer, Jim Morrison, a twenty-four-year-old graduate of U.C.L.A. who wore black vinyl pants and no underwear and tended to suggest some range of the possible just beyond a suicide pact. It was Morrison who had described The Doors as "erotic politicians." It was Morrison who had defined the group's interests as "anything about revolt, disorder, chaos, about activity that appears to have no meaning." It was Morrison who got arrested in Miami in December of 1967 for giving an "indecent" performance. It was Morrison who wrote most of The Doors' lyrics, the peculiar character of which was to reflect either an ambiguous paranoia or a quite unambiguous insistence upon the love-death as the ultimate high. And it was Morrison who was missing. It was Ray Manzarek and Robby Krieger and John Densmore who made The Doors sound the way they sounded, and maybe it was Manzarek and Krieger and Densmore who made seventeen out of twenty interviewees on *American Bandstand* prefer The Doors over all other bands, but it was Morrison who got up there in his black vinyl pants with no underwear and projected the idea, and it was Morrison they were waiting for now.

"Hey listen," the engineer said. "I was listening to an FM station on the way over here, they played three Doors songs, first they played 'Back Door Man' and then 'Love Me Two Times' and 'Light My Fire.'"

"I heard it," Densmore muttered. "I heard it."

"So what's wrong with somebody playing three of your songs?"

"This cat dedicates it to his family."

"Yeah? To his family?"

"To his family. Really crass."

Ray Manzarek was hunched over a Gibson keyboard. "You think *Morrison*'s going to come back?" he asked to no one in particular.

No one answered.

"So we can do some *vocals?*" Manzarek said.

The producer was working with the tape of the rhythm track they had just recorded. "I hope so," he said without looking up.

"Yeah," Manzarek said. "So do I."

My leg had gone to sleep, but I did not stand up; unspecific tensions seemed to be rendering everyone in the room catatonic. The producer played back the rhythm track. The engineer said that he wanted to do his deep-breathing exercises. Manzarek ate a hard-boiled egg. "Tennyson made a mantra out of his own name," he said to the engineer. "I don't know if he said 'Tennyson Tennyson Tennyson' or 'Alfred Alfred Alfred' or 'Alfred Lord Tennyson,' but anyway, he did it. Maybe he just said 'Lord Lord Lord.'"

"Groovy," the Clear Light bass player said. He was an amiable enthusiast, not at all a Door in spirit.

"I wonder what Blake said," Manzarek mused. "Too bad *Morrison*'s not here *Morrison* would know."

It was a long while later. Morrison arrived. He had on his black vinyl pants and he sat down on a leather couch in front of the four big blank speakers and he closed his eyes. The curious aspect of Morrison's arrival was this: no one acknowledged it. Robby Krieger continued working out a guitar passage. John Densmore tuned his drums. Manzarek sat at the control console and twirled a corkscrew and let a girl rub his shoulders. The girl did not look at Morrison, although he was in her direct line of sight. An hour or so passed, and still no one had spoken to Morrison. Then Morrison spoke to Manzarek. He spoke almost in a whisper, as if he were wresting the words from behind some disabling aphasia.

"It's an hour to West Covina," he said. "I was thinking maybe we should spend the night out there after we play."

Manzarek put down the corkscrew. "Why?" he said.

"Instead of coming back."

Manzarek shrugged. "We were planning to come back."

"Well, I was thinking, we could rehearse out there."

Manzarek said nothing.

"We could get in a rehearsal, there's a Holiday Inn next door."

"We could do that," Manzarek said. "Or we could rehearse Sunday, in town."

"I guess so." Morrison paused. "Will the place be ready to rehearse Sunday?"

Manzarek looked at him for a while. "No," he said then.

I counted the control knobs on the electronic console. There were seventy-six. I was unsure in whose favor the dialogue had been resolved, or if it had been resolved at all. Robby Krieger picked at his guitar, and said that he needed a fuzz box. The producer suggested that he borrow one from the Buffalo Springfield, who were recording in the next studio. Krieger shrugged. Morrison sat down again on the leather couch and leaned back. He lit a match. He studied the flame awhile and then very slowly, very deliberately, lowered it to the fly of his black vinyl pants. Manzarek watched him. The girl who was rubbing Manzarek's shoulders did not look at anyone. There was a sense that no one was going to leave the room, ever. It would be some weeks before The Doors finished recording this album. I did not see it through.

4.

Someone once brought Janis Joplin to a party at the house on Franklin Avenue: she had just done a concert and she wanted brandy-and-Benedictine in a water tumbler. Music people never wanted ordinary drinks. They wanted sake, or champagne cocktails, or tequila neat. Spending time with music people was confusing, and required a more fluid and ultimately a more passive approach than I ever acquired. In the first place time was never of the essence: we would have dinner at nine unless we had it at eleven-thirty, or we could order in later. We would go down to U.S.C. to see the Living Theater if the limo came at the very moment when no one had just made a drink or a cigarette or an arrangement to meet Ultra Violet at the Montecito. In any case David Hockney was coming by. In any case Ultra Violet was not at the Montecito. In any case we would go down to U.S.C. and see the Living Theater tonight or we would see the Living Theater another night, in New York, or Prague. First we wanted sushi for twenty, steamed clams, vegetable vindaloo and many rum drinks with gardenias for our hair. First we wanted a table for twelve, fourteen at the most, although there might be six more, or eight more, or eleven more: there would never be one or two more, because music people did not travel in groups of "one" or "two." John and Michelle Phillips, on their way to the hospital for the birth of their daughter Chynna, had the limo detour into Hollywood in order to pick up a friend, Ann Marshall. This incident, which I often embroider in my mind to include an imaginary second detour, to the Luau for gardenias, exactly describes the music business to me.

5.

Around five o'clock on the morning of October 28, 1967, in the desolate district between San Francisco Bay and the Oakland estuary that the Oakland police call Beat 101A, a twenty-five-year-old black militant named Huey P. Newton was stopped and questioned by a white police officer named John Frey, Jr. An hour later Huey Newton was under arrest at Kaiser Hospital in Oakland, where he had gone for emergency treatment of a gunshot wound in his stomach, and a few weeks later he was indicted by the Alameda County Grand Jury on charges of murdering John Frey, wounding another officer, and kidnapping a bystander.

In the spring of 1968, when Huey Newton was awaiting trial, I went to see him in the Alameda County Jail. I suppose I went because I was interested in the alchemy of issues, for an issue is what Huey Newton had by then become. To understand how that had happened you must first consider Huey Newton, who he was. He came from an Oakland family, and for a while he went to Merritt College. In October of 1966 he and a friend named Bobby Seale organized what they called the Black Panther Party. They borrowed the name from the emblem used by the Freedom Party in Lowndes County, Alabama, and, from the beginning, they defined themselves as a revolutionary political group. The Oakland police knew the Panthers, and had a list of twenty or so Panther cars. I am telling you neither that Huey Newton killed John Frey nor that Huey Newton did not kill John Frey, for in the context of revolutionary politics Huey Newton's guilt or innocence was irrelevant. I am telling you only how Huey Newton happened to be in the Alameda County Jail, and why rallies were held in his name, demonstrations organized whenever he appeared in court. LET'S SPRING HUEY, the buttons read (fifty cents each), and here and there on the courthouse steps, among the Panthers with their berets and sunglasses, the chants would go up:

Get your M–
31.
'Cause baby we gonna
Have some fun.
BOOM BOOM. BOOM BOOM.

"Fight on, brother," a woman would add in the spirit of a good-natured amen. "Bang-bang."

Bullshit bullshit
Can't stand the game
White man's playing.
One way out, one way out.
BOOM BOOM. BOOM BOOM.

In the corridor downstairs in the Alameda County Courthouse there was a crush of lawyers and CBC correspondents and cameramen and people who wanted to "visit Huey."

"Eldridge doesn't mind if I go up," one of the latter said to one of the lawyers.

"If Eldridge doesn't mind, it's all right with me," the lawyer said. "If you've got press credentials."

"I've got kind of dubious credentials."

"I can't take you up then. *Eldridge* has got dubious credentials. One's bad enough. I've got a good working relationship up there, I don't want to blow it." The lawyer turned to a cameraman. "You guys rolling yet?"

On that particular day I was allowed to go up, and a *Los Angeles Times* man, and a radio newscaster. We all signed the police register and sat around a scarred pine table and waited for Huey Newton. "The only thing that's going to free Huey Newton," Rap Brown had said recently at a Panther rally in Oakland Auditorium, "is gunpowder." "Huey Newton laid down his life for us," Stokely Carmichael had said the same night. But of course Huey Newton had not yet laid down his life at all, was just here in the Alameda County Jail waiting to be tried, and I wondered if the direction these rallies were taking ever made him uneasy, ever made him suspect that in many ways he was more useful to the revolution behind bars than on the street. He seemed, when he finally came in, an extremely likable young man, engaging, direct, and I did not get the sense that he had intended to become a political martyr. He smiled at us all and waited for his lawyer, Charles Garry, to set up a tape recorder, and he chatted softly with Eldridge Cleaver, who was then the Black Panthers' Minister of Information. (Huey Newton was still the Minister of Defense.) Eldridge Cleaver wore a black sweater and one gold earring and spoke in an almost inaudible drawl and was allowed to see Huey Newton because he had those "dubious credentials," a press card from *Ramparts*. Actually his interest was in getting "statements" from Huey Newton, "messages" to take outside; in receiving a kind of prophecy to be interpreted as needed.

"We need a statement, Huey, about the ten-point program," Eldridge Cleaver said, "so I'll ask you a question, see, and you answer it . . ."

"How's Bobby," Huey Newton asked.

"He's got a hearing on his misdemeanors, see . . ."

"I thought he had a felony."

"Well, that's another thing, the felony, he's also got a couple of misdemeanors . . ."

Once Charles Garry had set up the tape recorder Huey Newton stopped chatting and started lecturing, almost without pause. He talked, running the words together because he had said them so many times before, about "the American capitalistic-materialistic system" and "so-called free enterprise" and "the fight for the liberation of black people throughout the world." Every now and then Eldridge Cleaver would signal Huey Newton and say something like, "There are a lot of people interested in the Executive Mandate Number Three you've issued to the Black Panther Party, Huey. Care to comment?"

And Huey Newton would comment. "Yes. Mandate Number Three is this demand from the Black Panther Party speaking for the black community. Within the Mandate we admonish the racist police force . . ." I kept wishing that he would talk about himself, hoping to break through the wall of rhetoric, but he seemed to be one of those autodidacts for whom all things specific and personal present themselves as mine fields to be avoided even at the cost of coherence, for whom safety lies in generalization. The newspaperman, the radio man, they tried:

Q. Tell us something about yourself, Huey, I mean your life before the Panthers.

A. Before the Black Panther Party my life was very similar to that of most black people in this country.

Q. Well, your family, some incidents you remember, the influences that shaped you—

A. Living in America shaped me.

Q. Well, yes, but more specifically—

A. It reminds me of a quote from James Baldwin: "To be black and conscious in America is to be in a constant state of rage."

"To be black and conscious in America is to be in a constant state of rage," Eldridge Cleaver wrote in large letters on a pad of paper, and then he added:

"Huey P. Newton quoting James Baldwin." I could see it emblazoned above the speaker's platform at a rally, imprinted on the letterhead of an ad hoc committee still unborn. As a matter of fact almost everything Huey Newton said had the ring of being a "quotation," a "pronouncement" to be employed when the need arose. I had heard Huey P. Newton On Racism ("The Black Panther Party is against racism"), Huey P. Newton on Cultural Nationalism ("The Black Panther Party believes that the only culture worth holding onto is revolutionary culture"), Huey P. Newton On White Radicalism, On Police Occupation of the Ghetto, On The European Versus The African. "The European started to be sick when he denied his sexual nature," Huey Newton said, and Charles Garry interrupted then, bringing it back to first principles. "Isn't it true, though, Huey," he said, "that racism got its start for *economic* reasons?"

This weird interlocution seemed to take on a life of its own. The small room was hot and the fluorescent light hurt my eyes and I still did not know to what extent Huey Newton understood the nature of the role in which he was cast. As it happened I had always appreciated the logic of the Panther position, based as it was on the proposition that political power began at the end of the barrel of a gun (exactly what gun had even been specified, in an early memorandum from Huey P. Newton: *"Army .45; carbine; 12–gauge Magnum shotgun with 18" barrel, preferably the brand of High Standard; M–16; .357 Magnum pistols; P–38"*), and I could appreciate as well the particular beauty in Huey Newton as "issue." In the politics of revolution everyone was expendable, but I doubted that Huey Newton's political sophistication extended to seeing himself that way: the value of a Scottsboro case is easier to see if you are not yourself the Scottsboro boy. "Is there anything else you want to ask Huey?" Charles Garry asked. There did not seem to be. The lawyer adjusted his tape recorder. "I've had a request, Huey," he said, "from a high-school student, a reporter on his school paper, and he wanted a statement from you, and he's going to call me tonight. Care to give me a message for him?"

Huey Newton regarded the microphone. There was a moment in which he seemed not to remember the name of the play, and then he brightened. "I would like to point out," he said, his voice gaining volume as the memory disks clicked, *high school, student, youth, message to youth,* "that America is becoming a very young nation . . ."

I heard a moaning and a groaning, and I went over and it was—this Negro fellow was there. He had been shot in the stomach and at the time he didn't appear in any acute distress and so I said I'd see, and I asked him if he was a Kaiser, if he belonged to Kaiser, and he said, "Yes, yes. Get a doctor. Can't you see I'm bleeding? I've been shot. Now get someone out here." And I asked him if he had his Kaiser card and he got upset at this and he said, "Come on, get a doctor out here, I've been shot." I said, "I see this, but you're not in any acute distress." . . . So I told him we'd have to check to make sure he was a member. . . . And this kind of upset him more and he called me a few nasty names and said, "Now get a doctor out here right now, I've been shot and I'm bleeding." And he took his coat off and his shirt and he threw it on the desk there and he said, "Can't you see all this blood?" And I said, "I see it." And it wasn't that much, and so I said, "Well, you'll have to sign our admission sheet before you can be seen by a doctor." And he said, "I'm not signing anything." And I said, "You cannot be seen by a doctor unless you sign the admission sheet," and he said, "I don't have to sign anything" and a few more choice words . . .

This is an excerpt from the testimony before the Alameda County Grand Jury of Corrine Leonard, the nurse in charge of the Kaiser Foundation Hospital emergency room in Oakland at 5:30 A.M. on October 28, 1967. The "Negro fellow" was of course Huey Newton, wounded that morning during the gunfire which killed John Frey. For a long time I kept a copy of this testimony pinned to my office wall, on the theory that it illustrated a collision of cultures, a classic instance of an historical outsider confronting the established order at its most petty and impenetrable level. This theory was shattered when I learned that Huey Newton was in fact an enrolled member of the Kaiser Foundation Health Plan, i.e., in Nurse Leonard's words, "a Kaiser."

6.

One morning in 1968 I went to see Eldridge Cleaver in the San Francisco apartment he then shared with his wife, Kathleen. To be admitted to this apartment it was necessary to ring first and then stand in the middle of Oak Street, at a place which could be observed clearly from the Cleavers' apartment. After this scrutiny the visitor was, or was not, buzzed in. I was, and I climbed the stairs to find Kathleen Cleaver in the kitchen frying sausage and Eldridge Cleaver in the living room listening to a John Coltrane record and a number of other people all over the apartment, people everywhere, people standing in doorways and people moving around in one another's peripheral vision and people making and taking telephone calls. "When can you move on that?" I would hear in the background, and "You can't bribe me with a dinner, man, those *Guardian* dinners are all Old Left, like a wake." Most of these other people were members of the Black Panther Party, but one of them, in the living room, was Eldridge Cleaver's parole officer. It seems to me that I stayed about an hour. It seems to me that the three of us—Eldridge Cleaver, his parole officer and I—mainly discussed the commercial prospects of *Soul on Ice,* which, it happened, was being published that day. We discussed the advance ($5,000). We discussed the size of the first printing (10,000 copies). We discussed the advertising budget and we discussed the bookstores in which copies were or were not available. It was a not unusual discussion between writers, with the difference that one of the writers had his parole officer there and the other had stood out on Oak Street and been visually frisked before coming inside.

7.

To Pack and Wear:

> *2 skirts*
> *2 jerseys or leotards*
> *1 pullover sweater*
> *2 pair shoes*
> *stockings*
> *bra*
> *nightgown, robe, slippers*
> *cigarettes*
> *bourbon*
> *bag with:*
> > *shampoo*
> > *toothbrush and paste*
> > *Basis soap*
> > *razor, deodorant*
> > *aspirin, prescriptions, Tampax*
> > *face cream, powder, baby oil*

To Carry:

> *mohair throw*
> *typewriter*
> *2 legal pads and pens*
> *files*
> *house key*

This is a list which was taped inside my closet door in Hollywood during those years when I was reporting more or less steadily. The list enabled me to pack, without thinking, for any piece I was likely to do. Notice the deliberate anonymity of costume: in a skirt, a leotard, *and stockings,* I could pass on either side of the culture. Notice the mohair throw for trunk-line flights (i.e., no blankets) and for the motel room in which the air conditioning could not be turned off. Notice the bourbon for the same motel room. Notice the typewriter for the airport, coming home: the idea was to turn in the Hertz car, check in, find an empty bench, and start typing the day's notes.

It should be clear that this was a list made by someone who prized control, yearned after momentum, someone determined to play her role as if she had the script, heard her cues, knew the narrative. There is on this list one significant omission, one article I needed and never had: a watch. I needed a watch not during the day, when I could turn on the car radio or ask someone, but at night, in the motel. Quite often I would ask the desk for the time every half hour or so, until finally, embarrassed to ask again, I would call Los Angeles and ask my husband. In other words I had skirts, jerseys, leotards, pullover sweater, shoes, stockings, bra, nightgown, robe, slippers, cigarettes, bourbon, shampoo, tooth-brush and paste, Basis soap, razor, deodorant, aspirin, prescriptions, Tampax, face cream, powder, baby oil, mohair throw, typewriter, legal pads, pens, files and a house key, but I didn't know what time it was. This may be a parable, either of my life as a reporter during this period or of the period itself.

8.

Driving a Budget Rent-A-Car between Sacramento and San Francisco one rainy morning in November of 1968 I kept the radio on very loud. On this occasion I kept the radio on very loud not to find out what time it was but in an effort to erase six words from my mind, six words which had no significance for me but which seemed that year to signal the onset of anxiety or fright. The words, a line from Ezra Pound's "In a Station of the Metro," were these: *Petals on a wet black bough.* The radio played "Wichita Lineman" and "I Heard It on the Grapevine." *Petals on a wet black bough.* Somewhere between the Yolo Cause-way and Vallejo it occurred to me that during the course of any given week I met too many people who spoke favorably about bombing power stations. Some-where between the Yolo Causeway and Vallejo it also occurred to me that the fright on this particular morning was going to present itself as an inability to drive this Budget Rent-A-Car across the Carquinez Bridge. *The Wichita Lineman was still on the job.* I closed my eyes and drove across the Carquinez Bridge, because I had appointments, because I was working, because I had promised to watch the revolution being made at San Francisco State College and because there was no place in Vallejo to turn in a Budget Rent-A-Car and because nothing on my mind was in the script as I remembered it.

VISIONS OF AMERICA

9.

At San Francisco State College on that particular morning the wind was blowing the cold rain in squalls across the muddied lawns and against the lighted windows of empty classrooms. In the days before there had been fires set and classes invaded and finally a confrontation with the San Francisco Police Tactical Unit, and in the weeks to come the campus would become what many people on it were pleased to call "a battlefield." The police and the Mace and the noon arrests would become the routine of life on the campus, and every night the combatants would review their day on television: the waves of students advancing, the commotion at the edge of the frame, the riot sticks flashing, the instant of jerky camera that served to suggest at what risk the film was obtained; then a cut to the weather map. In the beginning there had been the necessary "issue," the suspension of a twenty-two-year-old instructor who happened as well to be Minister of Education for the Black Panther Party, but that issue, like most, had soon ceased to be the point in the minds of even the most dense participants. Disorder was its own point.

I had never before been on a campus in disorder, had missed even Berkeley and Columbia, and I suppose I went to San Francisco State expecting something other than what I found there. In some not at all trivial sense, the set was wrong. The very architecture of California state colleges tends to deny radical notions, to reflect instead a modest and hopeful vision of progressive welfare bureaucracy, and as I walked across the campus that day and on later days the entire San Francisco State dilemma—the gradual politicization, the "issues" here and there, the obligatory "Fifteen Demands," the continual arousal of the police and the outraged citizenry—seemed increasingly off-key, an instance of the *enfants terribles* and the Board of Trustees unconsciously collaborating on a wishful fantasy (Revolution on Campus) and playing it out in time for the six o'clock news. "Adjet-prop committee meeting in the Redwood Room," read a scrawled note on the cafeteria door one morning; only someone who needed very badly to be alarmed could respond with force to a guerrilla band that not only announced its meetings on the enemy's bulletin board but seemed innocent of the spelling, and so the meaning, of the words it used. "Hitler Hayakawa," some of the faculty had begun calling S. I. Hayakawa, the semanticist who had become the college's third president in a year and had incurred considerable displeasure by trying to keep the campus open. *"Eichmann,"* Kay Boyle had screamed at him at a rally. In just such broad strokes was the picture being painted in the fall of 1968 on the pastel campus at San Francisco State.

The place simply never seemed serious. The headlines were dark that first day, the college had been closed "indefinitely," both Ronald Reagan and Jesse

Unruh were threatening reprisals; still, the climate inside the Administration Building was that of a musical comedy about college life. "No *chance* we'll be open tomorrow," secretaries informed callers. "Go skiing, have a good time." Striking black militants dropped in to chat with the deans; striking white radicals exchanged gossip in the corridors. "No interviews, no press," announced a student strike leader who happened into a dean's office where I was sitting; in the next moment he was piqued because no one had told him that a Huntley-Brinkley camera crew was on campus. "We can still plug into that," the dean said soothingly. Everyone seemed joined in a rather festive camaraderie, a shared jargon, a shared sense of moment; the future was no longer arduous and indefinite but immediate and programmatic, aglow with the prospect of problems to be "addressed," plans to be "implemented." It was agreed all around that the confrontations could be "a very healthy development," that maybe it took a shutdown "to get something done." The mood, like the architecture, was 1948 functional, a model of pragmatic optimism.

Perhaps Evelyn Waugh could have gotten it down exactly right: Waugh was good at scenes of industrious self-delusion, scenes of people absorbed in odd games. Here at San Francisco State only the black militants could be construed as serious: they were at any rate picking the games, dictating the rules, and taking what they could from what seemed for everyone else just an amiable evasion of routine, of institutional anxiety, of the tedium of the academic calendar. Meanwhile the administrators could talk about programs. Meanwhile the white radicals could see themselves, on an investment of virtually nothing, as urban guerrillas. It was working out well for everyone, this game at San Francisco State, and its peculiar virtues had never been so clear to me as they became one afternoon when I sat in on a meeting of fifty or sixty SDS members. They had called a press conference for later that day, and now they were discussing "just what the format of the press conference should be."

"This has to be on our terms," someone warned. "Because they'll ask very leading questions, they'll ask *questions.*"

"Make them submit any questions in writing," someone else suggested. "The Black Student Union does that very successfully, then they just don't answer anything they don't want to answer."

"That's it, don't fall into their trap."

"Something we should stress at this press conference is *who owns the media.*"

"You don't think it's common knowledge that the papers represent corporate interests?" a realist among them interjected doubtfully.

"I don't think it's *understood.*"

Two hours and several dozen hand votes later, the group had selected four members to tell the press who owned the media, had decided to appear *en masse* at an opposition press conference, and had debated various slogans for the next day's demonstration. "Let's see, first we have 'Hearst Tells It Like It Ain't,' then 'Stop Press Distortion'—that's the one there was some political controversy about. . . ."

And, before they broke up, they had listened to a student who had driven up for the day from the College of San Mateo, a junior college down the peninsula from San Francisco. "I came up here today with some Third World students to tell you that we're with you, and we hope you'll be with *us* when we try to pull off a strike next week, because we're really into it, we carry our motorcycle helmets all the time, can't think, can't go to class."

He had paused. He was a nice-looking boy, and fired with his task. I considered the tender melancholy of life in San Mateo, which is one of the richest counties per capita in the United States of America, and I considered whether or not the Wichita Lineman and the petals on the wet black bough represented the aimlessness of the bourgeoisie, and I considered the illusion of aim to be gained by holding a press conference, the only problem with press conferences being that the press asked questions. "I'm here to tell you that at College of San Mateo we're living like *revolutionaries*," the boy said then.

10.

We put "Lay Lady Lay" on the record player, and "Suzanne." We went down to Melrose Avenue to see the Flying Burritos. There was a jasmine vine grown over the verandah of the big house on Franklin Avenue, and in the evenings the smell of jasmine came in through all the open doors and windows. I made bouillabaisse for people who did not eat meat. I imagined that my own life was simple and sweet, and sometimes it was, but there were odd things going around town. There were rumors. There were stories. *Everything was unmentionable but nothing was unimaginable.* This mystical flirtation with the idea of "sin"— *this sense that it was possible to go "too far,"* and that many people were doing it—was very much with us in Los Angeles in 1968 and 1969. A demented and seductive vortical tension was building in the community. The jitters were setting in. I recall a time when the dogs barked every night and the moon was always full. On August 9, 1969, I was sitting in the shallow end of my sister-in-law's swimming pool in Beverly Hills when she received a telephone call from a friend who had just heard about the murders at Sharon Tate Polanski's house on Cielo Drive. The phone rang many times during the next hour. These early reports were garbled and contradictory. One caller would say hoods, the next would say chains. There were twenty dead, no, twelve, ten, eighteen. Black masses were imagined, and bad trips blamed. I remember all of the day's misinformation very clearly, and I also remember this, and wish I did not: *I remember that no one was surprised.*

11.

When I first met Linda Kasabian in the summer of 1970 she was wearing her hair parted neatly in the middle, no makeup, Elizabeth Arden "Blue Grass" perfume, and the unpressed blue uniform issued to inmates at the Sybil Brand Institute for Women in Los Angeles. She was at Sybil Brand in protective custody, waiting out the time until she could testify about the murders of Sharon Tate Polanski, Abigail Folger, Jay Sebring, Voytek Frykowski, Steven Parent, and Rosemary and Leno LaBianca, and, with her lawyer, Gary Fleischman, I spent a number of evenings talking to her there. Of these evenings I remember mainly my dread at entering the prison, at leaving for even an hour the infinite possibilities I suddenly perceived in the summer twilight. I remember driving downtown on the Hollywood Freeway in Gary Fleischman's Cadillac convertible with the top down. I remember watching a rabbit graze on the grass by the gate as Gary Fleischman signed the prison register. Each of the half-dozen doors that locked behind us as we entered Sybil Brand was a little death, and I would emerge after the interview like Persephone from the underworld, euphoric, elated. Once home I would have two drinks and make myself a hamburger and eat it ravenously.

"Dig it," Gary Fleischman was always saying. One night when we were driving back to Hollywood from Sybil Brand in the Cadillac convertible with the top down he demanded that I tell him the population of India. I said that I did not know the population of India. "Take a guess," he prompted. I made a guess, absurdly low, and he was disgusted. He had asked the same question of his niece ("a college girl"), of Linda, and now of me, and none of us had known. It seemed to confirm some idea he had of women, their essential ineducability, their similarity under the skin. Gary Fleischman was someone of a type I met only rarely, a comic realist in a porkpie hat, a business traveler on the far frontiers of the period, a man who knew his way around the courthouse and Sybil Brand and remained cheerful, even jaunty, in the face of the awesome and impenetrable mystery at the center of what he called "the case." In fact we never talked about "the case," and referred to its central events only as "Cielo Drive" and "La-Bianca." We talked instead about Linda's childhood pastimes and disappointments, her high-school romances and her concern for her children. This particular juxtaposition of the spoken and the unspeakable was eerie and unsettling, and made my notebook a litany of little ironies so obvious as to be of interest only to dedicated absurdists. An example: Linda dreamed of opening a combination restaurant-boutique and pet shop.

12.

Certain organic disorders of the central nervous system are characterized by periodic remissions, the apparent complete recovery of the afflicted nerves. What happens appears to be this: as the lining of a nerve becomes inflamed and hardens into scar tissue, thereby blocking the passage of neural impulses, the nervous system gradually changes its circuitry, finds other, unaffected nerves to carry the same messages. During the years when I found it necessary to revise the circuitry of my mind I discovered that I was no longer interested in whether the woman on the ledge outside the window on the sixteenth floor jumped or did not jump, or in why. I was interested only in the picture of her in my mind: her hair incandescent in the floodlights, her bare toes curled inward on the stone ledge.

In this light all narrative was sentimental. In this light all connections were equally meaningful, and equally senseless. Try these: on the morning of John Kennedy's death in 1963 I was buying, at Ransohoff's in San Francisco, a short silk dress in which to be married. A few years later this dress of mine was ruined when, at a dinner party in Bel-Air, Roman Polanski accidentally spilled a glass of red wine on it. Sharon Tate was also a guest at this party, although she and Roman Polanski were not yet married. On July 27, 1970, I went to the Magnin-Hi Shop on the third floor of I. Magnin in Beverly Hills and picked out, at Linda Kasabian's request, the dress in which she began her testimony about the murders at Sharon Tate Polanski's house on Cielo Drive. "Size 9 Petite," her instructions read. "Mini but not extremely mini. In velvet if possible. Emerald green or gold. Or: A Mexican peasant-style dress, smocked or embroidered." She needed a dress that morning because the district attorney, Vincent Bugliosi, had expressed doubts about the dress she had planned to wear, a long white homespun shift. "Long is for evening," he had advised Linda. Long was for evening and white was for brides. At her own wedding in 1965 Linda Kasabian had worn a white brocade suit. Time passed, times changed. Everything was to teach us something. At 11:20 on that July morning in 1970 I delivered the dress in which she would testify to Gary Fleischman, who was waiting in front of his office on Rodeo Drive in Beverly Hills. He was wearing his porkpie hat and he was standing with Linda's second husband, Bob Kasabian, and their friend Charlie Melton, both of whom were wearing long white robes. Long was for Bob and Charlie, the dress in the I. Magnin box was for Linda. The three of them took the I. Magnin box and got into Gary Fleischman's Cadillac convertible with the top down and drove off in the sunlight toward the freeway downtown, waving back at me. I believe this to be an authentically senseless chain of correspondences, but in the jingle-jangle morning of that summer it made as much sense as anything else did.

13.

I recall a conversation I had in 1970 with the manager of a motel in which I was staying near Pendleton, Oregon. I had been doing a piece for *Life* about the storage of VX and GB nerve gas at an Army arsenal in Umatilla County, and now I was done, and trying to check out of the motel. During the course of checking out I was asked this question by the manager, who was a Mormon: *If you can't believe you're going to heaven in your own body and on a first-name basis with all the members of your family, then what's the point of dying?* At that time I believed that my basic affective controls were no longer intact, but now I present this to you as a more cogent question than it might at first appear, a kind of koan of the period.

14.

Once I had a rib broken, and during the few months that it was painful to turn in bed or raise my arms in a swimming pool I had, for the first time, a sharp apprehension of what it would be like to be old. Later I forgot. At some point during the years I am talking about here, after a series of periodic visual disturbances, three electroencephalograms, two complete sets of skull and neck X-rays, one five-hour glucose tolerance test, two electromyelograms, a battery of chemical tests and consultations with two opthalmologists, one internist and three neurologists, I was told that the disorder was not really in my eyes, but in my central nervous system. I might or might not experience symptoms of neural damage all my life. These symptoms, which might or might not appear, might or might not involve my eyes. They might or might not involve my arms or legs, they might or might not be disabling. Their effects might be lessened by cortisone injections, or they might not. It could not be predicted. The condition had a name, the kind of name usually associated with telethons, but the name meant nothing and the neurologist did not like to use it. The name was multiple sclerosis, but the name had no meaning. This was, the neurologist said, an exclusionary diagnosis, and meant nothing.

I had, at this time, a sharp apprehension not of what it was like to be old but of what it was like to open the door to the stranger and find that the stranger did indeed have the knife. In a few lines of dialogue in a neurologist's office in Beverly Hills, the improbable had become the probable, the norm: things which happened only to other people could in fact happen to me. I could be struck by lightning, could dare to eat a peach and be poisoned by the cyanide in the stone. The startling fact was this: my body was offering a precise physiological equivalent to what had been going on in my mind. "Lead a simple life," the neurologist advised. "Not that it makes any difference we know about." In other words it was another story without a narrative.

15.

Many people I know in Los Angeles believe that the Sixties ended abruptly on August 9, 1969, ended at the exact moment when word of the murders on Cielo Drive traveled like brushfire through the community, and in a sense this is true. The tension broke that day. The paranoia was fulfilled. In another sense the Sixties did not truly end for me until January of 1971, when I left the house on Franklin Avenue and moved to a house on the sea. This particular house on the sea had itself been very much a part of the Sixties, and for some months after we took possession I would come across souvenirs of that period in its history—a piece of Scientology literature beneath a drawer lining, a copy of *Stranger in a Strange Land* stuck deep on a closet shelf—but after a while we did some construction, and between the power saws and the sea wind the place got exorcised.

I have known, since then, very little about the movements of the people who seemed to me emblematic of those years. I know of course that Eldridge Cleaver went to Algeria and came home an entrepreneur. I know that Jim Morrison died in Paris. I know that Linda Kasabian fled in search of the pastoral to New Hampshire, where I once visited her; she also visited me in New York, and we took our children on the Staten Island Ferry to see the Statue of Liberty. I also know that in 1975 Paul Ferguson, while serving a life sentence for the murder of Ramon Novarro, won first prize in a PEN fiction contest and announced plans to "continue my writing." Writing had helped him, he said, to "reflect on experience and see what it means." Quite often I reflect on the big house in Hollywood, on "Midnight Confessions" and on Ramon Novarro and on the fact that Roman Polanski and I are godparents to the same child, but writing has not yet helped me to see what it means.

from BORN ON THE FOURTH OF JULY

Ron Kovic

Ron Kovic was born on July 4, 1946 and grew up in Massapequa, New York. In 1963 he graduated from high school and enlisted in the Marines. He was sent to Vietnam. In 1965, at the age of nineteen, he was wounded in action, paralyzed from the chest down. The following excerpt is from his memoir, *Born on the Fourth of July* (1976).

THE BLOOD IS STILL ROLLING OFF MY FLAK JACKET FROM THE HOLE in my shoulder and there are bullets cracking into the sand all around me. I keep trying to move my legs but I cannot feel them. I try to breathe but it is difficult. I have to get out of this place, make it out of here somehow.

Someone shouts from my left now, screaming for me to get up. Again and again he screams, but I am trapped in the sand.

Oh get me out of here, get me out of here, please someone help me! Oh help me, please help me. Oh God oh Jesus! "Is there a corpsman?" I cry. "Can you get a corpsman?"

There is a loud crack and I hear the guy begin to sob. "They've shot my fucking finger off! Let's go, sarge! Let's get outta here!"

"I can't move," I gasp. "I can't move my legs! I can't feel anything!"

269

I watch him go running back to the tree line.

"Sarge, are you all right?" Someone else is calling to me now and I try to turn around. Again there is the sudden crack of a bullet and a boy's voice crying. "Oh Jesus! Oh Jesus Christ!" I hear his body fall in back of me.

I think he must be dead but I feel nothing for him, I just want to live. I feel nothing.

And now I hear another man coming up from behind, trying to save me. "Get outta here!" I scream. "Get the fuck outta here!"

A tall black man with long skinny arms and enormous hands picks me up and throws me over his shoulder as bullets begin cracking over our heads like strings of firecrackers. Again and again they crack as the sky swirls around us like a cyclone. "Motherfuckers motherfuckers!" he screams. And the rounds keep cracking and the sky and the sun on my face and my body all gone, all twisted up dangling like a puppet's, diving again and again into the sand, up and down, rolling and cursing, gasping for breath. "Goddamn goddamn motherfuckers!"

And finally I am dragged into a hole in the sand with the bottom of my body that can no longer feel, twisted and bent underneath me. The black man runs from the hole without ever saying a thing. I never see his face. I will never know who he is. He is gone. And others now are in the hole helping me. They are bandaging my wounds. There is fear in their faces.

"It's all right," I say to them. "Everything is fine."

Someone has just saved my life. My rifle is gone and I don't feel like finding it or picking it up ever again. The only thing I can think of, the only thing that crosses my mind, is living. There seems to be nothing in the world more important than that.

Hundreds of rounds begin to crash in now. I stare up at the sky because I cannot move. Above the hole men are running around in every direction. I see their legs and frightened faces. They are screaming and dragging the wounded past me. Again and again the rounds crash in. They seem to be coming in closer and closer. A tall man jumps in, hugging me to the earth.

"Oh God!" he is crying. "Oh God please help us!"

The attack is lifted. They are carrying me out of the hole now—two, three, four men—quickly they are strapping me to a stretcher. My legs dangle off the sides until they realize I cannot control them. "I can't move them," I say, almost in a whisper. "I can't move them." I'm still carefully sucking the air, trying to calm myself, trying not to get excited, not to panic. I want to live. I keep telling myself. Take it slow now, as they strap my legs to the stretcher and carry my wounded body into an Amtrac packed with other wounded men. The steel trapdoor of the Amtrac slowly closes as we begin to move to the northern bank and back across the river to the battalion area.

BORN ON THE FOURTH OF JULY

Men are screaming all around me. "Oh God get me out of here!" "Please help!" they scream. Oh Jesus, like little children now, not like marines, not like the posters, not like that day in the high school, this is for real. "Mother!" screams a man without a face. "Oh I don't want to die!" screams a young boy cupping his intestines with his hands. "Oh please, oh no, oh God, oh help! Mother!" he screams again.

We are moving slowly through the water, the Amtrac rocking back and forth. We cannot be brave anymore, there is no reason. It means nothing now. We hold on to ourselves, to things around us, to memories, to thoughts, to dreams. I breathe slowly, desperately trying to stay awake.

The steel trapdoor is opening. I see faces. Corpsmen, I think. Others, curious, looking in at us. Air, fresh, I feel, I smell. They are carrying me out now. Over wounded bodies, past wounded screams. I'm in a helicopter now lifting above the battalion area. I'm leaving the war. I'm going to live. I am still breathing, I keep thinking over and over, I'm going to live and get out of here.

They are shoving tubes and needles in my arms. Now we are being packed into planes. I begin to believe more and more as I watch the other wounded packed around me on shelves that I am going to live.

I still fight desperately to stay awake. I am in an ambulance now rushing to some place. There is a man without any legs screaming in pain, moaning like a little baby. He is bleeding terribly from the stumps that were once his legs, thrashing his arms wildly about his chest, in a semiconscious daze. It is almost too much for me to watch.

I cannot take much more of this. I must be knocked out soon, before I lose my mind. I've seen too much today, I think. But I hold on, sucking the air. I shout then curse for him to be quiet. "My wound is much worse than yours!" I scream. "You're lucky," I shout, staring him in the eyes. "I can feel nothing from my chest down. You at least still have part of your legs. Shut up!" I scream again. "Shut the fuck up, you goddamned baby!" He keeps thrashing his arms wildly above his head and kicking his bleeding stumps toward the roof of the ambulance.

The journey seems to take a very long time, but soon we are at the place where the wounded are sent. I feel a tremendous exhilaration inside me. I have made it this far. I have actually made it this far without giving up and now I am in a hospital where they will operate on me and find out why I cannot feel anything from my chest down anymore. I know I am going to make it now. I am going to make it not because of any god, or any religion, but because *I* want to make it, *I* want to live. And I leave the screaming man without legs and am brought to a room that is very bright.

"What's your name?" the voice shouts.

"Wh-wh-what?" I say.

"What's your name?" the voice says again.

"K-K-Kovic," I say.

"No!" says the voice. "I want your name, rank, and service number. Your date of birth, the name of your father and mother."

"Kovic. Sergeant. Two-oh-three-oh-two-six-one, uh, when are you going to . . ."

"Date of birth!" the voice shouts.

"July fourth, nineteen forty-six. I was born on the Fourth of July. I can't feel . . ."

"What religion are you?"

"Catholic," I say.

"What outfit did you come from?"

"What's going on? When are you going to operate?" I say.

"The doctors will operate," he says. "Don't worry," he says confidently. "They are very busy and there are many wounded but they will take care of you soon."

He continues to stand almost at attention in front of me with a long clipboard in his hand, jotting down all the information he can. I cannot understand why they are taking so long to operate. There is something very wrong with me, I think, and they must operate as quickly as possible. The man with the clipboard walks out of the room. He will send the priest in soon.

I lie in the room alone staring at the walls, still sucking the air, determined to live more than ever now.

The priest seems to appear suddenly above my head. With his fingers he is gently touching my forehead, rubbing it slowly and softly. "How are you," he says.

"I'm fine, Father." His face is very tired but it is not frightened. He is almost at ease, as if what he is doing he has done many times before.

"I have come to give you the Last Rites, my son."

"I'm ready, Father," I say.

And he prays, rubbing oils on my face and gently placing the crucifix to my lips. "I will pray for you," he says.

"When will they operate?" I say to the priest.

"I do not know," he says. "The doctors are very busy. There are many wounded. There is not much time for anything here but trying to live. So you must try to live, my son, and I will pray for you."

Soon after that I am taken to a long room where there are many doctors and nurses. They move quickly around me. They are acting very competent. "You will be fine," says one nurse calmly.

"Breathe deeply into the mask," the doctor says.

"Are you going to operate?" I ask.

"Yes. Now breathe deeply into the mask." As the darkness of the mask slowly covers my face I pray with all my being that I will live through this operation and see the light of day once again. I want to live so much. And even before I go to sleep with the blackness still swirling around my head and the numbness of sleep, I begin to fight as I have never fought before in my life.

I awake to the screams of other men around me. I have made it. I think that maybe the wound is my punishment for killing the corporal and the children. That now everything is okay and the score is evened up. And now I am packed in this place with the others who have been wounded like myself, strapped onto a strange circular bed. I feel tubes going into my nose and hear the clanking, pumping sound of a machine. I still cannot feel any of my body but I know I am alive. I feel a terrible pain in my chest. My body is so cold. It has never been this weak. It feels so tired and out of touch, so lost and in pain. I can still barely breathe. I look around me, at people moving in shadows of numbness. There is the man who had been in the ambulance with me, screaming louder than ever, kicking his bloody stumps in the air, crying for his mother, crying for his morphine.

Directly across from me there is a Korean who has not even been in the war at all. The nurse says he was going to buy a newspaper when he stepped on a booby trap and it blew off both his legs and his arm. And all that is left now is this slab of meat swinging one arm crazily in the air, moaning like an animal gasping for its last bit of life, knowing that death is rushing toward him. The Korean is screaming like a madman at the top of his lungs. I cannot wait for the shots of morphine. Oh, the morphine feels so good. It makes everything dark and quiet. I can rest. I can leave this madness. I can dream of my back yard once again.

When I wake they are screaming still and the lights are on and the clock, the clock on the wall, I can hear it ticking to the sound of their screams. I can hear the dead being carted out and the new wounded being brought in to the beds all around me. I have to get out of this place.

"Can I call you by your first name?" I say to the nurse.

"No. My name is Lieutenant Wiecker."

"Please, can I . . ."

"No," she says. "It's against regulations."

I'm sleeping now. The lights are flashing. The black pilot is next to me. He says nothing. He stares at the ceiling all day long. He does nothing but that. But something is happening now, something is going wrong over there. The nurse is shouting for the machine, and the corpsman is crawling on the black man's chest, he has his knees on his chest and he's pounding it with his fists again and again.

"His heart has stopped!" screams the nurse.

Pounding, pounding, he's pounding his fist into his chest. "Get the machine!" screams the corpsman.

The nurse is pulling the machine across the hangar floor as quickly as she can now. They are trying to put curtains around the whole thing, but the curtains keep slipping and falling down. Everyone, all the wounded who can still see and think, now watch what is happening to the pilot, and it is happening right next to me. The doctor hands the corpsman a syringe, they are laughing as the corpsman drives the syringe into the pilot's chest like a knife. They are talking about the Green Bay Packers and the corpsman is driving his fist into the black man's chest again and again until the black pilot's body begins to bloat up, until it doesn't look like a body at all anymore. His face is all puffy like a balloon and saliva rolls slowly from the sides of his mouth. He keeps staring at the ceiling and saying nothing. "The machine! The machine!" screams the doctor, now climbing on top of the bed, taking the corpsman's place. "Turn on the machine!" screams the doctor.

He grabs a long suction cup that is attached to the machine and places it carefully against the black man's chest. The black man's body jumps up from the bed almost arcing into the air from each bolt of electricity, jolting and arcing, bloating up more and more.

"I'll bet on the Packers," says the corpsman.

"Green Bay doesn't have a chance," the doctor says, laughing.

The nurse is smiling now, making fun of both the doctor and the corpsman. "I don't understand football," she says.

They are pulling the sheet over the head of the black man and strapping him onto the gurney. He is taken out of the ward.

The Korean civilian is still screaming and there is a baby now at the end of the ward. The nurse says it has been napalmed by our own jets. I cannot see the baby but it screams all the time like the Korean and the young man without any legs I had met in the ambulance.

I can hear a radio. It is the Armed Forces radio. The corpsman is telling the baby to shut the hell up and there is a young kid with half his head blown away. They have brought him in and put him where the black pilot has just died, right next to me. He has thick bandages wrapped all around his head till I can hardly see his face at all. He is like a vegetable—a nineteen-year-old vegetable, thrashing his arms back and forth, babbling and pissing in his clean white sheets.

"Quit pissin' in your sheets!" screams the corpsman. But the nineteen-year-old kid who doesn't have any brains anymore makes the corpsman very angry. He just keeps pissing in the sheets and crying like a little baby.

There is a Green Beret sergeant calling for his mother. Every night now

BORN ON THE FOURTH OF JULY

I hear him. He has spinal meningitis. He will be dead before this evening is over.

The Korean civilian does not moan anymore. He does not wave his one arm and two fingers above his head. He is dead and they have taken him away too.

There is a nun who comes through the ward now with apples for the wounded and rosary beads. She is very pleasant and smiles at all of the wounded. The corpsman is reading a comicbook, still cursing at the baby. The baby is screaming and the Armed Forces radio is saying that troops will be home soon. The kid with the bloody stumps is getting a morphine shot.

There is a general walking down the aisles now, going to each bed. He's marching down the aisles, marching and facing each wounded man in his bed. A skinny private with a Polaroid camera follows directly behind him. The general is dressed in an immaculate uniform with shiny shoes. "Good afternoon, marine," the general says. "In the name of the President of the United States and the United States Marine Corps, I am proud to present you with the Purple Heart, and a picture," the general says. Just then the skinny man with the Polaroid camera jumps up, flashing a picture of the wounded man. "And a picture to send to your folks."

He comes up to my bed and says exactly the same thing he has said to all the rest. The skinny man jumps up, snapping a picture of the general handing the Purple Heart to me. "And here," says the general, "here is a picture to send home to your folks." The general makes a sharp left face. He is marching to the bed next to me where the nineteen-year-old kid is still pissing in his pants, babbling like a little baby.

"In the name of the President of the United States," the general says. The kid is screaming now, almost tearing the bandages off his head, exposing the parts of his brain that are still left. ". . . I present you with the Purple Heart. And here," the general says, handing the medal to the nineteen-year-old vegetable, the skinny guy jumping up and snapping a picture, "here is a picture . . ." the general says, looking at the picture the skinny guy has just pulled out of the camera. The kid is still pissing in his white sheets. ". . . And here is a picture to send home. . . ." The general does not finish what he is saying. He stares at the nineteen-year-old for what seems a long time. He hands the picture back to his photographer and as sharply as before marches to the next bed.

"Good afternoon, marine," he says.

The kid is still pissing in his clean white sheets when the general walks out of the room.

I am in this place for seven days and seven nights. I write notes on scraps of paper telling myself over and over that I will make it out of here, that I am going to live. I am squeezing rubber balls with my hands to try to get strong again. I write letters home to Mom and Dad. I dictate them to a woman named

Lucy who is with the USO. I am telling Mom and Dad that I am hurt pretty bad but I have done it for America and that it is worth it. I tell them not to worry. I will be home soon.

The day I am supposed to leave has come. I am strapped in a long frame and taken from the place of the wounded. I am moved from hangar to hangar, then finally put on a plane, and I leave Vietnam forever.

————

They came for him early that morning, walking up the wooden ramp and knocking on the front door of his house. He could hear them in the living room talking to his mom and dad about the parade and how important it was to have him marching with them on Memorial Day in his wheelchair.

"Parade time," his father said, walking into his room.

"I'll be right with you, Dad," he said, looking up from his bed. "I've got to get my pants on."

It was always hard getting dressed, but he was getting better at it. He turned from his back to his stomach, grabbing his pants and pulling them up until they reached his waist. Turning on his back again, he buckled his belt. Then he pushed himself with both hands in back of him until he was sitting up in the bed next to his wheelchair. He grabbed the chair with one hand, dragging his body across in a quick sweeping motion until he was seated, his legs still up on the bed.

Now his father knew it was time to help. He took each leg, carefully lowering them one at a time to the chair, spreading them apart to make sure the rubber tube wasn't twisted.

"Ready?" shouted the boy.

"Ready!" said his dad. And his father went in back of the chair as he always did and lifted him up underneath his arms so that he could pull his pants up again.

"Good," said the boy.

His father let him slowly down back onto the cushion and he turned around in his wheelchair to face the door and pushed his chair down the long, narrow hallway to the living room. His mom was there with a tall man he immediately remembered from the hospital; right next to him was a heavy guy. Both of them had on their American Legion uniforms with special caps placed smartly on their heads. He sat as straight in his chair as he could, holding on with one hand so he wouldn't lose his balance. He shook hands with the tall commander and with the heavy guy who stood beside him.

"You sure look great," said the tall commander, stepping forward. "Same tough marine we visited in the hospital," he said, smiling. "You know, Mr.

Kovic—" he was looking at his father now—"this kid of yours sure has a lot of guts."

"We're really proud of him," said the heavy guy.

"The whole town's proud of him and what he did," said the tall commander, smiling again.

"He's sacrificed a lot," said the heavy guy, putting his hand on the boy's shoulder.

"And we're gonna make certain," the tall commander said, "we're gonna make certain that his sacrifice and any of the others weren't in vain. We're still in that war to win," he said, looking at the boy's father. His father nodded his head up and down, showing the commander he understood.

It was time to go. The heavy guy had grabbed the back handles of the chair. Acting very confident, he reminded the boy that he had worked in the naval hospital.

The boy said goodbye to his mom and dad, and the heavy guy eased the wheelchair down the long wooden ramp to the sidewalk in front of the house. "I've been pushin' you boys around for almost two years now," he said.

The boy listened as the heavy guy and the commander stood for a moment in the front yard trying to figure out how they were going to get him into the back seat of the Cadillac convertible.

"You're goin' in style today," shouted the commander.

"Nothing but the best," said the heavy guy.

"I haven't learned how to . . ."

"We know, we understand," said the commander.

And before he could say another word, the heavy guy who had worked at the hospital lifted him out of the chair in one smooth motion. Opening the door with a kick of his foot, he carefully placed him in the back seat of the big open car.

"All right, Mr. Grand Marshal." The heavy guy patted him on the shoulder, then jumped into the car with the commander, beeping the horn all the way down Toronto Avenue.

"We're goin' over to Eddie Dugan's house," said the commander, turning his head. "Ya know Eddie?" He was talking very fast now. "Good boy," said the commander. "Lost both legs like you. Got plastic ones. Doin' great, isn't he?" He jabbed the heavy man with his fist.

"Got a lot of guts that kid Eddie Dugan," the heavy man said.

"I remember him . . ." The commander was turning the corner now, driving slowly down the street. "Yeah, I remember Eddie way back when he was . . . when he was playin' on the Little Leagues. And as God is my witness," said the commander, turning his head back toward him again, "as God is my witness,

I seen Eddie hit a home run on his birthday. He was nine or ten, something like that back then." The commander was laughing now. "I was coaching with his dad and it was Eddie's birthday. A lot of you guys got messed up over there." He was still talking very fast.

"Remember Clasternack? You heard of Clasternack, didn't you? He got killed. They got a street over in the park named after him." He paused for a long time. "Yeah . . . he got killed. He was the first of you kids to get it. And there were others too," said the commander. "That little guy, what was his name? Yeah I got it . . . Johnny Heanon . . . little Johnny Heanon . . . he used to play in the Little League with you guys."

He remembered Johnny Heanon.

"He tripped a land mine or something and died on the hospital ship during the operation. I see his folks every once in a while. They live down by the old high school. Fine kid," said the commander.

"He used to deliver my paper," said the heavy guy.

"There was the Peters family too . . . both brothers . . ." said the commander again, pausing for a long time. "Both of them got killed in the same week. And Alan Grady. . . . Did you know Alan Grady? He used to go to the boy scouts when you kids was growing up."

The boy in the back seat nodded. He knew Alan Grady too.

"He drowned," said the commander.

"Funny thing," said the heavy guy. "I mean, terrible way to go. He was on R and R or something and he drowned one afternoon when he was swimming."

"And Billy Morris," said the commander, "he used to get in all sorts of trouble down at the high school. He got killed too. There was a land mine or something and he got hit in the head with a tree. Isn't that crazy?" The commander was laughing almost hysterically now.

"He goes all the way over there and gets killed by a fucking tree."

"We've lost a lot of good boys," the heavy guy said. "We've been hit pretty bad. The whole town's changed."

"And it's been goin' on a long time." The commander was very angry now. "If those bastards in Washington would stop fiddlefucking around and drop a couple of big ones in the right places, we could get that whole thing over with next week. We could win that goddamn thing and get all our kids out of there."

When they got to Eddie Dugan's house, both of the men got out, leaving him in the back seat, and ran up to Eddie's doorstep. A few minutes passed, then Eddie came out the front door rocking back and forth across the lawn like a clown on his crutches until he had worked himself to the car door.

"I can do it," Eddie said.

"Sure," said the tall commander, smiling.

BORN ON THE FOURTH OF JULY

They watched as Eddie stretched leaning on his crutches, then swung into the car seat.

"Not bad," said the commander.

The commander and the heavy guy jumped back into the car and the boy could feel the warm spring air blowing on his face as they moved down Eddie's block. The leaves on the trees had blossomed full. They glistened in the sun, covering the streets in patches of morning shadow.

"You're not going to believe this," Eddie said to him, looking down at his legs. "I got hit by our own mortars." He was almost laughing now. "It was on a night patrol. . . . And you?" he asked.

"I got paralyzed from the chest down. I can't move or feel anything." He showed Eddie with his hand how far up he could not feel and then showed him the bag on the side of his leg. Usually he didn't like telling people how bad he had been hurt, but for some reason it was different with Eddie.

Eddie looked at the bag and shook his head, saying nothing.

"Let me see your new legs," he said to Eddie.

Eddie pulled up his trousers, showing his new plastic legs. "You see," he said, tapping them with his knuckles. He was very sarcastic. "As good as new."

They got to the place where the march was to begin and he saw the cub scouts and the girl scouts, the marching bands, the fathers in their Legion caps and uniforms, the mothers from the Legion's auxilliary, the pretty drum majorettes. The street was a sea of red, white, and blue. He remembered how he and all the rest of the kids on the block had put on their cub scout uniforms and marched every Memorial Day down these same streets. He remembered the hundreds of people lining the sidewalks, everyone standing and cheering and waving their small flags, his mother standing with the other mothers on the block shouting for him to keep in step. "There's my Yankee Doodle boy!" he'd hear her shouting, and he'd feel embarrassed, pulling his cap over his eyes like he always did.

There were scouts decorating the Cadillac now with red, white, and blue crepe paper and long paper banners that read WELCOME HOME RON KOVIC AND EDDIE DUGAN and SUPPORT OUR BOYS IN VIETNAM. There was a small sign, too, that read: OUR WOUNDED VIETNAM VETS . . . EDDIE DUGAN AND RON KOVIC.

When the scouts were finished, the commander came running over to the car with a can of beer in his hand. "Let's go!" he shouted, jumping back in with the heavy guy.

They drove slowly through the crowd until they were all the way up in the front of the parade. He could hear the horns and drums behind him and he looked out and watched the pretty drum majorettes and clowns dancing in the street. He looked out onto the sidewalks where the people from his town had gathered just like when he was a kid.

VISIONS OF AMERICA

But it was different. He couldn't tell at first exactly what it was, but something was not the same, they weren't waving and they just seemed to be standing staring at Eddie Dugan and himself like they weren't even there. It was as if they were ghosts like little Johnny Heanon or Billy Morris come back from the dead. And he couldn't understand what was happening.

Maybe, he thought, the banners, the ones the boy scouts and their fathers had put up, the ones telling the whole town who Eddie Dugan and he were, maybe, he thought, they had dropped off into the street and no one knew who they were and that's why no one was waving.

If the signs had been there, they'd have been flooding into the streets, stomping their feet and screaming and cheering the way they did for him and Eddie at the Little League games. They'd have been swelling into the streets, trying to shake their hands just like in the movies, when the boys had come home from the other wars and everyone went crazy throwing streamers of paper and confetti and hugging their sweethearts, sweeping them off their feet and kissing them for what seemed forever. If they really knew who they were, he thought, they'd be roaring and clapping and shouting. But they were quiet and all he heard whenever the band stopped playing was the soft purr of the American Legion's big Cadillac as it moved slowly down the street.

Even though it seemed very difficult acting like heroes, he and Eddie tried waving a couple of times, but after a while he realized that the staring faces weren't going to change and he couldn't help but feel like he was some kind of animal in a zoo or that he and Eddie were on display in some trophy case. And the more he thought about it, the more he wanted to get the hell out of the back seat of the Cadillac and go back home to his room where he knew it was safe and warm. The parade had hardly begun but already he felt trapped, just like in the hospital.

The tall commander turned down Broadway now, past Sparky the barber's place, then down to Massapequa Avenue, past the American Legion hall where the cannon they had played on as kids sat right across from the Long Island Railroad station. He thought of the time he and Bobby and Richie Castiglia used to sit on that thing with their plastic machine guns and army-navy store canteens full of lemonade; they'd sit and wait until a train pulled into the Massapequa station, and then they'd all scream "Ambush!" with Castiglia standing up bravely on the cannon barrel, riddling the train's windows.

He was beginning to feel very lonely. He kept looking over at Eddie. Why hadn't they waved, he thought. Eddie had lost both of his legs and he had come home with almost no body left, and no one seemed to care.

When they came to where the speakers' platform had been erected, he watched Eddie push himself out of the back seat, then up on his crutches while the heavy guy helped him with the door. The commander was opening the trunk, bringing the wheelchair to the side of the car. He was lifted out by the heavy guy and he saw the people around him watching, and it bothered him because he didn't want them to see how badly he had been hurt and how helpless he was, having to be carried out of the car into the chair like a baby. He tried to block out what he was feeling by smiling and waving to the people around him, making jokes about the chair to ease the tension, but it was very difficult being there at all and the more he felt stared at and gawked at like some strange object in a museum, the more difficult it became and the more he wanted to get the hell out of there.

He pushed himself to the back of the platform where two strong members of the Legion were waiting to lift him up in the chair. "How do you lift this goddamn thing?" shouted one of the men, suddenly staggering, almost dropping him. He tried to tell them how to lift it properly, the way they had shown him in the hospital, but they wanted to do it their own way and almost dropped him a second time.

They finally carried him up the steps of the stage where he was wheeled up front next to Eddie, who sat with his crutches by his side. They sat together watching the big crowd and listening to one speaker after the other, including the mayor and all the town's dignitaries; each one spoke very beautiful words about *sacrifice and patriotism and God,* crying out to the crowd to support the boys in the war so that their brave sacrifices would not have to be in vain.

And then it was the tall commander's turn to speak. He walked up to the microphone slowly, measuring his steps carefully, then jutted his head up and looked directly at the crowd. *"I believe in America!"* shouted the commander, shaking his fist in the air. *"And I believe in Americanism!"* The crowd was cheering now. *"And most of all . . . most of all, I believe in victory for America!"* He was very emotional. Then he shouted that the whole country had to come together and support the boys in the war. He told how he and the boys' fathers before them had fought in Korea and World War II, and how the whole country had been behind them back then and how they had won a great victory for freedom. Almost crying now, he shouted to the crowd that they couldn't give up in Vietnam. *"We have to win . . ."* he said, his voice still shaking; then pausing, he pointed his finger at him and Eddie Dugan *". . . because of them!"*

Suddenly it was very quiet and he could feel them looking right at him, sitting there in his wheelchair with Eddie all alone. It seemed everyone—the cub scouts, the boy scouts, the mothers, the fathers, the whole town—had their eyes on them and now he bent his head and stared into his lap.

The commander left the podium to great applause and the speeches continued, but the more they spoke, the more restless and uncomfortable he became, until he felt like he was going to jump out of his paralyzed body and scream. He was confused, then proud, then all of a sudden confused again. He wanted to listen and believe everything they were saying, but he kept thinking of all the things that had happened that day and now he wondered why he and Eddie hadn't even been given the chance to speak. They had just sat there all day long, like he had been sitting in his chair for weeks and months in the hospital and at home in his room alone, and he wondered now why he had allowed them to make him a hero and the grand marshal of the parade with Eddie, why he had let them take him all over town in that Cadillac when they hadn't even asked him to speak.

These people had never been to his war, and they had been talking like they knew everything, like they were experts on the whole goddamn thing, like he and Eddie didn't know how to speak for themselves because there was something wrong now with both of them. They couldn't speak because of the war and had to have others define for them with their lovely words what they didn't know anything about.

He sat back, watching the men who ran the town as they walked back and forth on the speaker's platform in their suits and ties, drinking their beer and talking about patriotism. It reminded him of the time in church a few Sundays before, when Father Bradley had suddenly pointed to him during the middle of the sermon, telling everyone he was a hero and a patriot in the eyes of God and his country for going to fight the communists. "We must pray for brave boys like Ron Kovic," said the priest. "And most of all," he said, "we must pray for victory in Vietnam and peace throughout the world." And when the service was over, people came to shake his hand and thank him for all he had done for God and his country, and he left the church feeling very sick and threw up in the parking lot.

After all the speeches, they carried him back down the steps of the platform and the crowd started clapping and now he felt more embarrassed than ever. He didn't deserve this, he didn't want this shit. All he could think of was getting out of there and going back home. He just wanted to get out of this place and go back right away.

But now someone in the crowd was calling his name. "Ronnie! Ronnie!" Over and over again he heard someone shouting. And finally he saw who it was. It was little Tommy Law, who had grown up on Hamilton Avenue with all the rest of the guys. He used to hit home runs over Tommy's hedge. Tommy had been one of his best friends like Richie and Bobby Zimmer. He hadn't seen him for years, not since high school. Tommy had joined the marines too, and he'd heard something about him being wounded in a rocket attack in the DMZ. No one had told him he was back from the war. And now Tommy was hugging him and they were crying, both of them at the bottom of the stage, hugging each other and crying in front of all of them that day. He wanted to pull away in embarrassment and hold back his feelings that seemed to be pouring out of him, but he could not and he cried even harder now, hugging his friend until he felt his arms go numb. It was so wonderful, so good, to see Tommy again. He seemed to bring back something wonderfully happy in his past and he didn't want to let go. They held on to each other for a long time. And when Tommy finally pulled away, his face was bright red and covered with tears and pain. Tommy held his head with his hands still shaking, looking at him sitting there in disbelief. He looked up at Tommy's face and he could see that he was very sad.

The crowd had gathered now watching the two friends almost with curiosity. He tried wiping the tears from his eyes, still trying to laugh and make Tommy and himself and all the others feel more at ease, but Tommy would not smile and he kept holding his head. Still crying, he shook his head back and forth. And now, looking up at Tommy's face, he could see the thin scar that ran along his hairline, the same kind of scar he'd seen on the heads of the vegetables who had had their brains blown out, where plates had been put in to replace part of the skull.

But Tommy didn't want to talk about what had happened to him. "Let's get out of here," he said. He grabbed the back handles of the chair and began pushing him through the crowd. He pushed him through the town past the Long Island Railroad station to the American Legion hall. They sat in the corner of the bar, watching the mayor and all the politicians. And Tommy tried to keep the drunken Legion members from hanging all over him and telling him their war stories.

The tall commander, who was now very drunk, came over asking Tommy and him if they wanted a ride back home in the Cadillac. Tommy said they were walking home, and they left the American Legion hall and the drunks in the bar, with Tommy pushing his wheelchair, walking back through the town where they had grown up, past the baseball field at Parkside School where they had played as kids, back to Hamilton Avenue, where they sat together in front of Peter Weber's house almost all night, still not believing they were together again.

from NO NAME IN THE STREET

James Baldwin

James Baldwin (1924–1987), preeminent American novelist and essayist, was
born in New York City, grew up in Harlem, and died in St. Paul de Vence,
France. He is the author of six novels, including *Go Tell It On the Mountain*
(1953), *Another Country* (1962), and *Just Above My Head* (1979); a short story
collection, *Going to Meet the Man* (1965); several volumes of personal essays
including *Notes of a Native Son* (1955), *Nobody Knows My Name* (1961), and
The Fire Next Time (1963); and two plays, *Blues for Mister Charlie* (1964)
and *The Amen Corner* (1965).

SINCE MARTIN'S DEATH, IN MEMPHIS, AND THAT TREMENDOUS DAY
in Atlanta, something has altered in me, something has gone away. Perhaps even
more than the death itself, the manner of his death has forced me into a judgment
concerning human life and human beings which I have always been reluctant to
make—indeed, I can see that a great deal of what the knowledgeable would call
my life-style is dictated by this reluctance. Incontestably, alas, most people are
not, in action, worth very much; and yet, every human being is an unprecedented
miracle. One tries to treat them as the miracles they are, while trying to protect
oneself against the disasters they've become. This is not very different from the
act of faith demanded by all those marches and petitions while Martin was still
alive. One could scarcely be deluded by Americans anymore, one scarcely dared
expect anything from the great, vast, blank generality; and yet one was compelled

to demand of Americans—and for their sakes, after all—a generosity, a clarity, and a nobility which they did not dream of demanding of themselves. Part of the error was irreducible, in that the marchers and petitioners were forced to suppose the existence of an entity which, when the chips were down, could not be located—*i.e.*, there *are* no American people yet: but to this speculation (or desperate hope) we shall presently return. Perhaps, however, the moral of the story (and the hope of the world) lies in what one demands, not of others, but of oneself. However that may be, the failure and the betrayal are in the record book forever, and sum up, and condemn, forever, those descendants of a barbarous Europe who arbitrarily and arrogantly reserve the right to call themselves Americans.

The mind is a strange and terrible vehicle, moving according to rigorous rules of its own; and my own mind, after I had left Atlanta, began to move backward in time, to places, people, and events I thought I had forgotten. Sorrow drove it there, I think, sorrow, and a certain kind of bewilderment, triggered, perhaps, by something which happened to me in connection with Martin's funeral.

When Martin was murdered, I was based in Hollywood, working—working, in fact, on the screen version of *The Autobiography of Malcolm X.* This was a difficult assignment, since I had known Malcolm, after all, crossed swords with him, worked with him, and held him in that great esteem which is not easily distinguishable, if it is distinguishable at all, from love. (The Hollywood gig did not work out because I did not wish to be a party to a second assassination: but we will also return to Hollywood, presently.)

Very shortly before his death, I had to appear with Martin at Carnegie Hall, in New York. Having been on the Coast so long, I had nothing suitable to wear for my Carnegie Hall gig, and so I rushed out, got a dark suit, got it fitted, and made my appearance. Something like two weeks later, I wore this same suit to Martin's funeral; returned to Hollywood; presently, had to come East again, on business. I ran into Leonard Lyons one night, and I told him that I would never be able to wear that suit again. Leonard put this in his column. I went back to Hollywood.

Weeks later, either because of a Civil Rights obligation, or because of Columbia Pictures, I was back in New York. On my desk in New York were various messages—and it must be said that my sister, Gloria, who worked for me then, is extremely selective, not to say brutal, about the messages she leaves on my desk. I don't see, simply, most of the messages I get. I couldn't conceivably live with them. No one could—as Gloria knows. However, my best friend, black, when I had been in junior high school, when I was twelve or thirteen, had been calling and calling and calling. The guilt of the survivor is a real guilt—as I was now to discover. In a way that I may never be able to make real for my countrymen, or myself, the fact that I had "made it"—that is, had been seen on television, and at Sardi's, could (presumably!) sign a check anywhere in the world, could, in short, for the length of an entrance, a dinner, or a drink, intimidate headwaiters by the use of a name which had not been mine when I was born and which love had compelled me to make my own—meant that I had betrayed the people who had produced me. Nothing could be more unutterably paradoxical: to have thrown in your lap what you never dreamed of getting, and, in sober, bitter truth, could never have dreamed of having, and that at the price of an assumed betrayal of your brothers and your sisters! One is always disproving the accusation in action as futile as it is inevitable.

I had not seen this friend—who could scarcely, any longer, be called a friend—in many years. I was brighter, or more driven than he—not my fault!— and, though neither of us knew it then, our friendship really ended during my ministry and was deader than my hope of heaven by the time I left the pulpit, the church, and home. Hindsight indicates, obviously, that this particular rupture, which was, of necessity, exceedingly brutal and which involved, after all, the deliberate repudiation of everything and everyone that had given me an identity until that moment, must have left some scars. The current of my life meant that I did not see this person very often, but I was always terribly guilty when I did. I was guilty because I had nothing to say to him, and at one time I had told him everything, or nearly everything. I was guilty because he was just another post-office worker, and we had dreamed such tremendous futures for ourselves. I was guilty because he and his family had been very nice to me during an awful time in my life and now none of that meant anything to me. I was guilty because I knew, at the bottom of my heart, that I judged this unremarkable colored man very harshly, far more harshly than I would have done if he were white, and I knew this to be unjust as well as sinister. I was furious because he thought my life was easy and I thought my life was hard, and I yet had to see that by his lights, certainly, and by any ordinary yardstick, my life was enviable compared to his. And if, as I kept saying, it was not my fault, it was not *his* fault, either. You can certainly see why I tended to avoid my old school chum.

But I called him, of course. I thought that he probably needed money, because that was the only thing, by now, that I could possibly hope to give him. But, no. He, or his wife, or a relative, had read the Leonard Lyons column and knew that I had a suit I wasn't wearing, and—as he remembered in one way and I in quite another—he was just my size.

Now, for me, that suit was drenched in the blood of all the crimes of my country. If I had said to Leonard, somewhat melodramatically, no doubt, that I could never wear it again, I was, just the same, being honest. I simply could not put it on, or look at it, without thinking of Martin, and Martin's end, of what he had meant to me, and to so many. I could not put it on without a bleak, pale, cold wonder about the future. I could not, in short, live with it, it was too heavy a garment. Yet—it was only a suit, worn, at most, three times. It was not a very expensive suit, but it was still more expensive than any my friend could buy. He could not afford to have suits in his closet which he didn't wear, he couldn't afford to throw suits away—he couldn't, in short, afford my elegant despair. Martin was dead, but *he* was living, he needed a suit, and—I was just his size. He invited me for dinner that evening, and I said that I would bring him the suit.

The American situation being what it is, and American taxi drivers being what they mostly are, I have, in effect, been forbidden to expose myself to the quite tremendous hazards of getting a cab to stop for me in New York, and have been forced to hire cars. Naturally, the car which picked me up on that particular guilty evening was a Cadillac limousine about seventy-three blocks long, and, naturally, the chauffeur was white. Neither did he want to drive a black man through Harlem to the Bronx, but American democracy has always been at the mercy of the dollar: the chauffeur may not have liked the gig, but he certainly wasn't about to lose the bread. Here we were, then, this terrified white man and myself, trapped in this leviathan, eyed bitterly, as it passed, by a totally hostile population. But it was not the chauffeur which the population looked on with such wry contempt: I held the suit over my arm, and was tempted to wave it: *I'm only taking a suit to a friend!*

I knew how they felt about black men in limousines—unless they were popular idols—and I couldn't blame them, and I knew that I could never explain. We found the house, and, with the suit over my arm, I mounted the familiar stairs.

I was no longer the person my friend and his family had known and loved—I was a stranger now, and keenly aware of it, and trying hard to act, as it were, normal. But nothing *can* be normal in such a situation. They *had* known me, and they *had* loved me; but now they couldn't be blamed for feeling *He thinks he's too good for us now.* I certainly didn't feel that, but I had no conceivable relationship with them anymore—that shy, pop-eyed thirteen-year-old my friend's mother had scolded and loved was no more. *I* was not the same, but *they* were, as though they had been trapped, preserved, in that moment in time. They seemed scarcely to have grown any older, my friend and his mother, and they greeted me as they had greeted me years ago, though I was now well past forty and felt every hour of it. My friend and I remained alike only in that neither of us had gained any weight. His face was as boyish as ever, and his voice; only a touch of gray in his hair proved that we were no longer at P.S. 139. And my life came with me into their small, dark, unspeakably respectable, incredibly hard-won rooms like the roar of champagne and the odor of brimstone. They still believed in the Lord, but I had quarreled with Him, and offended Him, and walked out of His house. They didn't smoke, but they knew (from seeing me on television) that I did, and they had placed about the room, in deference to me, those hideous little ash trays which can hold exactly one cigarette butt. And there was a bottle of whiskey, too, and they asked me if I wanted steak or chicken; for, in my travels, I might have learned not to like fried chicken anymore. I said, much relieved to be able to tell the truth, that I preferred chicken. I gave my friend the suit.

My friend's stepdaughter is young, considers herself a militant, and we had a brief argument concerning Bill Styron's *Nat Turner*, which I suggested that she read before condemning. This rather shocked the child, whose militancy, like that of many, tends to be a matter of indigestible fury and slogans and quotations. It rather checked the company, which had not imagined that I was a black militant could possibly disagree about anything. But what was most striking about our brief exchange was that it obliquely revealed how little the girl respected her stepfather. She appeared not to respect him at all. This was not revealed by anything she said to him, but by the fact that she said nothing to him. She barely looked at him. He didn't count.

I always think that this is a terrible thing to happen to a man, especially in his own house, and I am always terribly humiliated for the man to whom it happens. Then, of course, you get angry at the man for allowing it to happen.

And *how* had it happened? He had never been the brightest boy in the world, nobody is, but he had been energetic, active, funny, wrestling, playing handball, cheerfully submitting to being tyrannized by me, even to the extent of kneeling before the altar and having his soul saved—my insistence had accomplished that. I looked at him and remembered his sweating and beautiful face that night as he wrestled on the church floor and we prayed him through. I remembered his older brother, who had died in Sicily, in battle for the free world—he had barely had time to see Sicily before he died and had assuredly never seen the free world. I remembered the day he came to see me to tell me that his sister, who had been very ill, had died. We sat on the steps of the tenement, he was looking down as he told me, one finger making a circle on the step, and his tears splashed on the wood. We were children then, his sister had not been much older, and he was the youngest and now the only boy. But this was not *how* it happened, although I thought I could see, watching his widowed mother's still very handsome face watching him, how her human need might have held and trapped and frozen him. She had been sewing in the garment center all the years I knew them, rushing home to get supper on the table before her husband got home from *his* job; at night, and on Sundays, he was a deacon; and God knows, or should, where his energy came from. When I began working for the garment center, I used to see her, from time to time, rushing to catch the bus, in a crowd of black and Puerto Rican ladies.

And, yes, we had all loved each other then, and I had had great respect for

NO NAME IN THE STREET

my friend, who was handsomer than I, and more athletic, and more popular, and who beat me in every game I was foolish enough to play with him. I had gone my way and life had accomplished its inexorable mathematic—and what in the world was I by now but an aging, lonely, sexually dubious, politically outrageous, unspeakably erratic freak? his old friend. And what was *he* now? he worked for the post office and was building a house next door to his mother, in, I think, Long Island. They, too, then, had made it. But what I could not understand was how nothing seemed to have touched this man. We are living through what our church described as "these last and evil days," through wars and rumors of wars, to say the least. He could, for example, have known something about the anti-poverty program if only because his wife was more or less involved in it. He should have known something about the then raging school battle, if only because his step-daughter was a student; and she, whether or not she had thought her position through, was certainly involved. She may have hoped, at one time, anyway, for his clarity and his help. But, no. He seemed as little touched by the cataclysm in his house and all around him as he was by the mail he handled every day. I found this unbelievable, and, given my temperament and our old connection, maddening. We got into a battle about the war in Vietnam. I probably really should not have allowed this to happen, but it was partly the stepdaughter's prodding. And I was astounded that my friend would defend this particular racist folly. What for? for his job at the post office? And the answer came back at once, alas—yes. For his job at the post office. I told him that Americans had no business at all in Vietnam; and that black people certainly had no business there, aiding the slave master to enslave yet more millions of dark people, and also identifying themselves with the white American crimes: we, the blacks, are going to need our allies, for the Americans, odd as it may sound at the moment, will presently have none. It wasn't, I said, hard to understand why a black boy, standing, futureless, on the corner, would decide to join the Army, nor was it hard to decipher the slave master's reasons for hoping that he wouldn't live to come home, with a gun; but it wasn't necessary, after all, to defend it: to defend, that is, one's murder and one's murderers. "Wait a minute," he said, "let me stand up and tell you what I think we're trying to do there." *"We?"* I cried, "what motherfucking *we?* You stand up, motherfucker, and I'll kick you in the ass!"

He looked at me. His mother conveyed—but the good Lord knows I had hurt her—that she didn't want that language in her house, and that I had never talked that way before. And I love the lady. I had meant no disrespect. I stared at my friend, my old friend, and felt millions of people staring at us both. I tried to make a kind of joke out of it all. But it was too late. The way they looked at me proved that I had tipped my hand. And *this* hurt *me.* They should have known me better, or at least enough, to have known that I meant what I said. But the general reaction to famous people who hold difficult opinions is that they can't really mean it. It's considered, generally, to be merely an astute way of attracting public attention, a way of making oneself interesting: one marches in Montgomery, for example, merely (in my own case) to sell one's books. Well. There is nothing, then, to be said. There went the friendly fried chicken dinner. There went the loving past. I watched the mother watching me, wondering what had happened to her beloved Jimmy, and giving me up: her sourest suspicions confirmed. In great weariness I poured myself yet another stiff drink, by now definitively condemned, and lit another cigarette, they watching me all the while for symptoms of cancer, and with a precipice at my feet.

For that bloody suit was *their* suit, after all, it had been bought *for* them, it had even been bought *by* them: *they* had created Martin, he had not created them, and the blood in which the fabric of that suit was stiffening was theirs. The distance between us, and I had never thought of this before, was that they did not know this, and I now dared to realize that I loved them more than they loved me. And I do not mean that my love was greater: who dares judge the inexpressible expense another pays for his life? who knows how much one is loved, by whom, or what that love may be called on to do? No, the way the cards had fallen meant that I had to face more about them than they could know about me, knew their rent, whereas they did not know mine, and was condemned to make them uncomfortable. For, on the other hand, they certainly wanted that freedom which they thought was mine—that frightening limousine, for example, or the power to give away a suit, or my increasingly terrifying trans-Atlantic journeys. How can one say that freedom is taken, not given, and that no one is free until all are free? and that the price is high.

My friend tried on the suit, a perfect fit, and they all admired him in it, and I went home.

AMÉRKA, AMÉRKA:
A PALESTINIAN ABROAD IN THE LAND
OF THE FREE

Anton Shammas

Anton Shammas is a Palestinian born in Israel in 1950. He attended Hebrew University in Jerusalem and came to the United States in 1987 as a Rockefeller Fellow at the University of Michigan, where he is affiliated with the Near Eastern Studies Department. He is the author of a novel, *Arabesques* (1988). His essays have been published in *The New York Review of Books, Harper's, Granta,* the *New York Times,* and *Tikkun.*

SOME YEARS AGO, IN SAN FRANCISCO, I HEARD THE FOLLOWING tale from a young, American-educated Palestinian engineer. We had found a rustic, trendy place and managed to find a quiet table. Over lukewarm beers, rather than small cups of lukewarm cardamomed coffee, we talked about his family, which had wandered adrift in the Arab world for some time before finding its moorings on the West Coast, and in particular of a relative of his living to the south of San Francisco whom we were planning to visit the following day. We never did make that visit—that is a story, too—but the story about this man has fluttered inside my head ever since.

We will call him Abu-Khalil. Imagine him as a fortysomething Palestinian (he is now past sixty) whose West Bank homeland was, once again in his lifetime, caving in on him in June 1967 after what the Arabs call the Defeat of Hazieran

291

5 and the Israelis and Americans call the Six-Day War. Where was he to spend the occupation years of his life? Where could he get as far away from the Israeli "benign" presence as his captive mind could go? The choices were essentially two: He could cross the Allenby Bridge to His Majesty's Jordan, or he could take an unhijackable flight west, from Ben-Gurion Airport. He chose the latter, a plane that would carry him to the faraway U.S.A.—to those members of his large family (Arabs always seem to have *large* families) who had discovered the New World centuries after Columbus. (They had discovered the New World, as they would tell him later, in a sort of belated westbound revenge for the eastbound expulsion of their great ancestors from Andalusia/Spain the same year that Columbus's Spanish ships arrived on the shores of his imaginary India.)

To continue our tale: Abu-Khalil lands in San Francisco one warm September afternoon, clad in a heavy black coat that does not astonish his waiting relatives a bit, since they are familiar with the man's eccentricities. But what about the security guys at Ben-Gurion Airport? Didn't the out-of-season coat merit suspicion and a frisking? Apparently not. Abu-Khalil is, as far as I can tell, the only Palestinian to have seeped out through the thick security screenings at Ben-Gurion Airport—née Lydda—unsearched. How else to account for the fact that he had managed to carry on board with him a veritable Little Palestine—flora, fauna, and all?

His bags were heavy with small plants and seeds that went undetected by Israeli security. (It should be said, of course, that flora poised to explode is not what they look for in a Palestinian's luggage at Ben-Gurion Airport.) As for U.S. Customs Form 6059B, which inbound foreigners are graciously asked to fill out before they land—it prohibits passengers from importing "fruits, vegetables, plants, plant products, soil, meats, meat products, birds, snails, and other live animals and animal products"—our passenger, to the best of the storyteller's authorial knowledge (and mine), could not read English, and no American officer, lawful or otherwise, bothered to verify his declarations—albeit not made—through questioning, much less through physical search, these being two procedures that Palestinians are much accustomed to in their comings and goings in the Middle East.

So that's how Abu-Khalil managed to bring to California some representative plants of Palestine, many still rooted in their original, fecund soil. It seems, however, that he took pride mainly—think of it as a feather in his kaffiyeh—in his having managed to smuggle out of the West Bank, through Israel, and into the United States seven representative birds of his homeland. The duri, the hassoun, the sununu, the shahrur, the bulbul, the summan, and the hudhud, small-talk companion to King Solomon himself—they all surrounded him now in California, re-chirping Palestine away in his ears from inside their unlocked

A M É R K A , A M É R K A

American cages. "They will not leave their open cages," Abu-Khalil would say, or so the story went, "till I leave mine."

Abu-Khalil's was a cage of his own making; he has not left it to this very day. But I was mainly interested in the birds, in their mute, wondrous migration. In the years that followed, I asked the storyteller, did they forget their mother chirp? Did they eventually adopt the mellow sounds of California? And how, I asked, did he manage to smuggle in these birds in the first place? "Well," said my friend, "he had a coat of many pockets, you see."

I found the story hard to believe at the time; but one has to trust the storyteller, even a Palestinian. After all, where else could the birds of Palestine go "after the last sky," in the words of the poet Mahmoud Darwish, but to the Land of the Free.

My storyteller and I belong to a different generation from Abu-Khalil's. We, and others like us, are too young to think of smuggling roots and soil, though not young enough to forget all about the birds we left behind. We travel light, empty-pocketed, with the vanity of those who think home is a portable idea, something that dwells mainly in the mind or within a text. Celebrating the modern powers of imagination and of fiction, we have lost faith in our old idols—memory, storytelling. We are not even sure anymore whether there ever was a home out there, a territory, a homeland. We owe allegiance to no memory; and we have adopted as our anthem Derek Walcott's perhaps too-often-quoted line: "I had no nation now but the imagination." Our language, Arabic, was de-territorialized by another, and only later did we realize that Arabic does not even have a word for "territory." The act of de-territorialization, then, took place outside our language, so we could not talk, much less write, about our plight in our mother tongue. Now we need the language of the Other for that, the language that can categorize the new reality and sort it out for us in upper and lower cases; the language that can re-territorialize us, as imaginary as that might be, giving us some allegedly solid ground. It is English for my San Francisco storyteller-friend, French for others, Hebrew for me: the unlocked cages of our own choices. In short, we are Palestine's post–Abu-Khalilians, if you like.

Many Middle Eastern Abu-Khalils have immigrated to the U.S.A. over the years, driven out of their respective homelands by wars, greedy foreigners, and pangs of poverty. At the turn of the century, when the Ottomans—who had been ruling the Middle East since 1517—were practicing some refined forms of their famine policy, Arabs left their homes and families and sailed to the Americas. Brazil and Argentina had their charm; Michigan, too. Today, Michigan is home to the largest Arab-American community in North America. If you were to take a stroll through the streets of Dearborn, a south-by-southwest suburb of Detroit, the signs and names might remind you of some ancient legend.

Bereft of names and deeds, these Arabs came to Michigan to make names for themselves as a twentieth-century self-mocking variation on the old Mesopotamian tradition of the *shuma shakanu,* the preservation of one's name and deeds. That also was the original aim of those who followed Nimrod the Hunter in his biblical endeavor to reach heaven and said, "Let us make us a name for ourselves" (Gen. 11:4). An American heaven of sorts and, in this case, an American name; no concealed Nimrods.

Hoping for a happier ending than the biblical one, they have come from places whose names Mark Twain, the great American nomenclator, traveling with "the innocents abroad" some 123 years ago, found impossible to pronounce. "One of the great drawbacks to this country," he wrote in September 1867, from Palestine, "is its distressing names that nobody can get the hang of. . . . You may make a stagger of pronouncing these names, but they will bring any Christian to grief that tries to spell them. I have an idea that if I can only simplify the nomenclature of this country, it will be of the greatest service to Americans who may travel here in the future."

This may account for the notorious Hollywood tradition, many years after tongue-in-cheek Twain, of assuming that all men Middle Eastern—if fortunate enough to actually have names of their own in the films—should be called Abdul. (In fact, Abdul is but the first half of a common Middle Eastern compound.) So all these anonymous Abduls are here now, trying, so far away from home, to complete their names, in a new world that has been practicing the renaming of things now for five centuries and counting.

Twain might have bumped into the grandfathers of these Arab-Americans. The Arabs he happened upon reminded him "much of Indians," watching the innocents' every motion with "that vile, uncomplaining impoliteness which is so truly Indian, and which makes a white man so nervous, and uncomfortable and savage that he wants to exterminate the whole tribe." Luckily enough, perhaps because they'd already had far too many Indians of their own, the Americans did not see the Indians of the Middle East as their burden (as did the Europeans) until it was almost too late for brazen, self-assertive colonialism. Twain could wax a little White Man's Burdenish, though, as when he wrote: "These people are naturally good-hearted and intelligent, and with education and liberty, would be a happy and contented race."

"Education"? Maybe. "Liberty"? Well, not yet. "Happy"? Happiness in the Middle East is not something that you pursue as if it were a round, stiff pita tossed about like a Frisbee. Paradoxically enough (which Twain might have appreciated), the place where these Oriental Indians have been most likely to find "education and liberty" has been the United States, where they have also been

AMÉRKA, AMÉRKA

able to feel if not exactly "happy" then at least—in the words of Was (Not Was)—"better than James Brown" and much, much better than all the James Browns of Detroit.

America's debut in the Middle East was made some decades before Twain, in the 1820s, when the blue-eyed American Protestant missionaries in Lebanon started the big project—even in American terms—of converting the infidels of the Levant to Christianity and translating the Christian Bible into Arabic. One Dr. Eli Smith took the latter endeavor upon himself and even decided, in 1839, to cast the Arabic letters to be used in the printing process. In 1857, Dr. Smith passed away, survived only by the books of Genesis and Exodus in Arabic translation. There was no grace in Smith's Arabic letters; no grace in his translation (completed by others), though he had sought the assistance of some of the most brilliant Arab linguists of the time.

I came across Smith's translation anew the other day at the University of Michigan's graduate library; the language reminded me of Twain's description of Palestine. "Of all the lands on earth for dismal scenery," Twain wrote, "I think Palestine must be the prince. The hills are barren, they are dull of color, they are unpicturesque in shape. . . . It is the most hopeless, dreary, heartbroken piece of territory out of Arizona." Of course, to the Palestinian ear Twain's observation sounds like a rough draft of the famous Zionist slogan "A land without a people, to a people without a land."

I was born in that "most hopeless, dreary, heartbroken piece of territory out of Arizona," in the month of September. Come April, any American innocent abroad—perhaps a Gulf soldier in need of R and R—could notice the almost Eliotic breeding of lilacs out of the Galilean dead land, the mixing of memory and desire. Mr. Twain, I have been to Arizona, and, with all due respect, Arizona ain't no Galilee.

I first saw Phoenix one steamy afternoon in November of 1981. I was on my way to the Grand Canyon. Being, at the time, an official exchange visitor of the ICA (the International Communication Agency, now the United States Information Agency), I was forced, literally, to leave the serenity of Iowa City, the writer's haven, and tour the country, complying with the stated intent of my being brought to America—to get familiar with the ways of the land. My idea of seeing America was to visit émigré friends I had in cities on either coast, but the ICA would have none of it. I was unequivocally told that I was to "do some nature" too.

Arriving at the Phoenix airport overdressed for an Arizona November, I was met by an amiable local lady. All I wanted to do was to check in at the Ramada Inn, where I could hang my black, heavily redundant coat and take a decent shower. Instead, I was congenially, but firmly, escorted to the local zoo, where, under a scorching sun, I was offered the opportunity to admire three recalcitrant iguanas, five friendly snakes, and seven cacti. After a couple of hours I was told that my guide's father, who had some interest in things Near Eastern, was going to take me out for an early dinner, and then, maybe, I could check in. "How could anybody take me *out,*" I inquired of my guide, "if I haven't been *in* yet?"

Being a Phoenix first-timer, however, I thought I would stand a grave risk of being thought impolite if I refused. So I was taken to a place called Brookshires (how could I forget?) and there had what was, and still is, the quietest, most peaceful dinner of my life (twenty-three, twenty-five words max, just the bare necessities of menu small talk, were exchanged). A nice old man, taciturn—in the good sense of the word—he was.

Then, around eight, I finally reached the hotel and ended up in a room on the first floor, just off the swimming pool. (I should have shown up in the early afternoon if I wanted a better room.) This was not exactly my idea of peace and privacy, but it was one of those days. I took my long, long-overdue shower, then tried to open the huge sliding door so that I could go out and relax for a while near the pool. After some futile attempts, and almost on the verge of giving up, the phone rang, and on the other end of the line a woman's friendly voice said, "Hi, this is the front desk. All you need to do is remove the stick off the door's track." Which, embarrassed, I did.

A drink in hand, like any good tourist, I was watching the tranquil Arizona skies when a young black guy came by and started cleaning the pool with a net attached to a long rod. I remember thinking: What would this tool be called in English, let alone Arabic or Hebrew? Then I noticed, as he did, that the sounds I thought were coming from the sieved water were actually something else. The courtyard was surrounded by numerous sliding doors, curtained or otherwise, and it was hard to determine, engulfed in whispers and echoes, where exactly the sounds were coming from. But it turned out to be merely a net-throw away: a couple, ever so gently, making love. In a sudden ruse of discretion, we immediately retreated. I was no sooner back in my room when the phone rang, and what I thought was the same receptionist's voice, without identifying itself this time, abruptly said, "There's America for ya."

From Fassuta, my small village in the Galilee, émigrés went mainly to Brazil and Argentina. My grandfather and his brothers and brother-in-law left for Argentina in 1896, only to return home, empty-handed, a year later. Then, on the eve of the First World War, my grandfather tried his luck again, this time on his own, heading once more to Argentina (at least that's what he told my grandmother the night before he took off), where he vanished for about ten years, leaving behind three daughters and three sons, all of them hungry. His youngest son,

AMÉRKA, AMÉRKA

my uncle Jiryes, followed in his footsteps in 1928, leaving his wife and child behind, never to come back.

One of my childhood heroes, an old villager whom we, the children of Fassuta, always blamed for having invented school, had actually been to Salt Lake City. I don't have the foggiest idea what he did there for three years before the Depression; his deeds remain a sealed and, I suspect, quite salty book, but he certainly did not betray the Catholic faith, no sir. I still remember him in the late 1950s, breathing down my neck during Mass at the village's church. He used to wear impeccable white American shirts under his Arab *abaya,* even some thirty years after he had returned to the village. But that was the only American fingerprint on him; the rest was Middle Eastern.

The most famous American immigrant from my village, though, was M., my aunt Najeebeh's brother-in-law, Najeebeh being my father's sister. I hate to be finicky about the exact relationship, but that is simply the way it is in Arabic: There are different words to refer to the father's and the mother's side of the family. At any rate, M. left the village in the early 1920s and came back to visit his brothers some forty years later, with his non-Arabic-speaking sons. As a matter of fact, he was the only one of a long, winding line of immigrants who had really made it, or "had it fixed," as the Galileans would say. He came to own a chain of fast-food restaurants, quite famous in the Midwest. Before I myself left the Mideast for these parts, I went to see his nephews—my cousins—in the village and promised them, under oath, that I would certainly look M. up one day and introduce myself, or at least pop into one of his restaurants and, naturally, ask for a free meal. I have not yet done the former and am still keeping the latter for a rainy Michigan day. However, whenever I come across his chain's emblem, a plump plastic boy holding a plate high above his plumpily combed head, I remember my late aunt Najeebeh and think how disconcerted she would be had she known what kind of a mnemonic-device-in-the-form-of-a-cultural-shock she had become for her nephew, in faraway Amérka, as it is called in my part of the world.

Upon first arriving in Amérka, one of my first cultural shocks was the otherwise trivial American fact that shirts had not only a neck size but also a sleeve size. Fassuta's Salt Lake City visitor and I, we both come from a culture where, insofar as shirts are concerned, one's arm length doesn't matter much. People in the Middle East are still immersed in figuring out the length of their postcolonial borders, personal and otherwise, and all indications show that a long time will elapse before they start paying attention to the lonely business of their sleeve size.

Which may or may not have something to do with the fact that in a culture with an oral background of storytelling, where choices continue, even in post-colonial times, to be made for you (be they by God, fate, nature, or the ruler), you don't enjoy the luxuries of the novel's world, where characters make their own choices and have to live, subsequently, with the consequences, sleeve size and all. The storyteller's world revolved around memory; the novelist's, around imagination. And what people in places like the Middle East are struggling to do, I think, is to shrug off the bondage of their memory and decolonize their imagination. So, in this regard, for a Middle Easterner to have a sleeve size would be a sign of such a decolonization.

My first stroll ever on American soil took place in a park along the Iowa River, in Iowa City. I was thirty years old, and there were so many things I had not seen before. On that day I saw my first squirrel. There are many jittery, frail creatures in the Middle East, but, to the best of my zoological knowledge, there are no squirrels. However, people do talk of the *sinjabi,* the squirrelish color. I remember thinking, during my walk, that if there were no squirrels in the Middle East, how come the Arabs used the word *sinjabi?*

Not long after the day I took my walk, I found out, as I had expected, that there were *sinjabs* in Iran and that the word *sinjabi* was derived from the Persian, a language that had given Arabic, long before the Koran, so many beautiful words. Some 1,300 years later, at the very time of my stay in Iowa, the Ayatollah Khomeini was busy squirreling away some ideas about a new order, about the Mesopotamian tradition of the *shuma shakanu.* A half-world away, Salman Rushdie was, apparently, squirreling away some counter-ideas of his own. It was not hard to imagine, later, who would play the Crackers, and who—or on whose—Nuts.

My Galilean friend J., not to be confused with the biblical author, came to America some sixteen years ago. We'd met at the Hebrew University in Jerusalem, in the early Seventies. He was my instructor in the Introduction to Arabic Literature course, and I'm still indebted to him for teaching me the first steps of academic research and, most importantly, for being so decent a friend as to have unabash-edly explained to me how I would never have the proper discipline.

At that time he was mulling over the idea that he should perhaps come to this country to work on a Ph.D. in modern Arabic literature. Once he had made up his mind, he started frantically looking for a wife with whom to share the burden of American self-exile. I asked him once whether it wouldn't be wiser to find himself an already naturalized American lady, to which he replied: "I'm looking for a woman that when I put my weary head against her arm, I want to hear her blood murmuring in Arabic." He did eventually find one, and they both immigrated to Amérka and have been happily listening to each other's blood ever since.

AMÉRKA, AMÉRKA

J. was looking for the blood tongue, for the primordial language, wherein the names of things, long before the confusion of tongues, were so deeply lodged in the things they designated that no human eye could decipher the sign. Had he been a Cabalist, he would have believed that what God introduced into the world was written words, not murmurings of blood. But J. came from the oral Middle East to the literate West, and he knew upon arriving in Amérka that he would be expected to trade in his mother tongue and keep the secret language circulating only in his veins.

I saw the already "naturalized" J. again, in Jerusalem, some ten years after he'd left. At the end of a very long night of catching up, he picked up a Hebrew literary magazine from my desk and browsed through it. Something caught his eye; he paused for a moment. "What is *this* doing here?" "This" turned out to be an ad for a famous Israeli brand of women's underwear. I wasn't sure what he meant. It was a full-page ad, an exact replica of the famous photograph of Marilyn Monroe standing on a grate in the street, her dress blowing above her waist. "You know what the reference is to, right?" I asked. No, he did not. And I thought, How could a bright guy like J. live for so long in the U.S.A., be an *American citizen,* and not be familiar with what I thought were the basics of American iconography?

I had been settled for a year in Ann Arbor when I went to visit J. and his wife in Ohio. Having just returned from a short visit to our Galilee home, I brought J., who has a green thumb, what he had asked me to: some local lubia peas for his thriving backyard garden. We were reminiscing late at night, with Gayruz, the famous Lebanese singer, on the stereo in the background and some Middle Eastern munchies on the coffee table, when I suddenly remembered that night in Jerusalem years before and the ad with the Marilyn knockoff. It would be nice if you did recognize the American icon, I thought to myself, but it is nice too that you can live in this country for decades without being forced to go native. You can always pick up your own fold of the huge map and chart yourself into it.

Now it is my fourth year in Ann Arbor. I moved in early in September of 1987, and for three months my relationship with the squirrels outside my window was quite good. "Quite good," as my English professor at the Hebrew University in Jerusalem used to say, means "yes, good, but there's no need to be so excited about it." So I was developing an unexciting relationship with these creatures, especially with one of them, whom I told myself I was able to tell from the others, although they all did look alike, if I may so without prejudice. Anyway, I would open the door early in the morning to pick up the *New York Times* from the doorstep, and he would be goofing around its blue, transparent wrap (that's how the paper is home-delivered in Michigan), unalarmed by my invasion of *his* kingdom.

But one morning, as I reached down for the paper, he froze, all of a sudden, in the middle of one of his silly gesticulations, gaping at me in utter terror, and then fled away as if I were about to—well, throw a stone at him. Maybe it was a morning in December 1987, and he had peeked at the *Times*. Maybe I will never cease to look east for my images and metaphors.

For J., for my friend in San Francisco, for me, the Old World will never cease to hold us hostage in this way. Sometimes I think that no matter how deep I have traveled *into* the American life, I still carry my own miniature Abu-Khalils in my pockets and a miniature Middle East in my mind. There is little space for Amérka in the most private of my maps.

And speaking of maps, how many adult Americans know where the "heart-broken piece of territory" Mark Twain was talking about actually is? (Or Arizona, for that matter?)

Still, would it matter if they did?

I don't think it would. After all, modern colonialism (sometimes euphemisti-cally referred to as "our American interests"), unlike its old-fashioned, European counterpart, is not geographically oriented. Geographical literacy is defunct; its demise was caused by the invention of the remote control. And if you happen to live in this vast country, your sense of geography is necessarily numbed by what Aldous Huxley would have called one's "local validity." Paradoxically, the vastness of the land provides Americans with a continental alibi. A look at the map of the U.S.A. from, say, a Palestinian point of view would psychologically suffice to make a clear-cut distinction between the American people and their government's policy. Unlike England, for instance, where every Brit seems to be living in London and has something or another to do with the business of running the rather rusty machinery of a worn-out colonialism, there is an utter distinction when it comes to the United States between the Americans of Capitol Hill and the *real* Americans who, on a good day, want absolutely nothing to do with Washington's follies.

Maybe that's why Abu-Khalil can feel at home in California, surrounded by the artifacts of his lost Palestine. This country is *big;* it has enough room not only for the newcomers but also for their portable homelands. Among other achieve-ments, Amérka has made homesickness obsolete.

LIKE MEXICANS

Gary Soto

Gary Soto was born in Fresno, California, grew up in and around the fields of San Joaquin Valley, graduated magna cum laude from California State University, Fresno, and has an MFA in Creative Writing from the University of California, Irvine. Soto's first book, *The Elements of San Joaquin* (1976), won the U.S. Award of the International Poetry Forum; and his second book of poetry, *The Tale of Sunlight* (1978), was nominated for both the Pulitzer Prize and the National Book Award. He has written several additional volumes of poetry and numerous collections of narrative prose.

MY GRANDMOTHER GAVE ME BAD ADVICE AND GOOD ADVICE WHEN I was in my early teens. For the bad advice, she said that I should become a barber because they made good money and listened to the radio all day. "Honey, they don't work como burros," she would say every time I visited her. She made the sound of donkeys braying. "Like that, honey!" For the good advice, she said that I should marry a Mexican girl. "No Okies, hijo"—she would say—"Look my son. He marry one and they fight every day about I don't know what and I don't know what." For her, everyone who wasn't Mexican, black, or Asian were Okies. The French were Okies, the Italians in suits were Okies. When I asked about Jews, whom I had read about, she asked for a picture. I rode home on my bicycle and returned with a calendar depicting the important races of the world. "Pues si, son Okies tambien!" she said, nodding her head. She saved the calendar away

301

and we went to the living room where she lectured me on the virtues of the Mexican girl: first, she could cook and, second, she acted like a woman, not a man, in her husband's home. She said she would tell me about a third when I got a little older.

I asked my mother about it—becoming a barber and marrying Mexican. She was in the kitchen. Steam curled from a pot of boiling beans, the radio was on, looking as squat as a loaf of bread. "Well, if you want to be a barber—they say they make good money." She slapped a round steak with a knife, her glasses slipping down with each strike. She stopped and looked up. "If you find a good Mexican girl, marry her of course." She returned to slapping the meat and I went to the backyard where my brother and David King were sitting on the lawn feeling the inside of their cheeks.

"This is what girls feel like," my brother said, rubbing the inside of his cheek. David put three fingers inside his mouth and scratched. I ignored them and climbed the back fence to see my best friend, Scott, a second-generation Okie. I called him and his mother pointed to the side of the house where his bedroom was a small aluminum trailer, the kind you gawk at when they're flipped over on the freeway, wheels spinning in the air. I went around to find Scott pitching horseshoes.

I picked up a set of rusty ones and joined him. While we played, we talked about school and friends and record albums. The horseshoes scuffed up dirt, sometimes ringing the iron that threw out a meager shadow like a sundial. After three argued-over games, we pulled two oranges apiece from his tree and started down the alley still talking school and friends and record albums. We pulled more oranges from the alley and talked about who we would marry. "No offense, Scott," I said with an orange slice in my mouth, "but I would never marry an Okie." We walked in step, almost touching, with a sled of shadows dragging behind us. "No offense, Gary," Scott said, "but I would *never* marry a Mexican." I looked at him: a fang of orange slice showed from his munching mouth. I didn't think anything of it. He had his girl and I had mine. But our seventh-grade vision was the same: to marry, get jobs, buy cars and maybe a house if we had money left over.

We talked about our future lives until, to our surprise, we were on the downtown mall, two miles from home. We bought a bag of popcorn at Penneys and sat on a bench near the fountain watching Mexican and Okie girls pass. "That one's mine," I pointed with my chin when a girl with eyebrows arched into black rainbows ambled by. "She's cute," Scott said about a girl with yellow hair and a mouthful of gum. We dreamed aloud, our chins busy pointing out girls. We agreed that we couldn't wait to become men and lift them onto our laps.

But the woman I married was not Mexican but Japanese. It was a surprise to me. For years, I went about wide-eyed in my search for the brown girl in a white dress at a dance. I searched the playground at the baseball diamond. When the girls raced for grounders, their hair bounced like something that couldn't be caught. When they sat together in the lunchroom, heads pressed together, I knew they were talking about us Mexican guys. I saw them and dreamed them. I threw my face into my pillow, making up sentences that were good as in the movies.

But when I was twenty, I fell in love with this other girl who worried my mother, who had my grandmother asking once again to see the calendar of the Important Races of the World. I told her I had thrown it away years before. I took a much-glanced-at snapshot from my wallet. We looked at it together, in silence. Then grandma reclined in her chair, lit a cigarette, and said, "Es pretty." She blew and asked with all her worry pushed up to her forehead: "Chinese?"

I was in love and there was no looking back. She was the one. I told my mother who was slapping hamburger into patties. "Well, sure if you want to marry her," she said. But the more I talked, the more concerned she became. Later I began to worry. Was it all a mistake? "Marry a Mexican girl," I heard my mother say in my mind. I heard it at breakfast. I heard it over math problems, between Western Civilization and cultural geography. But then one afternoon while I was hitchhiking home from school, it struck me like a baseball in the back: my mother wanted me to marry someone of my own social class—a poor girl. I considered my fiancee, Carolyn, and she didn't look poor, though I knew she came from a family of farm workers and pull-yourself-up-by-your-bootstraps ranchers. I asked my brother, who was marrying Mexican poor that fall, if I should marry a poor girl. He screamed "Yeah" above his terrible guitar playing in his bedroom. I considered my sister who had married Mexican. Cousins were dating Mexican. Uncles were remarrying poor women. I asked Scott, who was still my best friend, and he said, "She's too good for you, so you better not."

I worried about it until Carolyn took me home to meet her parents. We drove in her Plymouth until the houses gave way to farms and ranches and finally her house fifty feet from the highway. When we pulled into the drive, I panicked and begged Carolyn to make a U-turn and go back so we could talk about it over a soda. She pinched my cheek, calling me a "silly boy." I felt better, though, when I got out of the car and saw the house: the chipped paint, a cracked window, boards for a walk to the back door. There were rusting cars near the barn. A tractor with a net of spiderwebs under a mulberry. A field. A bale of barbed wire like children's scribbling leaning against an empty chicken coop. Carolyn took my hand and pulled me to my future mother-in-law who was coming out to greet us.

We had lunch: sandwiches, potato chips, and iced tea. Carolyn and her mother talked mostly about neighbors and the congregation at the Japanese Methodist Church in West Fresno. Her father, who was in khaki work clothes, excused himself with a wave that was almost a salute and went outside. I heard a truck start, a dog bark, and then the truck rattle away.

Carolyn's mother offered another sandwich, but I declined with a shake of my head and a smile. I looked around when I could, when I was not saying over and over that I was a college student, hinting that I could take care of her daughter. I shifted my chair. I saw newspapers piled in corners, dusty cereal boxes and vinegar bottles in corners. The wallpaper was bubbled from rain that had come in from a bad roof. Dust. Dust lay on lamp shades and window sills. These people are just like Mexicans, I thought. Poor people.

Carolyn's mother asked me through Carolyn if I would like a *sushi*. A plate of black and white things were held in front of me. I took one, wide-eyed, and turned it over like a foreign coin. I was biting into one when I saw a kitten crawl up the window screen over the sink. I chewed and the kitten opened its mouth of terror as she crawled higher, wanting in to paw the leftovers from our plates. I looked at Carolyn who said that the cat was just showing off. I looked up in time to see it fall. It crawled up, then fell again.

We talked for an hour and had apple pie and coffee, slowly. Finally, we got up with Carolyn taking my hand. Slightly embarrassed, I tried to pull away but her grip held me. I let her have her way as she led me down the hallway with her mother right behind me. When I opened the door, I was startled by a kitten clinging to the screen door, its mouth screaming "cat food, dog biscuits, *sushi.* . . ." I opened the door and the kitten, still holding on, whined in the language of hungry animals. When I got into Carolyn's car, I looked back: the cat was still clinging. I asked Carolyn if it were possibly hungry, but she said the cat was being silly. She started the car, waved to her mother, and bounced us over the rain-poked drive, patting my thigh for being her lover baby. Carolyn waved again. I looked back, waving, then gawking at a window screen where there were now three kittens clawing and screaming to get in. Like Mexicans, I thought. I remembered the Molinas and how the cats clung to their screens— cats they shot down with squirt guns. On the highway, I felt happy, pleased by it all. I patted Carolyn's thigh. Her people were like Mexicans, only different.

REPORT FROM THE BAHAMAS

June Jordan

June Jordan was born in Harlem, New York of Jamaican parents, attended Barnard College and the University of Chicago. A significant poet, Jordan is also an educator, essayist, novelist, and writer of children's books, lyrics, and librettos. Her books of poetry include *Some Changes* (1971), *Things That I Do in the Dark* (1977), *Passion* (1980), *Living Room* (1985), and *Naming Our Destiny* (1989). Jordan's essay collections include *Civil Wars* (1981) and *On Call: New Political Essays 1981–1985* (1985).

I AM STAYING IN A HOTEL THAT CALLS ITSELF THE SHERATON BRITish Colonial. One of the photographs advertising the place displays a middle-aged Black man in a waiter's tuxedo, smiling. What intrigues me most about the picture is just this: while the Black man bears a tray full of "colorful" drinks above his left shoulder, both of his feet, shoes and trouserlegs, up to ten inches above his ankles, stand in the also "colorful" Caribbean salt water. He is so delighted to serve you he will wade into the water to bring you Banana Daquiris while you float! More precisely, he will wade into the water, fully clothed, oblivious to the ruin of his shoes, his trousers, his health, and he will do it with a smile.

I am in the Bahamas. On the phone in my room, a spinning complement of plastic pages offers handy index clues such as CAR RENTAL and CASINOS. A message from the Ministry of Tourism appears among these travellers' tips.

Opening with a paragraph of "WELCOME," the message then proceeds to "A PAGE OF HISTORY," which reads as follows:

> New World History begins on the same day that modern Bahamian history begins—October 12, 1492. That's when Columbus stepped ashore—British influence came first with the Eleutherian Adventurers of 1647—After the Revolutions, American Loyalists fled from the newly independent states and settled in the Bahamas. Confederate blockade-runners used the island as a haven during the War between the States, and after the War, a number of Southerners moved to the Bahamas . . .

There it is again. Something proclaims itself a legitimate history and all it does is track white Mr. Columbus to the British Eleutherians through the Confederate Southerners as they barge into New World surf, land on New World turf, and nobody saying one word about the Bahamian people, the Black peoples, to whom the only thing new in their island world was this weird succession of crude intruders and its colonial consequences.

This is my consciousness of race as I unpack my bathing suit in the Sheraton British Colonial. Neither this hotel nor the British nor the long ago Italians nor the white Delta airline pilots belong here, of course. And every time I look at the photograph of that fool standing in the water with his shoes on I'm about to have a West Indian fit, even though I know he's no fool; he's a middle-aged Black man who needs a job and this is his job—pretending himself a servile ancillary to the pleasures of the rich. (Compared to his options in life, I am a rich woman. Compared to most of the Black Americans arriving for this Easter weekend on a three/nights/four/days' deal of bargain rates, the middleaged waiter is a poor Black man.)

We will jostle along with the other (white) visitors and join them in the tee shirt shops or, laughing together, learn ruthless rules of negotiation as we, Black Americans as well as white, argue down the price of handwoven goods at the nearby straw market while the merchants, frequently toothless Black women seated on the concrete in their only presentable dress, humble themselves to our careless games:

"Yes? You like it? Eight dollar."

"Five."

"I give it to you. Seven."

And so it continues, this weird succession of crude intruders that, now, includes me and my brothers and my sisters from the North.

This is my consciousness of class as I try to decide how much money I can spend on Bahamian gifts for my family back in Brooklyn. No matter that these other Black women incessantly weave words and flowers into the straw hats and bags piled beside them on the burning dusty street. No matter that these other Black women must work their sense of beauty into these things that we will take away as cheaply as we dare, or they will do without food.

We are not white, after all. The budget is limited. And we are harmlessly killing time between the poolside rum punch and "The Native Show on the Patio" that will play tonight outside the hotel restaurant.

This is my consciousness of race and class and gender identity as I notice the fixed relations between these other Black women and myself. They sell and I buy or I don't. They risk not eating. I risk going broke on my first vacation afternoon.

We are not particularly women anymore; we are parties to a transaction designed to set us against each other.

"Olive" is the name of the Black woman who cleans my hotel room. On my way to the beach I am wondering what "Olive" would say if I told her why I chose the Sheraton British Colonial; if I told her I wanted to swim. I wanted to sleep. I did not want to be harassed by the middleaged waiter, or his nephew. I did not want to be raped by anybody (white or Black) at all and I calculated that my safety as a Black woman alone would best be assured by a multinational hotel corporation. In my experience, the big guys take customer complaints more seriously than the little ones. I would suppose that's one reason why they're big; they don't like to lose money anymore than I like to be bothered when I'm trying to read a goddamned book underneath a palm tree I paid $264 to get next to. A Black woman seeking refuge in a multinational corporation may seem like a contradiction to some, but there you are. In this case it's a coincidence of entirely different self-interests: Sheraton/cash = June Jordan's short run safety.

Anyway, I'm pretty sure "Olive" would look at me as though I came from someplace as far away as Brooklyn. Then she'd probably allow herself one indignant query before righteously removing her vacuum cleaner from my room; "and why in the first place you come down you without your husband?"

I cannot imagine how I would begin to answer her.

My "rights" and my "freedom" and my "desire" and a slew of other New World values; what would they sound like to this Black woman described on the card atop my hotel bureau as "Olive the Maid"? "Olive" is older than I am and I may smoke a cigarette while she changes the sheets on my bed. Whose rights? Whose freedom? Whose desire?

And why should she give a shit about mine unless I do something, for real, about hers?

It happens that the book that I finished reading under a palm tree earlier today was the novel, *Bread Givers*, by Anzia Yezierska. Definitely autobiographical, Yezierska lays out the difficulties of being both female and "a person" inside a traditional Jewish family at the start of the twentieth century. That any Jewish woman became anything more than the abused servant of her father or her husband is really an improbable piece of news. Yet Yezierska managed such an unlikely outcome for her own life. In *Bread Givers,* the heroine also manages an important, although partial, escape from traditional Jewish female destiny. And in the unpardonable, despotic father, the Talmudic scholar of that Jewish family, did I not see my own and hate him twice, again? When the heroine, the young Jewish child, wanders the streets with a filthy pail she borrows to sell herring in order to raise the ghetto rent and when she cries, "Nothing was before me but the hunger in our house, and no bread for the next meal if I didn't sell the herring. No longer like a fire engine, but like a houseful of hungry mouths my heart cried, 'herring—herring! Two cents apiece!' " who would doubt the ease, the sisterhood of conversation possible between that white girl and the Black women selling straw bags on the streets of paradise because they do not want to die? And is it not obvious that the wife of the Talmudic scholar and "Olive," who cleans my room here at the hotel, have more in common than I can claim with either one of them?

This is my consciousness of race and class and gender identity as I collect wet towels, sunglasses, wristwatch, and head towards a shower.

I am thinking about the boy who loaned this novel to me. He's white and he's Jewish and he's pursuing an independent study project with me, at the State University where I teach whether or not I feel like it, where I teach without stint because, like the waiter, I am no fool. It's my job and either I work or I do without everything you need money to buy. The boy loaned me the novel because he thought I'd be interested to know how a Jewish-American writer used English so that the syntax, and therefore the cultural habits of mind expressed by the Yiddish language, could survive translation. He did this because he wanted to create another connection between us on the basis of language, between his knowledge/his love of Yiddish and my knowledge/my love of Black English.

He has been right about the forceful survival of the Yiddish. And I had become excited by this further evidence of the written voice of spoken language protected from the monodrone of "standard" English, and so we had grown closer on this account. But then our talk shifted to student affairs more generally, and I had learned that this student does not care one way or the other about currently jeopardized Federal Student Loan Programs because, as he explained it to me, they do not affect him. He does not need financial help outside his family. My own son, however, is Black. And I am the only family help available to him and that means, if Reagan succeeds in eliminating Federal programs to aid minority students, he will have to forget about furthering his studies, or he or I or both of us will have to hit the numbers pretty big. For these reasons of difference, the student and I had moved away from each other, even while we continued to talk.

My consciousness turned to race, again, and class.

Sitting in the same chair as the boy, several weeks ago, a graduate student came to discuss her grade. I praised the excellence of her final paper; indeed it had seemed to me an extraordinary pulling together of recent left brain/right brain research with the themes of transcendental poetry.

She told me that, for her part, she'd completed her reading of my political essays. "You are so lucky!" she exclaimed.

"What do you mean by that?"

"You have a cause. You have a purpose to your life."

I looked carefully at this white woman; what was she really saying to me?

"What do you mean?" I repeated.

"Poverty. Police violence. Discrimination in general."

(Jesus Christ, I thought: Is that her idea of lucky?)

"And how about you?" I asked.

"Me?"

"Yeah, you. Don't you have a cause?"

"Me? I'm just a middle-aged woman: a housewife and a mother. I'm a nobody."

For a while, I made no response.

First of all, speaking of race and class and gender in one breath, what she said meant that those lucky preoccupations of mine, from police violence to nuclear wipe-out, were not shared. They were mine and not hers. But here she sat, friendly as an old stuffed animal, beaming good will or more "luck" in my direction.

In the second place, what this white woman said to me meant that she did not believe she was "a person" precisely because she had fulfilled the traditional female functions revered by the father of that Jewish immigrant, Anzia Yezierska. And the woman in front of me was not a Jew. That was not the connection. The link was strictly female. Nevertheless, how should that woman and I, another female, connect beyond this bizarre exchange?

If she believed me lucky to have regular hurdles of discrimination then why shouldn't I insist that she's lucky to be a middle-class white Wasp female who lives in such well-sanctioned and normative comfort that she even has the luxury to deny the power of the privileges that paralyze her life?

If she deserts me and "my cause" where we differ, if, for example, she abandons me to "my" problems of race, then why should I support her in "her" problems of housewifely oblivion?

Recollection of this peculiar moment brings me to the shower in the bathroom cleaned by "Olive." She reminds me of the usual Women's Studies curriculum because it has nothing to do with her or her job: you won't find "Olive" listed anywhere on the reading list. You will likewise seldom hear of Anzia Yezierska. But yes, you will find, from Florence Nightingale to Adrienne Rich, a white procession of independently well-to-do women writers. (Gertrude Stein/Virginia Woolf/Hilda Doolittle are standard names among the "essential" women writers).

In other words, most of the women of the world—Black and First World and white who work because we must—most of the women of the world persist far from the heart of the usual Women's Studies syllabus.

Similarly, the typical Black History course will slide by the majority experience it pretends to represent. For example, Mary McLeod Bethune will scarcely receive as much attention as Nat Turner, even though Black women who bravely and efficiently provided for the education of Black people hugely outnumber those few Black men who led successful or doomed rebellions against slavery. In fact, Mary McLeod Bethune may not receive even honorable mention because Black History too often apes those ridiculous white history courses which produce such dangerous gibberish as the Sheraton British Colonial "history" of the Bahamas. Both Black and white history courses exclude from their central consideration those people who neither killed nor conquered anyone as the means to new identity, those people who took care of every one of the people who wanted to become "a person," those people who still take care of the life at issue: the ones who wash and who feed and who teach and who diligently decorate straw hats and bags with all of their historically unrequired gentle love: the women.

> *Oh the old rugged cross*
> *on a hill far away*
> *Well I cherish the old rugged cross*

It's Good Friday in the Bahamas. Seventy-eight degrees in the shade. Except for Sheraton territory, everything's closed.

It so happens that for truly secular reasons I've been fasting for three days. My hunger has now reached nearly violent proportions. In the hotel sandwich shop, the Black woman handling the counter complains about the tourists; why isn't the shop closed and why don't the tourists stop eating for once in their lives. I'm famished and I order chicken salad and cottage cheese and lettuce and tomato and a hard boiled egg and a hot cross bun and apple juice.

She eyes me with disgust.

To be sure, the timing of my stomach offends her serious religious practices. Neither one of us apologizes to the other. She seasons the chicken salad to the peppery max while I listen to the loud radio gospel she plays to console herself. It's a country Black version of "The Old Rugged Cross."

As I heave much chicken into my mouth tears start. It's not the pepper. I am, after all, a West Indian daughter. It's the Good Friday music that dominates the humid atmosphere.

Well I cherish the old rugged cross

And I am back, faster than a 747, in Brooklyn, in the home of my parents where we are wondering, as we do every year, if the sky will darken until Christ has been buried in the tomb. The sky should darken if God is in His heavens. And then, around three P.M., at the conclusion of our mournful church service at the neighborhood St. Phillips, and even while we dumbly stare at the black cloth covering the gold altar and the slender unlit candles, the sun should return through the high gothic windows and vindicate our waiting faith that the Lord will rise again, on Easter.

How I used to bow my head at the very name of Jesus: ecstatic to abase myself in deference to His majesty.

My mouth is full of salad. I can't seem to eat quickly enough. I can't think how I should lessen the offense of my appetite. The other Black woman on the premises, the one who disapprovingly prepared this very tasty break from my fast, makes no remark. She is no fool. This is a job that she needs. I suppose she notices that at least I included a hot cross bun among my edibles. That's something in my favor. I decide that's enough.

I am suddenly eager to walk off the food. Up a fairly steep hill I walk without hurrying. Through the pastel desolation of the little town, the road brings me to a confectionary pink and white plantation house. At the gates, an unnecessarily large statue of Christopher Columbus faces me down, or tries to. His hand is fisted to one hip. I look back at him, laugh without deference, and turn left.

It's time to pack it up. Catch my plane. I scan the hotel room for things not to forget. There's that white report card on the bureau.

"Dear Guests" it says, under the name "Olive." I am your maid for the day. Please rate me: Excellent. Good. Average. Poor. Thank you."

I tuck this memento from the Sheraton British Colonial into my notebook. How would "Olive" rate *me*? What would it mean for us to seem "good" to each other? What would that rating require?

But I am hastening to leave. Neither turtle soup nor kidney pie nor any conch shell delight shall delay my departure. I have rested, here, in the Bahamas, and I'm ready to return to my usual job, my usual work. But the skin on my body has changed and so has my mind. On the Delta flight home I realize I am burning up, indeed.

So far as I can see, the usual race and class concepts of connection, or gender assumptions of unity, do not apply very well. I doubt that they ever did. Otherwise why would Black folks forever bemoan our lack of solidarity when the deal turns real. And if unity on the basis of sexual oppression is something natural, then why do we women, the majority people on the planet, still have a problem?

The plane's ready for takeoff. I fasten my seatbelt and let the tumult inside my head run free. Yes: race and class and gender remain as real as the weather. But what they must mean about the contact between two individuals is less obvious and, like the weather, not predictable.

And when these factors of race and class and gender absolutely collapse is whenever you try to use them as automatic concepts of connection. They may serve well as indicators of commonly felt conflict, but as elements of connection they seem about as reliable as precipitation probability for the day after the night before the day.

It occurs to me that much organizational grief could be avoided if people understood that partnership in misery does not necessarily provide for partnership for change: *When we get the monsters off our backs all of us may want to run in very different directions.*

And not only that: even though both "Olive" and "I" live inside a conflict neither one of us created, and even though both of us therefore hurt inside that conflict, I may be one of the monsters she needs to eliminate from her universe and, in a sense, she may be one of the monsters in mine.

I am reaching for the words to describe the difference between a common identity that has been imposed and the individual identity any one of us will choose, once she gains that chance.

That difference is the one that keeps us stupid in the face of new, specific information about somebody else with whom we are supposed to have a connection because a third party, hostile to both of us, has worked it so that the two of us, like it or not, share a common enemy. *What happens beyond the idea of that enemy and beyond the consequences of that enemy?*

I am saying that the ultimate connection cannot be the enemy. The ultimate connection must be the need that we find between us. It is not only who you are, in other words, but what we can do for each other that will determine the connection.

I am flying back to my job. I have been teaching contemporary women's poetry this semester. One quandary I have set myself to explore with my students is the one of taking responsibility without power. We had been wrestling ideas to the floor for several sessions when a young Black woman, a South African, asked me for help, after class.

REPORT FROM THE BAHAMAS

Sokutu told me she was "in a trance" and that she'd been unable to eat for two weeks.

"What's going on?" I asked her, even as my eyes startled at her trembling and emaciated appearance.

"My husband. He drinks all the time. He beats me up. I go to the hospital. I can't eat. I don't know what/anything."

In my office, she described her situation. I did not dare to let her sense my fear and horror. She was dragging about, hour by hour, in dread. Her husband, a young Black South African, was drinking himself into more and more deadly violence against her.

Sokutu told me how she could keep nothing down. She weighed ninety pounds at the outside, as she spoke to me. She'd already been hospitalized as a result of her husband's battering rage.

I knew both of them because I had organized a campus group to aid the liberation struggles of Southern Africa.

Nausea rose in my throat. What about this presumable connection: this husband and this wife fled from that homeland of hatred against them, and now what? He was destroying himself. If not stopped, he would certainly murder his wife.

She needed a doctor, right away. It was a medical emergency. She needed protection. It was a security crisis. She needed refuge for battered wives and personal therapy and legal counsel. She needed a friend.

I got on the phone and called every number in the campus directory that I could imagine might prove helpful. Nothing worked. There were no institutional resources designed to meet her enormous, multifaceted, and ordinary woman's need.

I called various students. I asked the Chairperson of the English Department for advice. I asked everyone for help.

Finally, another one of my students, Cathy, a young Irish woman active in campus IRA activities, responded. She asked for further details. I gave them to her.

"Her husband," Cathy told me, "is an alcoholic. You have to understand about alcoholics. It's not the same as anything else. And it's a disease you can't treat any old way."

I listened, fearfully. Did this mean there was nothing we could do?

"That's not what I'm saying," she said. "But you have to keep the alcoholic part of the thing central in everybody's mind, otherwise her husband will kill her. Or he'll kill himself."

She spoke calmly, I felt there was nothing to do but to assume she knew what she was talking about.

"Will you come with me?" I asked her, after a silence. "Will you come with me and help us figure out what to do next?"

Cathy said she would but that she felt shy: Sokutu comes from South Africa. What would she think about Cathy?

"I don't know," I said. "But let's go."

We left to find a dormitory room for the young battered wife.

It was late, now, and dark outside.

On Cathy's VW that I followed behind with my own car, was the sticker that reads BOBBY SANDS FREE AT LAST. My eyes blurred as I read and reread the words. This was another connection: Bobby Sands and Martin Luther King Jr. and who would believe it? I would not have believed it; I grew up terrorized by Irish kids who introduced me to the word "nigga."

And here I was following an Irish woman to the room of a Black South African. We were going to that room to try to save a life together.

When we reached the little room, we found ourselves awkward and large. Sokutu attempted to treat us with utmost courtesy, as though we were honored guests. She seemed surprised by Cathy, but mostly Sokutu was flushed with relief and joy because we were there, with her.

I did not know how we should ever terminate her heartfelt courtesies and address, directly, the reason for our visit: her starvation and her extreme physical danger.

Finally, Cathy sat on the floor and reached out her hands to Sokutu.

"I'm here," she said quietly, "because June has told me what has happened to you. And I know what it is. Your husband is an alcoholic. He has a disease. I know what it is. My father was an alcoholic. He killed himself. He almost killed my mother. I want to be your friend."

"Oh," was the only small sound that escaped from Sokutu's mouth. And then she embraced the other student. And then everything changed and I watched all of this happen so I know that this happened: this connection.

And after we called the police and exchanged phone numbers and plans were made for the night and for the next morning, the young South African woman walked down the dormitory hallway, saying goodbye and saying thank you to us.

I walked behind them, the young Irish woman and the young South African, and I saw them walking as sisters walk, hugging each other, and whispering and sure of each other and I felt how it was not who they were but what they both know and what they were both preparing to do about what they know that was going to make them both free at last.

And I look out the windows of the plane and I see clouds that will not kill me and I know that someday soon other clouds may erupt to kill us all.

And I tell the stewardess No thanks to the cocktails she offers me. But I

REPORT FROM THE BAHAMAS

look about the cabin at the hundred strangers drinking as they fly and I think even here and even now I must make the connection real between me and these strangers everywhere before those other clouds unify this ragged bunch of us, too late.

IMMIGRANT WAVES

Michael Stephens

Michael Stephens's most recent book is *Jigs and Reels* (1992). His other books include *Lost in Seoul* (1990), a memoir, and *Season at Coole* (Dutton, 1972; Dalkey Archive, 1984), a novel. Stephens has also written a play, *Our Father,* and his journalism is widely published in magazines and newspapers, including the *New York Times, Washington Post* and *Baltimore Sun.*

SHORTLY AFTER ARRIVING IN HAWAII TO TEACH FOR A SEMESTER, I came down with a strange fever. I never found out what it was, but a rare tropical disease doctor thought it might have been dengue, which had been wiped out in the Hawaiian Islands after the Second World War, though it was still epidemic in the South Seas and Southeast Asia. It would have been extremely unusual for me to have picked it up in Korea from where I had just come as it was a peninsula country jutting out of Siberia in Northeast Asia. During the day I managed to teach my classes, but when the sun set around five-thirty every night, and a cool breeze invaded the tropics, I broke out into high fever and cold sweats, and afterward, walking around Waikiki in a sweater and long black leather overcoat to keep off the chills, I noticed how blank and relaxed my mind became once this nightly ordeal subsided. One benefit—if such an absurd idea is possible with this weird illness I had—was that I found myself reading familiar books as if I had just discovered them. I would read *Dubliners,* say, as if for the first time, and this likewise happened reading Yeats's poetry. After the terror of my illness, this was quite rewarding, finding Joyce and Yeats again after a lifetime among them, only this time my Irish literary companions were reading under palm trees, watching forty-foot waves on the North Shore, or out on the lanai, thirty stories above Waikiki, sugar cane fires smoldering in the distant mountains toward the Leeward Side.

On the last day of school, the class had a party at the poolside of my hotel off the Ala Wai Canal in Waikiki; we drank and laughed and carried on until two tough-looking security guards came over and told us to quiet down, even though this had not been a wild party, or even a particularly big one. There were less than a dozen people gathered in a clutch around lawn chairs away from the pool and other hotel guests; most of them were serious-minded graduate students. The guards weren't the least bit friendly, but then again they had been trailing me around for a week, just waiting for me to do something wrong. I had offended a hotel clerk, grabbing and shaking him by the shirt when he called me a haole, this derogatory Hawaiian word that's used too frequently on the islands to refer to white people, but one which everyone seems to find acceptable speech. It means something like "spirit without breath," so that it's not really as neutral as people want you to believe if you do take offense at it, and it has less to do with white people versus people of color than it does with locals versus mainlanders. I told the class that's why the guards were so mean; they didn't like how I reacted to the nasty remark by the clerk.

I had been drunk and jumped over a counter and grabbed the clerk when he was getting my mail—"Boomertang," he had said to a Filipino worker, "get the haole his mail," and then I exploded. The two security guards were called after I grabbed the clerk and shouted in his face: "You don't know anything about me, mister, nothing, just a lot of presumption about who I am and what I do, and you don't have any idea what I might do to you right now, you aren't even sure if I am a haole, because maybe I'm not, maybe I'm Portuguese like you are or something else . . ."

It was the culmination of the fever, the job, a lack of human contact during my months there, but other things, too. A few months earlier a worker at the university cafeteria had asked me where I was from because, as she put it, I had "a funny accent," meaning, I think, that I had no pidgin in my English, no glide and lilt in my speech like the Hawaiians did, I was all mainland, this amorphous place to locals that is filled with haoles, bad speech, bad manners, no waves, no surf, no boards, no *howzit, brah* friendliness. Are you from the South? she asked. Georgia? she asked. Though to most anyone else I have what I think is an unmistakably New York accent, which, I realized, in Hawaii at least, is no different from a Southern accent, a Midwestern one, or one from Southern California. Less mainland speech, it is haolese, the speech of the spirit without breath from the mainland. But I didn't see it that way; I saw big differences between, say, myself and Jimmy Carter's speech, between Muddy Waters and Richard Nixon, Dr. John the Night Tripper and Dr. Spock, them and me. Once before I had exploded like this, at a local doctor who kept insisting—quite chauvinistically, I thought—that I had gotten the dengue in Korea, not in Hawaii. First of all, who cared where I got it; I just wanted to be cured of it, whatever it was. Secondly, the doctor had a Japanese last name, and I thought he was showing his prejudice toward Koreans by saying I got the dengue—a tropical fever—in Korea, a Siberian peninsula. I shouted that it was just his goddamn Japaneseness getting in the way of seeing Koreans for what they were.

Well, no.

You see, Dr. Inamine did have a Japanese last name, but like so many people from Hawaii, he had many different ethnic strains, including, as he told me in order to treat me and correct my presumptuousness, Irish, German, French, Hawaiian, and, of course, Japanese. But—

"My mother is Korean," he said, "so let's try to control yourself about what you say. I know you are under strain from this fever, but be careful about what you say."

I apologized.

Yet this fever, which would not go away and whose origin no one seemed to know, nor what it was exactly, and how long it would last, had oversensitized me to everything, not the least of it being how racially charged beautiful Hawaii was.

My students had this casual attitude about racial and ethnic put-downs and stereotypes. The Portuguese joked about the Chinese; the Chinese made fun of the Japanese; the Japanese goofed on the Koreans; the Koreans put down the Filipinos; the Filipinos had words for the Vietnamese; the Vietnamese, the Cambodians. Everyone made fun of the Tongans, why, I don't know, but maybe because they seemed to be the biggest people in the world. Then everyone, including the Tongans, gave stinkeye to the haoles. In this ethnic chop-suey that was Honolulu, no one had a high ground. Economically the Japanese—from Japan, not from Hawaii—owned the best real estate; the haoles (that hateful word again), of course, had their hands in everything from real estate to commerce to education. The only truly disenfranchised were the native Hawaiians, the speakers of one of the most beautiful spoken languages in the world; they lived in homelands, just like American Indians, and were shuttled off to the tropical edges in places like Waianae and Waimanalo.

IMMIGRANT WAVES

At my angriest moments, I liked to borrow a friend's car, drive out to Waianae, and drink in the funky, red-dust infested, rusty-rimmed beer joints, and I discovered that besides being big and plenty angry, Hawaiians were also some of the gentlest people on earth, great talkers and drinkers, but there was no way around the poverty and destitution in these homelands, and every once in a while it seemed like a terrifically bad idea to have driven out into the homelands to get drunk, just to fulfill my nasty New York City idea of a good old bad time.

The red sun would be going down over a dune; surfers would be out on the waves. I could see shark fins in the water; huge men who would be professional football players except for busted kneecaps drank large amounts of beer at these windowless cafes, growling to the rock-and-roll on the jukebox. I felt right at home. Meaning I felt more like a New Yorker than a haole, more street Irish workingclass than generic Brand X mainlander. When people found out I was from New York City, they wanted to know about the murders. At my most bitter, sinister self, I'd tell them that the murder rate had dropped considerably in New York City since I had come to Honolulu, and then I'd laugh in this deep-bellied male way I learned about in Korea, ordered another beer, drank it quickly and swirled out of there into the thick air of the waning daylight and the setting sun, the sweats descended, the fever spiking all around me.

This was complicated further by two things: I was at the deep end of twenty-five years of daily drinking with a bad case of alcoholism, which I wouldn't try to address and mend for two more years until I hit an even deeper bottom, and this in a place that, however, angry underneath, was mellow on the outside, so that outside the homelands there really weren't that many alcoholic-minded citizens. I know, because I befriended all of them in that six months, and would drink with them in such out of the way bistros as the backroom bar at the fastfood restaurant Zippy's, the Mexican restaurant in the Waikiki shopping mall, and various dives on Kuhio Avenue. And, secondly, even though I had not smoked marijuana for over twenty years—I spent a brief time in a New Hampshire jail to cure me of this obsession—I now was regularly smoking this awful stinky gungilike pakalolo-weed that comes from the Big Island, with its scent of burning rubber, and its effect like opiated hash. One joint lasted a week, this stuff was so powerful.

Yet the best things in Hawaii were the sun and sky and sea, the unownable universe, and that part of Hawaii inside its native people, whom I never thought of as angry men, no matter how angry I actually saw them, but rather as the sweetest tempered people—given all the circumstances—I ever saw. A case in point was the Mexican restaurant I went to regularly in a shopping mall in Waikiki, where a local band played nightly their specialty Motown songs—oh, how they sang The Temptations' "Just My Imagination"—and the biggest among them, a four-hundred-and-fifty-pound Hawaiian with a voice as wispy and silken as Aaron Neville's, another deceptively big man. Fights would break out, but they kept singing; the lead singer would be in a bad mood at the bar, drinking beers like there was no tomorrow, but he would get up and sing as though his vocal chords were heaven-sent, and he was blessed to be able to sing, and, in turn, we were blessed to hear him, and we were.

All was good in the land of the eternal tourist.

The dengue fever had me bent out of shape, not sure if I was coming or going. It felt like a kind of malaria, sweats, fever, dehydration, then that calmness afterwards; I had it nightly, but, as I said earlier, the days were manageable, and I worked, and before working, I did my own writing in the pre-dawn hours, adjusting to this tropical world. Sometimes it felt like—because of the tropical heat and this fever—as if all my brains had been fried; but then I started to get up at four in the morning, in the pitch black of the resort area, and walk over the Canal and then up the hill two miles to Manoa Valley and the University of Hawaii, working in my office until it got too hot, drinking water and looking out the glassless but jalousied windows down the hill and across the valley to Diamond Head and the blue-green coral-rich sea. As overwrought with tourism and even *kamaainas* (longtime island residents) as this place was, especially Honolulu, there was no denying how beautiful it was, the abundance of flowers on the roadside, there for the picking, mimosa and magnolia in perpetual bloom, bougainvillea lining back alleys, giant banyans filled with thousands of tiny cooing doves at sunset; or sunset, a show unto itself in Hawaii, as are the rainbows everywhere, so many that one almost becomes used to them; sometimes several rainbows in a row, off the road, up the hill, on the mountainside, in the distance, over the water.

Then there is the xenophobia. No one is immune to it, and so when the haoles experience it, the others nod approvingly, as if to say, it's about time they felt this, too. But I didn't think that I looked like any everyday haole; I wore the obligatory Hawaiian luau shirts in rayon, made in Tahiti, and adorned with flowers and colored pastel, and baggy white pants and sandals and a Panama hat. At the time I was forty years old and thought myself as dangerous as any drug dealer taking a room in my hotel, his bags filled with heroin from Southeast Asia, two huge Hawaiian bodyguards at his side, waiting for the man to come and cop his stuff, an automatic weapon strapped to his ankle and some bad dreams about "Miami Vice" in his crazy head. I'm black Irish, like my father, a sister and another brother; the others are fair-skinned, blond and blue-eyed, the laddies and colleens. These black ones in our clan had dark hair long after everyone else turned gray, and my sister Kaitlin and I didn't burn in the sun like the others; we turned dark, and by now I was plenty dark. I also had become quite fat with drinking around the clock and smoking incessantly. Six feet tall, I had become well over two hundred pounds, really closer to two-twenty, the size I was when I checked into a rehab two years later.

Once, in the lobby of a Waikiki hotel, waiting for a friend to show in order to go off to—what else?—drink and eat, a young tourist boy came over and asked if I was Sid Fernandez, the Mets speedball lefthander from Hawaii. Yes, I said, drunk, signing an autograph. After I throttled the desk clerk and told him that maybe I wasn't a haole after all, they all looked at me differently, too, or maybe I saw myself differently, which was probably more the case. I had taken on the grotesque plumage of an arrogant, misinformed minor deity, a freelance hitman, not the visiting writer at a university; or maybe I had become more like that drunken consul in Malcolm Lowry's *Under the Volcano,* though in my case I felt more sinister than he was, and yet no less muddled by everything. When this big wild haole went bonkers in the lobby of the Seaside Colony hotel, they figured it must be his fevers, his craziness, pakikihead jag-up swellhead lolo been-outside-in-the-sun-too-long kind of thing. Hey, what's a haole, brah? Somebody who put soy sauce on his rice. Big laugh, yah.

There was an older, retired Japanese woman in one of my writing classes; her name was Barbara, and she was one of the best students. A grandmother then, she had grown up on one of the outer islands, in the colonial world of a sugar plantation. Japanese was the spoken language of these immigrant workers, and Barbara had written a lovely story about a little plantation girl seeing a white person for the first time, a schoolteacher, and bursting into tears because the child thought she saw a ghost.

Obaki, obaki, the girl cried, running home to her mother.

Barbara writes honestly and well; she's got the rhythm of experience in her words. She understands what it's like to be discriminated against. Her memories go back to the time of Hawaii's colonial days, which after all is not that long ago, since it did not officially stop being colonial until it became a state in 1958. Some longtime residents will tell you that the state is still colonial. Probably they exaggerate, but only barely; they are not referring to actualities and facts, but rather drifts and currents, the unidentifiable discomfort and undeniable assertion of the ugly ethnicheaded us-against-them, outsiders and insiders, innies and outties, if you will. Racism. One race putting down another. Forgetting that we were all immigrants once. Most of our ancestors came indentured or broke, not leisurely, but fleet of foot, doubled up, and in haste. Here they came to the sugar and pineapple plantations; on the east coast of the mainland (my territory), it was into the tenant-world, the low-paying jobs, the heat and tension, bad feelings and grudges. Instead of plantations, it was sweat shops, day laboring, ditches and the like, working the docks, luffing the cargo skyward, longshoreman's spike on your shoulder. That was my family's introduction to America, at least, and not that long ago, just one generation back.

I liked everything about Barbara and her writing; she was spunky, courageous, forthright, outstanding. There was nothing old-fashioned about her, though she was more than fifty years older than most of the other students in my two classes, both undergraduate and graduate alike, and I knew she understood this, not the differences between us, the locals and the mainlanders, but our similarities.

Some people sat near the pool, drinking beer, being watched by the security guards who seemed to want us to do something wrong in order to break up the party; others stood around talking. The party was almost over, and soon people would go home when the sun set shortly. Some of the class talked about Barbara's story about the young girl seeing the white woman teacher and mistaking her for a ghost. A young Korean student left the party and I expressed my disappointment with his lack of output; Barbara defended him.

The kid was from Korea, she said, and only had a few years of high school in America before coming to the university. All of them, she said, were using English as a second language, and I didn't understand how difficult that was because my ancestors came to this country speaking English. But that's not true, I told her; yes it is, she said. Then I explained to Barbara that my father was from the Gaeltacht, the western part of Ireland where they spoke Irish, not English, and that English was just as foreign a language to him and his father as it was to her, the Korean boy, or any of the other students from immigrant families. I could see that Barbara thought I was making this up. How could I have come from a place that did not speak English?

Wasn't Stephens my last name and wasn't it an English name? Celtic, I told her, not really Irish but Welsh, I had heard. Still, a lot of Irish had it. James Stephens, the author of *The Crock of Gold,* that great Irish fairy tale; the other James Stephens, the founder of the Fenian Brotherhood, the precursor of the IRA.

Barbara frowned.

Welsh, Irish, English, what was the difference? she asked, meaning, unfortunately, they were all haoles, right?

So she left, unimpressed by what I said, and I cleaned up and went up to my hotel room, anticipating my departure in a few days. I went back to reading Yeats and Joyce for what felt like the first time again because it was sunset.

After the fever had spiked and the sweats had turned to chills, I walked around Waikiki in an Irish fisherman's sweater, which I bought in a local department store in Ala Moana shopping center, and my long black leather coat, which I had bought in Korea that summer but which seemed so quintessentially New York. When I thought about New York, I didn't picture skyscrapers and rush hours and hordes of people on the street, or glass towers on Avenue of the Americas (Sixth Avenue to us natives), or even the Statue of Liberty. I saw Brooklyn, East New York, that savage neighborhood deep inside the borough, highest crime area in the city, and so therefore maybe one of the most dangerous places on earth. Didn't those two security guards know where I came from? Or that dumb clerk? Didn't the guards know that their employer called them Harlem *popolos?* I had heard the manager of the hotel one day refer to them as being worse than the mokes in Waimanalo. My mother had sixteen children, and nine of us lived, starting out disadvantaged in that pulsing ghetto. My grandmother and her three crazy redheaded daughters were the last potatoheads left in the neighborhood; and soon after her death, my two aunts disappeared into the welfare system only to reappear twenty-five years later, poised to swan-dive into eternity, one of them at death's door with a bad case of lung cancer in Ojai, California, the other dying in sympathy for her twin; members of the underclass, sisters of the night and now West Coast social services. Their red hair matted, the twins bid us all goodbye in a final letter. I don't know for the life of me how to look upon those crazed redheaded daughters of the Brooklyn slums as haoles; they were more like banshees from Hell.

It's been years since I was last in Hawaii, but I still remember it, not the touristy part, but occasionally I go sentimental over the memory of a rainbow or sunset or sunrise or tropical rainstorm or a set of waves at the beach—especially the forty-foot ones in early December on the North Shore—or the color of the sky backdropping the Koolau mountains or the coral sea. I still think of those Waianae bars, even though I've had to give up drinking since then. Of course, I wonder whatever happened to good old Barbara, and I hope that Japanese child of the colonial world of the sugar plantations is well; what a lovely woman she was. I think about the falsetto singing in the Mexican bar at the shopping center, or friends at the university.

Recently I went out to East New York with a photographer friend. This backwater place, so desolate and bleak, drugged up and high, angry and dangerous, full of automatic weapons was unreal but not unfamiliar because I had dreamed about it all my life. I was on an journalistic assignment, but long after that visit back to the old neighborhood, I kept thinking about it, not the ruin it is, but the ruin it was, and how everything that went into making me a writer came out of those vagrant experiences I had on those stinky, dirty, poor streets. Everything I am as a person came out of that world, no matter how my parents tried to scrub it out of us in the working-class suburbs on Long Island. The language of the streets of my childhood was a mix of Spanish, Jamaican English, Yiddish, Irish, and Italian; my Irish grandmother spoke words from all these tongues.

Mostly, though, I remember those brooding, silent men in dark suits and wrinkled white shirts without ties; big black hobnailed boots on their feet. They were like an Irish equivalent of the equally mysterious and darkly clad, ancient-breathed Hasidic Jews on Pitkin Avenue in Brownsville on the other side of Eastern Parkway. These relatives' faces were blistery red, and going purple about their noses, and their eyes were hollow and sunken. They spoke little English to us children; they were my father's relatives from the old country, places like Mayo and Clare, rocky and heathen, they were transplanted fishermen and subsistence farmers who now painted houses and drove taxis in New York City. If they did speak, it was either in an English I could not comprehend, or, I realize now, in their native language, Irish, lilting, yes, but brooding and dark, too, like these blackhaired, silent men. The last time I saw any of them was thirty years ago at my grandmother's funeral underneath the el on Broadway, the funeral parlor's windows rattling from the passing subway trains, the noise deadening any sounds in that dark, gloomy room.

The only flowers in the room were a horseshoe of roses; in the back of the room was a table for a whiskey bottle and glasses and some cans of beer. My father's redheaded sisters all were drunk, and one of them was already half-gone in the head and her lungs would not last the winter from the packs of strong cigarettes she smoked; she was only forty years old. Her twin sisters, younger, less ferocious, did not speak English or Irish but rather a Brooklyn patois, and because they were goddesses of the slums, their speech was peppered with the most colorful of profanities, which drove my father crazy, and I guess that was its intended effect. He vowed never to return to the old neighborhood after they buried his mother. The last time I ever saw those Irish-speaking relatives was in the back of that room, their hands trembling as they drank the whiskey with beer chasers, and the room rattling from the passing subway trains. But Barbara from Honolulu was right; I have always spoken English. It came easy to me, and I loved it, but its rhythms had nothing to do with what was right and proper. Instead I spoke and wrote English from East New York, on the stoop of the shtetl, an immigrant from Brooklyn when my family eventually moved to the suburbs, a place where we never belonged and never were welcome, because the family was too big, too unruly, and never got East New York out of their systems, and from which I still am recovering to this day—Long Island, not Brooklyn, that is.

When I think of Hawaii these days I likewise recall almost nothing else but those rundown, seedy bars in Waianae in the homelands, the sun coming down, the surfers on the blue-green, shark-infested waters. I used to think Hawaiian was the most beautiful language I ever heard until I realized that my own native speech was the first most beautiful. It is the English of my childhood in East New York, immigrant yes, but not just Irish; it consisted of words from Eastern Europe, the Mediterranean, and the Caribbean. Plus Brooklyn itself. ("Hey, *tuse botz!* What a *schlemiel!* Ya no-good hooligan ya! Whattaya smokin', spliffs or somethin'?") This language of the street, the city, the poor, the hardworking and the lazy, gangsters and petty hoodlums, indolent teenagers with bad attitudes, and Spanish girls named Maria, Consuela, and Carmen. My English comes in immigrant waves; I found this out after getting over my dengue fever, reading Joyce and Yeats in Waikiki, and walking around at night in my long black leather jacket, right off the streets of Brooklyn.

HOMESICK

Jessica Hagedorn

Jessica Hagedorn was born in the Philippines. She is a performance artist, poet, playwright, and novelist. Her multimedia theater pieces are *Holy Food, Teenytown,* and *Mango Tango.* She is the author of two books of poetry and short prose pieces, *Dangerous Music* (1975) and *Pet Food and Tropical Apparitions* (1981), and of a novel, *Dogeaters* (1990).

"Homesick" was written while she was working on *Dogeaters.*

BLAME IT ON THE MAMBO AND THE CHA-CHA, VOODOO AMULETS worn on the same chain with tiny crucifixes and scapulars blessed by the Pope. Chains of love, medals engraved with the all-seeing Eye, ascending Blessed Virgins floating towards heaven surrounded by erotic cherubs and archangels, the magnificent torso of a tormented, half-naked Saint Sebastian pierced by arrows dripping blood. A crown of barbed-wire thorns adorns the holy subversive's head, while we drown in the legacy of brutal tropical generals stuffed in khaki uniforms, their eyes shielded by impenetrable black sunglasses, Douglas MacArthur-style.

And Douglas MacArthur and Tom Cruise are painted on billboards lining Manila's highways, modelling Ray-Ban shades and Jockey underwear. You choose between the cinema version starring Gregory Peck smoking a corncob pipe, or the real thing. "I shall return," promised the North American general, still revered by many as the savior of the Filipino people, who eagerly awaited his return. As the old saying goes, this is how we got screwed, screwed real good. According to Nick Joaquin, "The Philippines spent three hundred years trapped in a convent, and fifty-eight years in Hollywood . . ." Or was it four hundred years? No matter—there we were, seduced and abandoned in a confusion of identities, then granted our independence. Hollywood pretended to leave us alone. An African American saying also goes: "Nobody's *given* freedom." Being granted our independence meant we were owned all along by someone other than ourselves.

I step off the crowded plane on to the tarmac of the newly named Ninoy Aquino airport. It is an interesting appropriation of the assassinated senator's name, don't you think? So I think, homesick for this birthplace, my country of supreme ironies and fatalistic humor, mountains of foul garbage and breathtaking women, men with the fierce faces of wolves and steamy streets teeming with abandoned children.

The widow of the assassinated senator is Corazon Aquino, now President of the Republic of the Philippines in a deft stroke of irony that left the world stunned by a sudden turn of events in February, 1986. She is a beloved figurehead, a twentieth-century icon who has inherited a bundle of cultural contradictions and an economic nightmare in a lush paradise of corrupt, warring factions. In a Manila department store, one of the first souvenirs I buy my daughter is a rather homely Cory Aquino doll made out of brown cloth; the doll wears crooked wire eyeglasses, a straw shoulderbag, plastic high-heeled shoes, and Cory's signature yellow dress, with "I Love Cory" embroidered on the front. My daughter seems delighted with her doll and the notion of a woman president.

Soldiers in disguise, patrol the countryside . . . Jungle not far away. So goes a song I once wrote, pungent as the remembered taste of mangoes overripe as my imagination, the memory of Manila the central character of the novel I am writing, the novel which brings me back to this torrid zone, my landscape haunted by ghosts and movie-lovers.

Nietzsche once said, "A joke is an epitaph for an emotion." Our laughter is pained, self-mocking. Blame it on *Rambo, Platoon,* and *Gidget Goes Hawaiian.* Cory Aquino has inherited a holy war, a class war, an amazing nation of people who've endured incredible poverty and spiritual loss with inherent humor and grace. Member of the ruling class, our pious President has also inherited an army of divided, greedy men. Yet no one will probably bother assassinating her, as icons are always useful.

My novel sits in its black folder, an obsession with me for over ten years. Home is now New York, but home in my heart will also always be Manila, and the rage of a marvelous culture stilled, confused, and diverted. Manila is my river of dreams choked with refuse, the refuse of refusal and denial, a denial more profound than the forbidding Catholic Church in all its ominous presence.

Blame it on the mambo and the cha-cha, a Cardinal named Sin and an adviser named Joker. Blame it on *Imeldification,* a former beauty queen with a puffy face bailed out of a jam by Doris Duke. Blame it on children named Lourdes, Maria, Jesus, Carlos, Peachy, Baby, and Elvis. Blame it on the rich, who hang on in spite of everything. Blame it on the same people who are still in power, before Marcos, after Marcos. You name it, we'll blame it. The NPR, the vigilantes, rebel colonels nicknamed "Gringo" and a restless army plotting coups. Blame it on signs in nightclubs that warn: NO GUNS OR DRUGS.

Cards have been reshuffled, roles exchanged. The major players are the same, even those who suffered long years in prison under one regime, even those who died by the bullet. Aquino, Lopez, Cojuangco, Zobel, Laurel, Enrile, etc. Blood against blood, controlling the destinies of so many disparate tribes in these seven thousand islands.

I remember my grandmother, Lola Tecla, going for drives with me as a child down the boulevard along Manila Bay. The boulevard led to Luneta Park, where Rizal was executed by the Spanish colonizers; it was then known as "Dewey Boulevard," after an American admiral. From history books forced on me as a child at a convent school run by strict nuns, I learned a lopsided history of myself, one full of lies and blank spaces, a history of omission—a colonial version of history which scorned the "savage" ways of precolonial Filipinos. In those days, even our language was kept at a distance; Tagalog was studied in a course called "National Language" (sic), but it was English that was spoken, English that was preferred. Tagalog was a language used to address servants. I scorned myself, and it was only later, after I had left the Philippines to settle in the country of my oppressor, that I learned to confront my demons and reinvent my own history.

I am writing a novel set in the contemporary Philippines. It is a novel of fiction, a journey back I am always taking. I leave one place for the other, welcomed and embraced by the family I have left—fathers and brothers and cousins and uncles and aunts. Childhood sweethearts, now with their own children. I am unable to stay. I make excuses, adhere to tight schedules. I return, only to depart, weeks or months later, depending on finances and the weather, obligations to my daughter, my art, my addiction to life in the belly of one particular beast. I am the other, the exile within, afflicted with permanent nostalgia for the mud. I return only to depart: Manila, New York, San Francisco, Manila, Honolulu, Detroit, Manila, Guam, Hong Kong, Zamboanga, Manila, New York, San Francisco, Tokyo, Manila again, Manila again, Manila again.

TWO CUBAN DISSIDENTS:
HEBERTO PADILLA AND
BELKIS CUZA MALÉ

Pablo Medina

Pablo Medina was born in Havana, Cuba, in 1948, and has lived in the United States since 1960. He has received undergraduate and graduate degrees from Georgetown University. His poetry, prose, and translations from the Spanish language have appeared in many periodicals and anthologies. He is the author of two volumes of poetry, *Pork Rind and Cuban Songs* (1975) and *Arching into the Afterlife* (1991), and a collection of personal essays entitled *Exiled Memories: A Cuban Childhood* (1990).

"Two Cuban Dissidents" is part of a work-in-progress which treats the Cuban experience in the United States from a personal perspective.

MY KNOCK AT THEIR DOOR THAT SPRING DAY OF 1983 CAUSED SUCH an explosion of barks inside that I almost turned on my heels and went back home. A man's voice cursed the dogs in Spanish. They paid no heed and kept barking. A feminine voice interceded and the ruckus died down. When the door opened, there were no signs of the animals. The celebrated Cuban poet Heberto Padilla was heavier and bigger than I had imagined from the few photographs I'd seen. He seemed not to belong in Princeton, but I doubted if he belonged anywhere. His thick glasses reflected the sun and I could not see the eyes, but a quick, reluctant smile flashed across his face. Luckily I did not have to linger awkwardly before this man who had been burdened with the caprices of history.

Belkis, his wife and companion for over fifteen years, materialized out of a hallway, complaining about the dogs in much the same tones, I later learned, in

329

which she critiqued everything and everyone she loved. She took my coat and asked me to sit. I was offered Cuban coffee, which I gladly accepted, and Heberto sat down across from me while Belkis went into the kitchen. It was a routine that would repeat itself, with little variation, at every one of my visits.

Heberto and I spoke, interviewed each other, really, with him asking two questions for every one of mine. He wanted to know how long I'd been in the United States, what I did for a living, how far from them I lived, and so on. But it was not until he asked about my feelings with respect to writing in English that the interrogation became a conversation.

I explained that there had been a time when I wrote in both Spanish and English, but that necessity had forced me to limit myself to the language that surrounded me. Yes, he nodded, but how did I feel about that? Ambivalent, I responded. Did I consider myself a Cuban writer? Did I regret not writing in Spanish? I tried to answer each question as fully as I could. I wrote in English because I did—it was that simple—and I considered myself Cuban, but not necessarily a Cuban writer.

I asked about his feelings on the matter. One writes in whatever language one can, he answered. English is a great language, clean and precise. Just then Belkis appeared bearing a tray with the coffee, a bowl of sugar, and glasses with ice water.

I first heard of Heberto in October, 1968, when an international jury gathered in Havana, Cuba, unanimously awarded his poetry collection, *Fuera del juego (Out of the Game),* the prestigious Casa de las Américas prize. The Union of Artists and Writers of Cuba (UNEAC) disagreed with the jury's selection, calling Padilla a counterrevolutionary and his poems "ideologically in opposition to the revolution." Soon after that, *Verde Olivo,* the print organ of the Cuban Armed Forces, published a scathing attack against Padilla and his poetry, and against the jury that had awarded him the prize. As a result, Padilla lost his job and was ostracized from the Writers' Union. Almost a year later, Padilla wrote a letter to Fidel Castro explaining his situation and was given a job at the University of Havana.

Castro's largesse, however, did not stop the poet from continuing his criticism of the Revolution, and in a reading he gave at the headquarters of the Writers' Union in January 1971, from an unpublished manuscript titled, appropriately enough, *Provocaciones (Provocations),* Padilla railed against the strictures and limitations of revolutionary society. In one particular poem titled "A veces" or "At Times," he made a thinly veiled attack against Castro himself. Over the next two months Padilla became a provocateur. According to Jorge Edwards, the author of *Persona Non Grata* and the Chilean chargé d'affaires in Havana at the time, Padilla walked around the city with a copy of his novel *Heroes Are Grazing in My Garden* under his arm, complaining to anyone who dared to listen, of the failures of the Revolution. Certainly listening and taking note were agents of State Security, among them writer friends of the couple. The informants, some genuine supporters of the Revolution, others blackmailed into cooperating, believed only too firmly that the contents of the novel would be damaging to the Cuban government.

As Belkis joined us to enjoy the coffee on that first visit, I noticed that her face was not as heavily shadowed as Heberto's. She had dark shifting eyes, but when she spoke they fixed on me like radar on a target. Her hair was jet black and long and she tied it in a simple ponytail. There was something very Cuban about her. She spoke simply and directly, and she was mistress of that sharp, honest intelligence I noticed in her poems, which I read as an undergraduate years ago:

MY MOTHER'S HOMELAND

My mother always said
your homeland is any place,
preferably the place where you die.
That's why she bought the most arid land,
the saddest landscape,
the driest grass,
and beside the wretched tree
began to build her homeland.
She built it by fits and starts
(one day this wall, another day the roof;
from time to time, holes to let air squeeze in).
My house, she would say, is my homeland,
and I would see her close her eyes
like a young girl full of dreams
while she chose, once again, groping,
the place where she would die.
          (Translation by Pamela Carmell)

Belkis listened as Heberto and I talked about my grandfather, whose radio program in Havana he enjoyed. I presented them with a copy of my book of poems and then I asked if I could smoke. Heberto answered, "Of course, I will smoke with you and that will draw us closer." Belkis smacked her lips and looked away.

"She used to smoke two packs a day," Heberto said in apparent disdain. In subsequent visits I have learned that this banter is very much a part of their relationship. "But when she found out cigarettes kill you, she stopped immediately. Belkis is fainthearted when it comes to death."

"And well I should be," she answered.

Heberto puffed on his cigar and pointed out that he was from Pinar del Río, the Cuban province where the best tobacco is grown. This led him to describe in crystalline detail the process by which tobacco is planted, harvested, and produced. The account ended with a vivid description of cigar factories and the art of rolling cigars. Throughout the narrative, he had been asking me if I was bored. Though a treatise on tobacco-growing and production was the last thing I expected to hear when I knocked on their door, he piqued my interest and I wanted to learn much more than he was giving me. At this point Belkis interrupted. She wondered if I could stay for dinner—nothing fancy, mind you. I declined. My wife was expecting me.

They both looked at me quizzically. I had not mentioned her before and suddenly they wanted to ask all sorts of questions about her: Is she Cuban? No, she is American. (This answer seemed to clarify something for them.) How long have we been married? Two years. Any children? Yes, I have a son, she has a daughter, each from previous marriages. I saw more questions forming in their faces, but before they had a chance to continue, I shook their hands, said goodbye. "Come back whenever you want," Belkis said. "We are always here."

On March 20, 1971, Heberto and Belkis were arrested at their Havana house by agents of State Security. The police also confiscated five copies of Heberto's novel, but the original, hidden under a pile of their son's toys, was left behind. The arrest caused a flurry of activity among intellectuals of the free world and led a number of them, including Simone de Beauvoir, Jean-Paul Sartre, Alberto Moravia, Octavio Paz, and Susan Sontag, to sign a letter addressed to Fidel Castro expressing at once their solidarity with the Revolution and their distress at the couple's detention. The infamous Padilla case was now in full gear. Belkis was released after a few days, but she was not allowed to visit her husband for two weeks.

On April 27, after more than a month of interrogation and torture, Padilla signed a confession (under obvious duress) and was subsequently released. At a gathering of his colleagues in UNEAC headquarters that same night, Padilla read an extensive self-criticism that reiterated his "sins" and errors and implicated a number of his friends, among them Belkis and the dean of Cuban writers at the time, José Lezama Lima. Padilla's statements inspired another letter from the intellectuals and a response from Castro, delivered in a speech before the First National Congress of Education and Culture, in which he attacked bourgeois intellectuals and declared that the doors of Cuba would be indefinitely closed to them. Furthermore, he added that they would not be allowed to be jury members for Cuban contests and that awards would henceforth be given to "true poets, true revolutionaries."

Over the past eight years, I have come to visit Heberto and Belkis on a regular basis at their various residences in Princeton. I have listened to them, I have seen their fortunes rise and fall, I have watched them struggle with the new land in their attempts to make a life here. Belkis asked me to help with *Linden Lane,* which she had started soon after their arrival and singlehandedly made into the most important Spanish-language literary and intellectual publication in the United States. Heberto offered me cigars, which we shared as we talked, drawn closer, as he'd said, by the sweet smoke of the good tobacco.

He was interested then, and for a long time after, in the way that young Cubans had adapted to the United States. He was intrigued by how well I had mastered English and how expertly I appeared to swim through American society. The fact that I'd left Cuba when I was barely out of childhood did not convince him, nor did it really convince me. I was merely evading the real issue, and Heberto saw right through my evasion. For all intents and purposes, I was still very Cuban, and it was my Cubanness that directed my statements. One tries to be what one is not, I told him. One tries to fit in. At that point, a smile came over his face.

I must say that Heberto's smile is unusual in that it is inspired not by mirth but by intelligence. I imagined then, and I still hold the view, that Heberto Padilla is a man totally given to a life of the intellect. His mind is a sharp blade that cuts easily through falsehoods and intellectual pretensions. If there is any joy in his life, it comes from the exercise of his considerable mental acumen. If there is misery, it is a result of the failure of his intellectual faculties to save him from the caprices and meannesses of others.

From early on Belkis and Heberto entertained the hope that jobs in the United States would be offered, attention paid to them. Indeed, at first there was the usual flurry of manic interest from the press. Articles were written; interviews were done. And that small closed world of the grant givers responded with two quick awards, a Guggenheim and a Wilson Fellowship, the latter given to Heberto so that he could finish the manuscript of his novel, *Heroes Are Grazing in My Garden,* that he had miraculously smuggled out of Cuba. They spent a year in Washington and a year in Spain, but once the grants had run out and opportunities elsewhere narrowed, they found themselves back in New Jersey, and highbrow provincial New Jersey, to boot.

Of all the towns in the state, Princeton is perhaps the most difficult to settle in. Princely and arrogant, it would be happiest as a state in itself, floating above the Northeast like a focus of enlightened benevolence. Catholics and Jews go there to become WASPs. Belkis and Heberto both had concluded that living in

Miami, with its obsessive political climate and its insatiable demand for testimonials to the Castro debacle, would be intolerable for them. Princeton was secluded and quiet, and Belkis liked its quaintness and college-town charm; both of them were also under the impression that the university would show some hospitality to two writers of international reputation.

I, however, knew better. I'd lived in the area long enough to know that Princeton needs no one, especially not Cuban exiles. In 1985, Belkis approached me about organizing an exhibit of original art work that had appeared in *Linden Lane* since its beginning in 1981. The idea immediately appealed to me. The magazine had been printing not only some of the best Hispanic literature from throughout the world but also artwork by some of Latin America's most distinguished and accomplished artists. I suggested that the exhibit take place at one of the museums in Trenton. Belkis argued, not without reason, that events in Princeton drew a much larger audience than those in Trenton or any of its surrounding suburbs. At her insistence and despite my misgivings, I set up an appointment with the exhibits director at a popular arts space on Witherspoon Street.

Belkis brought with her a boxful of drawings and etchings. We introduced ourselves and spoke about the magazine. Then we pulled open the large Macy's box and passed the papers to the woman one by one. She was quite impressed by the quality of what she saw and started thinking aloud about how best to mount and advertise the exhibit. I was almost about to let go of my skepticism when Belkis mentioned that many of our fellow Cubans in the area would be interested in coming. Immediately the woman's countenance changed. I could imagine her enthusiasm escaping like the shadow of a cloud and the blank, indeterminate look of resistance replacing it. Then came her statement, as infuriating as it was unintelligent, even ludicrous: "You know, we support the Sandinistas here."

Belkis gave me one of her sidelong glances, eyes full of fire, took the artwork as graciously as she could from our host and put it back into the Macy's box.

Outside, the clouds had dissipated and a faint sun shined through the late winter haze.

"What do the Sandinistas have to do with any of this?" she asked knowing the answer full well. "There's nothing we can do, is there?"

"No," I responded. "I should have warned you."

"I would not have believed. She thinks we are fanatical arch-conservatives. They all think that way. She doesn't know how long we struggled to support socialism, how much we have sacrificed. It's comfortable for her to be a socialist in Princeton. This treatment is no better than what we got in Cuba."

"I don't know," I answered.

TWO CUBAN DISSIDENTS

But of course I knew. I'd had similar troubles on more than one occasion. I'd learned to keep a low profile and state my nationality only when asked. Cuba for Americans represents the last bastion of communism, but Cubans in America equal the reactionary right. One cannot win.

"There is no difference," she concluded. "We're being shunned. Except that the stakes here are very much smaller."

If Heberto and Belkis were searching for keys into the society through me, I could not offer them any. On the surface I appeared to be completely and comfortably assimilated, but the reality was another matter altogether. I'd been teaching in a college where I felt my abilitiess were underused and unappreciated. For years I had isolated myself from the rest of the Cubans in the northern part of the state. With time, Belkis and Heberto learned that I was as rudderless as they in the North American ocean. I'd just been in it longer, knew its currents and winds.

Belkis and Heberto remained in Cuba until 1979 and 1980 respectively. In the intervening years between the start of their troubles and their departure, Belkis was given a job at the Writers' Union and Heberto was provided with some translation work by a state publishing house. Neither was allowed to publish and both were watched constantly, obsessively, by State Security. According to Heberto in his extraordinary memoir, *Self-Portrait of the Other,* the authorities' greatest concern was that he would speak to foreigners. Thus, every effort was made to keep him away from visiting writers and dignitaries. By now it was clear to Castro that, though Padilla's arrest and self-criticism represented an internal victory over the voices of dissent, the Padilla affair had been far from a victory externally. The Cuban government's virulent reaction against a fine but at the time little-known poet further exacerbated the international intellectual community's alienation, which had begun earlier in 1968 in reaction to Castro's speech supporting the Soviet invasion of Czechoslovakia.

Given its exaggerated, even parodic tone, Padilla's self-criticism was hardly a sign that the couple had surrendered to the force of the state, or that a month in the hands of the security apparatus had made Heberto, and, by extension, Belkis, see the error of their ways. More likely, they saw little hope that further dissent would be of any benefit to them or in modifying the revolutionary government's increasingly Stalinist behavior. As it was, they had been spared the fate of other dissenters, such as Huber Matos, who had been framed with false charges and given long prison sentences.

Instead, Heberto and Belkis focused their efforts on trying to leave the country. Belkis wrote to anyone of note outside of Cuba whom she thought held political sway with Castro. And Heberto? He maintained his silence, saw few people, and, in the monotony of the ensuing years, felt increasingly isolated from the writing community as the initial outrage his case had created overseas died down. Concurrently he found himself fighting an overbearing sense of guilt— emphasized by conversations he had with the Cuban novelist Alejo Carpentier and the Colombian Gabriel García Márquez—that he had hurt the cause of socialism in Cuba and that he had no one to blame but himself. According to Heberto in *Self-Portrait of the Other,* both these men held "that in spite of the errors committed by the Revolution, one had to remain faithful to the cause and avoid making enemies of the international left." The transcendence of the Revolution above and beyond the needs of individual writers and artists was a theme that was brought up time and again by these two writers, and by others such as Julio Cortázar and Mario Benedetti, who found the Cuban government's actions on the whole justifiable, if not laudable.

And so I kept coming, drawn to Belkis and Heberto by a blend of curiosity, respect, and budding friendship. Their door was, as they promised, open to me. With time, their inner door opened as well. My visits became weekly events. We would sit in the living room for hours, talking, discussing politics. Belkis would bring me *Linden Lane* galleys to proofread. Heberto brought out the vodka. We drank, he and I, while I made corrections. The conversation continued all the while, and I heard stories about a writer who betrayed them to State Security, and of another well-known Cuban writer who was blackmailed into informing on them after he was discovered in a men's bathroom "sucking and tugging on an Argelian's ear," as Heberto euphemistically put it.

Once, Belkis told the story of a man who befriended her. Heberto interrupted and, voice dripping with irony, said that he had a crush on her. Belkis continued that he was an agent from State Security. Heberto agreed, but nevertheless insisted that the man was in love with Belkis.

"He visited for a long time," Belkis said. "And we always shared our food with him."

"We all knew what his role was. We accepted it," Heberto filled in.

"The three of us became friends," Belkis said. I have met very few couples who can tell the same story without stumbling over each other. "He admitted he was keeping his eye on us. Nevertheless, we received him, accepted his gifts."

Now Heberto took over.

"One day, after Belkis left, I heard news that he had taken ill and was in the hospital. I decided to visit him. I stayed until a suspicious-looking nurse drove me out. In Cuba all of the medical profession is at the service of the system. You cannot be a doctor or a nurse unless you are willing to do whatever the authorities ask."

It was Belkis's turn.

"The next day he was dead. They killed him."

"How do you know that?" I asked.

"When I saw him," Heberto said, "he had been given a clean bill of health. He'd been told he could leave the hospital that afternoon. He overstepped his bounds. They couldn't tolerate that. To this day I don't know if I did the wrong thing by visiting him."

"He was a nice man," Belkis added. "He could have harmed us if he wanted, but he never did."

"Because he was in love with you," Heberto concluded. *"El pobre."*

Belkis left Cuba first in 1979. Once in the United States, she resumed her incessant letter-writing on behalf of Heberto and sent missives to anyone of note she thought would help, from the pope to the president of the United States. Senator Ted Kennedy's office showed interest. Belkis even met with representatives of the Cuban delegation to the United Nations. In the meanwhile, Heberto had contacted Gabriel García Márquez at his hotel in Havana, and the Colombian novelist finally agreed to speak to Castro on Padilla's behalf. It was García Márquez' intercession, more than anything else, that convinced Castro to let Heberto go.

In one of the most gripping parts of *Self-Portrait of the Other,* Padilla describes his final meeting with Castro. The passage has a tone of unreality, as if the narrator were meeting with a god, a demented but nonetheless all-powerful one. Among the things Fidel tells him is to ". . . stay as long as you want, and when you want to come back, give me a call. If you are a true revolutionary, you will want to return . . . Don't get the idea that happiness is waiting for you on the other side; your exile will be nothing like you think it is going to be." Fidel continues and at one point asks Heberto if there is nothing of value that the Revolution has done in the cultural sector. Heberto mentions the many publishing houses that have been created and also the support given to the Cuban film industry through ICAIC, the Cuban film institute. This leads Fidel to remark on the collaborative nature of filmmaking and then to attack Jorge Edwards, the Chilean writer who had been in Cuba during the height of the Padilla affair. Fidel concludes the meeting with what, in hindsight, is a prophetic statement: "I know that this Revolution will grow in your memory, and you will find out that the best years of your life were lived when you were supporting it, before you got sick and embittered."

On one of my subsequent visits, I learned that Belkis and Heberto were moving to Miami. Belkis wanted to be closer to her parents, who were ailing, and Heberto was promised a job. I thought it a mistake but said nothing and we continued with our talk, centered on literature and the United States. Heberto focused on American poetry, unassuming and unpretentious, with the pure image as its foundation. He brought up Lowell, his favorite, and Elizabeth Bishop, I think.

My view was less admiring. Current American poetry, I maintained, was mired in the quotidian, lacked transcendence, insight. It was like Eliot belching. Heberto liked my simile and countered by saying that Latin American poetry was all transcendence and no substance, then launched into one of the best spontaneous parodies of Neruda I have heard. "That," he concluded "is Latin American poetry. We have yet to escape the Spanish yoke. But the North Americans, they are content to write about that dog."

He paused and pointed at Pup, the mutt they picked up on the streets of Madrid and brought to the New World.

"The way he wags his tail, the patterns of his spots, his teeth curling out of his mouth. That dog is the ultimate transcendence."

"You sound like Williams."

"Exactly. And it is time the Latin Americans and the Spaniards learned from him, but it is impossible. They are too taken with their rhetoric and their abstractions."

Belkis and Heberto lived in Miami for one year, in 1986. They returned almost as suddenly as they had left. Belkis said they'd gone to work as staffers for a new Spanish-language magazine, but when they got there they found the publication was in deep financial trouble. In short, they were never paid, but they had already put a down payment on a house and were more or less stuck there for the duration. Belkis spent her time taking care of her parents and listening to the political commentators on the countless Cuban-exile radio stations.

"One is crazier than the next," Belkis said. "And they all speak out of ignorance. They are living in another century. And they cannot stand us."

"Why not?" I asked.

"Because we supported the Revolution as long as we did. Because when we could no longer back the regime out of conscience, we decided to stay in Cuba and fight. Which is what they all should have done. Then Cuba wouldn't be the way it is."

"It is impossible," Heberto said.

"We could not have stayed in Miami," Belkis continued. "No culture. No respect for artists."

"You can get the best Cuban coffee at any corner," Heberto countered. "And all those stores in Calle Ocho. Miami is a parody of pre-Castro Havana, an invention of the Cuban exiles."

"Everyone expected us to drive an expensive car and live in an exclusive neighborhood. Just because our names are well-known, people there thought we had money to throw away. It never occurred to them that we did not have a penny to our names." By this point Belkis's voice was almost shrill.

"A Nicaraguan friend of mine who lives in a mansion on Brickell Avenue," Heberto added, "says that the only thing to do in Miami is to become a millionaire. He did. The whole time we were together we walked around his garden while he received calls on his portable phone."

"If you are not a millionaire or on the way there," Belkis concurred, "you might as well be a piece of carrion on Dixie Highway. Nobody cares."

I wanted to say that they were oversimplifying matters, that Miami was not as bad as they thought. I had never lived there, however, and my visits to family were invariably restful, close to idyllic. I liked the jazz and glitter of the city, and the sun on the brilliant blue sky. There was something alluring about Miami's relationship to the sea, something charming about its people, a promise almost of future greatness.

They had quite a different experience. Though both of them were quite willing to admit to the charms of the place, they had had their names bandied about, used and misused by any number of political hacks. Besides, in their minds, as in the mind of many an exile, glistened the legend of Havana, making Miami appear a poor and lacking cousin. I held my tongue and said nothing but listened to them, the tone of their voices growing increasingly bitter. Their complaints shifted now from the awful intrigue-laden atmosphere of Miami to the indifference universities in this country have shown them.

"Heberto has not yet received a job offer," Belkis said.

I felt my eyebrows arching. If I did not know her better, I would have said there was self-righteousness in her voice. I could have told them that the scene was much more diffuse than in Havana, that they had to search out the jobs, be aggressive, but the possibility of ostracism was all too real. There was little question that lesser people were being offered tenure-track jobs at universities up and down the East Coast. All told, it seemed that they were fighting a current much stronger than they, a current into which they had to jump swimming or drown.

I stayed away for months, in part because, in 1987, my marriage was falling apart, in part because the gloom of their existence was beginning to affect me. When I returned, Belkis asked me to drive with her to New York to pick up copies of *Linden Lane* at the printer. Over the traditional cup of coffee, I agreed to stop by the next morning, and then the conversation moved to their latest source of anxiety. Belkis's father was now quite ill with cancer and was not expected to live out the year. All his life he had been a heavy smoker and the smoking affected his wife as well, who was suffering from chronic emphysema. They had no idea what they would do with the old man, nor what would become of Belkis's mother once the father died. She was old, disabled, and penniless and had never worked outside the home a day in her life. Adding to Belkis's woes were the frequent phone calls from Cuba from her daughter by a previous marriage, asking for money, clothes, toys for her own daughter. Belkis, for her part, was trying to get the young woman off the island and had gone through no small expense in that endeavour.

In the meanwhile, jobs (temporary) and readings (poorly paid) trickled in for Heberto. None for Belkis. Her name was not notorious like his, and she was a woman. As she says in one of her poems, "Women don't make History, / but at nine months they push it out of their bellies / then sleep for twenty-four hours / like a soldier on leave from the front." Belkis stayed home, cooked, took care of their son Ernesto, produced *Linden Lane,* and wrote, always wrote.

The next morning Belkis insisted that we take her car, a six-year-old Mercury Topaz that burned almost as much oil as gasoline, into Manhattan to pick up the magazine. On the way, she once again brought up the question of her parents. The only solution, she thought, was for her to move back down and take care of them herself.

"I thought you and Miami do not get along," I said to her, rolling down the window. The oil smell and the summer sun beating down on the car were making me dizzy.

"What else can I do? I am the only one who can take care of them. They have no one else. My father is getting worse by the day and my mother is useless. In Cuba we never had these problems."

"You had others." I didn't mean to be short, but driving on the New Jersey Turnpike sapped my concentration and understanding.

"In Cuba they would have been taken care of. But here they are excess baggage. It was a mistake to leave."

"Your parents were already here," I reminded her. I was negotiating the middle lane between a slow car on the left and a tractor trailer on the right. Belkis was holding on to her seat.

"It was a mistake for them to leave too. It was a mistake for all Cubans to leave."

We arrived in New York at midmorning. We loaded up the car with bundles of magazines until it seemed that the bumper would scrape the road once we got going. We then drove to a few city bookstores and dropped bundles off. The crosstown traffic was taking its toll on me, and we got to the usual Lincoln Tunnel bottleneck way past lunch time. Sitting in traffic, I noticed that the temperature needle was dangerously close to the red zone and I asked Belkis when was the last time she added antifreeze to the radiator.

"Antifreeze? In the winter."

"Coolant. To keep the engine from overheating."

"I add water for that."

I closed my eyes and wiped the sweat from my forehead. In some ways she had never left Cuba. I looked at the temperature gauge again. The needle was less than a millimeter away from the danger zone. I moved the heat lever all the way to the right and turned the heater on full blast.

"What are you doing? Are you crazy?" she said.

"The car is about to overheat," I tried to explain.

"Turn that off!" she yelled out pointing to the vent. "It's midsummer. I can't stand it."

I glanced right and noticed she was holding her throat and beginning to sweat at the temples. Then she did a most extraordinary thing. She began to rip pages off a fresh issue of *Linden Lane* and stuff them into the heater vent. The vent kept regurgitating them onto the floor and so she balled up some more. Finally I grabbed her arm and explained that the heater drew heat away from the engine. It would keep the motor from overheating. I pointed to the gauge and indeed the needle had moved away from the red mark. Eventually the traffic began to move and we were out of danger. I vowed then never to get into that Mercury Topaz again.

A few weeks later the car I thought I had willed out of my life reappeared. By coincidence, we met at a party given by a Cuban poet and her husband, a superior court judge, in North Bergen, New Jersey. With me I brought my friend Ellen Jacko and the Cuban American writer, Carolina Hospital. It was a nice party and the host and hostess were gracious and charming. Afterwards, outside their door, Belkis mentioned that the car was giving them trouble once more. It was burning lots of oil and the motor was making a funny rumbling noise. She asked if we could follow them home, and I, oblivious of my vow a few weeks earlier, volunteered to drive their car. Ellen and Carolina would follow in mine.

We went one block down Bergenline Avenue and the Topaz died, steam hissing out of the engine and the temperature needle way into the red zone. Heberto next to me was half asleep, Belkis was nearly hysterical, and I was in a daze.

I walked into a restaurant and asked for some water to put into the radiator. The waiter handed me a pitcher from one of the empty tables and I rushed with it back to the car. When I tried to pour the water in, several ice cubes jammed the opening and the water spilled all around the engine, creating yet more steam and causing Belkis to exclaim that the car was about to explode. Finally we gave up trying to move it and arranged at a nearby gas station to have it towed. This meant, of course, that we would all have to pile into my diminutive Honda Civic for the hour-and-a-half drive back to Princeton. Ellen, Carolina, and Belkis took the back seat, while Heberto, who needed all the room he could get, took the passenger seat next to me. No sooner had I pulled the seat belt over him than he fell into a deep sleep.

Once on the New Jersey Turnpike, I sensed a medicinal smell wafting from the back seat, and through the rearview mirror I saw Belkis squeezing Ben Gay from a tube onto the palm of her hand and rubbing the side of her neck briskly.

"I have a neck spasm," she said sheepishly.

Next to me Heberto was moaning through his sleep something about Belkis being the only woman for him, and I heard Carolina ask Belkis why she had brought vinegar along. I looked into the rearview mirror once again and, indeed, I saw Belkis now holding a bottle of Heinz apple-cider vinegar while she rummaged in her oversize bag for something else.

"In case of a nose bleed," she answered.

"Do you get them often?" I asked.

"Never."

By the time we reached their house, Belkis and I were the only ones awake. I checked my watch. It was three-fifteen in the morning.

Not long after, Belkis was forced to return to Miami. Her father was dying and there was nothing to do but wait for the inevitable. Heberto stayed behind in Princeton. For a man for whom loneliness is the worst of prisons, the situation was a trial indeed. I came by as much as I could. He showed me the galleys of his latest book. We talked, we ate, we drank. Still, I have never seen a man so tormented by loneliness, by the prospect of himself without others. I could only begin to imagine the toll his political troubles took on his personality, and I came to realize that his one remaining buttress against the world was Belkis.

Belkis returned by train (she never flies) after a month, with her son and mother in tow. Heberto took ill that night and he called asking me to please meet them at the train station. I brought them home; only their one surviving dog seemed at ease. From then on, Belkis's mother, who, when she was not watching Spanish television, strolled around the house like a spectre, lived with them until her death a few months ago. At first the mother's impromptu appearances in the living room while I was visiting were quite disturbing. Eventually, though, I learned to ignore her in the same stoical way Belkis and Heberto did. "She is a constant reminder of our fate," one of them said.

My visits, rarer now that my life has become complicated, are not much different than they ever were. I still drink their coffee, and we talk of the same things—literature, politics, culture. Sadly, their lives have not changed for the better. Though Belkis is the most accomplished Cuban poet of her generation, she is still ignored and unread. She has given up trying to gain recognition for her work and instead focuses all her energies on the production and editing of *Linden Lane*. Heberto, the poet everyone admired when he stood up to the system, is sixty years old and has no steady job, in spite of the fact that his work has been published and critically acclaimed throughout the world. They have been shunned and resisted by those in position to offer them a modicum of security. They have been insulted by others, from both the left and the right, who would prefer them to be symbols easy to manipulate or decry. Though many are aware of their political importance and notoriety, few people are aware of their plight.

In spite of their problems, Belkis and Heberto remain steadfast in their support of the next generation of Cuban writers such as me, many of whom are now writing in English. As poets of the first rank, as socially committed individuals, as human beings for whom honesty in speech and in action has superceded political accommodation, they have been strong and constant models. Their home in Princeton is a place where literature and the island of Cuba coexist in easy and warm fellowship. I remember a poem of Belkis's titled "The Photogenic Ones," written in the late sixties, that ends,

> *At the foot of the photo a few lines*
> *attest to the fact:*
> *neither is sure of the other,*
> *but they sail, they sail with the island*
> *through all the seas of the world.*

Every time I leave their house, I feel I've taken on ballast, parts of my island. My sail fills, my rigging tightens, and I cast off into the North American ocean.

from HUNTING MISTER
HEARTBREAK: A DISCOVERY
OF AMERICA

Jonathan Raban

Jonathan Raban was born in England and is the author of the critically acclaimed *Old Glory: An American Voyage, Coasting* (1987), *For Love and
Money* (1989), *Hunting Mister Heartbreak: A Discovery of America* (1991) and
a novel, *Foreign Land* (1985). He lives in Seattle.

A SMALL KOREAN WOMAN WAS WRESTLING A LARGE MICROWAVE
oven through the swing doors on Broadway and Thirty-fifth. I made a show of
trying to help, but she muttered furiously at me, cuddled her precious oven to
her breast and broke into a run for the subway. Feeling foolish, I fed myself into
the avid Saturday crowd as it streamed into the store.

I'd been to Macy's once before, in 1972, when I went foraging in the
basement for a change of clothes. On a hot June afternoon the store had been
blessedly cool and cavernous. The motherly assistant had made an old-fashioned
fuss over my British accent and the clothes themselves had been, by European
standards, amazingly cheap. Made of some kind of acrylic stuff, they were smart,
bright, all-American. I bought a striped summer jacket in synthetic seersucker,
a pair of washable trousers with creases built in and guaranteed to last forever,

two button-down shirts with white collars and blue fronts. The bill for everything came to less than $70—which, at an exchange rate of $2.40 to the pound, seemed like a steal. Out on the street in my new American camouflage, I melted into the city, a regular guy at last.

Something had happened. Macy's in 1988 smelled of serious money. The air trapped in the swing door reeked of new leather and Rive Gauche. Inside, a man in white tie and tails was rattling off popular classics on a concert grand. Above the glassy aisles and mahogany-paneled boutiques there was a heraldic blazonry of expensive trade names—Louis Vuitton, Calvin Klein, Givenchy, Dior, Ralph Lauren. It was platinum-card country; a twinkling gallery, as big as a battlefield, of gold, silk, scent and lizardskin. When I'd last been here, there had been a slogan painted over the entrance: IT'S SMART TO BE THRIFTY. Sometime between the age of Richard Nixon and the last days of Ronald Reagan, that homely touch of American puritanism had been whitewashed over. Only frumps were thrifty now.

The crowd ran sluggishly through the long, marble-pillared corridors of jewelry, handbags and cosmetics. It eddied round the women in high heels, fishnet tights, frou-frou skirts and top-hats who were squirting scent samples at everyone, male and female, who came within their range. For a few moments, I was gridlocked with someone's reluctant husband, a tubby man wearing a bomber jacket and a leatherette helmet with earflaps who gave off a powerful odor of sweat and attar of roses. He was hauled away, whining, to the escalators by a twin-engined Brillo pad in a fox-fur stole, while the current of the crowd bore me along into Men's Furnishings.

These "furnishings" were disappointingly dull in themselves—plain cotton shirts and ties that in England would be the badge of having once belonged to an obscure county regiment or minor public school. It was the way they were displayed that was extraordinary. Each counter had been converted into a grotto of evocative junk. Between the shirts and ties were piles of antique fishing rods, golf clubs, snowshoes, hatboxes, tarnished silver cups, gumboots, antlers, broken leather suitcases with labels from hotels in Split, Prague, Venice, Florence; gold-banded walking sticks; a pair of crossed oars; a horn phonograph; a battered schoolroom globe; shotgun cartridges; bits of splayed cane furniture left over from the Raj; old family snapshots in ornate silver frames.

So this was what had been in the container billed as "Bric-à-brac" on the *Conveyor*'s cargo manifest. There was a new life waiting in America for all the rubbish in the attics of genteel England. Macy's must have ransacked half the Old Rectories and Mulberry Lodges in Cheshire in order to assemble this hoard of moth-eaten Edwardiana. The rubbish apparently served some alchemical purpose: after a day or two spent in the company of a croquet mallet, a hunting flask, a box of trout flies and a pair of old stirrups, an ordinary white shirt would, I supposed, begin to stiffen with exclusiveness and nobility as it absorbed the molecules of stables, servants, log-fires, field and stream. Certainly the shirt could only justify its ninety-dollar price tag if you were prepared to pay at least fifty dollars for the labor of the alchemist and not be too persnickety about the standard of shirtmaking.

The crowd poured onto the escalators. When Macy's opened in 1902, these escalators with their woodblock steps had been the latest thing; now they were of a piece with the antique luggage and the wind-up Victrola, valued the more highly for being old than being new. They rumbled up through timber-paneled shafts. We piled, hip to haunch, onto this creaky Jacob's ladder, talking in Spanish, Haitian French, Brooklyn, Russian. There was a noisy elation in the crowd, as if the act of going shopping was working like an inhalation of Benzedrine.

We climbed through a cloud bank of bras and negligées; a meadow of dresses went by. Suppose you'd just arrived from Guyana or Bucharest—here would be your vision of American plenty, the brimming cornucopia of the fruits of capitalism. Here goods queued up in line for people, not vice versa. Here you were treated as an object of elaborate cajolery and seduction.

Nothing was too much for you. At every turn of the moving staircase, Macy's had laid on a new surprise for your passing entertainment. You'd like to see the inside of an exclusive club for Victorian gentlemen? We've built one. A pioneer log cabin? Here it is. After the log cabin, a high-tech pleasuredrome of mirrors and white steel. After the pleasuredrome, a deconstructionist fantasy made of scaffolding, with banks of video screens all showing the same picture, of beautiful people modeling leisurewear. The whole store was wired for sound, and each architectural extravagance had its own musical signature. Duke Ellington . . . Telemann . . . Miles Davis . . . Strauss . . .

Macy's was scared stiff of our boredom. This was a world constructed for creatures with infantile attention spans, for whom every moment had to be crammed with novelties and sensations. To be so babied and beguiled, all for the sake of selling skirts and jackets, sheets and towels! It was gross, even by the relatively indulgent standards of London. Many of the people on the escalators were fresh from that other world of clothing coupons and short rations; had I been one of them, I'd have been swept by a wave of blank helplessness in the face of all this aggressive American fun.

To get by in Macy's, a sturdy sense of selfhood was required. Everything in the store whispered *For you! Just for you!*—and you needed to love yourself a very great deal to live up to this continual pampering, for there was an insidious coda to the message, whispering *Are you sure that* you *belong here?*

At each floor, we had to leave the escalator and walk round to the far side of the shaft; and on the way we were ingeniously tormented with mirrors, each one placed so that it appeared to be an innocuous part of the display. I kept on barging into a figure who darkly resembled Henry James's inconceivable alien. I first spotted him in the Victorian men's club: a lank and shabby character in scuffed shoes and concertina trousers whose hair (or what little was left of it) badly needed pruning. He could have done with a new set of teeth. Had I seen him in the subway station, shaking a polystyrene cup under my nose, I'd have given him a couple of quarters and walked on fast, but in Macy's there was no escaping him. He jumped out at me from behind a rack of padlocked fur coats, and was waiting for me at the bookstore. Wherever he was, he looked equally out of place and I grew increasingly ashamed of him.

Shame was a central part of the deal in this show. The luxurious artifice had been designed to soften you up; first, by making you feel good about yourself, then by slugging you below the belt with a surprise punch and making you feel rotten about yourself. It worked, too. By the time I was halfway up the store, I had an American haircut and a new pair of shiny oxblood Italian loafers. It was a pity that, though Macy's sold almost everything, they didn't seem to have a boutique where you could buy new teeth.

———

It was good to be back on the street, to escape this puzzling multistory fiction and return to the low realism of Broadway at dusk, with a hard nip in the air and a frank scowl of aggression on everyone's face as people shoved and jostled each other round the choked entrance to the subway. Two men were out of the race. One was blind and black; he stood his ground in the swarm, holding a tin mug and wearing a sandwich-board that said *I AM Blind / PleASE HELP me / thank you & / GOD BLESS YOU.* The other sat on a camp-stool, warbling on a bird-whistle, the self-appointed nightingale of Herald Square. He held the whistle to his lips with his left hand; the sleeve of his duffel jacket was fastened with a safety pin where his right elbow should have been. There was an expression of pure benignity on his face as he trilled and fluted at the angry crowd. His eyes were wide, their pale blue exactly matching the color of the faded denim cap that he'd pulled down over his Harpo Marx tangle of white hair. After the elaborate cunning of Macy's approach to the retail trade, his sales pitch was refreshingly direct. On a sheet of torn cardboard he had written in ballpoint *BIRD WHISTLE / ALL COLORS / $1.00 EACH WHISTLE.* I know a good bribe for four-year-olds when I see one, and bought five whistles, in red, yellow, green, white and blue. As I picked them out of the box at the man's feet, he smiled—a big, untidy, open smile that looked as if he really meant it.

"For to make the whistle, must first to put the water in the hole!" He shook his own whistle under my nose to show me.

"Where are you from? What country?"

"Me?" He seemed surprised and pleased that anyone should ask him such a question. "I come from Kiev. Kiev. In *Ukraine.*"

"How long in America?—how many years?"

"I come in . . . nineteen—eight-oh. I have eight years in New York."

"What was your job in the Ukraine? What did you do before you came here?"

He grinned, sighed, blinked. "Excuse me. Not understanding. Too bad English." His eyes, candid and friendly, remained on me as he piped a long, robinlike territorial demarcation call. It was a disappointment—I badly wanted to know why he seemed so happy. To escape from the Soviet Union, only to find yourself hawking plastic toys on a cold Manhattan street corner, would take an extraordinarily sunny disposition if you weren't to feel ground down by your fate. But the birdwhistle man didn't seem ground down at all. Nor did he seem mad or particularly slow-witted; just not much of a linguist. Down in the tiled warren of the subway station, I kept on hearing this blithe Ukrainian spirit sprinkling his plastic woodnotes on the New York air, and wondered how often, and how bitterly, he wished himself back to Kiev.

Still, he had a trade of sorts; by comparison with the beggars who took shelter in the subway stations, he was an *alrightnik.* Every station had its resident population of forlorn supplicants, and every journey across the city entailed a descent into a Third World of helpless distress.

The smartest beggars restored the literal meaning of the word "panhandler": they wielded long-handled saucepans with inward sloping sides to protect the alms within. When shaken, these pans made much the best noise: the mournful slather of quarters and dimes on Teflon was a sound in the same key as one's heartstrings. After the saucepan came the aluminum tankard, the tin plate, the greasy cap, the Styrofoam cup, the cracked and dirt-lined open palm. In as many yards, there were a dozen men and women—a desperate chamber orchestra of rattles, chinks and plunks.

Competition meant advertising. Some of the beggars rolled up their sleeves and trouser legs to expose weeping patches of violet scar tissue, growths, amputations, open sores. Others used techniques learned from radio and television. One well-dressed Third Avenue beggar was expert at delivering his slogan, which went, "I'm poor, I've had no breakfast/lunch/supper, and I want to work." He stood facing the drift of the crowd, and reeled off his words like an actor playing with variant meanings in a passage from *Hamlet.* He had a throwaway, cocktail party version: Oh, by the way, d'you know that "I'm poor, I've had no supper, and I want to work?" He shifted to truculence: *"I'*m poor! *I'*ve had no supper! And *I* want to work!" His voice took on a tearful, beseeching note: "I'm *poor*... I've had no *supper*... and I want to *work*..." He was a saucepan man.

Whenever I paused on the street, or hesitated over which subway line to take, someone new materialized beside me, and always the voice was discreet and confidential. I was a mailbox for muttered stories about lost wives, lost children, lost bus fares, lost jobs, hunger and thirst. Fifty cents or a dollar—never more—was what people asked for. With a bagel, a burger, a cup of coffee, a subway token, they said, their problem would be solved.

Always, I noticed, I was addressed as "sir." In the Great Depression, it had been "Buddy, can you spare a dime?"; fifty years on, we were buddies no longer. *They* were the outcast; *I* was the tenant of an apartment with uniformed doormen in the lobby—and there was no calling on my sense of fraternity to answer their need. I was sorry about the passing of that *buddy;* its disappearance registered something newly cruel in New York life.

The beggars slept much of the day away on benches on the subway platforms. The lighting was fierce, the noise of the trains was an incessant slamming and screeching. With their filthy topcoats pulled all the way up over their heads, the beggars looked like victims of a fatal accident; you knew they were alive only because they sometimes moaned and cried out in their sleep.

By night, they scavenged. Returning home late after dinner, I would meet them on the cross-streets around East Eighteenth, where small knots of them went tipping over trashcans in search of a bit of half-eaten pizza, or the lees of someone's can of Coors. They flopped and stumbled, far too feeble to be figures of menace, even on the darkest street—and at this hour none of them spoke to me; they knew that well-fed middle-class men take to their heels when strangers talk to them after dusk in Manhattan.

The current term for these misfortunates was "street people," an expression that had taken over from bag ladies, winos and bums. The Street People were seen as a tribe, like the Beaker Folk or the Bone People, and this fairly reflected the fact that there were so many more of them now than there had been a few years before. In New York one saw *a people;* a poor nation living on the leftovers of a rich one. They were anthropologically distinct, with their skin eruptions, their wasted figures, poor hair and bony faces. They looked like the Indians in an old Western.

The term was too easy by half. It casually lumped together the criminal and the innocent, the dangerous and the safe. It included long-term mental patients discharged from hospitals under what was called, in a sublime euphemism, the "de-institutionalization program," along with crack addicts, thieves, alcoholics, hobos, the temporarily jobless, the alimony defaulters, rent-hike victims and everyone else who'd fallen short of the appallingly high standards that Manhattan set for staying properly housed and fed.

VISIONS OF AMERICA

You were meant to be scared by the Street People, to take one look at this defeated crew and see—Crack! Mugging! Homicide! Pathological vice! This simplified things wonderfully for the apartment dwellers, for at a single verbal stroke it canceled a great chunk of the city from our vision.

Within hours of my arrival, I was pumped full of propaganda. Don't loiter— always walk purposefully and signal that you have an imminent destination. Keep to the outer edge of the sidewalk. Avoid doorways. Never make "eye contact." If asked the time, or for directions, don't reply. Don't go north of Ninety-sixth, south of Canal or west of Ninth Avenue. Stick to the "white" subways, like the Lexington Avenue line, and never use the subway system after dark. Treat every outing on the New York streets as a low-flying raid over enemy territory.

This advice had the ring of that given to Alice by the Red Queen:

> Now, *here,* you see, it takes all the running *you* can do, to keep in the same place. If you want to get somewhere else, you must run at least twice as fast as that . . . Speak in French when you can't think of the English for a thing—turn out your toes as you walk—and remember who you are!

Alicelike, I tried to follow it as politely as I could, with curious results.

I straightened my shoulders, focused on an imaginary point in the far distance, and marched, swinging my arms like a marathon walker. Almost imme- diately, I started to acquire Manhattan tunnel vision. The Street People moved from the center to the periphery of the frame; within a minute or two they became virtually invisible—bits of stationary furniture, on a level with the fire hydrants and the trashcans. Left, left, left, right, left . . . The stoplight flashed "Walk!" and I strode at a steady six miles per hour on the flank of the sidewalk; it flashed "Don't Walk!" and I halted, drawing my stomach in and throwing my chest out in the best parody I could manage of a guardsman on duty in a sentry box. There were no Street People now; just the marching backs of men in city suits. The entire physical fabric of New York had turned into a sheer trajectory, a bullet path (with one right-angled ricochet) between subway exit and apartment block.

It was a tiring exercise. My fixed stare kept on slipping, to include faces, shop windows, restaurant menus. On East Twenty-second at Broadway I found a vacant fire hydrant and settled on it, as into an armchair, like the Street People did, to watch the crowd file past. Everyone moved with the same stiff clockwork action; everyone wore the same boiled look on their faces. As they approached my fire hydrant, they accelerated slightly from the waist down, locked their eyes into the horizontal position, and swept by, giving me an exaggeratedly wide berth. I tried making eye contact, and managed to catch a few pairs of pupils offguard; they swerved away in their sockets, as quick as fish.

HUNTING MISTER HEARTBREAK

It was interesting to feel oneself being willed into nonexistence by total strangers. I'd never felt the force of such frank contempt—and all because I was sitting on a fire hydrant. Every one of these guys wanted to see me wiped out. I was a virus, a bad smell, a dirty smear that needed cleaning up. After only a minute or two of this, I began to warm with reciprocal feeling; had I stayed on my hydrant for an hour, I'd have been aching to get my fist round a tire iron or the butt of a .38, just to let a zombie know that I was human too.

There were the Street People and there were the Air People. Air People levitated like fakirs. Large portions of their day were spent waiting for, and traveling in, the elevators that were as fundamental to the middle-class culture of New York as gondolas had been to Venice in the Renaissance. It was the big distinction—to be able to press a button and take wing to your apartment. It didn't matter that you lived on the sixth, the sixteenth or sixtieth floor; access to the elevator was proof that your life had the buoyancy that was needed to stay afloat in a city where the ground was seen as the realm of failure and menace.

In blocks like Alice's, where doormen kept up a twenty-four-hour guard against the Street People, the elevator was like the village green. The moment that people were safely inside the cage, they started talking to strangers with cozy expansiveness. As we rattled up through the floors, it was "Hi!" and "Bye!" and "Where'd you *get* that?—I just love it" and "Don't you hate this weather?" . . . little trills and squawks of sociability that registered everyone's relief at having escaped the dreadful flintiness of the subway and the street.

Returning to Alice's apartment—to the camomile tea, the sheet music on the piano, the patchwork creature on the bed—I unlocked my own temporary castle in the air; a soap-bubble life, as far out of touch with the city below as if I'd pressed a rogue button on the elevator and been whisked from East Eighteenth Street to a sedate small town in Mississippi or a gnome's den in Zurich, Switzerland. Like the *tableaux vivants* on the top floor of Macy's, Alice's room was a fully furnished fantasy; not so much an actual living space as a fond idea of how you might live, if only you didn't live in Manhattan. Its shoebox tidiness, its over-careful taste, its museumlike display of little-girl things from Alice's childhood, were set against the encroaching city—its wild disorder, its vulgarity, its tough grown-upness. When Alice came home to New York, she was in flight from New York. I saw her closing the curtains against the street, putting a Bach cantata on the stereo system, and drifting up and away, a balloonist floating high over the lawless wreckage of the city.

Everyone I knew lived like this. Their New York consisted of a series of high-altitude interiors, each one guarded, triple-locked, electronically surveilled. They kept in touch by flying from one interior to the next, like sociable gulls swooping from cliff to cliff. For them, the old New York of streets, squares, neighborhoods, was rapidly turning into a vague and distant memory. It was the place where TV thrillers were filmed. It was where the Street People lived.

Diane, my friend of twenty years, had turned into an Air Person since I'd last seen her. Once, she'd been down on ground-level, in a small terraced house in Greenwich Village; now she had a twenty-ninth-floor rental in a new fortified apartment building on Thirtieth Street.

Paying a call on her nowadays was hardly less difficult than stopping by at Buckingham Palace to have a quiet word with the Queen. The vast marble lobby of the building was patrolled by men in braided caps and so much gold frogging on their jackets that they looked like officers in the service of some fierce South American dictatorship. Unsuccessful applicants for interviews sat about on upholstered benches, disconsolately waiting for their accreditation to come through. If you managed to be escorted to an elevator by a member of the Tontons Macoutes, you felt marked out as a conspicuous social success.

"It's what people boast about now," Diane said. "Everywhere you hear women talking about how many 'men' they've got. We've all got men now. Have you got men?"

Her apartment was a rectangle of sunlight, adrift in the thin air of High Manhattan. Long windows framed a heady view of brick pinnacles and pale sierras. Only the faint purr of the air conditioning disturbed the alpine silence. Diane's white drawing room was lightly furnished, as if she'd had to throw out all the ballast from her life in order to ascend this far. There were some framed photographs of her family on the walls, two small paintings, both by friends, a typewriter on a table, a single spray of flowers.

"It's sort of nowhere, really. That's what I like about New York—it's *nowhere*. Nowhere, with a view."

So it was. She'd found an airy vacancy.

"Look—you can see the East River—"

It took some finding. A very short section of it was sandwiched high up between the walls of two office buildings. A distant barge slid from behind a smoked-glass window and was immediately swallowed by an insurance company.

"I like to watch the ships when I'm working. Sometimes, at night, you hear their foghorns."

Extraordinary. All I ever heard in New York was the barbarous wailing of police sirens; in Diane's soap bubble, the sound of the city was of solitary ships at sea, riding downtide in the early-morning mist. Perhaps it did matter what storey you were on, after all. The higher up you were, the more free you were to live in a world of your own imaginative making. By the thirtieth floor, you could probably tear loose from reality altogether. By comparison with Diane's apartment, Alice's seemed flatly realistic, dragged down by the gravitational field of the street and its people.

HUNTING MISTER HEARTBREAK

Here you had to stand with your nose pressed against the double-glazing to see the street at all. Far below—a world away—was turmoil. Down around the knees and ankles of Diane's tall block, nineteenth-century tenements were being torn down by cranes and bulldozers in a low cloud of red dust. Stores were boarded up. Cabs were stalled at a light in an unbroken line of dirty yellow. With a really powerful telescope, you might pick out the sprawled beggars, the crack dealers with telephone bleepers in the back pockets of their jeans, the addict sweating off his high in the doorway of the derelict warehouse; but on the twenty-ninth floor you had no more reason to pay attention to these things than you would have to go rubbernecking down the sewage system of the city.

In her apprenticeship as an Air Person, Diane had learned how to stay aloft for days on end. Every morning her Romanian maid would arrive with bloodcurdling news from ground-level. A secretary came to type in the afternoons. At sunset, friends presented themselves to the guards and showed up—ears popping from their ascent—for drinks.

Her days were punctuated by the arrival of "men." "Men" brought cartons of groceries, ordered by telephone, to the door; "men" came with sticks of her French cigarettes, crates of wine and Stolichnaya vodka, fresh flowers, books, magazines and newspapers. I doubted if she knew where any of these commodities came from. Far down in the uninhabitable city there were stores that were just telephone numbers to the Air People; there things were counted, parceled, charged and posted up, via guards and elevators, like so many messages to another world.

Diane used her TV set as if it were a video intercom, to inspect what was happening in the street outside her front door. Four blocks to the west, a building collapsed, trapping a woman under a filing cabinet for thirteen hours. It was on television. One block south, a man was found shot dead in his laundry truck. It was, said a police spokesman on television, "a very professional job." Every day our neighborhood yielded a drug raid, a hold-up, a rape, a killing; it was constantly on television.

For Diane, places like Brooklyn and the Bronx were as remote as Beirut and Teheran. *Nobody* went there. The subway system was an ugly rumor—she had not set foot in it for years. She did quite often go walking alone in the knot of streets around East Thirtieth, as a seriously entrenched Air Person would not have dared to do; and sometimes what she saw on television led her to take the elevator down to the street, where she would prowl through her own neighborhood to the site of a disaster or the scene of a crime, like a war correspondent braving the battlefield for the sake of a story.

I sometimes joined her on evenings when she was dining out uptown—evenings that had the flavor of a tense commando operation. At eight o'clock, the lobby of her building was full of Air People waiting for their transport. A guard would secure a cab, and we'd fly up through New York to the West Sixties or the East Eighties. I thought the cabs far grimmer and more alarming than the subways. Their suspension had usually been long wrecked by the potholes on the Avenues; the bulletproof Plexiglas screen between us and the driver had knife scratches on it and had turned milky and opaque with age; the blood-colored seat covers were ripped and holed. The driver was nearly always in a state of uncontained fury, and inclined to treat his cab as a weapon, an Exocet missile in the War of New York. Swaying and shuddering over the terrible roads, while the driver burbled obscenities at everyone who came within his sight, was an experience calculated to make Air People fervently wish themselves back in their safe eyries.

On my first night-raid with Diane, the driver was forced to stop at the light on Lexington. The heating in the cab was savage, and I'd wound my window down and was gazing out of it with the unfocused curiosity of a man who's quite forgotten the cardinal rules of Manhattan street life. Obedient to the gaze, a long, skinny figure came limping out of a pool of shadow. He wore a greasy embroidered *yarmulke* on his head. "Sir . . ." Phrases I'd heard twenty times before during that day came dribbling listlessly out of his mouth. *Ain't had nothing to eat . . . no place to sleep . . . Sir, will you give me fifty cents?*

I fished out my wallet, searched for a one, but could find only a ten. A hand, with broken lampblack fingernails but delicate musician's fingers, seized it. The man stared at the note. He might as easily have been seventeen or thirty-five. "Ya gotta be kidding! Oh, God! Ya *got* to be kidding!"

Diane, embarrassed by this display, stared dead ahead, practicing her tunnel vision. The light was stuck solid on red.

The man held up the ten-dollar bill to the streetlamp, shouted *Oi veh!* and crushed the bill into a pocket. Then he began to dance—a crazy, limping, jittery dance—and as he danced he moaned words in what I took to be Yiddish. He went on dancing until the light turned green, when he stumbled back into the shadow where he lived.

As we pulled away, I saw the driver's eyes fixed on me in his rearview mirror. They were not friendly. He said, "Stoopid motherfucker—get that fuckin' window *up!*"

It was a white-knuckle ride. Diane sat bolt upright, wordless, clinging to the strap, while the cab flew through the dismal Thirties. At this level, at this hour, all of New York looked ugly, angular, fire-blackened, defaced—bad dream country. The sidewalks were empty now of everyone except the Street People. This was the time when things began to happen that you'd see tomorrow on breakfast television, and read about, in tombstone headlines, in the *Post* and *Daily News.* Father stabs three-year-old son, believing him to be Satan. Kin held in two bludgeonings. Woman slain as stray shot rips into hall. Mistaken identity—convicted murderer on run.

Few of these journeys lasted more than ten or eleven minutes, they were just long enough to let you catch a glimpse of the world you feared. Then, suddenly, there was another guard, dressed in a new exotic livery, putting you through Customs & Immigration in another lobby.

An elevator, identical to the one we had just left, spirited us upward with a long, low, mechanical whispering in its guts. At the appointed altitude, we stepped out into a mock-Tudor hall, where a Filipino servant was taking coats; and beyond, a splendid drawing room whose high ceiling was lavishly encrusted with mock-Georgian cornices. The guests who'd arrived before us were sitting on a brass-and-leather club fender, round a blazing log-fire in an open hearth decorated with *trompe l'oeil* plastic wood-ash. The carved timber mantelpiece was packed, end to end, with embossed invitation cards to charity dinners and memorial services.

There were several touches of Macy's ninth floor: a wall of books in claret leather bindings; a vast Japanese screen; a still life, French, of a spatchcocked hare with assorted fruits and flowers, which was three times the size of the one in Macy's. My first impression was that we had somehow stumbled on a house party assembled in the library of a castle, probably Scottish, in, perhaps, the middle of the 1920s.

I couldn't concentrate on the conversation, which was about German pedantry in the new edition of Joyce's *Ulysses;* a topic that I would have quickly warmed to in the ordinary way of things. Perched on the edge of the club fender, watching the gas flames leap from the make-believe logs, I was thinking of woman slain, father stabs, kin held, of the man in the *yarmulke* and of the word *motherfucker,* which was ringing unpleasantly in my head. *Up here,* you could barely credit the existence of *down there;* just as *down there* you couldn't conceive of the armored extravagance of *up here.*

This New York, the city of the Air People, was straining to break free of that other, accursed city of the same name. One day, perhaps, you'd feel a tremor under your feet and hear a sudden cracking and tearing as the fibers of steel and concrete gave way . . . At present the two cities were held together, one on top of the other, by the slender umbilical of the elevator, and by the Air People's dependence on the traffic that came up it—the *Times* and *Wall Street Journal,* beefsteak and zucchini, laundered shirts, Château Léoville-Barton, maids, flowers, guests, invitations.

Cry your heart out, man in the *yarmulke!* Up here, we're sailing through the sky where the air is keen and the view is of a flawless sweep of luminous indigo blue. You're way below the cloud ceiling. You're not even a dot to us, *buddy.*

"What was the name of that Dublin physician?"

"Did you read Susan's piece in the last issue?"

Fogheaded, unused to the altitude, I took my place at table.

Everyone was dreaming. The word came at one from every direction. On the subway platform at the Twenty-second Street station, one bench was permanently occupied by a head-covered sleeper who, as day followed day, I began to suspect was really dead. He (or she, or it) lay below a poster for the New York Lottery. It said, ALL YOU NEED IS A DOLLAR AND A DREAM. Whenever I switched on Alice's TV, I found politicians talking about their dreams. The Republican candidate for the presidency kept on reiterating his dream of a kinder, gentler America. The Democrat was reported by his advertising staff to have "lived the dream," because he was the son of an immigrant. Every congressperson and senator seemed under a weird compulsion to summon the ghost of Martin Luther King by slipping in the phrase "I have a dream" before going on to spell out their ghostwritten positions on Star Wars, or Medicare, or the federal deficit.

"In *our* country," said Alice rather sternly, "I'm afraid that we wouldn't much like it if politicians talked about their dreams as they do here. People would tend to think that they were a bit soft in the head. Where I come from, dreamers are impractical folk who have difficulty tying their own shoelaces. Still," she added politely, "I suppose that in America everything is as different as possible, and dreams are *far* more real to Americans than they are to us."

THE SOLACE OF OPEN SPACES

Gretel Ehrlich

Gretel Ehrlich's essays have appeared in *Harper's, The Atlantic, Time,* the *New York Times,* and *Antaeus.* Her books include *The Solace of Open Spaces* (1986); *Islands, the Universe, Home* (1991); and a novel, *Heart Mountain* (1988). She lives on a ranch in northern Wyoming.

IT'S MAY AND I'VE JUST AWAKENED FROM A NAP, CURLED AGAINST sagebrush the way my dog taught me to sleep—sheltered from wind. A front is pulling the huge sky over me, and from the dark a hailstone has hit me on the head. I'm trailing a band of two thousand sheep across a stretch of Wyoming badlands, a fifty-mile trip that takes five days because sheep shade up in hot sun and won't budge until it's cool. Bunched together now, and excited into a run by the storm, they drift across dry land, tumbling into draws like water and surge out again onto the rugged, choppy plateaus that are the building blocks of this state.

The name Wyoming comes from an Indian word meaning "at the great plains," but the plains are really valleys, great arid valleys, sixteen hundred square miles, with the horizon bending up on all sides into mountain ranges. This gives the vastness a sheltering look.

Winter lasts six months here. Prevailing winds spill snowdrifts to the east, and new storms from the northwest replenish them. This white bulk is sometimes dizzying, even nauseating, to look at. At twenty, thirty, and forty degrees below zero, not only does your car not work, but neither do your mind and body. The landscape hardens into a dungeon of space. During the winter, while I was riding to find a new calf, my jeans froze to the saddle, and in the silence that such cold creates I felt like the first person on earth, or the last.

Today the sun is out—only a few clouds billowing. In the east, where the sheep have started off without me, the benchland tilts up in a series of eroded red-earthed mesas, planed flat on top by a million years of water; behind them, a bold line of muscular scarps rears up ten thousand feet to become the Big Horn Mountains. A tidal pattern is engraved into the ground, as if left by the sea that once covered this state. Canyons curve down like galaxies to meet the oncoming rush of flat land.

To live and work in this kind of open country, with its hundred-mile views, is to lose the distinction between background and foreground. When I asked an older ranch hand to describe Wyoming's openness, he said, "It's all a bunch of nothing—wind and rattlesnakes—and so much of it you can't tell where you're going or where you've been and it don't make much difference." John, a sheepman I know, is tall and handsome and has an explosive temperament. He has a perfect intuition about people and sheep. They call him "Highpockets," because he's so long-legged; his graceful stride matches the distances he has to cover. He says, "Open space hasn't affected me at all. It's all the people moving in on it." The huge ranch he was born on takes up much of one county and spreads into another state; to put 100,000 miles on his pickup in three years and never leave home is not unusual. A friend of mine has an aunt who ranched on Powder River and didn't go off her place for eleven years. When her husband died, she quickly moved to town, bought a car, and drove around the States to see what she'd been missing.

Most people tell me they've simply driven through Wyoming, as if there were nothing to stop for. Or else they've skied in Jackson Hole, a place Wyomingites acknowledge uncomfortably because its green beauty and chic affluence are mismatched with the rest of the state. Most of Wyoming has a "lean-to" look. Instead of big, roomy barns and Victorian houses, there are dugouts, low sheds, log cabins, sheep camps, and fence lines that look like driftwood blown haphazardly into place. People here still feel pride because they live in such a harsh place, part of the glamorous cowboy past, and they are determined not to be the victims of a mining-dominated future.

Most characteristic of the state's landscape is what a developer euphemistically describes as "indigenous growth right up to your front door"—a reference to waterless stands of salt sage, snakes, jack rabbits, deerflies, red dust, a brief respite of wildflowers, dry washes, and no trees. In the Great Plains the vistas look like music, like Kyries of grass, but Wyoming seems to be the doing of a mad architect—tumbled and twisted, ribboned with faded, deathbed colors, thrust up and pulled down as if the place had been startled out of a deep sleep and thrown into a pure light.

I came here four years ago. I had not planned to stay, but I couldn't make myself leave. John, the sheepman, put me to work immediately. It was spring, and shearing time. For fourteen days of fourteen hours each, we moved thousands of sheep through sorting corrals to be sheared, branded, and deloused. I suspect that my original motive for coming here was to "lose myself" in new and unpopulated territory. Instead of producing the numbness I thought I wanted, life on the sheep ranch woke me up. The vitality of the people I was working with flushed out what had become a hallucinatory rawness inside me. I threw away my clothes and bought new ones; I cut my hair. The arid country was a clean slate. Its absolute indifference steadied me.

Sagebrush covers 58,000 square miles of Wyoming. The biggest city has a population of fifty thousand, and there are only five settlements that could be called cities in the whole state. The rest are towns, scattered across the expanse with as much as sixty miles between them, their populations two thousand, fifty, or ten. They are fugitive-looking, perched on a barren, windblown bench, or tagged onto a river or a railroad, or laid out straight in a farming valley with implement stores and a block-long Mormon church. In the eastern part of the state, which slides down into the Great Plains, the new mining settlements are boomtowns, trailer cities, metal knots on flat land.

Despite the desolate look, there's a coziness to living in this state. There are so few people (only 470,000) that ranchers who buy and sell cattle know one another statewide; the kids who choose to go to college usually go to the state's one university, in Laramie; hired hands work their way around Wyoming in a lifetime of hirings and firings. And despite the physical separation, people stay in touch, often driving two or three hours to another ranch for dinner.

Seventy-five years ago, when travel was by buckboard or horseback, cowboys who were temporarily out of work rode the grub line—drifting from ranch to ranch, mending fences or milking cows, and receiving in exchange a bed and meals. Gossip and messages traveled this slow circuit with them, creating an intimacy between ranchers who were three and four weeks' ride apart. One old-time couple I know, whose turn-of-the-century homestead was used by an outlaw gang as a relay station for stolen horses, recall that if you were traveling, desperado or not, any lighted ranch house was a welcome sign. Even now, for someone who lives in a remote spot, arriving at a ranch or coming to town for supplies is cause for celebration. To emerge from isolation can be disorienting. Everything looks bright, new, vivid. After I had been herding sheep for only three days, the sound of the camp tender's pickup flustered me. Longing for human company, I felt a foolish grin take over my face; yet I had to resist an urgent temptation to run and hide.

Things happen suddenly in Wyoming, the change of seasons and weather; for people, the violent swings in and out of isolation. But good-naturedness is concomitant with severity. Friendliness is a tradition. Strangers passing on the road wave hello. A common sight is two pickups stopped side by side far out on a range, on a dirt track winding through the sage. The drivers will share a cigarette, uncap their thermos bottles, and pass a battered cup, steaming with coffee, between windows. These meetings summon up the details of several generations, because, in Wyoming, private histories are largely public knowledge.

Because ranch work is a physical and, these days, economic strain, being "at home on the range" is a matter of vigor, self-reliance, and common sense. A person's life is not a series of dramatic events for which he or she is applauded or exiled but a slow accumulation of days, seasons, years, fleshed out by the generational weight of one's family and anchored by a land-bound sense of place.

In most parts of Wyoming, the human population is visibly outnumbered by the animal. Not far from my town of fifty, I rode into a narrow valley and startled a herd of two hundred elk. Eagles look like small people as they eat car-killed deer by the road. Antelope, moving in small, graceful bands, travel at sixty miles an hour, their mouths open as if drinking in the space.

The solitude in which westerners live makes them quiet. They telegraph thoughts and feelings by the way they tilt their heads and listen; pulling their Stetsons into a steep dive over their eyes, or pigeon-toeing one boot over the other, they lean against a fence with a fat wedge of Copenhagen beneath their lower lips and take in the whole scene. These detached looks of quiet amusement are sometimes cynical, but they can also come from a dry-eyed humility as lucid as the air is clear.

Conversation goes on in what sounds like a private code; a few phrases imply a complex of meanings. Asking directions, you get a curious list of details. While trailing sheep I was told to "ride up to that kinda upturned rock, follow the pink wash, turn left at the dump, and then you'll see the water hole." One friend told his wife on roundup to "turn at the salt lick and the dead cow," which turned out to be a scattering of bones and no salt lick at all.

Sentence structure is shortened to the skin and bones of a thought. Descriptive words are dropped, even verbs; a cowboy looking over a corral full of horses will say to a wrangler, "Which one needs rode?" People hold back their thoughts in what seems to be a dumbfounded silence, then erupt with an excoriating perceptive remark. Language, so compressed, becomes metaphorical. A rancher ended a relationship with one remark: "You're a bad check," meaning bouncing in and out was intolerable, and even coming back would be no good.

What's behind this laconic style is shyness. There is no vocabulary for the subject of feelings. It's not a hangdog shyness, or anything coy—always there's a robust spirit in evidence behind the restraint, as if the earth-dredging wind that pulls across Wyoming had carried its people's voices away but everything else in them had shouldered confidently into the breeze.

I've spent hours riding to sheep camp at dawn in a pickup when nothing was said; eaten meals in the cookhouse when the only words spoken were a mumbled "Thank you, ma'am" at the end of dinner. The silence is profound. Instead of talking, we seem to share one eye. Keenly observed, the world is transformed. The landscape is engorged with detail, every movement on it chillingly sharp. The air between people is charged. Days unfold, bathed in their own music. Nights become hallucinatory; dreams, prescient.

Spring weather is capricious and mean. It snows, then blisters with heat. There have been tornadoes. They lay their elephant trunks out in the sage until they find houses, then slurp everything up and leave. I've noticed that melting snow-banks hiss and rot, viperous, then drip into calm pools where ducklings hatch and livestock, being trailed to summer range, drink. With the ice cover gone, rivers churn a milkshake brown, taking culverts and small bridges with them. Water in such an arid place (the average annual rainfall where I live is less than eight inches) is like blood. It festoons drab land with green veins; a line of cottonwoods following a stream; a strip of alfalfa; and, on ditch banks, wild asparagus growing.

I've moved to a small cattle ranch owned by friends. It's at the foot of the Big Horn Mountains. A few weeks ago, I helped them deliver a calf who was stuck halfway out of his mother's body. By the time he was freed, we could see a heartbeat, but he was straining against a swollen tongue for air. Mary and I held him upside down by his back feet, while Stan, on his hands and knees in the blood, gave the calf mouth-to-mouth resuscitation. I have a vague memory of being pneumonia-choked as a child, my mother giving me her air, which may account for my romance with this windswept state.

If anything is endemic to Wyoming, it is wind. This big room of space is swept out daily, leaving a bone yard of fossils, agates, and carcasses in every stage of decay. Though it was water that initially shaped the state, wind is the meticulous gardener, raising dust and pruning the sage.

VISIONS OF AMERICA

. . .

I try to imagine a world in which I could ride my horse across uncharted land. There is no wilderness left; wildness, yes, but true wilderness has been gone on this continent since the time of Lewis and Clark's overland journey.

Two hundred years ago, the Crow, Shoshone, Arapaho, Cheyenne, and Sioux roamed the intermountain West, orchestrating their movements according to hunger, season, and warfare. Once they acquired horses, they traversed the spines of all the big Wyoming ranges—the Absarokas, the Wind Rivers, the Tetons, the Big Horns—and wintered on the unprotected plains that fan out from them. Space was life. The world was their home.

What was life-giving to Native Americans was often nightmarish to sodbusters who had arrived encumbered with families and ethnic pasts to be transplanted in nearly uninhabitable land. The great distances, the shortage of water and trees, and the loneliness created unexpected hardships for them. In her book *O Pioneers!*, Willa Cather gives a settler's version of the bleak landscape:

> The little town behind them had vanished as if it had never been, had fallen behind the swell of the prairie, and the stern frozen country received them into its bosom. The homesteads were few and far apart; here and there a windmill gaunt against the sky, a sod house crouching in a hollow.

The emptiness of the West was for others a geography of possibility. Men and women who amassed great chunks of land and struggled to preserve unfenced empires were, despite their self-serving motives, unwitting geographers. They understood the lay of the land. But by the 1850s the Oregon and Mormon trails sported bumper-to-bumper traffic. Wealthy landowners, many of them aristocratic absentee landlords, known as remittance men because they were paid to come West and get out of their families' hair, overstocked the range with more than a million head of cattle. By 1885 the feed and water were desperately short, and the winter of 1886 laid out the gaunt bodies of dead animals so closely together that when the thaw came, one rancher from Kaycee claimed to have walked on cowhide all the way to Crazy Woman Creek, twenty miles away.

Territorial Wyoming was a boy's world. The land was generous with everything but water. At first there was room enough, food enough, for everyone. And, as with all beginnings, an expansive mood set in. The young cowboys, drifters, shopkeepers, schoolteachers were heroic, lawless, generous, rowdy, and tenacious. The individualism and optimism generated during those times have endured.

John Tisdale rode north with the trail herds from Texas. He was a college-educated man with enough money to buy a small outfit near the Powder River. While driving home from the town of Buffalo with a buckboard full of Christmas toys for his family and a winter's supply of food, he was shot in the back by an agent of the cattle barons who resented the encroachment of small-time stockmen like him. The wealthy cattlemen tried to control all the public grazing land by restricting membership in the Wyoming Stock Growers Association, as if it were a country club. They ostracized from roundups and brandings cowboys and ranchers who were not members, then denounced them as rustlers. Tisdale's death, the second such cold-blooded murder, kicked off the Johnson County cattle war, which was no simple good-guy-bad-guy shoot-out but a complicated class struggle between landed gentry and less affluent settlers—a shocking reminder that the West was not an egalitarian sanctuary after all.

Fencing ultimately enforced boundaries, but barbed wire abrogated space. It was stretched across the beautiful valleys, into the mountains, over desert badlands, through buffalo grass. The "anything is possible" fever—the lure of any new place—was constricted. The integrity of the land as a geographical body, and the freedom to ride anywhere on it, were lost.

I punched cows with a young man named Martin, who is the great-grandson of John Tisdale. His inheritance is not the open land that Tisdale knew and prematurely lost but a rage against restraint.

Wyoming tips down as you head northeast; the highest ground—the Laramie Plains—is on the Colorado border. Up where I live, the Big Horn River leaks into difficult, arid terrain. In the basin where it's dammed, sandhill cranes gather and, with delicate legwork, slice through the stilled water. I was driving by with a rancher one morning when he commented that cranes are "old-fashioned." When I asked why, he said, "Because they mate for life." Then he looked at me with a twinkle in his eyes, as if to say he really did believe in such things but also understood why we break our own rules.

In all this open space, values crystalize quickly. People are strong on scruples but tenderhearted about quirky behavior. A friend and I found one ranch hand, who's "not quite right in the head," sitting in front of the badly decayed carcass of a cow, shaking his finger and saying, "Now, I don't want you to do this ever again!" When I asked what was wrong with him, I was told, "He's goofier than hell, just like the rest of us." Perhaps because the West is historically new, conventional morality is still felt to be less important than rock-bottom truths. Though there's always a lot of teasing and sparring, people are blunt with one another, sometimes even cruel, believing honesty is stronger medicine than sympathy, which may console but often conceals.

The formality that goes hand in hand with the rowdiness is known as the Western Code. It's a list of practical do's and don'ts, faithfully observed. A friend, Cliff, who runs a trapline in the winter, cut off half his foot while chopping a hole in the ice. Alone, he dragged himself to his pickup and headed for town, stopping to open the ranch gate as he left, and getting out to close it again, thus losing, in his observance of rules, precious time and blood. Later, he commented, "How would it look, them having to come to the hospital to tell me their cows had gotten out?"

Accustomed to emergencies, my friends doctor each other from the vet's bag with relish. When one old-timer suffered a heart attack in hunting camp, his partner quickly stirred up a brew of red horse liniment and hot water and made the half-conscious victim drink it, then tied him onto a horse and led him twenty miles to town. He regained consciousness and lived.

The roominess of the state has affected political attitudes as well. Ranchers keep up with world politics and the convulsions of the economy but are basically isolationists. Being used to running their own small empires of land and livestock, they're suspicious of big government. It's a "don't fence me in" holdover from a century ago. They still want the elbow room their grandfathers had, so they're strongly conservative, but with a populist twist.

Summer is the season when we get our "cowboy tans"—on the lower parts of our faces and on three fourths of our arms. Excessive heat, in the nineties and higher, sends us outside with the mosquitoes. In winter we're tucked inside our houses, and the white wasteland outside appears to be expanding, but in summer all the greenery abridges space. Summer is a go-ahead season. Every living thing is off the block and in the race: battalions of bugs in flight and biting; bats swinging around my log cabin as if the bases were loaded and someone had hit a home run. Some of summer's high-speed growth is ominous: larkspur, death camas, and green greasewood can kill sheep—an ironic idea, dying in this desert from eating what is too verdant. With sixteen hours of daylight, farmers and ranchers irrigate feverishly. There are first, second, and third cuttings of hay, some crews averaging only four hours of sleep a night for weeks. And, like the cowboys who in summer ride the night rodeo circuit, nighthawks make daredevil dives at dusk with an eerie whirring sound like a plane going down on the shimmering horizon.

In the town where I live, they've had to board up the dance-hall windows because there have been so many fights. There's so little to do except work that people wind up in a state of idle agitation that becomes fatalistic, as if there were nothing to be done about all this untapped energy. So the dark side to the grandeur of these spaces is the small-mindedness that seals people in. Men become hermits; women go mad. Cabin fever explodes into suicides, or into grudges and lifelong family feuds. Two sisters in my area inherited a ranch but found they couldn't get along. They fenced the place in half. When one's cows got out and mixed with the other's, the women went at each other with shovels. They ended up in the same hospital room but never spoke a word to each other for the rest of their lives.

THE SOLACE OF OPEN SPACES

. . .

After the brief lushness of summer, the sun moves south. The range grass is brown. Livestock is trailed back down from the mountains. Water holes begin to frost over at night. Last fall Martin asked me to accompany him on a pack trip. With five horses, we followed a river into the mountains behind the tiny Wyoming town of Meeteetse. Groves of aspen, red and orange, gave off a light that made us look toasted. Our hunting camp was so high that clouds skidded across our foreheads, then slowed to sail out across the warm valleys. Except for a bull moose who wandered into our camp and mistook our black gelding for a rival, we shot at nothing.

One of our evening entertainments was to watch the night sky. My dog, a dingo bred to herd sheep, also came on the trip. He is so used to the silence and empty skies that when an airplane flies over he always looks up and eyes the distant intruder quizzically. The sky, lately, seems to be much more crowded than it used to be. Satellites make their silent passes in the dark with great regularity. We counted eighteen in one hour's viewing. How odd to think that while they circumnavigated the planet, Martin and I had moved only six miles into our local wilderness and had seen no other human for the two weeks we stayed there.

At night, by moonlight, the land is whittled to slivers—a ridge, a river, a strip of grassland stretching to the mountains, then the huge sky. One morning a full moon was setting in the west just as the sun was rising. I felt precariously balanced between the two as I loped across a meadow. For a moment, I could believe that the stars, which were still visible, work like cooper's bands, holding together everything above Wyoming.

Space has a spiritual equivalent and can heal what is divided and burdensome in us. My grandchildren will probably use space shuttles for a honeymoon trip or to recover from heart attacks, but closer to home we might also learn how to carry space inside ourselves in the effortless way we carry our skins. Space represents sanity, not a life purified, dull, or "spaced out" but one that might accommodate intelligently any idea or situation.

From the clayey soil of northern Wyoming is mined bentonite, which is used as a filler in candy, gum, and lipstick. We Americans are great on fillers, as if what we have, what we are, is not enough. We have a cultural tendency toward denial, but, being affluent, we strangle ourselves with what we can buy. We have only to look at the houses we build to see how we build *against* space, the way we drink against pain and loneliness. We fill up space as if it were a pie shell, with things whose opacity further obstructs our ability to see what is already there.

ACKNOWLEDGMENTS

Grateful acknowledgment is made to the following authors, literary agencies, and publishers for permission to reprint the selections in this anthology.

JAMES BALDWIN: Excerpt from *No Name in the Street* by James Baldwin. Copyright © 1972 by James Baldwin. Used by permission of Doubleday, a division of Bantam Doubleday Dell Publishing Group, Inc.

WENDELL BERRY: Excerpt from "A Native Hill" from *Recollected Essays 1965–1980,* copyright © 1969, 1981 by Wendell Berry. Published by North Point Press and reprinted by permission of Farrar, Straus & Giroux, Inc.

CARLOS BULOSAN: Excerpt from *America Is in the Heart: A Personal History* by Carlos Bulosan is reprinted by permission of Harcourt Brace Jovanovich.

ACKNOWLEDGMENTS

JUDITH ORTIZ COFER: "Silent Dancing" is reprinted from *Silent Dancing: A Partial Remembrance of a Puerto Rican Childhood* by Judith Ortiz Cofer, copyright © 1989 by Judith Ortiz Cofer (Houston: Arte Publico Press-University of Houston, 1989) with permission of the publisher.

JOAN DIDION: "The White Album" from *The White Album* by Joan Didion. Copyright © 1979 by Joan Didion. Reprinted by permission of Farrar, Straus & Giroux, Inc.

GRETEL EHRLICH: "The Solace of Open Spaces" from *The Solace of Open Spaces* by Gretel Ehrlich. Copyright © 1985 by Gretel Ehrlich. Used by permission of Viking Penguin, a division of Penguin Books USA, Inc.

JAMES FARMER: "Tomorrow Is for Our Martyrs" from *Lay Bare the Heart* by James Farmer. Copyright © 1985 by James Farmer. Reprinted by permission of William Morrow & Company, Inc.

F. SCOTT FITZGERALD: "Echoes of the Jazz Age" from *The Crack-Up* by F. Scott Fitzgerald. Copyright © 1945 by New Directions Publishing Corporation. Reprinted by permission of New Directions Publishing Corporation.

MARY GORDON: " 'I Can't Stand Your Books': A Writer Goes Home," from *Good Boys and Dead Girls* by Mary Gordon. Copyright © 1991 by Mary Gordon. Used by permission of Viking Penguin, a division of Penguin Books USA, Inc.

VIVIAN GORNICK: "To Begin With" was originally published in somewhat different form in *The Romance of American Communism* by Vivian Gornick. Copyright © 1977, 1993 by Vivian Gornick. Reprinted by permission of the author.

JESSICA HAGEDORN: "Homesick" by Jessica Hagedorn. Copyright © 1987, 1988, 1993 by Jessica Hagedorn. Reprinted by permission of the author and the author's agents, Harold Schmidt Literary Agency.

BARBARA GRIZZUTI HARRISON: "Going Home: Brooklyn Revisited," from *Off Center* by Barbara Grizzuti Harrison. Copyright © 1980 by Barbara Grizzuti Harrison. Used by permission of Doubleday, a division of Bantam Doubleday Dell Publishing Group, Inc.

EVA HOFFMAN: Excerpt from *Lost in Translation* by Eva Hoffman. Copyright © 1989 by Eva Hoffman. Used by permission of the publisher, Dutton, an imprint of New American Library, a division of Penguin Books USA, Inc.

JUNE JORDAN: "Report from the Bahamas" by June Jordan, Copyright © 1982, 1985 by June Jordan. Published in *On Call: New Political Essays 1981–1985* by South End Press, and reprinted by permission of the author.

ACKNOWLEDGMENTS

MAXINE HONG KINGSTON: Excerpt from *The Woman Warrior* by Maxine Hong Kingston. Copyright © 1975, 1976 by Maxine Hong Kingston. Reprinted by permission of Alfred A. Knopf, Inc.

KIM YONG IK: "A Book-writing Venture" by Kim Yong Ik. Copyright © 1965, 1993 by Kim Yong Ik. Originally published in *The Writer.* Reprinted by permission of the author.

RON KOVIC: Excerpt from *Born on the Fourth of July* by Ron Kovic. Copyright © 1976 by Ron Kovic. Reprinted by permission of McGraw-Hill Book Company, Inc.

BELKIS CUZA MALÉ: "My Mother's Homeland" quoted in Pablo Medina's essay "Two Cuban Dissidents: Heberto Padilla and Belkis Cuza Malé" is from *A Woman on the Front Lines* by Belkis Cuza Malé, translated by Pamela Carmell (Greensboro, N.C.: Unicorn Press). Copyright © 1987 by Belkis Cuza Malé and Pamela Carmell. Reprinted by permission of the author.

PAULE MARSHALL: "The Making of a Writer: From the Poets in the Kitchen" by Paule Marshall, from *Reena and Other Stories.* Copyright © 1983 by Paule Marshall. Published by The Feminist Press at The City University of New York. Reprinted by permission. All rights reserved.

PABLO MEDINA: "Two Cuban Dissidents: Heberto Padilla and Belkis Cuza Malé" by Pablo Medina. Copyright © 1993 by Pablo Medina. First published in *Visions of America: Personal Narratives from the Promised Land* by arrangement with the author and the Elaine Markson Literary Agency.

N. SCOTT MOMADAY: Excerpt from *The Names* by N. Scott Momaday. Copyright © 1976 by N. Scott Momaday. Reprinted by permission of the author.

BHARATI MUKHERJEE: "Love Me or Leave Me" by Bharati Mukherjee. Copyright © 1991 by Bharati Mukherjee. Reprinted by permission of the Elaine Markson Literary Agency.

GEOFFREY O'BRIEN: Excerpt from *Dream Time* by Geoffrey O'Brien. Copyright © 1988 by Geoffrey O'Brien. Used by permission of Viking Penguin, a division of Penguin Books USA, Inc.

GREGORY ORFALEA: "The Messenger of the Lost Battalion" by Gregory Orfalea. Copyright © 1993 by Gregory Orfalea. First published in *Visions of America: Personal Narratives from the Promised Land* by arrangement with the author.

ACKNOWLEDGMENTS

SONIA PILCER: "2G" by Sonia Pilcer. Copyright © 1990, 1993 by Sonia Pilcer. Originally published in a somewhat different form in *7 Days* magazine. Reprinted by permission of the author.

MARIO PUZO: "Choosing a Dream: Italians in Hell's Kitchen" is reprinted from *The Godfather Papers and Other Confessions* by Mario Puzo. Copyright © 1972 by Mario Puzo. Reprinted by permission of Donadio & Ashworth, Inc.

JONATHAN RABAN: Excerpt from *Hunting Mister Heartbreak: A Discovery of America* by Jonathan Raban. Copyright © 1991 by Jonathan Raban. Reprinted by permission of HarperCollins Publisher.

ADRIENNE RICH: "Split at the Root: An Essay on Jewish Identity" is reprinted from *Blood, Bread, and Poetry, Selected Prose 1979–1985* by Adrienne Rich. Copyright © 1986 by Adrienne Rich. Reprinted by permission of W.W. Norton & Company, Inc.

RICHARD RODRIGUEZ: Excerpt from *Hunger of Memory* by Richard Rodriguez. Copyright © 1982 by Richard Rodriguez. Reprinted by permission of David R. Godine, Publisher.

ANTON SHAMMAS: "Amérka, Amérka: A Palestinian Abroad in the Land of the Free" by Anton Shammas. Copyright © 1991 by *Harper's Magazine.* All rights reserved. Reprinted from the February issue by special permission.

MONICA SONE: "Pearl Harbor Echoes in Seattle" from *Nisei Daughter* by Monica Sone. Copyright © 1953 by Monica Sone, copyright renewed 1981 by Monica Sone. Reprinted by permission of Little, Brown and Company.

GARY SOTO: "Like Mexicans" from *Small Faces* by Gary Soto. Copyright © 1986 by Gary Soto. Used by permission of Delacorte Press, a division of Bantam Doubleday Dell Publishing Group, Inc.

MICHAEL STEPHENS: "Immigrant Waves" by Michael Stephens. Copyright © 1993 by Michael Stephens. First published in *Visions of America: Personal Narratives from the Promised Land* by arrangement with the author.

ANZIA YEZIERSKA: "The Myth that Made Hollywood" is reprinted from *Red Ribbon on a White Horse* by Anzia Yezierska. Copyright © 1950 by Anzia Yezierska; copyright renewed 1978 by Louise Levitas Henriksen. Reprinted by permission of Persea Books, Inc.